AMERICA'S STRUGGLE
AGAINST POVERTY
1900-1994

AMERICA'S STRUGGLE AGAINST POVERTY 1900-1994

James T. Patterson

Harvard University Press
Cambridge, Massachusetts
London, England

In memory of my wife, Nancy
1937-1980

This book is an enlarged edition of *America's Struggle against Poverty, 1900-1985,* published in 1986 by Harvard University Press.

Library of Congress Cataloging-in-Publication Data

Patterson, James T.
    America's struggle against poverty, 1900–1994 / James T.
Patterson.
        p.   cm.
    Enl. ed. of: America's struggle against poverty, 1900–1985. 1986.
    Includes bibliographical references and index.
    ISBN 0-674-03123-7
    1. United States—Social policy.   2. United States—Economic
conditions.   3. Public welfare—United States—History—20th
century.   4. Poverty—Government policy—United States—
History—20th century.   I. Patterson, James T.   America's struggle
against poverty, 1900–1985.   II. Title.
HN59.P39   1995
361.6'1'0973—dc20   94-22736
                                                                                    CIP

PREFACE, 1994

This third revision reflects my continuing belief that poverty in the United States is not only a major concern—perhaps the biggest the nation faces—but also a source of angry controversy which reveals much about American culture and politics. For these reasons I have added a chapter that explores developments affecting the struggle against poverty in the United States between 1985 and early 1994.

The title of this new chapter, "Welfare Reform: No Consensus," hints at my interpretation of this struggle: a major overhaul of the nation's welfare system—and alleviation of poverty—proved elusive in the decade after 1985. Poverty, indeed, deepened in the early 1990s. Americans grew increasingly agitated about the "underclasses," the breakup of families, illegitimacy, welfare dependency, and crime. Liberals who warred against poverty fought historically powerful attitudes that resisted providing welfare to the "undeserving." They also confronted formidable fiscal, political, and institutional barriers to welfare reform, however defined. Still, these were also years of fascinating debates concerning the sources of poverty and the programs to combat it. If there was no consensus, the arguments nonetheless were more vital and serious than they had been in the late 1970s and early 1980s. My notes identify the range of these discussions and may lead readers to new conclusions of their own.

My thanks go to several experts who answered my last-minute calls for criticism and read drafts of my chapter: Steven Gillon of Brown University, Eugene Smolensky of the University of California, Berkeley, David Rochefort of Northeastern University, Edward Berkowitz of George Washington University, Lowell Gallaway of Ohio University, Jason DeParle of the *New York Times,* and William Galston, Office of the Assistant to the President.

PREFACE, 1985

When I wrote the earlier edition of this book, I was pleased to be able to carry the story of poverty and welfare in modern American history to 1980. At that time it seemed that 1980 marked a logical stopping point. The subject of poverty had ceased to be of much popular concern. The Great Society programs of the 1960s were undergoing sustained assault from conservatives, who pronounced those policies counterproductive. Confirming the conservative mood, Ronald Reagan swept to victory in the 1980 election. It appeared unlikely that the problem of poverty would soon recapture the attention of most Americans.

In the five years between 1980 and 1985, however, poverty again became a source of considerable discussion and controversy, in part because the Reagan administration continued to assail various aspects of the welfare state. His rhetoric and that of other conservatives placed liberals on the defensive and sparked renewed debate over social policy.

Two other developments did still more to make poverty and welfare controversial in the 1980s. First, the recession of 1980–1982 had a severe and lasting impact on poor people, whose numbers greatly increased, from approximately 26 million in 1979 to 35.5 million by 1983. Economic gains after 1983 reduced these numbers only slightly, to 33.7 million in 1984. This striking deterioration between 1979 and 1983 naturally provoked new concern for the plight of the poor in the United States. Second, many Americans became much alarmed in the 1980s about the rise of a so-called underclass of mostly black and Hispanic school dropouts, hustlers, criminals, dope addicts, welfare mothers, and (most numerous) long-term or permanently unemployed people. Their numbers and, more important, their behavior frightened conservatives and liberals, blacks and whites alike.

The return of concern about poverty to the front pages of the news-papers and magazines prompted me to look again at the subject, and convinced me to write a brief new chapter bringing my history to the mid-1980s. That addition necessitated altering the title of the book and changing the epilogue to Chapter 13. Otherwise, this edition is unchanged from the version published in 1981.

As my notes reveal, the new chapter depends heavily on newspaper and magazine articles published since 1980, and especially on publications sponsored by the Institute for Research on Poverty. This organization, originally funded by the Office of Economic Opportunity (OEO), produces from its base at the University of Wisconsin at Madison many up-to-date and carefully researched papers and articles on a range of subjects relating to poverty. The IRP sponsored an important conference in December 1984 at Williamsburg, Virginia, featuring leading writers on poverty; their papers have proved of great value to me. I thank Aida Donald, Harvard University Press, for suggesting that I update this book. I also thank Steven Gillon of Yale University, Peter Gottschalk of Bowdoin College, John Dittmer of Depauw University, Sheldon Danziger and Eugene Smolensky of the University of Wisconsin, George Bass of Brown University, and Hugh Heclo of Harvard University, all of whom offered constructive comments on drafts of this chapter.

PREFACE, 1981

Wʜᴇɴ I ʙᴇɢᴀɴ ᴛᴏ ᴇxᴘʟᴏʀᴇ the history of poverty and welfare in the United States, I was struck by the number of good books that might still be written. No historian had yet published a broad demographic history of the poor, a social history of poor people, or a synthetic study of the changing causes of poverty in the United States. My book touches on these matters but makes no claim to being comprehensive.

My focus, rather, resembles that of Robert Bremner's account of attitudes toward poverty prior to 1920, *From the Depths*. Like him, I am interested in exploring changing perspectives, especially of reformers, toward poverty and welfare. Unlike him, I largely ignore artists and novelists, and I focus on the twentieth century, mainly the period after 1930. Because these were years of increasing governmental involvement in social welfare, my book tries to integrate intellectual history and analysis of public policy. It attempts to show how popular views of poverty, prescriptions of reformers, and governmental programs have affected poor Americans during these years. To the degree that sources permit, it places the American experience within the context of international developments and depicts what poor people themselves thought of efforts on their behalf.

Several main themes recur in this history. These include the persistence of attitudes popular among the middle classes: that many, if not most, of the destitute are undeserving; that large numbers of poor people exist in an intergenerational "culture of poverty"; that social insurance is preferable to welfare, which is wasteful and demoralizing; that wise public policy seeks to prevent destitution, not to provide income maintenance; that work, not welfare, is the essence of the meaningful life.

But these popular attitudes have not always shaped policy. Among the other forces that have resulted in the developing welfare state are demographic change: the aging of the population, mass movements from farm to city, the rise in the number of broken families. Other forces are political and institutional: the accelerating nationalization of politics after 1933, the growing power of pressure groups such as the aged, and the bureaucratic expansion of established public programs. Perhaps most important have been economic forces, which have influenced attitudes and policies in very different ways. In the Depression of the 1930s, economic catastrophe called for new responses; in times of great prosperity, confidence in the future has tended to stimulate the "discovery" of poverty and more generous public responses to the poor.

Pursuing these themes, I chase a more ambitious goal: to explore how and why Americans, especially authorities on poverty and welfare, have (and have not) changed their fundamental assumptions about the good society during the industrial and postindustrial age. In this effort I build on R. H. Tawney's observation that "there is no touchstone, except the treatment of childhood, which reveals the true character of a social philosophy more clearly than the spirit in which it regards the misfortunes of those of its members who fall by the way" (*Religion and the Rise of Capitalism* [New York, 1926], p. 268). Like Tawney, I think that attitudes and policies toward poor people, important in themselves, provide clues about broader "social philosophies"—popular and otherwise—of the nation.

In searching for these social philosophies, I have divided the book into four parts chronologically, using dates—1930, 1960, 1965—that marked shifts in the social thought of experts on poverty and welfare. The first part discusses the drive for "prevention" that motivated reformers prior to 1930. The second concerns the Depression and the rudimentary welfare state that developed in the next two decades. At that time, many Americans continued to yearn for prevention—a constant theme—and to hope that poverty would soon "wither away." The third part concentrates on the rediscovery of poverty in the early 1960s and the subsequent war on it. Though the assumptions and goals of this war were different from those of the 1930s, it continued to emphasize prevention, this time in the guise of expanding "opportunity." The fourth part deals with the extraordinary developments in social welfare that occurred in the late 1960s and early 1970s, years of little-noticed but virtually revolutionary changes in welfare. The 1960s, I think, marked a sharp break with the past in many aspects of social policy. Chapter 13 discusses the stalemate over welfare reform that characterized the mid- and late 1970s.

Like most broad historical studies, this one risks overgeneraliza-tion. Phrases such as "the poor" or "middle-class attitudes" may obscure considerable differences within such groups and in so doing underplay the importance of cultural divisions in American society. Focusing on "the poor" may also exaggerate the differences that dis-tinguish them from near-poor working people. I use "may" here be-cause historians do not really know enough yet to make very solid statements differentiating the values and life-styles of various groups of poor people from those of the middle and upper classes. I try to make generalizations about "the poor" only with caution.

Readers will note that I am trying to write history, not a guide to welfare reform in the future. For that reason I have resisted the advice of some friends who urged that any book on this subject *must* explain where the story will end. I wish I knew.

The notes list many scholars whose research made it possible for me to write this book. I am also indebted to Donald Spaeth, John S. Gilkeson, and Stephanie Gardner, all of Brown University, who typed the manuscript. The following scholars assisted me greatly by reading earlier drafts: Robert McElwaine of Millsaps College (chapters three and four), Robert Plotnick of the Institute for Research on Poverty (chapters ten through thirteen), and John Gilkeson, who ably criti-cized the entire manuscript. Stephan Thernstrom of Harvard Univer-sity and Robert Bremner of Ohio State University read the whole manuscript and saved me from many errors. Edward Berkowitz of the President's Commission for a National Agenda for the Eighties and Carl Brauer of the University of Virginia gave earlier drafts especially careful attention and induced me to make many necessary changes. I owe a debt also to my colleague John L. Thomas of Brown University, whose expert eye helped transform a bunch of chapters into a book. Winifred Barton and Karen Mota performed countless secretarial tasks for me, usually with good humor. Peg Anderson of Harvard Press did an excellent job of editing. I thank especially Nancy's fam-ily, whose support during very difficult times made the book possible: Dr. David and Ruth Weeks, Robert and Ruth Clark, Rich and Bar-bara Miner. My children, Steve and Marnie, inspired me to persist.

CONTENTS

I. The Preventive Impulse, 1900-1930

1. Snapshots of the Poor   3
2. The Gospel of Prevention, Progressive Style   20

II. Coping and Rehabilitation, 1930-1960

3. The Poor in the Depression   37
4. The Early Welfare State   56
5. Withering Away   78

III. Doors to Opportunity, 1960-1965

6. The Rediscovery of Poverty   99
7. A Culture of Poverty?   115
8. Girding for War on Poverty   126
9. OEO: A Hand Up, Not a Handout   142

IV. The Unsung Revolution, 1965-1973

10. The Revolution in Social Welfare   157
11. The Welfare Explosion   171
12. Floors and Doors   185

V. Reactions, 1980-1994

13. Stalemate   199
14. Regression in the Early 1980s   210
15. Welfare Reform: No Consensus   224

     Notes   243
     Resources   301
     Index   305

AMERICA'S STRUGGLE
AGAINST POVERTY
1900-1994

I
THE PREVENTIVE
IMPULSE
1900-1930

1
SNAPSHOTS
OF THE POOR

SETTLEMENT HOUSE WORKERS, muckraking journalists, and social reformers sang a monotonous dirge about poverty in the half century before the Great Depression of the 1930s. That dirge repeated a powerful and recurrent theme—that poor people suffered mainly from weaknesses in the economy, not from moral flaws. A few examples from this litany suffice:

Low Wages, New York City, 1890: There were nine in the family: husband, wife, an aged grandmother, and six children; honest, hard-working Germans, scrupulously neat, but poor. All nine lived in two rooms, one about ten feet square that served as parlor, bedroom, and eating room, the other a small hall-room made into a kitchen. The rent was seven dollars and a half a month, more than a week's wages for the husband and father, who was the only bread-winner in the family. That day the mother had thrown herself out of the window, and was carried up from the street dead. She was "discouraged," said some of the other women of the tenement.

Women's Work, 1890: Here is the case of a woman employed in the manufacturing department of a Broadway house. It stands for a hundred like her own. She averages three dollars a week. Pays $1.50 for her room; for breakfast she has a cup of coffee; lunch she cannot afford. One meal a day is her allowance. This woman is young, she is pretty. She has "the world before her." Is it anything less than a miracle if she is found guilty of nothing worse than the "early and improvident marriage" against which moralists exclaim as one of the prolific causes of the distress of

3

the poor? Almost any door might seem to offer welcome escape from such slavery as this.

"Sweating" in Tenements, 1905: The workers, poor, helpless, ignorant foreigners, work on in dirt, often in filth unspeakable, in the presence of all contagious and other diseases, and in apartments in which the sun enters only at noon or never at all. In such an apartment I attended a woman ill with tuberculosis, finishing trousers . . . Three years of life in this apartment killed the woman . . . As soon as a little child can be of the least possible help, it must add to the family income by taking in a share of the toil . . . The other day a girl of 8 years was dismissed from the diphtheria hospital after a severe attack of the disease. Almost immediately she was working at women's collars, although scarcely able to walk across the room.

Slack, Seasonal Work, Pittsburgh, 1920s: Mr. Contillo is one of nine children. His whole family came to America in 1907. Mrs. Contillo was also born in Italy, coming here in 1911. In the sixteen years of their married life, the Contillos have had seven children . . . Mr. Contillo has always been a laborer, working for whatever company advertised for workers. A year and a half is the longest time that he has ever worked for any one company, but his periods between jobs were rarely more than a week . . . This past winter, 1928-29, he has had no steady work for five months, and only ten days of special work.

The greatest disaster resulting from Mr. Contillo's unemployment has been its effect on his point of view. Before this last winter he was cheerful, fond of the children, content with Mrs. Contillo's management of the house and very neighborly. The two factors, unemployment and his neighborliness, have proved his undoing . . . He has become a steady drinker, though before he was never drunk except on holidays . . . Mrs. Contillo says that half the time he sits by the fire drunk; occasionally he is violent toward the children and frequently threatens to kill the boarders.

Racial Discrimination, 1920s: William Lovejoy, a carpenter of Cleveland, is a Negro. The Negro is harder hit in dull times than the white, although differently. During the course of a year he will have had more jobs but also more unemployment than the average white worker . . . Lovejoy finished grammar school and the first year of high school in Georgia. His wife, too, had a fairly good education at a girls' school. Her mother had been a school-teacher. Lovejoy's father and older brothers had been carpenters, and he had learned his trade from them. He was forced to join the carpenters' union in 1923. Then, because union wages were as high for colored workers as for others, his white employers dropped him from the payroll and hired white help instead. For the past seven years he has depended on odd jobs of any kind . . .

During spells of unemployment they have lived on next to nothing, so the children [they had nine] have been much undernourished . . . Often the whole family went hungry, particularly the father and mother . . . Somehow they have managed to exist without calling upon agencies for help . . . Through every vicissitude, it has been the family aim to keep the children in school at all costs . . .

Depressed Areas, 1920s: Say that trade shifts oust you. You are Nicholas Poulos of Boston. In the nineteen years since you came from Greece, you have worked in shoe factories there. But the shoe industry has increasingly left New England. In your early days you had no work for one month, part time for three months, and full time the rest of the year. Now you work full time for one month, and part time for five, and for the remaining six you do not work at all. Since even for full time you never received more than $25 a week, on which your wife Helen and your three children have had to live, it is thanks to Helen's extraordinary thrift that you made any savings at all. What has the decentralization of the shoe industry done to you?

This is what happened to the Nicholas Poulos family. First they lost two insurance policies. Rent fell in arrears, so the mother, Helen, found work in a laundry. During the weeks in which Mr. Poulos also had work, her weekly earnings of $12 enabled the family to pay back some of the money they owed to their friends.

But Mrs. Poulos worked beyond her strength. In spite of her utmost efforts at management, her children had to be neglected. The youngest was reported by the school as being undernourished and had to be fed at the School Diet Kitchen. She resented her husband's idleness, said he did not try to find work. He became inert and fatalistic. They quarreled and were under constant domestic strain.[1]

The social workers who wrote these reports did not sympathize with all the poor. Some of the needy, they believed, were "paupers," improvident people dependent on relief. Other poor people, they thought, belonged to the "dangerous classes." The experts of that rapidly urbanizing age were easily disgusted by crowding and dirt, often obsessed with the need for open spaces, playgrounds, and cleanliness. The social workers habitually used a "case study" method that focused on the problems of individual families and unintentionally blurred the underlying environmental forces they wished to expose. Readers of their case studies might pity poor families without appreciating fully the broad base of poverty in late nineteenth- and early twentieth-century America.

But social workers of 1900 should not be judged by the different standards of public policy since the 1930s, for few other Americans paid any attention to the poor at that time. Moreover, the case studies, however monotonous, inevitably exposed the major causes of poverty, including personal problems such as illness, disability, drink, old age, and death of a breadwinner. This was "case" poverty, a curse in any society. But poverty, social workers recognized, also afflicted millions among the young and able-bodied. These people suffered from a range of social and economic problems: technological disruption, economic recessions, business failures, and depressed areas. The basic causes of poverty were not personal weakness but two deeper problems: an economy insufficiently abundant to provide subsistence for all the able-bodied, and a social order that inequitably distributed what wealth there was. In these fundamental ways poverty was then and continued to be a structural, not a moral, matter.

Fortunately for historians, a few writers prior to 1930 did something more than tug at the emotions of readers. Two snapshots of poverty— one around 1900, the other of the late 1920s—reveal the major points about poverty in those times: first, that it rested on a frighteningly broad base around 1900, and second, that it declined slowly but appreciably during the next thirty years of economic progress.

The earlier snapshot was taken by Robert Hunter. The son of a Terre Haute, Indiana, carriage manufacturer, Hunter was an impressionable nineteen-year-old when the depression of 1893 threw millions out of work. After graduating from Indiana University in 1896, he moved to Chicago, where he lived at Jane Addams's Hull House settlement as a social worker. He traveled to Europe, where he met important socialist and radical leaders. Hunter read the contemporary published studies of poverty and lower-class life: Jacob Riis's *How the Other Half Lives* (1890), Amos Warner's *American Charities* (1894), Charles Booth's multivolume monument, *Life and Labour of the People in London* (1889-1903), and B. Seebohm Rowntree's influential study of York, England, *Poverty: A Study of Town Life* (1901). Drawing upon these and other books, Hunter published in 1904 *Poverty*, a classic of the literature.

In his book Hunter admitted that "the extent of poverty in the United States [was] absolutely unknown." He nonetheless snapped a picture of destitution that, although flawed in important respects, exposed its structural foundation. He estimated that 10 million Americans—12 percent of the population of 82 million—were poor in 1904. Most of this poverty, he wrote, was in northern industrial areas, where about 6.6 million people, or 20 percent of the population, were poor. The incidence of poverty in the South, he guessed wrongly, was about half as great. He showed that 20 percent of the people of Boston were in distress in 1903, that 19 percent of New York State's population was needy in 1897, and that 14 percent of Manhattan's families were evicted from their homes in 1903. Citing Riis, he observed that one-tenth of New York City's dead received a pauper's burial between 1885 and 1890, and that only about 4 million of the 10 million poor in America received any public relief.[2]

Hunter, who turned to socialism at the time he wrote the book, was well aware that income was badly distributed. He knew that poverty was a relative concept and that drawing an absolute "poverty line" was arbitrary; moving the line up or down a little greatly changed the number defined as poor. Still, like all the pioneering writers on the subject, Hunter used an absolute definition of poverty, which he set as $460 a year for an average-sized family (five people) in northern industrial areas, and $300 for such a family in the rural South. Families with lower incomes were "not able to *obtain those necessaries which will permit them to maintain a state of physical efficiency*" and were "underfed, underclothed, and poorly housed." To live at the poverty line, Hunter explained, was to adopt the "same standard that a man would demand for his horses or slaves."[3]

This absolute definition, based on estimates by social workers and nutritionists of people's elementary needs, employed the same reasoning used by Booth, who found 30.7 percent of London in poverty between 1887 and 1892, and Rowntree, who discovered that 27.8 percent of York's population was poor in the relatively prosperous year of 1899. American readers could take some small consolation in finding that poverty in the United States was probably less prevalent than in England.[4]

Even those people slightly above Hunter's poverty line struggled every day to stay afloat. Urban families with three children and earnings of $500-$800 in 1900 typically owned little furniture and no real estate. They rented two- or three-room flats without hot or even running water and without indoor flush toilets. They subsisted on bread and potatoes. Illness or loss of a job quickly wiped out whatever savings the provident were able to amass. There was no unemployment insurance, little public welfare, virtually no old-age pensions. If all else failed, most poor persons could turn only to local politicians and charities or take refuge overnight at the police station. Seeking charity was a time-consuming, frustrating, and stigmatizing experience.

In identifying the needy, Hunter and other writers distinguished between the poor, victims of the economic system, and paupers, who had long been labeled as "undeserving," who had "lost all self-respect, who rarely, if ever, work, who are aimless and drifting, who like drink, who have no thought for their children, and who live more or less contentedly on alms."[5] How many of the indigent fit this unflattering description was not clear. Warner's authoritative book on charity, published in 1894, concluded that 25 percent of poverty stemmed from what he called personal misconduct. Edward Devine, a leading New York charity worker, was probably closer to the mark in holding that 12 percent of a sample of 5,000 relief cases (the most dependent among the poor) in 1907-1908 were improvident. Such experts, believing that paupers dragged down the "deserving" poor, wasted little sympathy on them. Warner recommended the "permanent isolation of the essentially unfit." Booth wanted them to be "gradually harried out of existence." The improvident, he thought, should be placed in work camps and removed from the labor market. Even Hunter was cold. "It would be unwise," he concluded, "to legislate out of existence, even were it possible to do so, that poverty which penalizes the voluntarily idle and vicious . . . The poor who are always with us, are, it seems to me, in poverty of their own making."[6]

Much more numerous than the paupers were the unfortunate dependents who fell into poverty through no fault of their own, such as the disabled, the chronically ill, the aged, and women with dependent children. Devine found that 12 percent of poor households were headed by a man temporarily disabled or mentally ill, 30 percent by widows or permanently disabled men, and 6 percent by old people. Two-thirds of the individuals in his sample were either women or children under fourteen. Devine's figures pointed to an enduring truth about modern American poverty. Then and later, dependency was a major source of destitution.[7]

Hunter's focus was more on the problems of low wages and unemployment, which he regarded as the curse of industrialization. His was in fact a classic structural analysis of poverty as it affected able-bodied working people. Using the census of 1900, he estimated that 6.4 million workers, or 22 percent of the labor force, were unemployed at some time during that year. He guessed that about 2.5 million of these people—mostly unskilled—were jobless for four to six months, and 780,000 for seven to twelve months. None of these workers received unemployment insurance, which almost no one in America endorsed at the time.[8]

Other writers reported a similar focus on the relationship among industrialization, underemployment, and poverty. Rowntree blamed low wages for 52 percent of York's poverty; Devine figured that 69 percent of his heads of households in 1907-1908 were employable but out of work; and Booth thought three-fifths of London's poor were jobless. Booth and others refused to draw from such data the Marxian tenet that industrialization spawned a vast "reserve army" of unemployed workers.[9] But Hunter was more bold:

> Much of our poverty is directly due to a whole series of economic disorders which seem actually to make waste of human life necessary. And in so far as poverty is a result of such deeply seated and fundamental economic disorders, due either to the method by which industry is organized or the present ownership of the means and materials of production, it will, in all probability, find a solution only through struggles between the workers and the capitalists.[10]

This, then, was Hunter's snapshot of poverty in 1900: 20 percent poor in northern industrial areas, 10 percent in the South; a little malingering and pauperism; much dependency; serious unemployment; industrialization threatening further to impoverish the nation.

Hunter's portrait was incomplete. It did not provide a historical or comparative dimension to the problem of poverty. In his zeal to focus on industrialization in his time, he did not discuss the truly terrible poverty that had existed in preindustrial Europe. Probably one-half the population of England before 1720 suffered from poverty and constant underemployment. Undernourished, living in unsanitary conditions, these people suffered from tuberculosis, gastric ulcers, influenza, smallpox, dysentery, and in the seventeenth century, bubonic plague. In London, a refuge for the land-starved poor, about 60 percent of the boys in the mid-seventeenth century died before the age of sixteen. To make life tolerable, the English turned heavily to drink. Alcohol, indeed, was "an essential narcotic which anaesthetized men against the strains of contemporary life."[11]

Life in seventeenth- and eighteenth-century France was no better. In the late seventeenth century thousands of land-poor peasants poured out of hill villages into the plains of Languedoc, where, too weak to walk farther, they died of starvation. Widespread malnutrition in the area around Beauvais in the 1690s caused infertility among the women and killed whole families that were too weak to resist disease. These rural folk subsisted almost entirely on cereals; they suffered from typhoid, typhus, enteric fevers, scarlet fever, pneumonia. Desperate, they commonly abandoned children, and some practiced infanticide. In their frenzy, they banded together and raided neighboring villages. On the eve of the French Revolution in 1789, one-third to one-half the population was destitute.[12]

America was spared such conditions. Though never a wholly egalitarian society, it did not at first develop sharply defined social classes or mass rural poverty. But from the start many American farmers lived on the margin, in circumstances that appalled contemporaries who took the trouble to find them. In 1800 Michael Gaffney, a wealthy resident of Charleston, South Carolina, visited the backcountry near Spartanburg. He wrote:

> The country for about one hundred and fifty miles from Charleston is extremely low and unhealthy. The people looked yellow, poor, and sickly. Some of them lived the most miserably I ever saw any poor people live . . . Their dress is generally a hunting shirt and some trousers of coarse cotton yarn . . . The women of this country live the poorest lives of any people in the world. It is directly opposite to Charleston; here they must do everything from cooking to plowing and after that they have no more life in them than Indian squaws.[13]

These conditions had nothing to do with industrialization, which did not affect the United States at that time. Rather there was poverty wherever Americans attempted to farm poor land or competed unsuccessfully with larger operators in the commercial market. Unable to make a living, many rural people began flocking to cities as early as the mid-eighteenth century, where they were joined by immigrants from abroad. Even then, urban poverty was pressing. In 1772, 25 percent of the free men in Philadelphia were poor or near poor. By 1815 New York City gave public aid to 19,000 people, one-fifth of its population. Some historians have gone so far as to claim—on admittedly sketchy evidence—that as many as one-fifth of whites and virtually all blacks lived in poverty during the late eighteenth century.[14]

Like Hunter, other urban-oriented writers such as Riis also slighted the problem of agricultural poverty. But it was unfortunate that they did not talk about the problems of rural areas in general and of the South in particular, for both prior to Hunter's time and for decades thereafter the South showed by far the highest incidence of poverty in the nation. Hard times after 1860 perpetuated a deeply depressed lower class of sharecroppers and tenant farmers, who suffered heavily from hookworm, pellagra, and malnutrition. Thousands were driven to eating clay from the chinks in their rough-hewn cabins. Oppressed, they straggled into mill villages, where conditions were frightful: average wages in the 1890s of $3 for a seventy-hour work week—$150 per year. But because whole families could earn a little, they were able to live better than they had in the backcountry.[15]

The flight of poor southern farmers from the land was but a part of the vast urban migration in western industrialized countries in the nineteenth and twentieth centuries. And from the standpoint of income, they usually bettered their economic condition. In the United States and Great Britain the real wages of factory workers improved in the late nineteenth century. So did diets and health standards; people who had once lived on bread and potatoes began to enjoy a more varied diet. Though cities sometimes were the sinkholes of concentrated human misery perceived by nostalgic writers like Riis, they were also places that promoted economic progress. Neither in 1900 nor at any time since has the connection between urbanization and poverty been so simple as Hunter suggested.

Hunter might also have been a little more precise in labeling industrialization as the villain. It was true, of course, that industrial fluctuations caused widespread unemployment, but it did not necessarily follow that workers in nonindustrial urban occupations were better off. Both before and after heavy industrialization, casual labor, low wage work, and underemployment in commerce, transportation, and retail trade contributed mightily to poverty in the United States and elsewhere. In failing to give due emphasis to these aspects of poverty, Hunter and his contemporaries reflected the almost mesmerizing effect of industrialization on people raised in that more rural generation.

Because Hunter set his poverty line so low ($460 a year for a family of five), he was conservative in his estimate of the extent of poverty. John Ryan, a leading advocate of a "living wage," thought that $600 ($800 in some places) was the minimum necessary for a family with three children. Under this definition, millions whom Hunter did not count as poor slipped under the line. Using a line of $700 for a family with three children, more than 40 percent of wage earners and clerical workers were living in poverty at the time.[16]

Employing estimates such as Ryan's, it is possible to set the total poverty population of America at between 30 and 50 million—three to five times Hunter's estimate. This is not to say that Hunter was ill-informed—he used what data he had carefully—but to suggest that all absolute definitions of poverty depend on the standards employed.

Hunter's were conservative, even for his own time. Given the wide base of America's income pyramid since 1880, there are inevitably as many (or more) near-poor as there are those who fit official definitions.

It is worth remembering also the modest expectations of people in that era. One scholar who has estimated the cost of living over time has suggested that Hunter's standard of $460 was equivalent in real earning power to around $3,000 in 1977. Yet in that year the Social Security Administration set a poverty line more than twice as high, or $5,981 for an urban family of four. The 1977 definition reveals what all students of poverty have recognized: definitions of poverty have grown steadily more generous over time. If one applied the standards of 1977 (or even of 1937) to Hunter's time, only a very small percentage of Americans would be defined as living above the poverty line.[17]

The snapshot approach, as Hunter also realized, finally fails to distinguish the short-term from the long-term poor, and therefore tends to underestimate the poverty problem. Were the 12 percent who were poor in 1904 the same individuals who had been poor in 1903 and were to be in 1905? How many of the unemployed in 1900 had been out of work in 1899 or might lose their jobs in 1901? Neither Hunter nor anyone else knew the answer to these questions. But 20 million or so "nonpoor" Americans had family incomes of only $100 to $300 more per year than Hunter's poverty population. Any misfortune—illness, loss of a job—could throw them under the line. So could hardships common in the life cycles of heads of families, in the years when they had to support children too young to work, and later, in their forties and fifties, when they were turned out of their jobs without pension. The number of individuals therefore who experienced poverty at various times in their lives was vastly higher than Hunter's 10 million, higher than any snapshot could ever reveal. This problem of marginality, indeed, was rarely to receive in America the attention it deserved.

Imprecision about the dimensions of poverty over time makes it impossible to answer the still broader question: how was poverty in 1900 different from poverty since that time? Some writers in the 1960s, such as Michael Harrington, gave the impression that most poverty at the turn of the century was rooted in essentially economic weaknesses that were great at that stage of capitalism. The "new" poor of the 1960s, by contrast, were, according to Harrington, deprived minorities who were immune to the country's economic progress. Abandoned and hopeless, they wallowed in a "culture" of poverty. As another writer proclaimed, "Hunter's enigma was acute and cyclical; that of the sixties seems chronic and structural."[18]

Other writers reject this "bad new days" view. They stress that the poor in 1900, especially blacks, had been mired for generations in poverty and lived in a quite different culture from the middle class. In the North workers in company towns and immigrants in urban ghettos were more cut off from middle-class ways of life and aspirations than were poor Americans in the age of mass media and mass education after 1950. Isolated, indeed trapped, the poor of 1900 knew not what they missed and therefore subsisted in a barren world. One scholar, employing this "bad old days" approach, concluded that the poor in late-nineteenth-century America had "different values" and formed a kind of "subculture." "Poor people were not merely rich people with less money, ability, and opportunity. In many ways they were in different societies altogether."[19]

The absence of longitudinal studies of poor people makes it very difficult to assess either perspective on poverty over time. Inferring from subsequent developments, however, it appears that the bad-old-days argument is statistically accurate in an economic sense: the percentage of Americans defined as poor by consistent standards was as high in the late nineteenth century as it ever had been or was to be. Hunter, in short, was right in pointing to the high incidence of poverty in 1900, though wrong in implying that industrialization was inevitably and progressively impoverishing. Using some contemporary definitions of poverty (which have risen over time), it is roughly accurate to say that 40 percent of Americans were poor in 1900, 33-40 percent in the Great Depression, 25 percent in the mid-1950s, and 6-15 percent between 1970 and 1980. If one applies the stringent standards of 1900 to later periods, the improvement is still more dramatic.

Those who employ the bad-old-days perspective to talk about a culture of poverty in late-nineteenth-century America seem at first to have a plausible case. Well before then observers had perceived lower-class subcultures that reveled in cockfights, taverns, and fairs and believed in witches and fortune-telling. Other observers, especially after the wave of immigration in the 1840s and 1850s, trembled before the specter of the dangerous classes and of "wild Irish slums." Hunter, like most reformers at the turn of the century, loathed some of the lowest classes, who existed in a "culture bed for criminals, paupers, vagrants, and for such diseases as inebriety, insanity, and imbecility." Ignore this cancer, he said, and "the dependency of the adults infects the children, and the foulest of our social miseries is thus perpetuated from generation to generation."

Allowing for the special color of Hunter's medical metaphor and remembering that he meant to describe a small minority of those in need, it is obvious that he perceived a real problem. The "dregs" (the lazy and apathetic) and "skidders" (alcoholics, drug addicts) tended to congregate in the poorest sections of the cities, and to reinforce a lower lower class that lived without hope. They suffered not only from personal weaknesses but also from low income and exploitation of all sorts: by juvenile gangs, the underworld, grasping landlords, and corrupt police. Writers like Riis, though nostalgic for the simpler life of the countryside, did not much exaggerate the squalor, misery, and disorder of their lives.[20]

But this approach distorts reality. It is doubtful that the "culture bed for criminals, paupers, and vagrants" represented more than about 5 percent of the poverty population in 1900. Many other poor people—landless workers, new immigrants—lived in close physical proximity to the hopeless 5 percent without becoming "infected" with the disease of pauperism. They developed a network of self-help activities, including unions, churches, mutual aid societies, building and loan associations, and urban political connections. They depended especially on kin and ethnic ties. These people never expected to get much help from social workers, let alone the government. They worked long hours at manual labor; they sent their children into the factories, mines, and mills; their wives took in boarders. They yearned to rise, and many of them did. One careful study of social mobility concluded that between 30 and 40 percent of the sons of blue-collar workers in American cities attained middle-class occupational status between 1880 and 1930. Blacks, the poorest Americans, moved to cities after 1914, showing that they shared many of the economic aspirations of nonpoor Americans. They clung to their own cultural traditions, but they neither inherited nor passed on a "culture of poverty."[21]

The image of a culture of poverty nonetheless persists. If 40 percent of the sons of blue-collar people moved out of manual occupations, what about the remaining 60 percent? Some—perhaps a sixth—became skilled workers. But how many of the rest passed on to their children a more-or-less permanent poverty, as opposed to low occupational status? Probably not many, but that is a guess inferred mainly from statistics on occupational distribution over time and on poverty in the 1960s and 1970s. More puzzling, what was the role of cultural inheritance? Were particular groups, such as Jews, especially well equipped to escape poverty while others were not? Writers at the time did not much explore this question, and some (including Riis) tossed about what later generations recognized as crude and damning stereotypes of ethnic groups. Historians still cannot confidently single out the role of cultural inheritance in the transmission of economic poverty across the generations.

Talk of an intergenerational culture of poverty, however intriguing, obscures the highlight of any snapshot of 1900: the economy at that time was not abundant enough to prevent a uniquely high percentage of Americans of all ethnic backgrounds from falling into poverty. From this economic perspective, an emphasis on the familial or cultural attributes of the poor is highly misleading, and nostalgia about the good old days is nonsense.

In the 1920s optimistic businessmen and social scientists thought the United States had entered a "new era." As Herbert Hoover said in 1928, "We shall soon, with the help of God, be in sight of the day when poverty will be banished in the nation."

So assured and statistically minded a social engineer as Hoover could not have been altogether wrong. And he was not. The national income, in constant 1913 dollars, increased from $24 billion in 1900 to $37 billion in 1929. Income per capita, in the same 1913 dollars, rose from $320 to $473 in the same period. After a sharp depression in 1921, per capita income rose every year until 1929. Though students of the question haggle over statistics, it is fair to conclude that real per capita income was one and a half times as great in 1929 as in 1900.[22]

Improved standards of living accompanied these gains. However one measured such standards—diet, size and quality of housing, number of home appliances—most Americans were better off in the 1920s than they had ever been. Even a working-class family could afford to buy a Model T Ford, which cost less than $300 in the late 1920s. Most dramatic were improvements in health, reflected in statistics on longevity. Life expectancy at birth was 47.3 years in 1900, 59.7 in 1930. The aging of the population during these and later years was one of several demographic developments (migration from poor rural areas to the cities was another, and family breakup was a third) that dramatically affected poverty and public policy in modern America. Aging increased the extent of dependency, promoted organized movements for pensions, and led ultimately to sustenance of a social security system that by 1980 represented a staggering expense.

But statistics on health or housing do not measure poverty. Indeed few writers attempted such measuring in the years between Hunter's findings and the Great Depression. Although social scientists in the intervening decades sponsored numerous studies of the cost of living and charted the amounts spent by various income groups on food, clothing, and shelter, they did not attempt very sophisticated overviews of poverty per se.[23] Like Hoover, they assumed that economic progress would drive poverty away.

In 1934 the Brookings Institution came close to remedying that neglect when it published its volume, *America's Capacity to Consume.*

As the title suggested, the book focused on income maldistribution, not on poverty, and offered a case for the expansion of purchasing power. Its premise, that experts could direct economic growth, exposed its faith in social engineering. Nonetheless, the book described a structurally deep economic want that had been hidden in the optimistic years before 1930.[24]

The Brookings authors used a family poverty line (without calling it that) of $2,000. This was higher in real purchasing power than Hunter's $460 (it corresponded to about $700-$800 1904 dollars) and higher than other contemporary estimates (which ran as low as $1,200). But the line of $2,000 was not overly generous, for it was "sufficient to supply only basic necessities." The authors estimated that 16 million American families, about 60 percent of the total, involving at least 70 million people, received less than that amount in 1930.

Words like "poverty" and "destitution" appeared rarely in this and other studies, but it took no great imagination to see what such figures meant. The Brookings authors noted that a family of five had to earn $3,000—an amount amassed by only 25 percent of America's 21.6 million nonfarm families—to pay for an "adequate diet at moderate cost." The 7.5 million nonfarm families (30 million people) earning less than $1,500 could afford to spend only $350 to $500 a year on food—enough for "restricted diets for emergency use" or "adequate diets at minimum cost," respectively.

The Brookings study depicted rural poverty more clearly than Hunter had. The average income of the nation's 5.8 million farm families, it showed, was only $1,240. Moreover, the authors estimated that 54 percent of farm families, about 17 million people, earned less than $1,000 a year. These were the poorest of America's poor. Within fifteen years these people, many of them black, began a mass migration to cities that dramatically urbanized poverty and provoked anguished talk of a "welfare crisis" in the United States.

Given the depressed condition of agriculture, it was not surprising that the South showed the lowest income levels. The Brookings study observed that per capita income ranged from a high of $1,107 in New York, New Jersey, and Pennsylvania, to a low of $344 in Kentucky, Tennessee, Alabama, and Mississippi. In twelve states, all in the South, the per capita income of the farm population was below $200. These data suggested that one long-range answer to America's poverty could be large shifts of population out of the rural areas of the South and the plains and into the cities and suburbs. In any event the statistics gave little comfort to those who yearned for decentralization of the population and restoration of the small family farm.

What, then, of Hunter's worries about the insecurity and dependency that accompanied industrialization? It was testimony to the optimism of the New Era that few unemployment statistics were collected before the Great Depression; those that did exist offered both good and bad news. The good was a downward movement over time in unemployment rates. Where Hunter had found 22 percent of the nonagricultural work force out of a job at some time in 1900, subsequent studies suggested that the average between 1910 and 1929 was closer to 8-10 percent, three to five million people, in manufacturing, transportation, building trades, and mining. Also, industrial workers in the 1920s apparently moved less often than they had in 1900 and held jobs for longer periods of time. This trend reflected not only the relative prosperity of the period, but also the conscious effort of business leaders to cut back on job turnover and of unions to write seniority rules into contracts. Hunter and other socialists of the time had underestimated the ability of capitalists to mold a productive, geographically more stable, though by no means docile work force.[25]

Statistics on employment for some of the best years were especially heartening. In 1929, for instance, there were 47 million people in the work force, 19 million more than the 28 million in 1900, and the economy was able to employ all but 1.6 million of them. For that good year, the census showed only 3.2 percent of the labor force as unemployed. The apparently limitless capacity of the economy to absorb an ever-larger number of workers understandably impressed contemporaries and led to illusions about the abolition of want.

The bad news exposed persistent social and economic problems. One appeared in impressionistic surveys of hobos, of whom an estimated 300,000 to 500,000 a year—not always the same individuals in each year—passed through Chicago alone in the early 1920s. These were not floating industrial workers so much as a "hard-living" bunch of drifters displaced from the countryside.[26] Blacks, moreover, remained so deprived and isolated as to be virtually invisible to reformers. The Brookings study did not mention race. George Schuyler, a prominent black intellectual, explained later, "The reason why the Depression didn't have the impact on the Negro that it had on the whites was that the Negroes had been in the Depression all the time."[27]

The deepest problem remained the insecurity stemming from low wages and unstable jobs. Large-scale movements of industries, such as the shift of textiles from New England to the Piedmont, desolated whole regions. Mining and agriculture were depressed occupations throughout the 1920s. Frequent, unheralded downturns in the business cycle, in 1907-1908, 1913-1914, and 1921-1922, ravaged a work force that was still without unemployment insurance. In the worst of these downturns, in 1921-1922, estimates of unemployment among manufacturing workers began at a conservative 14 percent. A careful study of Philadelphia in the supposedly prosperous month of April 1929 revealed that 77,000 (16 percent) of the city's 481,000 families were suffering from unemployment. Of these, 50 percent were out of work for three months, 28 percent for six months or more, and 12 percent for at least a year.[28]

The human dimensions of this structural poverty are best captured by novelists or by the case studies of social workers. In the main, however, improvements in living conditions between 1900 and 1929 did not much affect the poor. The rural poor still crowded into ramshackle, drafty structures without hot or running water, indoor plumbing, or electricity. They had only the most rudimentary social services, including education. The urban poor lived better, but still inhabited run-down, ill-furnished, crowded flats and tenements. These poor—as opposed to regularly employed skilled workers—did not own real estate or amass savings. Poor Americans, abandoned in the hinterland or penned in urban enclaves, had little sense of common cause. They were insecure, and their lives were sore afraid.

What they thought about their existence can scarcely be generalized, for the poor have never been an undifferentiated mass. Hard-living hobos, migrant farm laborers, and floating industrial workers resembled one another superficially in that they all moved about. But they had different backgrounds and different aspirations. Immigrants, many of whom remained poor, seemed to some outsiders a homogeneous mass. But their distinctive cultural heritages affected family organization, work habits, and goals. Moreover, in the 1920s the sons and daughters of immigrants looked at a world brighter than that of their fathers and mothers in 1900—and much brigher than that of the blacks penned in the ghettos or stranded in the backcountry of the South. And how could anyone generalize easily about the values of "the poor"? Those of a fourteen-year-old-boy, classified as a dependent in a poverty-stricken family, could hardly be equated with those of a sixty-year-old widow or a fifty-five-year-old man who had lost his job or a thirty-year-old mother of three small children whose father had deserted. Yet all were likely to be poor. The great diversity of American poverty undermines any glib generalizations about lower-class values in 1929.

Still, millions of poor Americans seemed to share certain attitudes. Whether in 1900 or 1929, most did not perceive of themselves as proletarians. Despite their trials, they still nourished some hopes of success, however incremental, for themselves or their children. Nor were most of them apathetic, docile members of a culture of poverty. Many preserved meaning and dignity in their lives and promoted order in their communities. Far from living for the moment, those who could worked long and hard. When abused, they were ready to strike or stage demonstrations.

It may be that poor adults in 1930 shared more middle-class aspirations of economic success than they had in 1900—that a mainstream value system was developing. A smaller percentage of the whites were foreign-born; a smaller percentage of blacks had grown up in slavery. Improved communications by 1930 made many of the needy a little less isolated than they had been and more aware of what they were missing. Above all, economic growth was real, and it inevitably led some of the poor to share in the improved standards of living. Social scientists and social workers thought the poor needed more, and they constructed slightly more generous budgets (in real dollars) for poor families in the 1920s than they had in the 1890s. The liberalization of such budgets over time, like the raising of the poverty line, reflected the experts' awareness that poor people themselves expected a little more in 1929 than they had thirty and fifty years before.[29]

But everyday life taught the poor to expect only marginal gains at best. Although they aspired to a better life, few thought they had a right to a minimum standard of living—or even to charity. Before 1930 the notion rarely crossed their minds that government would offer much help. As one poor person later observed, "Always going to be more poor folks than them that ain't poor, and I guess always will be. I ain't saying that's the government's fault. It's just down right truth, that's all."[30] Above all, the poor were too deprived and scattered to organize or to develop political power. Social workers propagandizing for better welfare in the 1920s therefore found little organized support for their cause from the poor, who coped as best they could on their own. Until pressure groups of or for the poor arose, there was little else the destitute could do.

2

THE GOSPEL OF PREVENTION, PROGRESSIVE STYLE

THE ECONOMIC GROWTH between 1900 and 1929 prompted great optimism among social scientists. As living conditions improved for the middle classes, many began to think that the work ethic could be relaxed, that there was room in life for play. The immensely popular magazine *Success* began carrying titles like "Why Take Life So Seriously, Anyway?" and "Fun is a Necessity." The eminent sociologist E. A. Ross explained that the nation was passing from a "pain" to a "pleasure" economy.[1]

Economic progress also expanded expectations of improving the lot of the poor. In a post-Malthusian world of abundance poverty could not only be alleviated; it could be prevented. This faith in prevention helped account for the "discovery" of poverty by many writers in the progressive era. It fostered also a plethora of antipoverty ideas from contemporary reformers. Prevention of poverty represented the dominant social philosophy of an optimistic, forward-looking age. It was a goal that continued to captivate Americans into the 1980s.[2]

Of course, many Americans inherited timeless notions about poverty and welfare, or relief, as it was called in that more voluntarist age. Some accepted complacently the words of Jesus, "The poor ye have always with you." Cardinal Gibbons had explained in 1891, "As well attempt to legislate vice out of existence as to legislate poverty and suffering out of the world . . . It is in accordance with the economy of Divine Providence that men should exist in unequal conditions in society."[3] Others enshrined the work ethic. As developed in England under the infamous Poor Law of 1834, this ethic included the idea of "less eligibility"—that life on relief must be less eligible (less desira-

20

ble) than life enhanced by work: "If any would not work, neither should he eat." The Poor Law sharpened the ageless distinction between the deserving poor—those in need through no fault of their own —and the lazybones who would not work.[4]

In the United States the strong Charity Organization Societies (COS) of the 1880s and 1890s applied this philosophy by attempting to abolish all "outdoor" aid—handouts to people in their own homes (as opposed to "indoor" institutional aid)—on the grounds that "the folly of indiscriminate giving" encouraged the "thriftlessness, extravagance, and general culpability of many workers." Relief cost money and damaged the work ethic. No one expressed these ideas better than Josephine Shaw Lowell, perhaps the most respected COS leader. "What shall it profit a man," she quoted, "if he shall gain the whole world and lose his own soul?" She added, "The real condemnation of relief-giving is that it is material, that it seeks material means, and therefore must fail . . . For man is a spiritual being, and if he is to be helped, it must be by spiritual means."[5]

While this rhetoric seemed quaint by the turn of the twentieth century, the work ethic it sustained was far from passé. So scrupulous an observer as Amos Warner, an expert on charity and welfare, believed that public relief invited political corruption and waste; he preferred private charity. He held firmly to the principle of less eligibility: the more public relief was available, the more recipients would prefer it to work. He had concluded in 1894, "Nearly all the experiences in this country indicate that outdoor relief is a source of corruption to politics, of expense to the community, and of degradation and increased pauperization to the poor." Ten years later Robert Hunter added, "Relief is almost sure to result in injury to the applicants . . . support in idleness and dependence does an additional injury to a class already unfairly treated."[6]

Other Americans at the time persisted in popularizing stereotypes about the masses in the slums of the large cities. Two of these stereotypes were almost diametrically opposed. Some writers repeated the nineteenth-century reformer Charles Loring Brace who had raised the specter of the dangerous classes; others stereotyped the poor as they did blacks at the time—as lazy, apathetic, childlike, and sensual. Both descriptions crudely outlined a culture of poverty. Applying this notion, Francis Walker, an economics professor who headed the U.S. Census, concluded in 1897 that "pauperism is largely voluntary . . . Those who are paupers are so far more from character than from condition. They have the pauper trait; they bear the pauper brand."[7]

By the 1900s this fear of the masses was projected especially against immigrants in the cities. Joseph Lee, the nationally renowned leader of the movement for urban playgrounds, agreed that "the problems with which American philanthropy has at present to deal have been largely imported along with the greatly increased volume of immigration that has come during the last fifty or sixty years." To counter the immigrant menace, reformers like Lee endorsed Americanization to heat up the melting pot and, after 1920, birth control. Robert Kelso, a leading writer on poverty in the 1920s, who believed overpopulation to be one of its key causes, called for "such control and regulation of . . . propagation as will result in a selective birth rate."[8]

Other writers refurbished the notion that poverty was part of a vicious circle that encompassed both hereditary and environmental forces. This metaphor, indeed, became almost a popular cliché. Jamieson Hurry, an English doctor, wrote *Vicious Circles in Disease* in 1911 and followed it in 1921 with *Poverty and its Vicious Circles*. He began with the poem:

> Alas! that poverty so oft breeds more
> And greater poverty than went before;
> That social ills in Vicious Circles spin
> And growing strength by constant circling win.

Despite this grim beginning, Hurry shared the optimism of his contemporaries. A lengthy chapter entitled "Breaking of the Circle" attested to his faith that poverty could be attacked.[9]

Robert Kelso also believed in the vicious circle. In 1929 he listed many causes of poverty, including crime, mental defectiveness, the "natural helplessness" of children and old people, overpopulation, physical handicaps, political and economic change, sickness, "unwise remedies" (such as poor relief, which pauperized people), war, and "wasteful or exhausting habits." But he, too, was a progressive environmentalist, an optimist, an evangel for prevention. He even called, though softly, for social insurance and redistribution of wealth. Along with other writers after the turn of the century, he jettisoned many nineteenth-century moralisms. These writers stressed above all the dominance of environment over heredity. "The only safe generalization to make about the dependent poor," an editorialist in *Charities and the Commons*, a social work journal, proclaimed in 1908, "is that they are poor . . . The differentiating factors are economic rather than moral or religious, social rather than personal, accidental and remedial rather than functional." Edward Devine added, "Personal depravity is as foreign to any sound theory of the hardships of our modern poor as witchcraft or demonic possession . . . these hardsnips are economic, social, transitional, measurable, manageable."[10]

No one expressed this characteristically progressive combination of environmentalism and optimism better than Jacob Hollander, a Johns Hopkins professor of political economy who set out in 1913-1914 to test Robert Hunter's findings. Somewhat to his surprise, Hollander found that Hunter had not exaggerated in concluding that 10 million Americans lacked subsistence income. He, too, dispensed with moralisms: "Neither race qualities nor national characteristics account for the presence of such poverty. It persists as an accompaniment of modern economic life, in widely removed countries among ethnically different peoples. It cannot be identified with alien elements in native race stocks."

Where Hunter, then discovering socialism, had been grim and uncompromising, Hollander displayed the optimism of the preventive faith. His book, published in 1914, was titled *Abolition of Poverty.* Poverty, he said, was not so structurally connected to capitalism as Hunter thought. It was "an incident of historical evolution, not an essential of economic structure." He added, "Its presence implies maladjustment, not normal working; its control may be effected by wise social policy; and its ultimate disappearance is a fair inference from the facts of economic experience." Thus spoke the new social science: environmentalist, self-confident, sure that economic efficiency, expertise, and growth would conquer all.[11]

Although environmentalism sounds congenial to modern ears, the progressives' remedies featured new labels on old bottles. The philosophy of prevention, far from succoring a gospel of welfare, in some ways sustained nineteenth-century practices that distinguished, often harshly, between the deserving and the undeserving poor. The progressive glorified the work ethic, usually by making the poor as miserable as possible when they got relief. For all their environmentalism, they still tried to change the needy—to take the poverty out of people —as well as to take the people out of poverty.

Advocates of tenement house reform and urban playgrounds revealed this sort of environmentalism. Jacob Riis, remembering the violence of Mulberry Bend, a foul New York slum, said that "men became pigs in that foul spot." But when the slum was torn down, "The sunlight came in, that was all, and grass, and flowers and birds, and with them peace." Joseph Lee, in calling for more urban playgrounds, was equally optimistic about the ways that environmental change could actually make better people. "The boy without a playground," he wrote, "is father to the man without a job; and the boy with a bad playground is apt to be father to a man with a job that had better have been left undone." Riis and Lee came close to asserting that prevention of slums could change people, or at least change the young. Once changed, they would display the traits of the middle classes, and poverty would fade away.[12]

Prevention was equally the goal of progressives who wished to abolish the evils associated with "houses of correction" and other institutions, including almshouses, where juveniles were incarcerated. All agreed that young people had to be taught the virtues of self-discipline and the joys of work. With these traits, boys would develop "character"—a key goal. "A man's best years," Lee wrote, "and his best strength—the main force with which his character and his life are to be built up if he is to have any character and live any life worth living—are spent upon his daily work." Lee and others praised the efforts of Booker T. Washington, whose Tuskegee Institute attempted to help young blacks develop manual skills. They called for juvenile courts and especially a system of "industrial schools," because only by beginning with the young could the seeds of prevention find fertile soil.[13]

Most settlement houses, which proliferated between 1900 and 1915, enthusiastically supported preventive reforms. The left wing of the settlement house movement went further, favoring a broad range of such social reforms as minimum wages for women and children, unemployment insurance, the abolition of child labor, and racial justice. Younger and more idealistic than the Lady Bountifuls of the Charity Organization Societies, these settlement house workers tried to divest themselves of demeaning stereotypes about the poor and to accept the lower classes, including immigrants, as they were. "Character," they recognized, was largely a social creation. No group of reformers was more knowledgeable about or more sympathetic to reforms in American welfare.[14]

But they too wanted to prevent dependency and social tension, not to expand cash handouts to the poor. Like the COS representatives, the settlement workers worried that "outdoor" relief encouraged pauperism. Like the playground reformers, they hoped to restore a sense of "community" to the neighborhoods and to prevent disorder. Robert Woods, a conservative spokesman for the settlement house movement, explained that "the settlement is an outpost for the discovery, by scientific method, of the next step toward social peace." This elusive goal of establishing community—defined usually as sustaining the neighborhood—was a geographical solution to poverty that skirted the wider economic basis of destitution and insecurity. It underestimated the desire of working-class people to get out of run-down neighborhoods and buy homes in the suburbs. It did not consider comprehensive programs of social welfare. In its most conservative guises it was frankly nostalgic—as was the playground movement

—in seeking to implant the countryside in the slum. The goal of community nonetheless persisted for decades—in groups promoting community organization in the 1920s and again in community action agencies in the 1960s. It remained one of the most durable goals of antipoverty warriors in twentieth-century America.[15]

Another goal of settlement workers—instilling middle-class aspirations among the poor—also encountered difficulties. This is not to say that all settlement workers were paternalistic: Thorstein Veblen was unfair in describing them as "young ladies with weak eyes and young gentlemen with weak chins fluttering confused among heterogeneous foreigners, offering cocoa and sponge cake as a sort of dessert to the factory system." But they did hope to impress upon immigrants the value of education. In this aim they had indifferent success. Some poor people, notably Jews, responded enthusiastically to the educational and cultural offerings of settlement houses. But most heads of family spent ten to twelve hours daily at a job, or looking for one. Men in particular were actively suspicious of the cultural and educational "frills" offered by the Yankee do-gooders down the block. Fathers struggling to support their families exercised their usually unchallenged paternal authority to demand that wives and children spend their time working. The settlement could not reach these men.[16]

Settlement house workers lacked the resources to do much about the poorest of the poor. In Chicago, home of Jane Addams's much-touted Hull House, the police were a much more important source of relief for unemployed men. In 1901, 92,500 men found overnight lodgings in police stations. Upset by this drain on public resources, the city streamlined its care in 1902. The police were instructed to refuse the men refuge in the stations unless applicants appeared after ten at night or in severely cold weather. The homeless could then be housed but were warned that the next time they would be prosecuted as vagrants and beggars. As a result of this reform, the number of men given overnight lodging in Chicago dropped in one year from 92,500 to 16,800, 11,000 of whom stayed in a new municipal house and 5,800 of whom found refuge with the police. Neither Hull House nor any other organization, private or public, succeeded in promoting institutions to augment police welfare (or of the "welfare" provided by political bosses) in succeeding years.[17]

For these and other reasons, the settlement house movement lost force in the teens and twenties, and the organized charitable agencies again assumed a more visible role. By then these were more self-consciously scientific and professional than in the COS's glory days of the 1880s. By 1919 there were seventeen schools of social work, organized into the American Association of Professional Schools of Social

Work. Communities, meanwhile, had begun to establish federations of charities, created on what the city of Cleveland, a pioneer, publicized as a "solid systematic and scientific basis." These were the forerunners of the Community Chests of the 1920s. Like the COS's they replaced, the charity federations carefully investigated each case to ensure against waste or fraud. They relied on private funding, and they resisted public welfare. Josephine Shaw Lowell would have approved of their preventive aims.[18]

The elite of the charity establishment, trained in schools of social work, naturally wanted to practice what it had been taught: expert case work, not social reforms. Some thoughtful leaders, like Mary Richmond, did investigate general social conditions, but many relied heavily on psychiatric case work. "All social case work," one expert explained, "is mental hygiene. Case work not founded on the point of view of personality and adjustment for which mental hygiene contends is simply poor case work, superficial in diagnosis and blind in treatment."[19] Outraged social reformers complained about this emphasis. Paul Kellogg, editor of the reform-minded Survey magazine, grumbled that it portrayed the "drama of people's insides rather than the pageantry of their group contacts and common needs." The radical A. J. Muste noted simply that social work had "gone psychiatric in a world which has gone industrial." Though many social workers were not so psychiatrically oriented, it was true that they focused on counseling and other preventive techniques, obscuring and even ignoring larger structural problems.[20]

The increasingly activist American Association for Labor Legislation (AALL), founded in 1906, also spread the gospel of prevention. Though it supported long-range goals such as Social Security, minimum wages, and stronger trade unions, before 1920 its focus was on prevention of unemployment and of accidents on the job. Work accidents, it stressed, harmed industrial efficiency and led to a loss in 1910 of $1.5 billion, or 5 percent of the national income. Workmen's compensation was therefore a sound "investment in human capital," as was unemployment insurance. The AALL leaders drew on the plan enacted in 1911 in England, which taxed employers and employees, added funds from the public purse, extended payments for up to fifteen weeks, and provided for refunds to individual employers with good records in avoiding layoffs.[21]

The refund provision was not so important in England, where unemployment was widely understood to be a broad industrial problem over which individual employers had little control. The cost of paying insurance had to be pooled among all employers. In the United States, however, AALL leaders made the refund idea a core of their preventist philosophy. In part they believed that the United States, lacking reliable statistics on unemployment, could not easily devise a system of pooling; in part, as progressives they tended to blame individual corporate leaders for what more often than not were structural problems. But their root faith was in prevention. In the 1930s the planners of America's social security system, following the lead of the AALL, encouraged states to include in their plans for unemployment compensation "merit rating" provisions to reward employers with records of stable employment.

Preventist aspirations were only a little less important in the movement to offer public aid to mothers with dependent children. Beginning in Illinois in 1911, the movement spread quickly to include all but eight states in 1926. Clearly such pensions could "prevent" nothing except hardship; they were outdoor relief to a needy class of people. From the beginning, however, supporters perceived this type of relief as an inexpensive alternative to taking care of widows and their dependent children in public institutions. Advocates made sure that money went only to "deserving" mothers who passed a means test, which tended to exclude all but poor widows, 81 percent of known cases in 1931. Leaving nothing to chance, legislators wrote into mothers' aid statutes provisions denying assistance to women who were not "physically, mentally, and morally fit." They regularly refused help to mothers who had been deserted or who had given birth to illegitimate children. Homer Folks, a leading progressive advocate of better care for children, argued in 1914 that "to pension desertion or illegitimacy would, undoubtedly, have the effect of a premium upon these crimes against society." For Folks and other reformers, it was vitally important to prevent waste and fraud and to limit carefully the welfare functions of government.[22]

These attitudes toward poverty between 1900 and 1930 had a mixed impact on actual practice. Some reformers, reflecting the optimism of the age, rejoiced that "public welfare" was replacing the older "charities and corrections" philosophy. They observed happily that twenty-five states established "Social Welfare" or "Public Welfare" agencies between 1917 and 1929. Kelso explained in 1923 that "government, keeping in step with deeper currents of thought and understanding, has gone from a watchdog of public expenditures for the housing of the poor to leader in the constructive social work of the community."[23]

Other progressive writers offered statistics suggesting that welfare spending increased both absolutely and per capita from 1900 to 1930. Though nationwide statistics are sketchy and unreliable, one solid study of sixteen cities showed that public outdoor aid rose from $1 million in 1911 to $7.4 million in 1928. Public aid to mothers of dependent children increased during the same period from $14,000 to $11 million. Another study concluded that "social welfare expenditures," including education, rose from 2.4 percent of the gross national product (GNP) in 1890 to 3.9 percent in 1929. The economist Wesley Mitchell, noting such progress, spoke for many social scientists when he wrote in 1929: "Research and study, the orderly classification of knowledge, joined to increasing skill, well may make complete control of the economic system a possibility."[24]

But neither Mitchell nor anyone else scrutinized such figures very carefully. No one paid enough attention to poverty between 1905 and 1930 to determine how many Americans actually received aid or for how long. The best one can do is to interpolate from government statistics, which suggest that spending for social insurance and welfare at all levels of government rose from around $114 million in 1913 to $500 million in 1929. This did not include aid for health and education or to veterans; it did include both indoor (institutional) and outdoor relief. Private charity for youth services, welfare, and race relations, at about one-third to one-half such amounts, may have increased the totals to as much as $180 million and $750 million, respectively. Other statistics suggest that between 4 and 10 percent of the population received either public or private aid during those years. Using the higher figure of 10 percent, the overall relief picture looks like this:[25]

	1913	1929
Total welfare spending (*public and private, in millions of constant dollars*)	180	750
Total population (*in millions*)	97	122
Spending per capita (*in dollars, annual*)	1.85	6.25
Total recipients (*in millions*)	9.7	12.2
Spending per recipient (*in dollars, annual*)	$18.50	$62.50
% of GNP (*current prices*)	.45%	.73%

Considering these figures, it is not surprising that many activists were discouraged. For the need remained considerable in 1929, when approximately 70 million Americans lived in families with total earnings of less than $2,000 a year—the amount that the Brookings Institution researchers thought was "sufficient to supply only basic necessities." Perhaps 40 million lived in families earning less than $1,200, a low subsistence line in use at the time. There was no way that the relief offered in that year could sustain these people.

Activists were equally discouraged about the prospects for public action. In 1930 they were only beginning to establish nationwide networks and lobbies. Reformers then formed the American Association for Public Welfare but lacked the funds to hire a staff or engage in any important activities. The American Association for Old Age Security, created as a lobby in 1927, had collaborated with the AALL to push for old-age pensions, but with little success: in 1929, eleven states paid a grand total of $222,000 in pensions for all of 1,000 old people. Advocates of social insurance, such as Isaac Rubinow and Abraham Epstein, felt they were crying in the wilderness. As of 1930 no state had enacted an unemployment insurance plan, and spending for mothers' aid remained pitifully small. In 1931, only 93,260 of the 3.8 million female-headed families in the United States received mothers' assistance. The average monthly family grant ranged from $4.33 in Arkansas to $69.31 in Massachusetts.

The states, moreover, did not require their subdivisions to provide either pensions or mothers' aid. The federal government spent no money on relief in 1929, except for Indian wards, seamen, veterans, and some institutions, and the states persisted in opposing outdoor assistance. Eight states actually instructed local governments on the maximum amounts they might spend on such aid, ranging from $8 per month per person in Alabama to $200 a year in New Jersey. But most state spending on relief and welfare in the 1920s went for indoor aid, including funding for almshouses—old, shabby structures serviced by aging staffs. The most up-to-date nationwide survey, in 1923, revealed that 2,046 almshouses maintained custody of 85,899 inmates. No one pretended that these were other than custodial institutions.[26]

Old state laws, a fair test of inherited attitudes, in 1929 still authorized towns to "warn out" recent settlers who were thought likely to become public charges, to let contracts to private citizens for care of the needy, and to prosecute people who refused to support their poor relatives. Fourteen state constitutions deprived paupers of the right to vote or to hold office. South Carolina disfranchised "persons who are idiots, insane, paupers supported at the public expense, and persons confined in any public prison."[27]

Under the wide discretion of such laws, local governments, acting as they had for years, turned over administration of relief to selectmen or other elected officials, who, anxious to cut costs, relied heavily on residency laws that remained unchanged from the seventeenth and eighteenth centuries. Most of these laws still required applicants for relief to have lived in the town for a year; eighteen state laws required a stay of two years or more. Localities bent these laws to suit their purposes, often denying aid even to needy people who claimed to have established settlement. In such cases the poor had no right to a hearing. Conflicts were endless between towns trying to pass on their responsibility. In New York between 1928 and 1932 litigation in such disputes cost $192,000, compared to the $215,000 that could have been spent to maintain those poor people during the time of litigation. In these years 11,234 New Yorkers—more than 2,000 per year—were "removed" from one town to another as a result of such suits.

Three cases suggest the working of local poor laws as late as 1933-1935. In Syracuse, New York, a woman who had established her settlement married an immigrant, who then traveled to Canada to straighten out his papers, only to be denied reentry to the United States. When the woman and her children applied for aid, the town demurred, arguing that her marriage to an immigrant without the right of settlement made her ineligible for relief. She received aid only after extended legal hassling. In the second case, the town of Plymouth, Massachusetts, tried to avoid supporting a young illegitimate girl whose mother had died. The town tried to force the grandfather to pay, but he refused, and a law case followed. After protracted maneuvering, the grandfather won his case—not because the town was decreed to have the responsibility but because by seventeenth-century state law, an illegitimate child was legally the obligation of no one! In the third case, when a temporarily unemployed Maine man applied for aid, the town not only denied his claim but insisted on defining him as a "pauper," and thus ineligible to vote.[28]

That was in 1935. By then Germany had had a social insurance system for fifty years, Great Britain and Sweden for almost twenty-five. Most Western European nations paid family allowances designed in part to help the poor. Though reliable international statistics on relief spending do not exist, contemporary reformers were sure that America lagged far behind Europe in the size of its payments, the comprehensiveness of its coverage, and the spirit in which aid was provided. Historians have agreed and have asked the obvious question: why was welfare so attenuated in the United States?[29]

One answer stresses the peculiar racial and ethnic heterogeneity of America's lower classes, especially in the years between 1870 and 1930. Divided racially and ethnically and highly mobile geographically, working-class and poor Americans could not easily coalesce. In particular, they did not have a strong Socialist or Labor party to unite behind, such as developed in Germany and Great Britain. This interpretation assumes that welfare legislation is most likely to occur where a politicized working class perceives a common grievance and applies pressure for change.

This argument, although relevant in most respects, requires some modification. Ethnic divisions in countries such as Belgium, Canada, and the Netherlands did not prevent adoption of more comprehensive health and welfare programs. Also it is uncertain that American workers were much more mobile geographically than those in western Europe, where comparably massive movements from farm to city were taking place. Nor is it clear that a powerful Socialist or Labor party is a necessary condition for a welfare state. In Germany Bismarck instituted the social insurance system in part to defuse working-class unrest; socialists opposed him. Similar legislation in Sweden in 1913 and in England in 1908-1911 depended on broad support from the political center, which viewed it as beneficial to national efficiency, and was enacted by the Liberal parties in both countries.[30]

Another argument stresses the pernicious role of the elite classes. According to this perspective, American reformers were motivated not by the suffering of the poor but by more functional, less altruistic reasons: achieving religious salvation, enhancing their social status, restoring a less urban age, promoting social stability, ensuring a vast supply of cheap labor, controlling the dangerous classes.[31] One nineteenth-century reformer warned of "that fermenting mass of vice and ignorance which . . . [threatens] the safety of our social and political institutions." A charity worker stated in 1854: "Let [poverty] be neglected, and the present number of paupers and vagrants continue to multiply in the same ratio as at present, and the time may not be distant when the division of classes—the poor arrayed against the rich —may give us a revised edition of such scenes as have been once and again enacted in the streets of Paris."[32]

A psychologically oriented variant of such arguments holds that reformers, indeed all people, become anxious when facing people who, like the poor, look or act differently from themselves. Challenged, they have a psychic need to stereotype the poor. They project their guilt by calling the others deviants, by "blaming the victim." Only in this way can middle-class people be satisfied that theirs is the "normal" world and persuade themselves that they need not support spending for welfare.[33]

Some of these functional arguments make sense. Elites who sought to instill the work ethic tried to keep people off relief, thus ensuring a supply of cheap labor. Groups like the Chamber of Commerce, the

National Association of Manufacturers, and the Farm Bureau Federation drew their strength in the twentieth century from employers and large farmers who reaped economic gains by keeping poor people in their places and psychological comfort from clinging to damning stereotypes. American welfare owed its grudging character in part to an enduring middle-class coolness toward the poor and in part to the cost-consciousness of taxpayers and local officials. It stemmed also from the purposeful and powerful activity of interest groups that had solid functional reasons for opposing generous welfare and from elitist institutions, including the courts, that sustained these interests.

It is not clear, however, that reformers and experts were consciously serving elite groups or curbing the dangerous classes. Many reformers thought they could bring religion to the poor, and others regarded social reform as their civic duty. Still others cherished republican ideals of equal opportunity. Those who sought to ensure social order were neither unique to America nor, given the turbulence of the late nineteenth century, acting irrationally. Historians who lament the "quest for social control" would do well to remember the complexity of human motivation and to recognize that reforms which indeed did little to help the poor were not necessarily so intended. They might also ask if the obvious alternatives in that voluntarist age to the gospel of prevention—total neglect or social upheaval—would better have served the poor. And they must remember that the economy, for all its growth by 1930, still had not generated enough abundance—even if equitably distributed—to prevent significant incidence of poverty.[34]

Most explanations of the attenuated state of American welfare before 1930 agree, however, on the importance of one force that was especially powerful in America, affecting elites and many of the poor alike. This force was the faith that hard work led to economic advancement; public aid was therefore unnecessary (save in an emergency). Franklinesque homilies on the virtues of thrift and self-discipline had long sustained a series of immensely popular writers, including the almost legendary Horatio Alger. The Populists in 1892, though favoring public works in hard times, reaffirmed, "If any will not work, neither will he eat." A few years later Theodore Roosevelt, himself a hero of the people, celebrated the "strenuous life." "Nothing in this world," he said, "is worth having or worth doing unless it means effort, pain, difficulty."[35]

A second force operating against a welfare state in America before 1930, especially before World I, was the lack of experience with or confidence in governmental answers to public problems. This attitude was not unique among western industrial countries, but it was especially strong in the United States. Any term such as "welfare state" was simply unthinkable in the American context, which celebrated voluntarism, federalism, rugged individualism, and political decentralization. Until 1917 most ordinary Americans had little if any direct experience with government beyond the local level.[36]

Voluntarism in America meant more than qualified laissez faire. For many, including trade union leaders, it involved active distrust of government, which traditionally had sided with corporate elites. Samuel Gompers, head of the American Federation of Labor, never tired of exhorting his followers to rely on their own economic powers —notably the strike—and to avoid political involvement. Though he himself formed a loose alliance with the Democratic party after 1906, he bitterly opposed socialism. Union leaders were cool even to the AALL program, which called for expansion of governmental authority. They knew from experience that the government could take away with one hand what it had given with the other.

Many reformers doubted the very capacity of American government. When Germany and England adopted social insurance systems, those countries already had trained, respected civil servants to whom the administration could be entrusted. The United States, by contrast, had a spoils-ridden, inefficient bureaucracy. As one reformer complained in 1904, "The German success, such as it is, has been owing to a strictly competent and independent administration. With an administration like that which has controlled our army pensions, what would become of social insurance?" Lawrence Veiller, a leading advocate of tenement house reform, opposed public housing. He asked, "Are our streets being properly cleaned? Is our police force being wisely administered? . . . Do public officers sell privileges to practice iniquity? . . . It will seem that we can widely postpone so important an experiment until we have achieved better municipal administration of those functions of government which now engage the attention of the authorities."[37]

Another reason for the lack of public welfare was the European experience with social insurance. To many Americans during World War I, social insurance was distrusted as a "German" product. Worse, the ill-financed English system of unemployment insurance virtually broke down under the strain of trying to care for the massive distress of the postwar period. Corporate elites were quick to pronounce unemployment insurance a ghastly mistake, as were some political leaders who studied the matter. The Massachusetts Special Commission on Unemployment, Unemployment Compensation, and the Minimum Wage proclaimed in 1922 that "unemployment insurance bids fair to encourage shiftlessness and improvidence . . . To the industrious and independent American worker, unemployment insurance apparently makes little appeal."[38]

Hostility to social insurance was part of a broader consensus after the war among elites concerning the necessity for "sound economic thinking." At one level the phrase meant that private enterprise should be entrusted with whatever welfare measures were developed. The 1920s saw the spread in large corporations of "welfare capitalism"—employee benefit plans based on "businesslike" principles designed to maximize efficiency within the factory or office. At another level, sound economic thinking meant that governments must economize if they were to survive the postwar economic chaos. Talk of an egalitarian society, or even of using government to enhance opportunity, was not timely. Socialist parties in England and Sweden after the war demanded economy in government, as did leading political spokesmen in the United States. Social policymaking must operate within the latitude of current beliefs, which in the 1920s was rather confining throughout the western industrialized world.[39]

Underlying all these beliefs was the fundamental attitude, especially among reformers, of optimism about the future of the economy. After 1900 it seemed that the bad old days of heavy work, hard times and labor strife were fading away. Old-fashioned moralisms and hereditarian notions about the lower classes seemed less relevant, for the economic environment was improving every day. And reformers expected progress to continue. These expanded expectations underlay the "discovery" of poverty during the progressive era, and in the long run they made possible, indeed unavoidable, the great changes in social policy of the 1960s, when unparalleled affluence banished the old world of fear and scarcity.

Among reformers, this optimism concocted a strange brew of complacency and utopianism. A few structuralists, like Robert Hunter, prescribed state intervention on a broad scale. Most others shrank from such strong medicine—in part because legislators would not swallow it, in part because their goals were stability and economic progress, not an egalitarian society. So they contented themselves with reforms to improve efficiency and prevent dislocation, in the expectation that a modest amount of social engineering would soon put matters right. In hindsight this faith in prevention seems complacent. In its complacency, its paternalism, and its hostility to public welfare, prevention progressive-style differed only in degree, not in kind, from the harsher gospel of prevention that had characterized earlier generations of reformers.

II
COPING AND
REHABILITATION
1930-1960

3
THE POOR
IN THE DEPRESSION

ACTIVIST SOCIAL WORKERS in the catastrophic Depression of the 1930s probably came closer to poor people than did any other middle-class groups. Their reports seethed with outrage:

Massachusetts, 1934: About the unemployed themselves: this picture is so grim that whatever words I use will seem hysterical and exaggerated. And I find them all in the same shape—fear, fear driving them into a state of semi-collapse; cracking nerves; and an overpowering terror of the future . . . I haven't been in one home that hasn't offered me the spectacle of a human being being driven beyond his or her powers of endurance and sanity . . . They can't pay rent and are evicted. They . . . are watching their children grow thinner and thinner; fearing the cold for children who have neither coats nor shoes; wondering about coal.

Homestead, Pennsylvania, 1934: I went through block after block of houses in nauseating condition of filth and congestion where roofs and walls offer little protection from the weather. In some houses I could put my doubled fist through holes in outside walls.

Sullivan County, New York, 1938: Truly rural slums are worse than city slums. Homes are, almost without exception, old frame farm or camp buildings on shallow foundations. They are heated by wood-burning stoves. In the past few years wood has become scarce and almost as costly as coal. Families from five to seven members have been obliged to move beds into kitchen and crowd up the best way possible to sleep and keep from freezing

... Hardly without exception, roofs leak, plastering is off walls and ceilings, and cracks let in cold air to add to the cold, damp mildewed air of the unheated rooms.

St. Louis, 1938: Inadequate diet and unhygienic living conditions have produced widespread malnutrition in St. Louis among persons on the relief rolls . . . and those who are eking out an existence upon near-starvation wages . . . Those close to the situation—doctors, nurses, welfare workers, and educators —believe that the future health of the community is at stake. They believe that the subnormal mental and physical impairments that follow undernourishment in the cases of children will swell the increasing ranks of "unemployables." Children so affected will become adults who cannot, even if they would, work for a livelihood and will thus become public charges.

Chicago, 1936: One woman wrote to a relief station as follows: "I am without food for myself and child. I only got $6.26 to last me from the tenth to the twenty-fifth. That order is out and I haven't anything to eat. We go to bed hungry. Please give us something to eat. I cannot stand to see my child hungry."

Another woman requesting rent wrote: "I must have rent for my flat. I am not strong enough to fight for anything so if I don't get attention in my desperate situation I just can't survive any more. It isn't worth it."

Chicago, 1938: Mr. X fainted while waiting his turn in the relief line. He was picked up and taken to the Cook County Hospital, where he later died of stomach hemorrhages. It is believed that his illness was aggravated by poor diet.[1]

Social workers had reported cases such as these for years, describing situations that had existed long before the Depression of the 1930s. The "old" poverty that had aroused Riis, Hunter, and others was concentrated among the same groups that had always suffered the most: "unemployables" (the aged, the sick, the disabled, children in female-headed families); disadvantaged minority groups; workers in unstable or low-paying jobs; and displaced employees in depressed areas or trades.

The most deprived members of this old poverty were small farmers, especially sharecroppers and tenants in the South. A total of 8.5 million people (3 million of whom were blacks) lived in 1.7 million southern tenant and cropper families in 1930. This was one-fourth of the southern population. Typically they lived in two- to three-room unpainted cabins without screens, doors, plumbing, electricity, running water, or sanitary wells. They subsisted on salt pork, flour, cornmeal, molasses, dried peas, and beans. Most tenants had not received any cash income in years; the average annual income in 1932 of those who did was $105.43 per family. Disease was rampant—two million cases of malaria alone in 1938. One report in 1938 concluded that the cotton states were a "belt of sickness, misery, and unnecessary death." Another concluded that tenant families were "schooled in dependency and unaccustomed to responsibility."[2]

The poorest areas of the rural South were virtually cut off from the broader society. Macon County, Alabama, a cotton-growing area that included Tuskegee, was 82 percent black. Charles Johnson, who studied the area in the early 1930s, concluded that it displayed a "static economics not unlike that of the Mexican *hacienda*, or the condition of the Polish peasant—a situation in which the members of a group are 'muffled with a vast apathy.' " Of the 612 households Johnson surveyed, 443 rented as tenants or croppers, and 108 lived in cabins on plantations. Most of the cabins were more than thirty years old and lacked windows. Of the 443 tenant dwellings, 310 had open privies, 296 no sewage disposal at all, 81 no water on the premises. Johnson concluded: "The crowding together of families in these small rooms destroys all privacy, dulls the desire for neatness and cleanliness, and renders virtually impossible the development of any sense of beauty. It is a cheerless condition of life for those who keep alive a flickering desire for something better."[3]

Johnson emphasized the disorganization of black family life. Of the 612 households, 404 were common-law, and 152 lacked a male head; 144 of the families had 181 illegitimate children. Others who studied black life at the time reached similar conclusions. Allison Davis and John Dollard concluded that one-tenth of black births in New Orleans and one-third of those in Natchez in 1938 were illegitimate. The anthropologist Hortense Powdermaker, observing "Cottonville" in Mississippi, considered free sex, illegitimacy, and female-headed households as givens, perhaps to be preferred to the tenser life of whites. "The typical Negro family throughout the South," she wrote in 1939, "is matriarchal and elastic [extended], in striking contrast to the more rigid and patriarchal family organization of occidental white culture." Dollard agreed. "There is much behavior," he wrote, "that is sheer gratification of indolent tendencies, the mark of a relaxed and aimless existence in exact contrast to the intense 'time is money' attitude of mobile middle class people."[4]

These views, verging on romanticism, reflected the cultural relativism that thrived in anthropology at the time. Other writers saw nothing to romanticize; to the sociologist E. W. Burgess, "an unorganized and disorganized family life'' was the American Negro's ''chief handicap.'' The writings of E. Franklin Frazier, although subject to differing emphases, stressed the breakdown of black family life during and after slavery. And the Swedish scholar Gunnar Myrdal later drew heavily on Frazier and others to offer the bleakest picture of all. ''In practically all its divergences,'' he wrote, ''American Negro culture is not something independent of general American culture. It is a distorted development, or a pathological condition, of the general American culture.'' This structural emphasis was echoed again in 1965, when Daniel Moynihan, then assistant secretary of labor, wrote of the ''tangle of pathology'' that gripped black families in the United States.[5]

Neither the romantic nor the pathological view is very reliable. Subsequent studies suggest that places like Macon County were unusually poor, that on the whole two-parent families were the norm among blacks as well as whites, and that illegitimacy rates, if controlled for income, did not differ substantially by race. As Powdermaker and others noted at the time, a major reason for female-headed black households was the shorter life expectancy of black males. Still, southern blacks did suffer grievously from an especially deep economic poverty.[6]

A sample of 165,000 urban households on relief in 1934 drew almost as bleak a picture of old, pre-Depression poverty. It showed that 20 percent of these households had no employable member, and that of the rest, 25 percent depended on jobs that paid below-subsistence wages. The others were headed by the unemployed, 14 percent of whom had lost their last jobs at their usual occupation prior to the spring of 1929. In nine cities, including Detroit, 20 percent of men on relief rolls were pre-Depression unemployed. The survey concluded that there was a ''residual group of long-term unemployed who are at the core of a permanent relief problem,'' who suffered from the plagues that Hunter had warned against: the insecurity and dependency of an industrial age. Utterly dependent on wages, they were helpless in hard times. As the report put it, they were ''stranded in every sense of the word.''[7]

Long-term structural developments essentially unrelated to the Depression compounded the poverty problem in the 1930s and thereafter. One was the aging of the population. The number of Americans over sixty-five increased from 4.9 million in 1920 to 9 million in 1940, from 4.6 to 6.9 percent of total population. Even in good times, old people were among the last hired and first fired; a majority of them were poor. Another scourge was depletion of the soil, culminating in the Dust Bowl. A third development was the increase in the labor force; 500,000 more people sought jobs each year. It required a very expansive economy to keep pace. Finally, there was residual unemployment even in the good years of the 1920s, beginning with a low estimate of a million per year.

The dimensions of this old poverty in the 1930s defy precise measurement. No one had bothered to collect adequate statistics on poverty before the Depression, and government officials in the 1930s were slow to count even unemployment. As Harry Hopkins, head of federal relief efforts, admitted in 1936, "A major obstacle in the path of meeting the problem of unemployment has been the absence of really adequate unemployment figures." He might have added that knowledge of poverty unrelated to unemployment was equally sketchy. Robert Hunter's complaint in 1904 was still valid: "The United States spends more money than any other nation in the world upon statistical investigations, and yet we know less about the poverty of the people than almost any other great nation of the Western world."

It is nonetheless possible, by interpolating from vital statistics, to outline the dimensions of the old poverty. In 1930 the number of people in disadvantaged families was approximately 18 million (6.6 million aged, 1 million disabled, 10.5 million women and children in female-headed families). Perhaps 12 to 15 million of these, 10 to 15 percent of the population of 123 million in 1930, lived under a low line of subsistence (around $1,200 for urban families of four in 1930).

These people, however, were not even a majority of the perhaps 40 million Americans who lived below such a line at the time. Almost all of the 10 million nonwhites living in male-headed, nonaged households were poor. Added to these were at least 10 million people in families headed by nonaged, able-bodied, white male workers. Poorly paid and irregular employment continued to be major causes of poverty in the United States.[8]

In 1942 the National Resources Planning Board (NRPB) issued useful estimates of the long-range dimensions of this old poverty. It concluded that around 18 million people, nearly 14 percent of the population, in more than 4 million households would always fall short of earning a subsistence income, even in a healthy economy. These, mainly the unemployable aged, disabled, and dependents, were not all the same people year after year. Some climbed out of poverty, others fell in, so the incidence of this poverty was much higher than 14% over a several-year span.

The NRPB went on to emphasize the larger problem of low income. In fiscal 1936, a bad year, 18.3 million families and single people received less than $1,000. That was around 60 million people. A total of 6.7 million families and single people got less than $500 per year. Franklin D. Roosevelt's statement in 1937 that "one-third of [the] nation" was "ill-housed, ill-clad, ill-nourished" was by almost any contemporary definition of poverty conservative. The percentage was closer in fact to 40 or 50 percent.[9]

Contemporaries concentrated neither on old poverty nor on low income. Their focus, so intense that it virtually blotted all else from vision, was unemployment, which the unprecedented depression drove to catastrophic proportions. According to official government estimates, unemployment rose from 1.6 million in 1929 to a high of 12.8 million in 1933—or 25 percent of the labor force. It dipped to 7.7 million in 1937, but was still 9.5 million, or 17 percent, in 1939. Other estimates placed the high in early 1933 at around 15 million and concluded that the number of people indirectly affected approached one-third of the population of 125 million. Add to these the unemployables and those who worked irregularly or at low wages, and the dimensions of the catastrophe of the 1930s are clear.[10]

Statistics, of course, need some comparative dimension. In some ways, perhaps, the poverty of the 1930s was easier to bear than that of, say, the 1960s. About half of the poor during the Depression years grew some of their food; thirty years later about 85 percent of poor people lived off the farm. For them, nothing was free. Americans in the 1930s, moreover, did not expect to own many expensive gadgets. (Fully 40 percent of all households in 1940 lacked bathtubs, and 58 percent lacked central heating). By the 1960s, however, the poor thought they had to have phones, television sets, electricity, and cars. Finally, poor people in the 1930s did not have television to remind them every day of what they were missing. More than people in the 1960s, they were outside the consumer culture. Their provinciality, especially in the rural areas of the South and West, helped account for their essential invisibility in the public eye and for their neglect by policymakers prior to the 1930s.

The estimates of poverty in the 1930s—even those that showed 50 percent of the people below a poverty line—also do not appear disastrously large in historical or international perspective. In Hunter's time similarly high percentages lived at or below subsistence, even by the more stringent definition of subsistence at that time. And even in the 1930s America was a phenomenally rich country by world standards. When Russians viewed the film, *The Grapes of Wrath*, they marveled that the Okies had cars. Will Rogers quipped that the United States was the only nation in history that went to the poorhouse in automobiles.[11]

But Americans in the 1930s did not much care how the Russian people lived; they measured their well-being by their own standards and expectations. Though these expectations were much lower than they were to become thirty years later, they were higher than they had been in Hunter's time, and they had been formed in an era, the 1920s, that had promised progress and prosperity. Americans in the 1930s were stunned especially by unemployment. The surprise and shock, indeed the agony, of the Great Depression made privation especially hard to bear for the new, unemployed poor.

Experts and policymakers, too, were taken by surprise, and neither their diagnoses nor their prescriptions solved the problems of unemployment and poverty; only the defense spending to prepare for World War II ended the Great Depression in America. After that, those categories of people who had been poor before the Depression struggled about as much as ever.

In hindsight one can point out the major blind spots of top policymakers in the 1930s. Until the early 1940s few were prepared to follow the advice of John Maynard Keynes, Brookings Institution economists, and others who stressed the problem of income maldistribution or who appreciated the utility of countercyclical fiscal policy. At a time of economic stagnation few could foresee that great economic growth and affluence were possible. Shaken by unemployment, few people devoted much attention to the longer-range structural problems of low income, of farm tenancy, of old poverty generally. Even liberals, obsessed with the need for economic recovery, devoted little time to planning a more egalitarian society. It was a time to deal with unemployment—the scourge of the era—not to attack low income generally.

But some leading figures in the fields of relief and welfare did believe that government must vastly increase welfare spending and develop social insurance. Harry Hopkins, a social worker with wide experience in the field, was chief among them. As head of the New Deal's Federal Emergency Relief Administration (FERA) from 1933 to 1935 and then of the Works Progress Administration (WPA), he recognized the magnitude and complexity of the poverty problem. His solution, work relief, rested on the quasi-Keynesian conviction that purchasing power was the key to recovery. Distress, he said in 1934, "cannot be settled in a day. We are on our way, but make no mistake about it, we are going to have unemployment on our hands for years to come." The Depression, he wrote, "uncovered for the public gaze a volume of chronic poverty unsuspected except by a few studies and by those who have always experienced it . . . The poorest have in large numbers been kept alive by the slightly less poor."[12]

Many social work activists were to the left of Hopkins. The National Federation of Settlements had been so worried about unemployment even in the 1920s that it had commissioned studies of the subject, which were published in 1931.[13] Social workers coalesced within such organizations as the American Public Welfare Association and the American Association of Social Workers (AASW) and lobbied hard in the early 1930s for federal public works and unemployment relief. Throughout the decade they challenged Hopkins, whom they respected, to expand federal welfare. Some of them worked in the FERA or WPA as roving field observers; their reports to Hopkins and other Washington officials rang with indignation about conditions and offered far-seeing plans for relocating people out of depressed areas, for retraining, and for legislation to promote better wages and working conditions. Social workers never showed more interest in public welfare than they did in the Depression years.[14]

Some social workers echoed Hunter's structuralist arguments. Harry Lurie, chairman of an AASW subcommittee on Federal Action, wrote in 1934 that "the dislocations and malfunctioning of the economic functions which produce unemployment and distress are not of an accidental character but are inherent in the nature of our economic organization." He called for "establishment of minimum standards of security applying to the entire population." Ewan Clague of the AASW (and later of the Social Security Administration) concluded a few months later that "there is justification for grave doubts concerning the effectiveness of the present capitalistic system for the well-being of the population . . . the idea of 100 percent security against all hazards for individuals is not immediately practicable under any other than some form of socialism." Lurie and Clague echoed other social workers and economists, including I. M. Rubinow, a father of social insurance in America, and Paul Kellogg, the influential editor of the reformist *Survey* magazine.[15]

They were convinced that the federal government must not leave relief spending to states and localities, that it must abolish the old poor-law philosophy of less eligibility, and that it must recognize that poverty would never wither away. Some urged a Cabinet-level Department of Welfare to oversee national relief and health coverage. As the AASW's committee on relief problems observed in 1935, "The need, as we see it, is for the Administration to . . . assume . . . a continuing, long term partnership with the states in a generalized public assistance program." William Hodson, chairman of the AASW's national division on government and social work, explained in 1937 that "in the end we shall have a relief load much larger than any we have known in the past. It will include not only those who are unemployable, but who did not receive public assistance prior to the depression; it will also include persons who are receiving substandard wages; it will include the sick and the mentally unadjusted. We know also that progress in machine production will mean a larger number of persons than ever before who will not be employed again."[16]

These experts stressed the evils of insecurity, and a few, like Rubinow, were ahead of their time in presenting the idea that need was a relative matter. Escaping poverty, he said, meant the "opportunity to *enjoy life*."[17] His perspective exposed the long-range influence on economic thought of material advances in western society: the higher the average standard of living, the higher contemporaries set the minimum subsistence. Poverty lines rose over time.

Rubinow and others also considered poverty as but one evil in an economic system that was in many ways dysfunctional and inefficient. Accordingly, they urged governmental stimulation of the economy; promoting purchasing power would drive away the old Malthusian world. They also favored redistribution of wealth. These prescriptions promised much, especially for the working poor who could benefit readily from growth. They advanced well beyond older cultural interpretations that had stressed the "improvidence" of the poor and beyond the notion that the economy would stabilize on its own. Government-aided economic growth, plus redistribution of income, were their alternatives to the gospel of prevention. These were the basis for what was becoming a new "social philosophy" in America.[18]

Although they were articulate and well-informed, the social workers and activists did not make much of an impression on the opinions of middle-class Americans. The results of polls are not very reliable for the 1930s, but they suggest that a majority of the people recognized the obligation of the government to provide aid to the truly deserving poor, including the newly unemployed. When asked if government should aid the "needy," they said yes. But polls showed also that a majority preferred work relief to the dole, which was almost universally condemned. Majorities favored turning over relief to states and localities, where welfare was certain to reflect the old poor-law philosophy. Heavy majorities appeared to approve of old-age pensions, but only if paid for according to insurance principles; few wanted to pay old people from general revenue funds. Revealing uses of words— "beneficiaries" of old-age pensions, "recipients" of public aid— exposed a barely articulated popular feeling that social insurance was a proper function of government and that welfare—except for a few deserving needy—was not.[19]

By the late 1930s, popular attitudes seemed harsher. Reflecting this hardening, Congress regularly cut relief appropriations proposed by the administration. Majorities in polls said that most poor people could get off relief if they tried hard enough. Respondents began to distinguish between the unemployed—perhaps deserving—and "reliefers," "good-for-nothing loafers," and "pampered poverty rats," who were as reprehensible as "paupers" had been in Hunter's day.[20] Jokes exposed the tenacity of old stereotypes about the "idle," lazy poor, and took aim at government welfare projects. "Why is a relief worker like King Solomon?" "Because he takes his pick and goes to bed." Or: "There's a new cure for cancer, but they can't get any of it. It's sweat from a WPA worker." The initials WPA, people said, stood variously for "We Pay for All," "We Piddle Around," "We Putter Around." It was said that the Okies sang, "Merrily we dole along, dole along, dole along, across a dark blue sea."

The tendency of some people to endow even the Okies with the traits of sloth and shiftlessness revealed the function of stereotypes in chasing away the guilt of more fortunate Americans. Historically, those traits had been thought to characterize mainly blacks and paupers. By contrast, farmers on the plains were imagined to be hardworking, self-reliant yeomen. For some people (notably Californians) the Depression changed that image, for it drove the Okies out of their natural environs, threatening others with competition for jobs. Stereotypes then spread, showing that poverty could lead to discrimination. Against blacks, the process had often worked the other way around.

Those who attempted to cut down these popular stereotypes countered with well-meaning stereotypes of their own. The unemployed, Hopkins said in 1935, were "not ne'er do wells, not paupers, not bums, but fine people, the workers, a cross-section of America's payrolls." He added in 1936, "The poor are not a class apart who are to be pitied, but are human beings, average run-of-mill citizens just like the rest of us, and with the same hopes, aspirations, and appetites." Hopkins, attempting to strip away the stigma of being unemployed and to enhance the political prospects for relief spending, did his best to destroy notions about a culture of poverty or the dangerous poor. But it was misleading to imply that the unemployed were an undifferentiated group, let alone to obscure class and cultural divisions in American society. This approach also tended to slight the pre-Depression poor, whose misery had little to do with unemployment.[21]

Some popular writers, on the other hand, portrayed poor people as fundamentally different from the mainstream. One approach showed them as downtrodden and suffering. The extreme of this genre was Erskine Caldwell's novel *Tobacco Road* (1932), which purported to expose the degenerate lives of southern sharecroppers, who were, in

Caldwell's hand, virtually subhuman. The respectful attention given the book provoked one liberal southerner, W. T. Couch, to complain of Americans' "merriment over psychopaths."[22]

With the photographer Margaret Bourke-White, Caldwell achieved a more balanced view in *You Have Seen Their Faces* (1937), which aimed at the reader's nerve of pity. In the process, however, they again stressed the misery and hopelessness of sharecroppers' lives. One caption, under a picture of a black girl and her deformed little brother, read, "Little brother began shrivelling up eleven years ago." Another featured a full face of a very sad, very old woman. The caption said, "I've done the best I know how all my life, but it didn't amount to much in the end." Another, of a dirty, middle-aged woman sitting on a foul mass of a mattress, was entitled "Sometimes I tell my husband we couldn't be worse off if we tried."[23]

Many collections of case studies published during the decade ennobled the poor. One was the WPA's volume on poor people in Tennessee, North Carolina, and Georgia, *These Are Our Lives* (1939). Its brief interviews purported to let the poor speak for themselves, often in local dialect. Couch, who led the project, aimed among other things to counteract Caldwell. Perhaps for that reason, the interviews emphasized the humanity of poor people, making some into virtual saints. The lead interview, entitled "You're Gonna Have Lace Curtains," exemplified this attitude. It closed with a poor white farmer named John turning to his wife: "John coughed gently. 'You're gonna have lace curtains some day, Sarah. Just as shore as God spares my life for a little longer, you're gonna have them lace curtains.'" Another, entitled "Them That Needs," praised the entrepreneurial spirit of a farmer: "I want to buy me about three acres of land. That'd be as much as I could work. Build me a nice little house on it. I'd raise chickens, have a garden, two or three good cows and some pigs . . . I tries to do the best I knows how. I guess the Lord don't ask more of nobody than that. But I'd be a lots easier in my head if I could get together enough to buy that farm for me and Ella and the kids. A lots easier." The WPA volume ended with a portrait of Gracie, a black sharecropper. "Every night I prays to de Lord: 'Please keep death off till I get out'n dis shape. Dey ain't a decent rag to bury me if I was to die right now, and I hates for de county to have to put me away!'"[24]

Caldwell, Bourke-White, and the WPA volume extolled the patience of the poor. Many of Bourke-White's photos aimed from below at people, thereby silhouetting them grandly against the sky. One such photo, of a solid farm woman, had a caption that read, "We Manage to Get Along." The caption under a photo of a Georgia farm couple added, "A man learns not to expect much after he's farmed cotton most of his life." Portions of Caldwell's text explicitly denounced exploitation and racism, but many of the pictures and captions—the parts most accessible to a large audience—tended to stress people's patience under appalling conditions.[25]

Volumes such as these exploited what appeared to be an almost vicarious popular interest in rural poverty, especially in the South and the plains states, echoing the old American hymns to the land. Caldwell and Bourke-White included a shot of a man plowing a hillside, with the sky spreading out around him. The caption read, "Plowing the land and harvesting crops gives a man something that satisfies him as long as he lives." Photographers employed by the Farm Security Administration fanned out through the nation's rural byways to capture the "folk" of America. The photographer Lewis Hine, whose pictures had exposed inhumane industrial conditions during the progressive era, devoted much of his work in the 1930s to rural scenes. John Steinbeck's *Grapes of Wrath*, though dealing with exploitation, ultimately reaffirmed the ideals of family life, private property, and the land. One striking image of the poor in the 1930s was of small town folk and farmers, who were seen as fundamentally good, God-fearing, hard-working folk—the sort that had made America great.[26]

Many liberals welcomed such humanitarian volumes. But the new visions of poverty in the 1930s were ambivalent. Were the poor just like everyone else, as Hopkins sometimes said? Were they the beaten folk of Caldwell's *Tobacco Road?* Was it possible, as Caldwell and Bourke-White suggested, that the poor were both—that they could be at once admired and pitied?

The uncertainty of these approaches stemmed in part from their intended function of reaching a popular audience. Hopkins knew that poverty was a complex phenomenon affecting long-term as well as new poor, but he wanted above all to promote economic recovery and to help the unemployed. He was faced with the dilemma of choosing to stress the normality of poor people and get rid of old stereotypes or of emphasizing their degradation so as to arouse sympathy. The first tactic was unsensational, but the second led to overdramatization and sentimentality and risked confirming the vision of a culture of poverty. Both views encouraged oversimplification that homogenized the poor.

The new visions of the poor were incomplete also because they focused on farmers, ignoring the urban poor. In Europe, George Orwell paid more attention to poverty, as Hunter had, in the "smoke and filth" of industrial areas where "you lose yourself in labyrinths of little brick houses blackened by smoke, festering in planless chaos round miry alleys and little cindered yards where there are stinking dustbins of grimy washing . . ."[27] This was a grim, deliberately unromanticized depiction of poverty. The United States, however, was still a nation mainly of people raised on farms and in small towns. It was not yet the urban society it became after 1945. So rural poverty seemed especially awful. Moreover, the Great Depression prompted a search for roots, for a usable past. Writers, artists, and photographers searching for the "true" America returned to the small towns and the countryside, where they were appalled to find poverty in what had always been imagined as the world of fresh air and good health. The large northern cities, besides, remained a more "ethnic" environment; these people had always been poor, so why write extensively about them? No Jacob Riis emerged in the 1930s to expose the squalor of the slums, which was left for a later generation to rediscover.

Few popular writings dealt sympathetically with a special class of the pre-Depression poor, what the photographer Dorothea Lange called the "bindlestiffs, the drifters, the tramps, the unfortunate, aimless, dregs of a country." Indeed, the poor were rarely portrayed as angry, violent, or class-conscious; rather, they were considered meek and weak. This was a one-sided, almost sanitized vision. The case study or documentary approach partly accounted for this view. It highlighted poverty as it affected individuals or families, not as it hit slum neighborhoods or social classes. It said more about the impact of hard times on a person's psychological defenses than about the cultural traditions of various groups of poor people. This resolutely empirical focus was less theoretical and structural than those of scholars in Europe.[28]

Excepting some radicals, and (to some extent) reformers like Steinbeck, other writers also tended to downplay rebelliousness and class consciousness among the poor. In so doing they recognized that poor people, although frequently angry and militant, found it hard to organize. Their protests, such as rent strikes and demonstrations against cuts in pay, were often violent in those very turbulent times. But they were largely local and easily contained. Another reason why observers underplayed rebelliousness was the virtual invisibility of the urban, slum-dwelling masses who had prompted talk thirty years earlier about the dangerous classes. By 1935, it had been twenty years since the last large-scale immigration, and first-generation immigrants were a significantly smaller proportion of the population. Many once-poor foreigners had left the old urban slums, which now—the Studs Lonigans aside—seemed a little less threatening. And turbulence in the black ghettos, though widespread, was suppressed. Even when racial rioting occurred, as in Harlem in 1935, Americans elsewhere did not get alarmed. It was not until the 1960s, when these ghettos erupted, that the angry black American became a dominant image whenever more affluent citizens thought about the poor.

People like Hopkins, too, had good reason to downplay class consciousness and rebelliousness. To highlight such activity would not endear the poor to middle-class Americans; instead it would raise the specter of a divided, perhaps class-ridden society. It was safer politically—and perhaps more accurate before 1934-1935—to portray the poor as restless but otherwise peaceable citizens. Or to stress their long-suffering patience even at the risk of being sentimental. Or focus on the problems of rural, small-town America, the bedrock of virtue. So it was that the concept of the dangerous classes faded somewhat in the 1930s, not to reappear until the city-dwelling offspring of the poor farmers of the 1930s joined in the urban riots of the 1960s. In the meantime, many middle-class Americans preferred to think that the poor were people down on their luck—unhappy but uncomplaining.

Did this image of the poor really fit a dominant reality in the 1930s? Social workers and academics who made it their business to see poverty at close hand thought the answer to that question might offer clues about the future stability of the American social order.

Some social workers did not share the view that the poor were normal. Poverty and unemployment, they believed, degraded and stultified people, broke up families, and led to social disorder. One observer concluded that the Depression promoted "immorality and crime . . . and undermined the basic security of our entire social structure." He claimed to find increases in stealing and prostitution and declines in thrift and respect for the law. A team of sociologists, reporting on the lowest classes in "Elmtown" in the late 1930s, found a "scum of the city"—people "resigned to life in a community that despises them for their disregard of morals, lack of 'success' goals, and dire poverty." This "distinctive subculture" was "isolated from organized community activities." It featured family disorganization, criminal behavior, and psychological maladjustment.[29]

Concern about the psychology of the poor, about "morale," grew during the decade. The unemployed, writers observed, were more likely to grow morose (some committed suicide, many deserted their families) than to commit crimes. They blamed themselves, not society. One of Hopkins's many field observers reported that "mental deterioration is reported to be extremely serious . . . a mere job is not enough for these people, for their morale is broken." Another lamented that "there is a terrible problem here of salvaging human material, or letting it permanently rot . . . this ailment [of poverty] is chronic and needs long-time constructive planning." Some feared especially the impact of poverty on jobless young people, who were growing up without what one sociologist later called the "energizing experience of middle class adolescents." One social worker cried that "the young are as disheartening as any group, more so, really. They are apathetic, sinking into a resigned bitterness . . . They don't believe in man or God, let alone private industry. The only thing that keeps them from suicide is this amazing loss of vitality."[30]

Some liberal observers complained about the lack of rebelliousness among the poor. "There are no protest groups," one noted as late as November 1934. "There are no 'dangerous reds.' If anything, these people are a sad grey; waiting, hoping, trusting. They talk of the President as if he were Moses, and they are simply waiting to be led into the Promised Land." Another reported at the same time sadly that "the more articulate of [relief recipients] go into the offices and kick. Mostly, however, their attitude is one of patience—a rather terrible sort of patience, I think." Reporters witnessing the so-called Bonus Army of veterans who came to Washington in 1932 to ask for help were struck by the veterans' "curious melancholy." It was not a dangerous bunch of radicals, but an "army of bewilderment."[31]

Some social workers were sure that the loss of "morale" was destroying the work ethic and creating a permanent relief class. One of Hopkins's aides in November 1934 reported a "decline in morale of our relief clients as each month goes by . . . we are beginning to notice what I would class a complacency on relief." Another told Hopkins a month later that "the psychology of relief has seeped so far through the population that there is a potential additional five million people who will come on the rolls under the present setup . . . The scope of the new relief psychology embraces fully a quarter of the population." He added in another report that "clients are assuming that the government has a responsibility to provide. The stigma of relief has almost disappeared except among white collar groups."[32]

Comments such as these reveal the obvious: not all poor Americans in the 1930s remained ordinary working people temporarily down on their luck. Many were demoralized; others adopted what Martha Gellhorn, a liberal writer, called a "maddening attitude of gimme-gimme." But such comments reveal as much about the values of the observers as about the observed. They exposed in particular a widespread anxiety that the Depression would ultimately destroy initiative, the essence of the American dream.[33]

More careful observers discounted the view that poverty was promoting an apathetic lower class. They discovered the rebelliousness that was widespread among the down-and-outers. This anger rarely found expression as consious radical ideology—few poor Americans conceptualized society in such terms. Rather, it broke forth in rage against the rich and powerful. One poor man in Colorado complained in 1930, "Why don't the big corporations dig down and donate a little? It's always the poor devil that has to fork over . . . Now is the time for all RICH MEN to come to the aid of their country." An unemployed Pennsylvanian wrote Hopkins five years later, "when the half-starved unemployed get a job cutting grass these days, they sing, every tuft of grass, a big shot's head. That gives them strength: when I come to your head, I get roots and all."

Angry Americans usually tended to blame the "big shots" in business, or state and local politicians, not Roosevelt. The president, they thought, was their friend, even their savior. A black Georgian addressed him in 1935 as "you honor sir and your Royalty, Majesty." A Wisconsin woman added, "If ever there was a Saint, He is one. As long as President Roosevelt will be our leader under Jesus Christ we feel no fear." But even Roosevelt was not immune to the rage that gripped the supposedly patient poor. "You are not doing the Poor people Wright," a Kentuckian complained in 1936. "The ones that has a good Living is getting more than the ones are starving to Death." Another man wrote FDR in 1935, "We are tired of hearing this New Deal a Starvation Plan and what do we poor people get . . . you are afraid you will hirt the rich but Not a fraid to hurt the poor . . . or have you sold out to Wall Street." A third added, "Those in charge of relief have never lain awake at night worrying about unpaid rent, or how to make a few groceries do for the seemingly endless seven days . . . it is always the people with full stomachs who tell us poor people to keep happy."

In the first years of the Depression, these Americans were slow to express their anger openly. For the new poor, especially, the shock of hard times was overwhelming. Unemployment made them ashamed, defensive, reclusive. Some contemplated suicide. "A man over forty might as well go out and shoot himself," a Chicago man wrote in 1934. Another asked a Washington relief official in 1934, "Can you advise me as to which would be the most humane way to dispose of myself and family, as this is about the only thing that I can see left to do." But by 1934 the new poor, numbering in the many millions, had huddled together in bread lines, relief offices, and on work gangs. Sharing experiences, they discarded some of their self-blame and grew more outspoken. Many supported the crusade for old-age pensions led by Dr. Francis Townsend or the "Share Our Wealth" nostrums of Senator Huey Long of Louisiana. By 1935, according to one nation-wide poll, 89 percent of respondents supported the view that "the government should see to it that every man who wants to work had a job.'' Compared to popular views in the 1920s, this represented increased expectations of government. Roosevelt responded shrewdly by calling for stiffer taxes on the wealthy. Congress paid him little heed, but his gesture helped mute Long's thunder and preserved his own standing among the down-and-out.[34]

Although the most careful observers recognized the extent of rebelliousness, they also stressed that the unemployed poor continued to seek work, reflecting their passionate yearning to escape the stigma still attached to the dole. Lorena Hickok, one of Hopkins's roving aides, underlined this feeling among the unemployed. "I'd do anything if only I could get a job," one told her, "even to cleaning cuspidors, or doing any other Nigger work." An accountant on a work project said, "I'd rather stay out there in that ditch the rest of my life than take one cent of direct relief." A middle-aged insurance man proudly showed her his card certifying him for work relief. "When I got that card, it was the biggest day in my whole life. At last I could say, 'I've got a job.' "[35]

The head of a New York relief agency confirmed Hickok's observations. "At least 75 percent of the people who came to us," he told Mayor Fiorello La Guardia, "wanted just one thing, and that was work; the last thing they wanted was a charity dole of any kind." A careful study revealed that only 24 percent of 998 people who were unemployed in 1933 had applied for aid two years later. Half of this 24 percent were pre-Depression poor. Wight Bakke, the sensitive sociologist who conducted the study, emphasized the loathing of the newly unemployed for relief. "I'd rather be dead and buried," one said. Another, forced finally to apply for aid, said, "I would hide my face in the ground and pound the earth."[36]

To Bakke, the quest for work proved that the unemployed were not easily "demoralized." Researchers also suggested the need to make distinctions among the poor; one who tried repeatedly though unsystematically to do so was Martha Gellhorn. At one point she distinguished between teenagers, who showed a "terrifying cynicism" and "hopelessness," and older people, "who can remember an easier life, a less stringent world, and refuse to believe the end has come." At another time she speculated that "the foreign born (or one generation American) reacts better to hardship than the native. The reaction of the native to these circumstances is demoralization and breakdown . . . whereas the foreigner attempts still, despite hopelessness and poverty, to maintain his home." Both of these hypotheses were facile. Poor teenagers indeed suffered, but as newcomers to the job market they were less likely to blame themselves for idleness than were the older unemployed. Their "cynicism" later dissipated in the more affluent 1940s. Dichotomizing native and foreign born was simply crude. But those who attempted such distinctions at least struggled to avoid homogenizing the poor.[37]

Social workers and sociologists made other distinctions that were more plausible. One distinguished between the long-term and the new poor. People who had been poor in the 1920s were much more likely than the newly unemployed to display apathy or low morale. They were among the first to apply for relief and the last to get off. Many, indeed, had succumbed to a "relief psychology" before the Depression. Similarly, families that had been under stress in the 1920s were the most likely to disintegrate under the trials of hard times in the 1930s. Some of the pre-Depression poor had lived in want so long that they were virtually hopeless even before 1929. The new poor, by contrast, were less hopeless than bewildered. Trapped in a strange world, they tended at first to castigate themselves. At least until 1934, neither group was much inclined to join the radical movements of intellectuals and activists.[38]

Other observers made useful distinctions about the ways that social class and occupation influenced people's responses to the Depression. Americans who had enjoyed steady jobs or middle-class incomes in the 1920s found unemployment a novel and terrifying experience. They were the most likely to berate themselves, the last to go to the relief office. As Bakke put it, "The higher they climb, the harder they fall." Many blue-collar workers, however, had never enjoyed much freedom or control over their work, and insecurity had been the lot of their daily lives. For them the work ethic was a middle-class slogan. They were practiced in coping with hard times, and the fact of being unemployed, or even on relief, Bakke noted, "does not alter the basic character of the worker." There was not a " 'decay of self-reliance,' but merely . . . altered tactics in view of the fact that the source of maintenance has been changed." No one described such tactical responses better than George Orwell, who wrote of similar circumstances in England: "It may be that the psychological adjustment which the working class are visibly making is the best they could make in the circumstance. They have neither turned revolutionary nor lost their self-respect; merely they have kept their tempers and settled down to make the best of things on a fish-and-chip standard."[39]

Although the working classes tried to avoid the stigma of relief, they seemed better able to accept life on welfare once circumstances had left them no choice. Some, indeed, grew adept at using the system. Once on relief, they shrewdly refused jobs in private employment that seemed likely to be temporary; if they took a private job that did not last, they were quick to reapply for welfare. Leaving nothing to chance, they learned to hide good shoes or other possessions from the eyes of social work investigators. Some grew angry or cynical. "Oh, Christ!" one man on relief said to a squeamish neighbor. "You'll never get anything if you tell the truth. You gotta be wise, give them a good story." This sort of attitude prompted anguished cries about "chiseling" on welfare. To Bakke, however, it was merely a sign that blue-collar workers were intelligently coping with a world that had never treated them well. "The man with initiative," he wrote, "uses every means at his disposal to increase his standard of living."[40]

Bakke's findings did not mean that working-class people necessarily coped any more happily than did the middle-class unemployed. They did suggest, however, that it is wrong to generalize about loss of morale. What stands out is the toughness of the values that working-class people brought to the Depression. These guaranteed a certain continuity and stability. Most people—whether long-term poor, working-class new poor, or middle-class unemployed—used strategies and tactics that harmonized with their past ways of doing things; in a word, they were resilient. There was nothing surprising or especially noble about this.

What stands out also is the qualified expectations of people in that generation. Even the middle classes had lived frugally in the 1920s. Though they had been optimistic about the future, they had not been utopian. They had expected little from government, and they were used to working hard. This cultural heritage helps account for the reluctance of the newly unemployed to go on relief or to join in radical causes. Though increasingly impatient and angry by 1935, they were not organized nationally and they had little choice but to ride out the disaster. It was not until the 1960s, when a much more expectant and highly organized generation began demanding its "rights," that there emerged striking changes in the values and treatment of poor people.

4

THE EARLY
WELFARE STATE

"**D**URING THE TEN YEARS between 1929 and 1939," wrote an informed social worker in 1940, "more progress was made in public welfare and relief than in the three hundred years after this country was first settled." Left-wing reformers conceded this progress but added angrily that much more had to be done. Debate over the accomplishments in relief and welfare in the 1930s resonated for years thereafter, because the setup of the early welfare state in America profoundly affected its subsequent form. Nothing—good times or bad, liberal or conservative administrations, demographic and social change—had a greater long-range impact on the structure of the American welfare state than the jerry-built framework with which it began.[1]

During the first few years of the Depression, progress in public aid was slow. Americans continued to hope that private charity, which performed heroically under the circumstances, and private pension plans, which remained woefully inadequate, could cope with the situation. Total government expenditures for welfare—federal, state, and local—increased from less than $100 million a year in the 1920s to only $208 million in 1932. That was $1.67 per inhabitant in 1932, 1.5 percent of all governmental expenditures, and 0.5 percent of the national income.[2] This spending, almost all of it by local governments, fell far short of the need. The situation in Philadelphia, which developed what one historian called the "most imaginative and effective" municipal relief operation in the country, showed how much remained to be done. That city enlisted cooperation between private agencies and municipal resources, to the tune of $1 million per month in 1931. Nothing like such sums had ever been spent in the city, yet so many people turned out for help that needy families could get but $1.50 to

$2 per person per week in grocery orders. Families of six received $5 worth of food per week plus a bit of coal, secondhand clothes, and shoes. The demands persisted, and the United Fund chipped in $5 million, which was used up in three months. By June 1932 there was no more local money for relief, and neither the state nor the federal government acted resolutely to fill the vacuum, so 57,000 families were abandoned to their own resources.[3]

At that point Franklin D. Roosevelt's New Deal moved to relieve distress. In early 1933 Congress appropriated $500 million for direct relief, and Roosevelt set up the FERA under Harry Hopkins, to provide "sufficient relief to prevent physical suffering and to maintain living standards." Hopkins, wasting no time, spent more than $5 million in his first two hours in office. Most of the money went as a cash dole to the needy; some people got work relief. Later that year Roosevelt authorized the Civil Works Administration (CWA) to tide people over the potentially disastrous winter of 1933-34. This work relief program, available to the needy without a means test, aided more than four million workers at its peak in January 1934 and paid wages averaging more than $15 a week—two and a half times the average FERA benefit. No New Deal creation was more generous or more thankfully received than the CWA. Without it, the country would have faced widespread malnutrition and unrest.

By February 1934, the FERA, CWA, and Civilian Conservation Corps (CCC), which employed young men in a variety of forestry and conservation projects, reached nearly 8 million households, or 28 million people. This was 22.2 percent of the population—a high in public welfare for any time in American history. Though spending declined in the summer months and in the winter of 1934-35, total government expenditures (federal, state, and local) for such public aid amounted to $3 billion in 1935, or fifteen times the sum spent three years earlier. Most of this money came from the federal government, much of it under the auspices of the FERA. No wonder that one observer called the FERA "our most promising experiment in public welfare."[4]

Such rapid innovation did not please everyone in the charity field. Many private agencies, whose top people had been trained in psychiatrically oriented case work, resisted the intrusion of government. Like the Charity Organization Society spokespeople in the 1880s, they were cool at best to "almsgiving" or welfare. Angry at this attitude, the board of directors of the National Federation of Settlements stated that "the policy of private agencies in refusing to work with the public agencies leads to poor work on the part of the public departments." The managing editor of *Survey* commented bitterly in 1933 about such private agencies. "To some of us," she wrote, "it is as though a lot of good people ran around protecting bird life on a raging battlefield. Where a lot of these high-hat family society people miss it, it seems to me, is in assuming that the public workers of the future . . . are going to be content to remain indefinitely the grocery peddlers of social work while the private society people take the part of the work that has some intellectual challenge . . . I wish the boys and girls would forget vested interests and come clean."[5]

Activists complained also about the political opportunism of state officials under the FERA. The states were expected to provide as much as $3 for every $1 from Washington, but many governors and state legislators could not or would not provide the money. The governor of Oklahoma, one FERA observer complained, perceived social work as "that performed in cleaning up a political situation, with possibly some value in work done by ladies of the W.C.T.U. or the Elks in distributing Christmas baskets." The situation in Alabama, another wrote, was "entirely unsatisfactory as being run. The Governor knows very little about the situation." Arkansas's relief setup, said a third, was "deeply rooted in small political groups in the counties." Hopkins, frustrated, ultimately federalized relief administration in six states, but conflict persisted. It was not easy to shake hard-pressed state and local officials from old poor-law philosophies of relief.[6]

The dispensation of aid under FERA provoked outrage from some contemporary observers. To qualify for FERA assistance, people had to appear at a relief station, declare themselves in need, and pass a means test certifying that they were poor. This process often subjected the poor to time-consuming, humiliating investigations. One of Hopkins's aides noted that "few [recipients] understand even the simplest alphabetical designation for the various welfare activities, and the bewildering showers of alphabets wherever they apply for aid leaves nerves that are already jangled, raw and protesting." Another assistant, Lorena Hickok, observed simply that the "public is beginning to resent all this social service business" and the "red tape involved in applying this damned budget system." A third aide, visiting the relief station in Phoenix, was appalled to find more than a hundred people jammed into a small room in 100-degree heat, with an overflow crowd waiting for hours in a nearby garage. He added: "When I see the lack of intelligence, not to say common, ordinary human sympathy which characterizes the handling of destitute families in some places, I am ashamed of what we are doing."[7]

FERA's greatest weakness was lack of funds. Hopkins himself said in 1936, "It is curious that among the almost innumerable criticisms we have experienced, the one most truthful allegation is never made except by the families who depend upon us. *We have never given ade-*

quate relief." In 1934-1935, the FERA paid $25-$29 per family per month, the average *weekly* pre-Depression wages of a regularly employed industrial worker. The FERA did not pay hospital bills or assume the cost of institutionalizing people, and it rarely helped with rent. A family getting $25 a month—$300 a year—fell far short of the $1,200 regarded as a minimum subsistence. Millions more got no aid at all.[8]

Several forces accounted for the shortage of funds: the inability or unwillingness of states and localities to spend more money; the sheer magnitude of need, which dwarfed all efforts to cope; and, to some degree, Roosevelt's attitude. The president, anxious to save money and to prevent relief from becoming what he called a "habit with the country," refused to preach the gospel of income maintenance. He sought tirelessly to obviate the need for long-term relief spending. For these reasons he forced Hopkins to scuttle the CWA early in 1934. "Nobody," he said, "is going to starve during the warm weather." Within a couple of months Hopkins had to fire 4 million CWA workers.[9]

Hopkins, too, thought that the dole demoralized recipients. "I don't think anybody can go on year after year, month after month," he said, "accepting relief without affecting his character in some way unfavorably. It is probably going to undermine the independence of hundreds of thousands of families." He added, "Give a man a dole, and you save his body and destroy his spirit. Give him a job and pay him an assured wage and you save both the body and the spirit." Similar thinking prompted Roosevelt to add in January 1935 that "continued dependence upon relief induces a spiritual and moral disintegration fundamentally destructive to the national fibre. To dole out relief in this way is to administer a narcotic, a subtle destroyer of the human spirit." The federal government, he closed, "must and shall quit this business of relief."[10]

Roosevelt said that those on public aid who were employable should henceforth work for their relief check. He had in mind paying them a "security wage" of about $50 a month—below prevailing wage rates for skilled labor but twice what the needy had received under the dole. The unemployables, whom he estimated at around 1.5 million people, were to be turned over to the care of states and localities. That is what he meant by getting the federal government to "quit this business of relief."

In making the distinction between employables and unemployables the president relied heavily on his Cabinet-level Committee on Economic Security, which envisioned the new relief setup as part of a much broader social insurance program. With the forthcoming enactment of Social Security, the committee argued in January 1935, "the residual relief problem will have diminished to a point where it will be possible to return primary responsibility for the care of people who cannot work to the state and local governments." It urged that states "substitute for their ancient, out-moded poor laws modernized public assistance laws, and replace their traditional poor law administrations by unified and efficient state and local public welfare departments."

The administration's most fundamental assumption was that the federal government ought to handle only "residual" needs. Social insurance, not welfare, was to lead the fight against poverty. As Hopkins put it, "It goes without saying that the plan which helps to make further relief unnecessary is the best and cheapest form of relief." Top officials in the field of social welfare repeated endlessly that a "program for the poor is a poor program," meaning mainly that it was politically vulnerable. So they stressed the virtues of Social Security, a preventive program, under which poverty would gradually "wither away."[11]

Congress, happy to quit the business of federal relief, did Roosevelt's bidding in 1935. At that time the American welfare state assumed its fateful form. Its four main parts were: general relief, funded by states and localities, mainly for so-called unemployables; work relief, paid by the federal government, for employables; categorical public assistance, for the needy blind, aged, and dependent children; and social insurance, which provided pensions to retired workers and temporary compensation to the jobless.[12]

From the beginning the general relief program was largely a failure. Migrants, in particular, suffered after 1935. Under the Transients Division of the FERA, a small minority of these people—perhaps 300,000 at the peak—had been helped, but under the new organization the Transients Division was abolished, throwing the migrants into limbo. States and localities ordinarily defined them as employable and referred them to federal work relief offices, but 90 percent of work relief jobs were reserved for local people on the rolls. In 1936, when twenty-one governors urged Roosevelt to make care of migrants a federal responsibility, the president replied by reiterating that the federal government "has definitely withdrawn from the field of direct relief and cannot accept this responsibility for any one group of the population."[13]

States and localities, unwilling to help the numbers in need, responded coldly to the migrants' plight. Many increased the residency requirement to two or three years. Massachusetts, New Hampshire, and Connecticut enforced a five-year rule; Rhode Island, ten years.

Migrants received harsh treatment almost everywhere. Colorado's governor proclaimed that the state was "threatened with invasion" and placed police at the borders to stop unwanted transients. Migrants elsewhere usually got one day's work and were then jailed for vagrancy. Signs in Deming, New Mexico, warned newcomers: "Do not ask for relief. You can be fed and slept at the jail in return for ten days hard labor." In Los Angeles, mecca for thousands of migrants, police patrolled the city borders. The local paper defended this practice by observing that "Los Angeles has stopped being a national Santa Claus, not from choice but from bitter, desperate necessity . . . We have taken our stand and we will stick to it—even if Arizona's governor calls out the troops."[14]

Many of these migrants were the same small farmers, Okies, tenants, and croppers who attracted so much attention from writers like Steinbeck. They were victims not only of hard times and soil erosion, but also of New Deal agricultural policies that curbed production of major crops. These policies unintentionally forced small operators off the land and into the migrant population. Larger farmers, meanwhile, got federal bonus payments and higher farm prices—virtually guaranteed income maintenance. No other group received more generous treatment in the 1930s. The New Deal's farm policy revealed the differential treatment of America's rural people: subsidies for farm owners (some of them very needy, some not) and neglect and abuse for the rest. Its policy toward migrants exposed the refusal of officials —then and later—to encourage geographical mobility. To develop a stake in the system, one had to stay put.

Those people who did manage to secure general assistance fared only a little better than the migrants, because the states and localities simply did not provide enough money. Roosevelt badly underestimated the extent of need: states and towns in 1936 had to support 4.7 million on general relief—not the 1.5 million the president had anticipated. His miscalculation rested in part on using as a benchmark the late 1920s, when somewhere around 1.5 million "unemployables" had needed state-local relief. By 1935 old age, sickness, and family breakup had tossed thousands more into the pool. Roosevelt miscalculated especially in assuming that economic recovery would be more rapid. If it had, the need for work relief would have subsided. But hard times persisted, and the funds for work relief could not take care of employable people in need. With nowhere else to turn, the jobless looked desperately to state and local relief authorities.

The situation in Illinois revealed the scope of distress. In 1933-1934, local governments had paid only 4 percent of total public aid; the balance had come from state and mainly federal funds. When the

FERA closed its doors in December 1935, it was assumed that work relief would pick up the employables, leaving only a "residue" to be taken care of locally. This was a terrible miscalculation. Limits on funds for work relief left approximately 92,000 employable poor people and their families without aid in Illinois. Naturally, they turned to the state and localities, which were swamped already by 76,000 people previously covered by the FERA. For a while the localities struggled to help both groups, to the dissatisfaction of both. A survey revealed that "relief now being granted in the majority of communities is considerably less than the subsistence level of relief." The state then stepped in with $2 million a month which, like other states, it raised by levying regressive taxes. The growth of the sales tax movement in the 1930s owed much to the administration's decision to make states and towns handle general relief.[15]

Surveys also showed that local relief officials rarely abandoned the poor law philosophy. On the contrary, such officials tended to be the same untrained, often elected political figures who had handled public aid in the past. Without federal help, they had to economize, and they tried to keep all but the most unemployable people off the general relief rolls. Aging workers without skills, women with dependent children, the temporarily disabled—all were likely to be told that they could work and were therefore ineligible for assistance. Or they were treated curtly at the relief office. "A man took sick and couldn't work," one supervisor said. "Now his wife pesters me for relief. I told her he won't be sick forever and they should manage . . . but she won't let me alone."[16]

To save money, many communities stopped providing any allowance for clothing, rent, or medical assistance; others tried to make unemployables work for their check. Some reverted to paying people in goods rather than cash. Many tightened residency requirements or enforced statutes that had been on the books since the seventeenth century. There were great variations in payments for general assistance. In April 1939 the average was $23.86 per month for 4 million families, as opposed to $28.96 four years earlier under the FERA. Ten southern states, however, paid less than $10 per month. Turning over general assistance to the states meant that the wealthiest states of the North and East approximated the low FERA level of spending per recipient, while the poorer states fell far short.[17]

Advocates of better welfare began to despair by the late 1930s. One expert complained that the "end of the FERA has been one of the tragedies of the Administration's program." An observer in Florida reported in 1938 that "the relief population is increasing far faster than funds to take care of them. Submarginal families still live in shacks, in crowded town sections, or on isolated farms. Families of six and seven are known to be in homes with maybe two beds and few other articles of furniture." A social worker in Washington, D.C., stated, "There is no other large city in the country of which I am aware in which there is so acute a situation of need . . . The situation is not only inhuman, but is discreditable to the capital of the wealthiest nation in the world."[18] From any standpoint, America needed a nationally financed program of general relief. Under state-local auspices, relief supported more than 4 million families per year between 1936 and 1940: no other program at the time affected so many people. But both then and later, general relief remained a state-local responsibility, and a weak link in the emerging welfare system.

Work relief promised to be more satisfactory. Roosevelt pledged that the work done would be "useful . . . in the sense that it affords permanent improvements in living conditions or that it creates future new wealth for the nation." The projects would be labor intensive and not competitive with private industry. Hopkins added that work relief would conserve human skills and enhance purchasing power. Above all, it "preserves a man's morale. It saves his skill. It gives him a chance to do something useful." He liked to cite the gratitude of relief workers no longer dependent on the dole. One worker's wife explained, "We aren't on relief any more, my husband is working for the government."[19]

The Works Progress Administration, set up in 1935, accomplished some of Roosevelt and Hopkins's objectives. It employed not only blue-collar workers but also some white-collar and professional people. Its theater, arts, and writers' projects were bold ventures in government support of cultural activities. The National Youth Administration, an offshoot of the WPA, provided part-time jobs to more than 2 million students and assisted 2.5 million more who were not in school. WPA and NYA workers did much to build and improve the nation's schools, hospitals, and playgrounds. By any pre-Depression standard, the WPA was a striking advance in welfare.[20]

But like general relief, the WPA fell well short of being a generous arm of a welfare state. One major problem was structural—between 1929 and 1935, around 3.5 million young people joined the throngs of displaced workers. That number approximated the maximum put to work at any one time by the WPA. Another problem was lack of funds. The 1935 relief appropriation of $4.54 billion represented a peacetime record high, but only $1.39 billion went to the WPA; the rest was scattered among agencies such as the CCC, the Bureau of Roads, and the Public Works Administration. The WPA never supported at any one time more than 39 percent of the unemployed; most of the time it helped around 30 percent of the 8 to 10.7 million who were without jobs between mid-1935 and mid-1940. Its average wages per recipient, around $55 per month, were twice as high as those under FERA, but in some rural areas unskilled WPA workers got only $21 a month. Even $55 per month—$660 per year—was a pittance.[21]

From the beginning, some congressmen and social workers protested against certain WPA rules, including one that required 90 percent of WPA workers to be taken from existing relief rolls. Although this regulation was intended to help the neediest, it discriminated against all kinds of poor people, especially workers who were laid off after 1935. Another rule said that only one member of a family could sign on with the WPA, thus discriminating against women, who generally made up only 12 to 19 percent of WPA rolls. This rule also worked against large families, some of which were worse off under the WPA than they had been under FERA. States and towns regularly refused to pick up the slack and removed from their rolls any relief family that included a WPA worker.[22]

Many WPA projects were of the make-work variety for several reasons, notably the injunction that the WPA not compete with private industry. Even the more useful projects were not so cost effective as they might have been under private auspices. The requirement that 90 percent be hired from the relief rolls led to a chronic shortage of skilled supervisory personnel, and to the use of many barely employable, often elderly workers who lowered productivity as well as the morale of other workers. Even the able-bodied employees were often unsuited for the project they were assigned to. Although supervisors struggled to place people in proper openings, they were too pressed for time— especially in 1935-1936—to inquire very carefully about applicants' backgrounds. And the applicants, desperate for work, told the supervisors whatever they thought would help them get on the payroll quickly.

Another obstacle to efficiency in the WPA was equipment shortages; only by saving on machinery could the limited WPA funds go into the pockets of workers. It was also difficult to discharge inefficient workers; supervisors understandably shrank from firing people in the midst of the Depression. Still another problem was short-term planning. WPA administrators were dependent upon uncertain congressional appropriations, and local supervisors could never assure their workers of a future on the job. The workers' insecurity damaged productivity and morale. Finally, the WPA's working-hours policy created difficulties. For several reasons—to provide a decent hourly wage, to spread the work around—WPA hours were short, usually thirty hours a week or less, and the most skilled workers, including foremen, tended to work the shortest hours. The result was frequent shifts of supervisory personnel, with attendant lapses in continuity and efficiency.

Unfortunately for advocates of government-sponsored employment, several aspects of WPA administration exposed these inefficiencies to public view. At the start, in 1935, the WPA took on workers faster than project planners could use them so that on some jobs there was a "curbstone payroll" of workers who stood around with little to do. Other projects tried hard to keep their workers busy but could not, for lack of equipment. Insufficient trucks inevitably meant that WPA employees had to stand around, apparently loafing, while waiting to load up. Many blue-collar projects were most heavily enrolled during the winter when private construction was slack, but the workers had to take frequent breaks to keep warm. Bystanders observing men huddling about a stove or at the door of a shack often assumed that the WPA was a colossal waste of taxpayers' money.

Some people complained that the WPA did nothing to improve the workers' skills or to help them get better private jobs. They had a point. New Dealers, indeed, never claimed to be doing much more than keeping people busy. Anxious to relieve unemployment in the here and now, they did little to develop manpower training programs. They hoped that the need for such special programs, like the need for relief, would wither away. They concentrated on tiding workers over until the emergency disappeared.

In this emphasis the New Deal differed from the war on poverty unleashed thirty years later by President Lyndon Johnson. That program, like the ideas of many progressives before 1929, developed in a generally prosperous, confident time. Its goals were more preventive and more optimistic than the relatively modest ambitions of the WPA. During the Depression public officials were coping with an emergency situation and did not have time for social engineering. They were relatively free of paternalistic notions about changing people.[23]

Perhaps the most stinging criticism of the WPA refuted the claim that work relief did wonders for morale. On some white-collar projects it did. Morale seemed high also on those blue-collar projects in which the workers were well-fitted for their jobs by past experience and in which there were few misfits padded onto the rolls. These projects tended to use skilled workers receiving the highest WPA wage scales. At such work sites, one official observed, "The WPA workers stood up. There was less cringing."[24]

But such projects were exceptional. Most WPA jobs paid poorly and operated on the very dubious middle-class premise that all blue-collar workers were alike—equally able to perform any manual labor, no matter how demanding or unfamiliar. For all these reasons, workers on WPA projects were restless and unhappy. Although grateful for assistance, they knew they had come down in the world. As the social worker Grace Abbott observed in 1938, "If employment is long continued on a relief basis with hours limited so that earnings are on a near-destitution level, and if there are sudden contractions of the employment program so that there is no security even on this level, then work relief is also destructive of morale. The worker finally accepts a lower standard of living than he formerly had and gives up planning for the future, and finally a kind of demoralization sets in."[25]

Some observers insisted that the WPA could be improved, that government-sponsored employment could be a key strategy against poverty and unemployment. The CWA, after all, had eschewed means tests, paid fairly decent wages, and sustained morale over a bitter winter season. But taxpayers chafed at the expense of work relief, which because of project costs was higher per worker than was direct relief. Contractors grumbled that WPA projects cut into their business, and some of the skilled craft unions thought the "security wage" undermined wage scales. As the sense of crisis subsided in the mid- and late 1930s, Americans generally seemed to sour on the WPA. A poll in 1936 found only 25 percent saying that people taken off the rolls would have an "easy time" finding work. By August 1937, however, the economy seemed stronger, and 55 percent responded that "many people" in WPA "could get jobs if they tried." When skilled workers in New York City, protesting WPA wages, staged a walkout in 1939, 74 percent of city residents told pollers for the American Institute of Public Opinion that the strikers should be fired. The WPA, they said, was a "form of charity, and the workers should be glad of what they get."[26]

Some liberals doubted the long-range potential for large-scale public employment, but they did not jettison the idea of public welfare. Instead they called for greater reliance on direct relief to supply everybody with a basic minimum income. This would be income maintenance as a right, with no snooping social workers or meddlesome politicians. Because it would be universal, no one would feel demoralized by being a part of it. It would avoid the nettlesome problems that beset the WPA or any program of public work.

The idea of universal income maintenance was too radical for the time. Only large farmers, a potent pressure group, received this kind of guarantee in the 1930s. This lack of interest was unfortunate, for advocates of the idea were correct that demoralization came mainly from being unemployed and poor, not from accepting relief. They were correct also in pointing out that universal income maintenance was less stigmatizing and potentially a more secure source of support than was work relief as administered under the WPA.

By the end of the decade, however, the whole idea of work relief was under attack from increasingly conservative critics, who said the flaws of the WPA were inherent in any system of public employment. Even New Dealers, put on the defensive, were not eager to claim in the late 1930s that work relief promised much more than temporary relief. In the next three decades few people used the WPA as an example of a "successful" agency that would justify public employment as a major weapon against poverty.

The third part of the early welfare state was categorical assistance for the needy over sixty-five, blind people, and dependent children. As passed in the Social Security Act of 1935, the "categorical" aid programs promised limited amounts of matching funds; $1 of federal money for every $1 spent by states for the needy aged and blind, and $1 for every $2 spent for aid to dependent children (ADC). The program affirmed the old belief that these people were the "deserving" poor who, unlike the other unemployables, had to have federal help.

The categorical assistance programs represented a modestly liberal step. In approving them, Congress established public assistance to these special people as a federal responsibility. The programs specified that aid be given in cash, not in kind, and not in institutions. The law also modified some old-fashioned practices by reducing state residence requirements to five years for such categories and abolishing local residence requirements. Further striking against localism, it mandated that states had to operate the programs in all their subdivisions. Amendments in 1939 enlarged the federal presence by increasing the federal matching grant for dependent children to $1 for $1 of state money.[27]

The early evolution of ADC—ultimately the largest and most important of the three categorical assistance programs—occasioned grudging admiration from some liberals. Jane Hoey, the social worker who headed the Bureau of Public Assistance that ran the program, devoted herself to ensuring state and local compliance with these regulations. One result of her zeal was a maze of rules that irritated local officials. Her firmness, however, led to slight improvements in the training of case workers, some controls over the size of case loads, and safeguards against corruption and political intrusion. Her tenure, which lasted until she was eased out of office in 1953, at least placed some limits on the attempted evasions of local officials.[28]

Some gains in coverage were made during these early years. When the ADC program was started in 1935-1936, only 300,000 dependent children were receiving help under existing state mothers' aid programs. By 1939 ADC was caring for 700,000. Amendments to Social Security in that year placed some widows under an Old Age and Survivors Insurance plan (OASI), and over time, as OASI covered more and more widows, the ADC program catered primarily to children of divorced or deserted mothers. This extension of public welfare provoked conservative complaints, for no one in 1935 imagined throwing millions of dollars into broken homes; the mothers' aid plans had been restricted almost entirely to widows in "suitable homes."[29]

But liberals were unhappy over ADC's spotty coverage. States were not required to join the categorical assistance plans, and ten states had not done so by early 1939. Those that did made little effort to publicize the plan or to dispense aid kindly: at least two-thirds of eligible dependent children were not covered by 1940. And benefits were scarcely generous. According to the original act the federal government would match a maximum of $12 of state money per month for the first dependent child, and a maximum of $8 of state money for the others. The eldest children in states spending the maximum (not all did), therefore got $18 ($12 plus $6 in federal money); younger children got $12. The national average in 1940 was only $32.10 per month per assisted family. By contrast, the needy aged, who had a stronger lobby in Congress, secured a provision setting the maximum to be matched at $15 per month. These individuals therefore got $30, as opposed to only $18 for a mother and her dependent child.[30]

Reformers lamented especially the pervasive curse of localism. The legislation had originally included a provision that required states, as a condition of getting federal aid, to provide a "reasonable subsistence compatible with decency and health." During hearings on the bill, however, proponents conceded that the provision would permit the federal government to cut off aid to states that did not comply. Conservatives, led by Virginia Senator Harry Byrd, feared that federal intervention would destroy states' rights, especially over racial relations. As a staff man for the Committee on Economic Security conceded, "The Southern Democrats are very anxious not to give to any federal administrator the power to tell the sovereign state of Arkansas how it shall administer . . . social legislation." The southerners joined fiscal conservatives to enlarge local discretion. As finally passed, the key clause merely asked states to fund the programs "as far as practicable under the conditions in such states."[31]

Similar concessions permitted states to apply prejudicial conditions. Some denied aid to mothers with criminal records; others imposed harsh income or property qualifications. Others, while complying with the provision to operate the program in all subdivisions, favored some areas at the expense of others. Most common, especially after passage of OASI, were regulations limiting ADC to families with "suitable homes," a euphemism for homes in which there were no illegitimate children, and to families that could prove American citizenship. These provisions provided convenient covers to states, especially in the South, that discriminated against black and Mexican-American households.[32]

To some observers, the ADC program seemed designed to encourage family breakup. Until 1950 ADC provided no "caretaker" grant for the mother—only for her children. Because the grants were so low, moreover, many mothers were forced out of the home and into the cheap labor market. Mothers fortunate enough to find a job had to report their income to relief officials, who promptly subtracted the money from the next relief check. This 100 percent tax on earnings was not revised until 1967. Many states also included "absent father" clauses, denying aid to dependent children whose father (or any other employable male) was suspected of visiting or living in the home from time to time. Aimed at preventing "chiseling," these provisions sanctioned midnight raids by welfare investigators and other invasions of privacy and even, it was said, drove unemployed fathers out of the home so that the children might qualify for aid. Only in 1961 was ADC amended to authorize the granting of aid to two-parent families with unemployed fathers, and half the states did not avail themselves of this option.

Localism also resulted in wide interstate variations in payments. In the early days of federal welfare, there was hardly a thought of establishing a national minimum—only a maximum. For states participating in the ADC program, payments ranged in 1939 from an average of $8.10 per family per month in Arkansas to a high of $61.07 in Massachusetts, which supplemented the program beyond the maximum matched from Washington. As in the case of general relief, payments were lowest in the poorest southern states, highest in the North and East. Benefits showed no discernible relationship to the average size of poor families or to the extent of need. Liberals, while conceding that regional differences in the cost of living justified some variation in benefits, repeatedly urged Congress to revise the formula to increase the federal share in low-income states, but got nowhere until 1958.[33]

Critics thought they recognized deliberate motives behind these inequities in ADC. Some said corporate interests (including large commercial farmers) kept benefits low to force people to work, thus ensuring a vast supply of cheap labor. Others blamed racism. Some observers, noting how the program could divide families, viewed ADC as one example (another was the WPA rule limiting work relief to one person per family) of the way that American welfare directed itself toward individuals not families. Compared with European countries, which were experimenting at the time with family allowances, the American welfare state did not seem supportive of hearth and home.[34]

There is no doubt that the ADC program gave racists a free hand and forced mothers into low-paying jobs. The framers of the legislation, however, did not plan things that way. They were liberals, not corporate spokesmen. Although they had no thought of upsetting existing institutions or of radically redistributing income, they did think they were making the system more generous. This meant broadening the hopelessly inadequate mothers' pension plans then run by the states. By that standard, ADC was a liberal venture.

Why, then, did the framers not devise a better plan? Why, especially, was the federal government obliged to provide only one-third of the money for ADC, as opposed to one-half for the needy aged and blind? The answer does not point to the power of corporate groups, but to the political circumstances. The ADC formula was adopted from an existing federal program to aid the widows and dependent children of war veterans. That program included an additional "caretaker" grant to the widows and was therefore more generous than the ADC program as finally passed. In the rush of putting together a package, however, no one in 1935 included a grant for the mothers. Edwin Witte, executive secretary of the Committee on Economic Security, observed at the time that the formula "was adopted [by the House committee] without any of the members grasping what they were doing." When Witte remonstrated, calling the proposed formula a "most illogical situation which will result in great havoc," no one paid him much heed. Simple negligence by the framers—nothing more —best accounts for the relative stinginess of the ADC formula and for the lack of caretaker grants for mothers. Congress plugged these gaps in 1939 and 1950, respectively.[35]

One reason for this negligence was that the Committee on Economic Security was more concerned with developing politically acceptable plans for unemployment compensation and old-age pensions. Joblessness, after all, was the most visible crisis of the era. With such programs in operation, the planners thought, poverty would ultimately wither away, and welfare would play only a residual role.

Above all, Congress worried about satisfying the great political pressure from advocates of the so-called Townsend plan, which would have required the government to give everyone over sixty pensions of $200 per month, providing they stopped gainful work and spent the money within one month inside the United States. Old people joined

Townsend's crusade in droves; there were at least 10 million supporters of petitions for the plan. Responding to this pressure, Witte and others urged that there be no limit to the amounts of money that the federal government would match for old-age assistance. "With this limitation taken out," he wrote in February 1935, "the pressure for higher pensions will be taken away from Washington and directed toward the State Capitols." The final bill did not remove all limits, but it did set the maximum at $15, higher than the $12 and $8 for dependent children. That anomaly occurred as a response to demographic change and to the pressure from organized lobbies, which then and later meant much in the formulation of policy; it had nothing to do with the role of corporate groups or with ideas about family policy.[36]

Even the coalition developed by Senator Byrd owed less to the influence of large farmers or racists than to congressional doubts, among liberals as well as conservatives, about federal power. Roosevelt himself favored decentralization and federalism—the more so because of a hostile Supreme Court.[37] Like many others in the 1930s, he thought state experimentation valuable and federal "dictation" dangerous. States' rights in 1935 was a vital ideology, not just a functional cover for racism. Byrd's allies also included many who were concerned about the impact of heavy federal spending on the national credit. Roosevelt, although prepared to unbalance the budget in the emergency, was actually a fiscal conservative. And many congressmen believed that the original financial commitment to provide a "reasonable subsistence compatible with decency and health" was economically impossible amid the depressed conditions of the time. Given the budgetary constraints imposed by the fiscal orthodoxy of the era, and the real difficulties of raising more taxes during the Depression, that was an understandable feeling.

This is not to say that Byrd's amendment made no difference in the long run. On the contrary, it played into the hands of interest groups who stood to gain by oppressing the poor or discriminating against minorities. But that was not Congress's main intention in 1935. The dangers became obvious only later, when cost-conscious states and localities used the law to sustain the principle of "less eligibility," the saving of public funds, and the tendency to place as many poor people as possible in the category of "undeserving." In this sense the ADC program testified to the enduring vitality of pre-Depression notions—among them the equation of democracy with local control.

Unemployment compensation and old-age pensions, the fourth major part of America's early welfare state, were not "welfare" at all. Both

programs, featured items in the Social Security law of 1935, were
financed largely from the private sector. A payroll tax paid by employers provided the money for unemployment compensation. The
federal government authorized employers to deduct 90 percent of the
taxes in figuring their own obligations to Washington. Old-age pensions were financed by employer and employee payroll taxes. Those
who benefited from these programs were not necessarily poor; they
were working people—in later years the vast majority of Americans—
who contributed to "insurance." Still, the early evolution of these
programs illuminates much about attitudes toward welfare in America
and helps explain the weaknesses of public assistance.

Unemployment compensation and old-age pensions marked great
steps forward in the development of social services. For the first time
such benefits were established as rights, not rewards given by paternalistic employers. The programs owed their passage to many forces:
promotion by groups such as the American Association for Labor
Legislation; the support, finally (as late as 1932!), of the American
Federation of Labor; growing public confidence in the capacity of appointed government officials, most of whom were civil service employees by the 1930s; and above all the Depression, which brought
New Dealers to power and intensified demands for government aid.
The success of the old-age pension bill in particular owed much to
long-range demographic trends. The number of people over sixty-five
increased from 5.7 million in 1925 to 7.8 million in 1935, by which
time the group was becoming organized and insistent. The old-age
lobby added urgency to passage of pensions as well as of old-age assistance. Witte concluded later that without pressure from the elderly, "I
doubt whether anything else would have gone through at all."[38]

Many activists were not satisfied with the unemployment program,
which drew its funds from taxes on employers on the highly dubious
theory that individual corporate leaders could prevent layoffs. Reformers argued unsuccessfully that because unemployment was a national structural problem, it should be funded by federal subsidies
from general tax revenues. Liberals failed also to get the program extended to employees of small firms or to domestic and agricultural
workers—the classes most in need. Women, blacks, and migrants suffered especially from this policy.

Activists also lost the battle for national standards of unemployment compensation. Reflecting the contemporary faith in states'
rights, the plan set no national minimum and permitted the states wide
latitude, which resulted in large variations. The most common standards—sixteen weeks of benefits at half pay—ordinarily set a maximum of $15 a week, approximating the average WPA rate. In En-

gland, workers got about three-fourths of their weekly wages. America's plan also stranded workers after their coverage expired; no "second tier" took over. Roosevelt had imagined that the WPA would fill in, but most work relief went to people already certified in 1935 for relief. The newly unemployed thereafter had to struggle to sign on with the WPA.[39]

The old-age pension plan also exempted large categories of the poorest workers, notably domestics and agricultural laborers. When payments began in 1940, only 20 percent of workers qualified. Its payroll taxes (1 percent at first, rising to 3 percent of the first $3,000 of income by 1949 and to 6.65 percent of $29,700 by 1981) exerted a regressive effect on purchasing power. Unlike social insurance systems elsewhere in the western world, the law did not authorize any federal contribution. It did not provide for health insurance or permanent disability, and it did not cover widows or survivors until 1939.[40]

The pension plan reflected three elusive forces that had coalesced by the 1930s, none of which suggested liberal attitudes toward welfare. The development of private pension plans in the 1920s and of government retirement programs for civil servants and railroad workers provided familiar models for the old-age program passed in 1935. Unlike the system in England, which aimed at paying all old people equal pensions to at least a subsistence level, the American program linked pensions to each retiree's past earnings. Workers were to receive monthly checks equal to about 50 percent of their average wages, or between $10 and a maximum of $85. This provision, similar to those in advanced corporate pension plans, attempted to ensure that the incomes of covered workers over sixty-five would have the same relation as before retirement. The emphasis of the American system was equity—the model was insurance—not a national minimum or guaranteed subsistence income. Indeed, the framers hailed the contributory principle as a fiscally responsible alternative to Townsendite pressure for subsidies from the treasury. "If we do not get a contributory system started," Witte warned, "we are in for free pensions for everybody with constant pressure for higher pensions, far exceeding anything that the veterans have ever been able to exert."[41]

Adoption of the contributory principle did not mean that in practice the pension plan strictly followed insurance principles. The benefit formula in fact favored employees who reached sixty-five soon after 1935, because these workers contributed for only a few years and received much more in pensions than they ever put in. Because only a fraction of income was taxed for Social Security, the benefits supported lower-income recipients at a level relatively closer to their wage levels than was the case for richer workers. In this sense it exerted a slightly egalitarian force toward income redistribution—a force that later amendments increased. Still, insurance principles became the key selling point used by advocates of the system, who even implied that workers paid "premiums" toward individual "old-age accounts" with the government. This argument was false: workers did not make a contribution, they paid a tax. But the claim highlighted the distinction Americans insisted on drawing between social insurance and welfare. As one expert said ruefully, "The apparent analogy with private insurance made the change acceptable to a society which was dominated by business ethics and which stressed individual economic responsibility."[42]

A second source of support for pensions was the desire for economic efficiency, and here again, the existing private plans served as models. Pensions were considered a wise investment in preventing "superannuation" on the job. By encouraging old workers to retire, pensions would open the gates for younger, more productive employees, and the carrot of long-range benefits would also reduce wasteful turnover within firms. Such terms as "superannuation" and the idea of a fixed retirement age were relatively new, revealing that the work ethic—once applied to all workers until they dropped dead in the traces—was being directed more sharply at younger, productive workers.

The Depression merely deepened this passion for efficiency. Senator Robert Wagner of New York, the most influential congressional supporter of Social Security, declared in 1935, "The incentive to the retirement of superannuated workers will improve efficiency standards, will make places for the strong and eager, and will increase the productivity of the young by removing from their shoulders the uneven burden of caring for the old."[43] Similar thinking motivated the Committee on Economic Security, which favored contributions from workers as well as from employers, partly on the theory that double benefits would make retirement more attractive. The committee also called for, and Congress approved, a limit of $15 per month that workers over sixty-five might earn without losing their benefits. This provision especially exposed the lawmakers' desire to get old people out of the labor market. The imperatives were opening up employment and improving productivity, not providing "welfare" for older Americans.

The third force assisting the pension movement, and the hardest to document, was the accelerating segmentation of age groups in American society. With economic progress in the 1920s, the middle classes had begun to get accustomed to better life-styles. They had fewer children, and they frequently moved far away from their parents. They did not want to lose what they had by being forced to take in the old folks. For these people, the allure of old-age insurance was not the benefits they would ultimately receive themselves, which few Americans calculated carefully. Rather, it was the assurance that they would not have to take care of their parents in the here and now. To this extent, the pension movement drew upon and abetted the segregation of generations in twentieth-century American society.

Although few contemporaries perceived these long-range forces behind the Social Security Act, many reformers were quick to spot its inequities and limitations. Unhappy social workers blamed conservative pressures, including the Supreme Court, which was expected to rule against a strictly national plan of unemployment compensation; the medical profession, which helped to stop serious consideration of health insurance; and organized farmers, who objected to taxes on their payrolls. "The Social Security Act," one social worker noted, "can only be called a measure to furnish such means of security as do not arouse serious opposition."[44]

As with public assistance, broad ideological forces abetted these conservative pressure groups and worked against more comprehensive, generous social insurance. These forces included fears of the cost; faith in federalism; and disagreements among the liberal experts who devised the plan. Secretary of Labor Frances Perkins, who headed the Committee on Economic Security, recalled the "headaches" associated with the "violent differences of opinion among the experts and advisers." Getting out a program at all, she said, was "like driving a team of high-strung unbroken horses."[45] Considering the magnitude and novelty of the undertaking, disagreements—mainly over the degree of federal involvement in the plans—were understandable. But they delayed introduction of the proposals until early 1935 and made Congress wary of moving too far too fast. Defending this caution, welfare expert Wilbur Cohen, an aide to Witte, later commented that it was better "to digest one meal at a time rather than eating breakfast, lunch, and dinner all at once and getting indigestion."[46]

Most accounts of the early welfare state in America arrive at a balance of debits and credits. The debits were easy to see. The four-part system of general assistance, work relief, categorical aid, and social insurance did not offer much aid to people, did not end the Depression, and did not develop a coherent family policy. It sanctioned widespread variations in benefits and catered to local pressures. It was concerned more with restoring jobs and morale than with attacking poverty, which was seen less as a long-range structural problem than as a by-product of the business cycle. It did not include health insurance or much public housing—omissions that long distinguished the American welfare state from those of the other advanced western nations. Policies that would have redistributed income or established the idea of minimum income as a right were scarcely considered. In these and other ways the early welfare state reflected past attitudes, contemporary political realities, real fiscal constraints, and the pressure to promote economic recovery in the short run.[47]

The most obvious characteristic of the new order was its primary reliance on contributory social insurance and its concomitant distaste for welfare, a reliance reflecting the age-old distinction between the deserving and the undeserving poor. The American emphasis, moreover, was unique; other western nations developed a blend of social policies, including family allowances, health services, housing allowances, and assistance, that benefited poor and nonpoor alike and obscured the distinction between social insurance and welfare. The separation of the two policies in the United States narrowed severely the scope of welfare, segregating general assistance and categorical aid as *the* cash-relief, means-tested programs and making the stigma for those who participated all the greater.[48]

The credits of the early welfare system were also obvious. One was its recognition that poverty was mainly an economic, not a cultural, problem. As obvious as that perception may seem in retrospect, it began to break with many old notions about the dangerous or idle poor and with visions of a culture of poverty. Though institutionalizing the distinction between the deserving and undeserving, the New Dealers turned to an unromantic, practical reliance on cash payments. This approach was considerably less paternalistic than other policies, such as rehabilitation through psychiatric case work or services to "multiproblem families." Long popular with social workers, these approaches gained ground again in the 1950s. The focus on cash payments also had the advantage of putting some money directly into the hands of low-income people. Compared to programs of the early 1960s—notably job training and community action—public assistance and social insurance were liberal in giving money to the poor.

Even in this tentative form, the early welfare state marked a substantial advance in American treatment of the poor. During the 1930s some 46 million people, 35 percent of the population, received public aid or social insurance at one time or another. Public funds for these programs scarcely existed in 1929; in 1939 they amounted to $5 billion, 27 percent of government expenditures at all levels and 7 percent of the national income. Most of this money went for work relief and general and categorical assistance. Though the long-range priority was social insurance, the early welfare state, developed under the pressure of emergency, responded with a level of public aid scarcely imaginable in 1929.[49]

The return of good times after 1940 significantly reduced the amounts spent on welfare ($1.5 billion in 1943), but it did not erase the commitment to social insurance. On the contrary, the framers were correct in foreseeing that the contributory principle guaranteed its long-range political appeal and solidified social insurance as the core of the nation's social services. Had old-age pensions been financed out of general revenues, as some activists demanded, they would have been subject to the vagaries of congressional politics. If they had had to compete for money with other programs (including spending for defense), Social Security might have suffered, as later happened to some degree in other nations. Even the matching-grant approach to categorical assistance had its political uses. Congress could modify the formulas (and did, by increasing federal shares), but it could not easily renege on its long-range commitment to assume part of the responsibility. Thus was ADC protected from annual struggles for congressional appropriations. With political bases established, the early welfare state in America had the potential to grow.

The Depression years, in expanding the social welfare functions of government, also shaped popular expectations then and in the future. In the 1930s poor people did not put great pressure on public officials: they were too shaken, too unorganized, to develop much direct political influence. But the overwhelming needs of the time left policy-makers with no choice but to heed the groups that were organizing, some of whom spoke for low-income citizens: labor unions, old people, the United States Conference of Mayors. Security-conscious after the shock of Depression, these groups lobbied hard for better benefits. Having set these groups in motion, government had to respond to rising expectations, and as government reacted, appetites were whetted still more, expanding in the process a bureaucracy whose business was to serve its customers. The early welfare state thereby acquired two assets that proved invaluable as time elapsed: an organized constituency and a bureaucratic momentum that could not easily be stopped.

5

WITHERING AWAY

When Americans "rediscovered" poverty in the early 1960s, social scientists were appalled to realize how little they knew about it. The economist Kenneth Boulding lamented that knowledge of poverty was "scanty"; the statistician Herman P. Miller complained that it was "deplorable." The sociologist Daniel Bell recalled, "When the poverty issue arose, nobody was really prepared, nobody had any data, nobody knew what to do."[1]

Social scientists also bemoaned the paucity of serious studies that might assist welfare policymakers. A sociologist complained later, "During the 1940s, the 1950s, and the first few years of the 1960s, the topic of poverty was virtually nonexistent in the sociological literature." Two students of welfare concluded in 1963: "It is not known for certain how many [on relief] have the basic external and internal resources to become self-sufficient in a short time with just a little temporary aid, how many when provided with a number of external socio-cultural and economic resources can make a go of it, or how many, regardless of assistance, will find it difficult to move into the mainstream."[2]

This imperfect understanding reflected a benign neglect of the scattered data on the subject during the 1940s and 1950s. If these years had been as prosperous as many contemporaries believed, this neglect would not have mattered much, but in the late 1950s, a host of social problems remained, with poverty affecting nearly 40 million people, or one-fifth of the population. The majority of these poor people received little help from a welfare system that was less generous and comprehensive than those of western Europe.[3]

This benign neglect of poverty and welfare exposed the readiness of

Americans, once prosperity returned in the 1940s, to put the awful Depression years out of memory and to reaffirm the attitudes, only slightly altered, that had characterized progressives in the 1920s. Chief among these attitudes—one that always seemed to flourish in good times—was optimism that economic growth would ultimately conquer all. The market, along with gradual increases in social insurance, Americans believed, would soon eliminate privation. And welfare, a blight on the good society, would "wither away."

Prosperity, mainly a result of heavy government spending during World War II, was both sudden and striking. And though growth was sluggish in the late 1950s, the overall upward trend endured, all but erasing from memory the Malthusian forebodings of the 1930s. Between 1936 and 1946 the average personal income of families and unattached individuals increased (in constant 1954 dollars) from $3,343 to $5,150; by 1960 it was $6,193. This real economic progress understandably excited contemporaries. By the early 1960s, reformers echoed Herbert Hoover and the optimists of the 1920s in assuming that poverty was un-American and could be abolished.

This real economic growth inevitably decreased the percentage of Americans with incomes below the poverty line, however defined. One careful study by the statistician Herman Miller, using contemporary definitions of minimum subsistence—life deemed compatible with "decency and health"—found that the percentage of families in poverty rose from around 40 percent in 1929 to 48 percent (61 million people) in 1935-1936 and then fell steadily—to 33 percent (44 million) in 1940, 27 percent (41 million) in 1950, and 21 percent (more than 39 million) in 1960. James Tobin, a member of President John F. Kennedy's Council of Economic Advisers, reported even more striking gains:

Percentage of families with annual incomes below $3,000
(1965 dollars)

Year	Percent
1896	67
1918	63
1935-36	51
1950	30
1960	20
1965	17

Other definitions of poverty arrived at slightly different figures, but there was no doubting that absolute poverty diminished rapidly between 1939 and 1941, continued to fall during World War II, and decreased, though much less spectacularly, from 1946 to 1956.⁴ The key to this progress was not welfare, which was relatively insignificant, but economic growth.

By world standards the American poor of the 1940s and 1950s were staggeringly well off. The per capita income of Harlem ranked with that of the top five nations in the world. Blacks in Mississippi—among the poorest groups in the nation—had a median income in 1959 of $944, compared to a median for Puerto Ricans of $819. Puerto Rico then ranked in the top fourth of the world's nations in per capita income. In Harlan County, Kentucky, one of the country's poorest counties, two-thirds of the homes in 1960 were "substandard," and one-fourth lacked running water. Yet, 67 percent had television, 42 percent had a telephone, and 59 percent had a car.⁵

This progress was part of a continuing downward trend in the incidence of absolute poverty, which according to official definitions fell to between 12 and 15 percent in the 1970s. These gains, moreover, reflected contemporary standards of a subsistence level of living, which rose more rapidly than ever in the affluent postwar years. So people under the poverty line as defined in 1960 tended to live much better than poor people had in the past.

Some major changes in the composition of the poor population accompanied these trends. Far and away the most significant change stemmed from the technological revolution in agriculture. In 1943 the mechanical cotton picker began its recklessly progressive path, reducing the number of man-hours necessary to gather a bale of cotton from 160 to 25 and displacing perhaps 2.3 million family farm workers. Economic growth in the area absorbed only a fourth of these workers. Many of the rest left the South, which experienced a net loss from interregional migration of 2.2 million in the 1940s and 1.4 million in the 1950s.

Most of these migrants settled in urban areas, which became the main locus of poverty. By 1960 some 55 percent of the poor lived in cities, 30 percent in small towns, and only 15 percent on farms, as opposed to around 50 percent in the mid 1930s who had done some farming. This shift of poverty to the North and the cities was the most significant change in modern American history. By the mid-1960s it helped make poverty visible again and facilitated community organization and political pressure from the poor.

The main dimensions of poverty were otherwise fairly stable during the 1940s and 1950s. As ever, small farmers suffered—they were twice as susceptible to poverty as nonfarmers. In 1963, 43 percent of America's 3.1 million farm families, almost 5 million people, lived in poverty (defined as $3,000 or less per year in 1962 prices), compared to 17 percent of the nation's 44 million nonfarm families. About half of these poor farm families lived in the South, which still had the highest incidence of poverty. Indeed, 45 percent of all poor families lived in the South. In Alabama and Mississippi, half of these families (three-fourths of them white) earned less than $2,000 per year in 1960.[6]

Other groups historically susceptible to poverty—the aged, non-whites, and members of broken families—also continued to struggle against destitution. The consistently high incidence (40 to 50 percent) of poverty among the aged and female-headed families was an important statistic often overlooked by opponents of welfare: more than one-third of people in all poor families were children, and half of the poor were not in the labor market. Three-fifths (25 million of 40 million in 1960) were under eighteen or over sixty-five. For these very young and very old Americans (and for the disabled and mothers of little children), public transfer payments were vital.[7]

These figures did not mean that poverty was restricted only to specially disadvantaged groups. In 1960 approximately one-fifth of poor families with two or more members were headed by able-bodied white males who worked a full week every week of the year. These were the white working poor. Two-fifths of all poor families were headed by people in the prime working years, twenty-five to forty. Still, the proportion of the poverty population that belonged to specially disadvantaged families rose in the 1940s and 1950s because economic growth nudged many of the white working poor over the poverty line. So it was that Michael Harrington could claim in 1962 to discover a "new" hard-core poor of old people, female-headed households, and minority groups.[8]

Although these trends are clear, writers on poverty in the 1940s and 1950s fought endlessly over other aspects of the problem, disagreeing especially over where to place poverty lines. Experts, indeed, distinguished among incomes providing "minimum subsistence," "minimum adequacy," and "minimum comfort." One application of these three definitions resulted in estimates of 11, 26, and 40 percent, respectively, of poor households in 1960.[9]

Attempting to still some of the debate, the Social Security Administration in the early 1960s adopted a single system for measuring poverty. The SSA accepted the Department of Agriculture's "economy" food budget and multiplied it by three to get a minimum subsistence for families. Rounding figures off, the Council of Economic Advisers set a poverty line of $3,000 before taxes for a family of four and $1,500 for a single individual in 1962. Experts admitted that this line was low—50 percent lower in fact than the "modest but adequate" budget used by the Bureau of Labor Statistics for a city worker's family and about half the median family income. For this and other reasons, debate over the location of the line continued.

Debate mounted especially over the utility of any absolute measure of poverty. Critics of these measures observed that millions of officially "nonpoor" Americans lived, as the expert Mollie Orshansky put it in 1966, "with privation as their daily portion." Many of these slipped in and out of poverty. In a mass media age they could not help but be aware of the growing gap that separated them from the middle classes. Experts who focused on this gap later recognized that absolute poverty was but a small part of the broader problem of income maldistribution and relative deprivation.[10]

Experts hardly possessed the data even in the 1960s to settle another important question about poverty in the 1940s and 1950s: what percentage of poor people, however defined, were long-term, and what percentage were borderline types who slipped in and out? Analysts who considered this question in the 1950s and early 1960s did not complete comprehensive studies of poverty populations over extended periods of time and did not always ask hard questions of their data. Thus, early reports suggested that approximately 40 percent of parents who got federal relief in 1960 had themselves been children in welfare families.[11] A common conclusion from this widely cited finding was that 40 percent of welfare families were multigeneration, multiproblem families—a hard core poor living in an intransigent "culture of poverty." Yet, when it is remembered that at least 35 percent of Americans received relief at some time in the 1930s, this statistic tells little. As the historian Stephan Thernstrom observed in 1965, "Those who are convinced that poverty is increasingly being meted out in life sentences have yet to do the homework to substantiate the claim."[12]

These disputes among experts writing since 1960 seem technical, even arcane. The most important trend was the diminution of poverty, however defined. But they are relevant to any historical account of American poverty between 1940 and 1960, if only because they reveal the limited amount of solid information available to that generation of welfare reformers. Historians concerned with postwar poverty must cope with what one expert has aptly called "cross-sectional snapshots" instead of "longitudinal motion pictures" of America destitution.[13]

World War II did more than promote economic growth; it also set in motion a host of political and social changes. Together, these prompted long-range revolutionary increases in popular expectations that helped absolutely to improve the lot of the poor in the late 1960s and 1970s.

Some of these changes were apparent in the 1940s. The war enhanced the political power of organized labor, which by then included some unskilled and low-wage workers; it promoted the spread among economists of Keynesian notions concerning the role of fiscal policy; and it led Congress to approve generous veterans' benefits, which affected nearly one-half of the population. The war also expanded the federal bureaucracy, even in the field of social welfare. In the long run, this bureaucracy responded to pressures for better social services.

The growth of government bureaucracy was part of a broader, ultimately powerful nationalization of politics and policies, a movement generated by the war. The federal government grew dramatically in these years; in 1940 the federal budget had been $9 billion; in 1946 it was $64 million. Such increases in spending, which dwarfed those of the supposedly wasteful New Deal, brought to life increasingly well-organized interest groups, all scrambling for pieces of a pie that was growing irresistibly large because of economic growth. This nationalizing process was slow to affect welfare, which people hoped would wither away. But by the late 1960s, it had centralized and therefore liberalized the mainly state-local welfare state of the 1930s.

These developments, however, were the long-run legacies of the war. In the short run, the war strengthened conservative popular attitudes toward public aid, resulting in benign neglect, and in this the American experience was distinctive. Most western European countries had suffered appalling loss of life and property during the war. Their experience generated a sense of common cause which immediately intensified demands for social services. France, Denmark, Norway, and the Low Countries embarked on major expansions of social insurance programs in the 1940s and 1950s. England endorsed the Beveridge plan, which asserted that all citizens were entitled to a minimum income.[14] No such developments occurred in the United States, where only veterans—not the poor—were perceived to have sacrificed much. Instead, the war enhanced the power of corporate groups, the military, and the conservative coalition in Congress, which scuttled New Deal relief agencies. Until the mid-1960s, when long-range political and economic forces compelled change, conservative middle-class attitudes toward poverty and welfare dominated the scene.

Prosperity made it easy to ignore the poor. Blinded by their sudden good fortune, Americans were eager to believe that the Depression had been but a lengthy trough in the inevitable business cycle. With unemployment—the scourge of the recent past—now "solved," it was easy to ignore the pre-Depression structural poverty that persisted even in good times. Few Americans in the 1940s and 1950s talked much about what John Kenneth Galbraith was to call "case" poverty, affecting people too young, too sick, too old, or too tied down by family duties to get a job. The substantial increases in the numbers of people over sixty-five (9 million in 1940, 16.7 million in 1960), aroused relatively little concern. Until the late 1950s few writers paid much attention to low-wage or casual labor, to urban poverty, or to so-called insular poverty affecting depressed areas.[15]

The return of prosperity also encouraged the notion that America was a classless, consensual society. In part, this notion stemmed from the fantastic economic growth generated by heavy government spending, which improved the income pyramid a little. In part, this belief was the product of deliberate efforts by groups anxious to promote national unity in the common cause against fascism. "Hate the Enemy" ads, war bond drives, and mock air raids cultivated this spirit. World War II provided a heaven-sent opportunity for Americans to soften the class divisions that had sharpened in the Depression years.[16]

Reflecting this view, social scientists in the immediate postwar years tended to put less emphasis on social conflict than had sociologists like Robert and Helen Lynd in the more tumultuous 1930s. Some, the conservative functionalists, seeking the source of consensus so apparent in World War II (and so desirable in the Cold War era), asked what makes a society stable. They concluded that social classes served the function of differentiating economic rewards and social status; economic inequality was therefore omnipresent and inevitable. This view had the virtue of recognizing the existence of social stratification. It did not deal in crude and subjective stereotypes of poor people. But at the same time it was an unsentimental approach to social structure. Conservative functionalism—at the peak of its credibility among academics in the 1940s—was matter-of-fact if not complacent about poverty and economic inequality.

Other sociologists came close to celebrating lower-class life. This view, inspired by psychology, contended that middle-class people were repressed and unhappy. The lower classes, in contrast, raised their children in a permissive environment and indulged their whims; their lives were colorful. If the functionalists accepted economic inequality as unavoidable, these writers seemed to cherish it. They, too, enjoyed some credibility among social scientists in the 1940s.[17]

Neither of these academic traditions really reached policymakers, let alone a wide popular audience, but they were important reflections of the complacency in social science circles about poverty. Yes, poor people existed, and they always would. But they were happy, and times were getting better. So be it.

Continuing prosperity gradually promoted a still more optimistic sense of national well-being. Some observers of the growth of suburbs, ignoring their variety, concluded that suburbanization was fashioning a purely middle-class nation. Other writers thought that America had shed its ethnic, racial, and class divisions. Even critics who were uncomfortable with what they perceived as the conformity of American life conceded that the old conflicts had subsided. A prominent sociologist, Robert Nisbet, concluded in 1959 that the United States was a consensual, largely egalitarian society. "As far as the bulk of Western society is concerned," he said, "and especially in the United States, the conception of class is largely obsolete."[18]

The Cold War accentuated the belief in classlessness. Social scientists labored diligently to contrast the class cleavage and rigidity of Soviet society with the mobility and opportunity available in America. They congratulated themselves on living in a country where ideological dogmas—communism or socialism—did not take hold. Pluralism, they thought, was an ideal that had become reality in the American setting. As one sociologist said, in *Life*, "The saving grace of the American social system is that our social positions are not fixed artificially, as they are in the so-called 'classless' society in Russia."[19]

Writers easily, and correctly, identified the source of America's fortunate condition as economic growth. By the mid-1950s younger Americans who had not been adults during the Depression began to take prosperity for granted. Economists, too, grew increasingly confident. By that time many had been converted to Keynesian notions about the positive role of fiscal policy in promoting prosperity. These Keynesians were not complacent, but they were optimistic. Like many Americans in the 1940s and 1950s, they shared the faith that economic growth was the single greatest guarantee that poverty ultimately would wither away.[20]

This notion of withering away, which remained a dominant motif of thinking about poverty into the early 1960s, helped explain why even the reformers in the Social Security Administration paid little attention to the Bureau of Public Assistance, their ugly and unwanted stepchild. A program for the poor, these experts continued to believe, was politically a poor program. The main goal should be to broaden the contributory Social Security plans to provide insurance against disability and old age. Meanwhile, economic growth would curb unemployment and put an end to poverty.[21]

What was the role of welfare policies in these years? From many perspectives, it seemed, welfare policies were progressive. By contrast to 1930, public policies in 1960 were staggeringly broad in coverage and generous in benefits. The number of people receiving old age, survivors, and disability insurance (OASDI) increased from 1.3 million in 1945 to 14.8 million in 1960. The number receiving aid to families of dependent children—by 1960 the largest federal welfare program—increased from 701,000 to 3 million during the same period. Average monthly payments for AFDC increased from $33 to $124 between 1940 and 1962, a hike of 77 percent in real purchasing power. Total social welfare expenditures, including social insurance and public assistance (but excluding education and veterans' benefits), represented in 1960 more than 40 percent of the total income of the poor.[22]

But neither social insurance nor welfare was comprehensive or generous enough to satisfy many observers in the 1940s and 1950s. Social Security was insufficient in itself to remove people from poverty. Financed by regressive taxes on employee salaries and employer payrolls, it drained off potential purchasing power. It supported many nonpoor as well as poor, and about half of America's poor families were not covered by Social Security in 1960.[23]

Reformers were especially alarmed at what they considered the inadequacy of welfare. Only a fifth to a sixth of the country's poor families in the 1950s got either categorical or general assistance. Money spent on them represented less than 1 percent of the gross national product. Those who did get aid were not to be envied. Of households on AFDC, 28 percent in 1960 lacked flush toilets and hot water, and 17 percent did without running water at all. Some half of these households relied entirely on welfare, which averaged $30 per recipient and $115 per family per month in 1960. What they got depended on where they lived, for levels of aid varied widely.[24]

The condition in 1960 of AFDC families in New York City, where social agencies set the subsistence level budget at $2,660 per year for a family of four, suggests how recipients had to live if they expected welfare workers to certify them as in need. Such families were permitted to rent a five-room flat. The living room could have two chairs, a mattress and springs on legs to serve as a couch, a drop-leaf table for eating, and two straight chairs. The floor could be covered with linoleum, not rugs. There could be one or two lamps, but electricity was to be carefully used. The family could have a refrigerator and an electric iron and could play the radio an hour a day—there was no provision for using TV. The weekly food budget allowed for meat, but not for frozen foods, tobacco, beer, or telephone calls. The clothing allowance provided for protection against the weather but left no room for impulse buying or fashion and barely coped with the problem of wear. A woman's coat was to last for five years. Breakage (say of light bulbs) or spillage (of flour) meant that the family did without. This budget provided no "frills"—haircuts more than once a month, home permanents more than once a year, drugs other than aspirin, candy or ice cream for the children, movies, coffee for visitors.

New York's standard of $2,660 offered more in real dollars than budgets used there in the mid-1930s. It was high compared to the national average in 1960 of $2,150 per year and well above the $1,600 defined as subsistence in the five least generous states. Families with outside income managed on it. But (as almost everywhere) the standard was below the $3,000 generally regarded at the time as a poverty line and far below the $5,464 that the more liberal Bureau of Labor Statistics considered the "minimum comfort" standard for a family of four in 1960. Moreover, these standards were sums that social workers thought should be reached, not money paid by public authorities in practice. Most states could not or would not pay public clients the amount their social agencies set for subsistence.[25]

Reformers complained also that American welfare policies were less generous and comprehensive than those of western Europe. Experts agreed that America lagged behind most industrialized countries in the percentage of national income spent on social insurance plus public assistance.[26] They lamented especially the spirit under which aid was given. In western Europe, administrators usually tried to maximize coverage and minimize the stigma of accepting public aid; by contrast, American relief administrators sought to cut expenses and exclude from the rolls all people considered able to care for themselves. As one expert complained, "The general public does not know what you are talking about when you talk about professional competence and the need for better skills [in welfare administration]. A good administrator is one who can keep chiselers off the rolls—public welfare is as simple as that to them."[27]

This niggardly spirit pervaded the AFDC program; in the 1940s and 1950s states developed a range of ingenious regulations designed to evade liberal federal guidelines. Many states denied aid to families with "employable mothers," dawdled in processing applications, established lengthy residence requirements (usually a year or more), and intimidated prospective applicants—sometimes by stationing police outside relief offices. Irritated officials in the Bureau of Public Assistance issued endless regulations to force states to comply with federal guidelines: by the 1960s its Handbook of Public Assistance Administration was more than five inches thick. But this effort resulted mainly in heaps of paperwork for case workers. In the absence of pressure from the poor themselves, who were ill organized at that time, or from potent lobbies, the bureau lacked the means and the will to engage in debilitating skirmishes with cost-conscious politicians in the states and localities.[28]

States proved particularly adept at denying AFDC to children whose absent fathers were suspected of being able to provide support or of living in the vicinity. This concern was minor in the early 1940s, but it intensified with the increase in broken families—and therefore in the case load—in the late 1940s and 1950s. Alarmists feared that AFDC, originally intended to take care of "deserving" widows with children, was becoming a haven for "immoral welfare mothers." As early as 1950 Congress passed an amendment mandating local welfare agencies to notify law enforcement officers whenever aid was granted to children whose father had deserted the family. Many states and towns dispatched agents on "midnight raids" to catch men visiting overnight in welfare homes.

States relied especially on "suitable home" regulations aimed at denying aid to "undeserving" mothers. To enforce such regulations case workers had to pry into the private lives of recipients. Arkansas cut off aid to mothers engaged in a "nonstable, nonlegal union"; Michigan, to families with "male boarders"; Texas, to "pseudo-common law marriages." To receive aid some mothers had to sign affidavits like this one:

> I . . . do hereby promise and agree that until such time as the following agreement is rescinded, I will not have any male callers coming to my home nor meeting me elsewhere under improper conditions.
>
> I also agree to raise my children to the best of my ability and will not knowingly contribute or be a contributing factor to their being shamed by my conduct. I understand that should I violate this agreement, the children will be taken from me.

Louisiana carried such practices to an extreme in 1960. Strictly administering its "suitable home" regulations, it cut off aid to 6,281 families with 23,489 children, families in which the mothers, since receiving assistance, had given birth to one or more illegitimate children. Because the new regulation was applied retroactively, it affected legitimate as well as illegitimate children in such families, 95 percent of which were black. Cries of outrage prompted federal intervention and reinstatement of about half of the affected families. The others, however, went without public assistance.[29]

Federal officials who wanted better welfare found very few allies. In the 1930s they had been able to count on some activist social workers, but the return of better times seemed to sap the reformist spirit in the profession. The majority of well-trained workers went into private charity, where they got better pay and the chance to apply their courses in psychiatrically oriented case work. These courses stressed rehabilitation of individuals and of families, not reform of public welfare. Conferences of social workers regularly featured sessions on such subjects as "Working with the Child in His Own Home," "The Hard to Reach Multiple Problem Families," "Managing a Case Load," "Opportunities for Professional Social Work Training."[30] Sessions on public welfare were less numerous, for many social workers continued to believe that public assistance, as one worker explained, was "an albatross around the neck of social service." The dirty work of public welfare often fell by default to elected, nonprofessional town and county officials, whose goal was to control costs.[31]

Many social work professionals, of course, did concern themselves with public welfare, and they began mobilizing lobbies in the mid- and late 1950s. Among the most important of these was the Committee on Social Issues and Policies of the National Social Welfare Assembly (which was itself a holding company for a variety of social work organizations). The leaders of this effort focused their efforts on HEW, where many of them worked or had close contacts. But they had difficulty developing support for wholesale changes in Congress, whose specialized subcommittees scrutinized proposals on a narrow program-by-program basis. Reformers in the 1950s therefore had to settle for modest changes in Social Security.

Reformers had to contend also with many contemporary authorities in the field who overoptimistically believed that economic progress would ultimately wipe out destitution, leaving only a few individual problems to deal with. These authorities were not complacent —they worked patiently for incremental improvements in social insurance. But they had great hopes for the potential of economic growth, and especially for achieving the age-old goal that had possessed experts in the prosperous years before 1930: prevention via rehabilitation. This goal of rehabilitating people—and ultimately of saving public money on welfare—was the gospel of the 1950s. As the director of the American Public Welfare Administration explained in 1957, "We can expect the volume of public assistance cases to decrease in the future. [He was wrong.] As this happens, hopefully public welfare workers can begin to realize one of their major objectives, namely the opportunity to focus more attention on the preventive and rehabilitative aspects of their work."[32]

Advocates of improved aid found equally little support from popular magazines. The few articles on poverty tended to carry scare headlines and to fret about the cost of welfare. One headline read, "When It Pays to Play Pauper." Another article proclaimed, "The Hillbillies Invade Chicago." A third, entitled "I Say Relief is Ruining Families," publicized the views of a New York City domestic relations court judge, who intoned, "The relief setup is sapping the will to work . . . encouraging cynicism, petty chiselling and bare-faced immorality."

Another article, entitled "Welfare: Has It Become a Scandal?"

complained that "relief without rehabilitation has spawned a vicious circle in welfare, so that now a second generation of reliefers is maturing on welfare rolls." It cited as a "typical case" a forty-year-old man with four children and twenty-nine grandchildren, all illegitimate. "The girls take their pregnancies as a matter of course. The home is like Grand Central Terminal. Members vanish and stay away five days at a time. All the girls should have been put in homes . . . It's a vicious circle." Another article, "Detroit Cracks Down on Welfare Chiselers," was certain that "relief clients have thought this whole thing out carefully, weighing the advantages of being on relief against working for a living," and choosing welfare. "When perfectly executed, this consists of a person going off the aid-to-dependent children rolls upon reaching his twenty-first birthday, immediately establishing himself upon the relief rolls, and remaining there forever, if possible."

Champions of more generous welfare feared that such articles appealed to millions of middle-class readers. One liberal sadly quoted a Chicago cab driver: "What do I think about welfare? It ought to be cut back. The goddam people sit around when they should be working and they're having illegitimate kids to get more money. You know, their morals are different. They don't give a damn. Stop it. That's what I say. These people they don't work. They don't pay taxes." Another citizen added, "All of the people on relief should be made to work because I think half of them are bums." Outbursts such as these seemed to reflect a growing popular concern that family breakdown, illegitimacy, and welfare were weakening the moral fiber of the nation and developing an intergenerational culture of poverty.[33]

That concern was not so widespread as reformers feared. Polls in fact suggested ambivalent feelings among middle-class Americans. When asked about "welfare" or "relief," people took the conservative line that public assistance was wasteful and demoralizing. But when asked if the government should help those in "need," they responded affirmatively. Polls revealed also that a majority of Americans supported a broadening of Social Security, which was widely (though inaccurately) perceived as a strictly insurance proposition.

Still, advocates of more generous welfare were probably correct in concluding that most middle-class Americans distinguished between Social Security, which they considered a necessity, and public welfare —a wasteful handout. Congress, reflecting this distinction, took the simple way out by liberalizing social insurance and maintaining a policy of benign neglect toward welfare. It refused to mandate a national minimum for welfare payments, to force states to pay benefits up to their inadequate definitions of need, to involve the federal government in general assistance, or to give public aid to two-parent families in need. Congress was reflecting both the lack of organized pressure for change, since the poor did not participate in interest group politics, and the dominant middle-class coolness to welfare. Despite war and dramatic economic change, that coolness changed little, either then or later.[34]

Given the power of such attitudes in the 1940s and 1950s, it was not surprising that other perspectives on poverty were ignored. Of these perspectives, three offered overlapping insights which, if heeded, might have enhanced public understanding. These may be called the cultural, liberal, and structuralist views.

The cultural perspective was the antithesis of older views of a sodden culture of poverty. It argued instead that different ethnic groups and social classes possessed distinctive, even admirable, cultural traditions that sustained them in crisis times. The sociologist William F. Whyte, whose work influenced many academics in the 1940s, labored especially to demolish the notion that "social disorganization" afflicted the slums. Not so, he argued. Groups that seemed disorganized and deviant were actually adhering to recognizable and useful values.

Another writer who echoed this focus on distinctive cultural patterns was E. Wight Bakke, whose studies of jobless Americans in the 1930s had revealed that working-class people cherished sturdy traditions. Bakke, like Whyte, did not romanticize these patterns, but he thought them functional. Although such values differed in subtle ways from those of the middle classes, they enabled the unemployed to cope fairly well even after prolonged periods out of work.[35]

The studies of W. Lloyd Warner and his many followers also challenged indirectly the thesis that the lower classes lived in "social disorganization." Applying techniques of cultural anthropology to small and middle-sized communities, Warner and others emphasized the persistence of social divisions in American life. Members of the different strata had different values: the poor were not would-be middle-class people in tattered clothing and ramshackle homes. Warner stressed that lower-class values were functional, not deviant. As an associate of Warner's said in 1951, "Behavior which middle-class teachers, clinicians, and psychiatrists often regard as 'delinquent' or 'hostile' or 'unmotivated' in slum children is usually a perfectly realistic, adaptive, and—in slum life—socially acceptable response to reality."[36]

Cultural anthropologists like Warner came under attack from some sociologists, who denounced both the community study approach and what they said was an unsystematic reliance on interviews. These critics complained that cultural anthropologists concentrated on values and life-styles and spread the notion that class and poverty were cultural instead of economic. Critics added that Warner defined social class as the prestige and status people had in the eyes of others, slighting more important, extra-community matters involving income, wealth, and economic power. The true tests of class, they said, were economic, not cultural.[37]

More outspoken were the critics who simply denied the importance of social class. These writers were so sure of the ultimate homogenization of American society that they slighted ethnic and regional traditions and forgot that many lower-class people do not want to adopt middle-class values. Working in an age supposedly of consensus, these observers left the impression that the poor were culturally undifferentiated, either from each other or from the nonpoor. Against this prevailing view, potentially useful arguments that stressed the persistence of class and cultural divisions made little headway in the 1940s and 1950s.

A second insightful approach to poverty, the liberal view, came especially from the handful of social scientists, social workers, and bureaucrats who had been closely associated with New Deal welfare programs. Many of these people were familiar with statistical studies of unemployment and relief done by the Works Progress Administration, the National Resources Planning Board (NRPB), and other federal agencies in the 1930s. Unlike most Americans, who thought the economic revival of 1940-1942 would solve the problem of destitution, they insisted that welfare must remain an important element in public policy.

No group was more persuaded of this continuing need than the NRPB. After substantial study it produced in December 1941 a report much like the more widely publicized Beveridge report in England in 1942. The NRPB observed frankly that "even in so-called 'good' times a disturbingly large proportion of the population has a precarious existence as a result of inadequate or no private income." The Great Depression, it argued, was "different in degree . . . and in kind" from previous depressions in that unemployment had lasted longer, effectively severing many old workers, who were increasing as a percentage of the total population, from the job market. To address national needs, the report said, the government should take from localities the burden of general assistance, require states to liberalize residency and eligibility standards, increase federal contributions for various forms of assistance, and change the matching grant formulas for categorical aid to reflect regional needs and the states' varying fiscal capacities.

Though the NRPB actually underestimated the extent of need, its report was in every way a far-seeing document. It called in effect for a federally supported floor under income. President Roosevelt waited sixteen months before forwarding the report to Congress, but he ultimately reflected the NRPB's point of view in his Economic Bill of Rights of January 1944. All citizens, he said, deserved useful and remunerative jobs; income to provide sufficient food, clothing, and recreation; decent lodgings; medical care; protection against the hazards of old age, sickness, accident, and unemployment; and a good education.[38]

At about the same time, the leadership of the Social Security Board was reaching equally liberal conclusions. In the mid-1930s it had stressed that Social Security must be a strictly businesslike insurance operation, based on employer and employee contributions. The government, far from dispensing welfare, was to be a piggy bank, storing contributions and paying them back with interest at age sixty-five. By 1938, however, an advisory council appointed to help the SSB liberalize Social Security began to discard this piggy bank concept and to favor, for example, support of the disabled at levels approximating their wages in their best-paid years. Such a program, of course, would mean giving many disabled workers far more than they had contributed to the system. Private insurance executives, recognizing this lapse from the prevailing orthodoxy, opposed it. But the Social Security Board adopted the principle in 1941 and lobbied for it in Congress throughout the 1940s.

This deviation from insurance principles appears unexciting in retrospect, but the change in perspective reflected a movement toward merging Social Security and welfare and was so recognized by the planners who adopted it. As one participant put it, "We went through not just a political but sort of an intellectual and religious reformation. We began to come out with a perspective that none of us had when we first began doing these things. Between 1939 and 1942 we were changed persons."[39]

Thanks to the efforts of an ever-expanding and shrewdly persistent social welfare bureaucracy, which labored for incremental improvements in social policy, this liberal outlook slowly advanced under both Democratic and Republican administrations in the 1940s and 1950s. As early as 1939, Congress tied old age benefits not to lifetime contributions but to average earnings over a shorter covered period. The result was to establish minimum benefits related to need as well as to contributions—a departure in practice from the supposedly sacrosanct actuarial principles of social insurance. At the same time Congress added liberal amendments to categorical assistance by increasing the federal contribution to aid to dependent children from one-third to one-half. By 1964 it had raised the federal share to this and the other categorical assistance programs nine more times.

Other amendments, especially in the 1950s, quietly added millions of workers to the OASI system and began to increase welfare benefits. In 1950 Congress rectified its original neglect of mothers of dependent children by offering them a "caretaker" grant. It also set up a matching grant program for a new category of poor people, the permanently and totally disabled. In 1956 it added disability insurance to Social Security, and in 1958 it adopted a partial sliding scale for assistance grants that resulted in more generous federal contributions to states with low per capita incomes. These advances were hardly dramatic, but they were significant.[40]

A structuralist approach, the third useful line of thinking about poverty and welfare, resembled the liberal view in that it assumed the long-term need for extensive public welfare. Most of its practitioners were Keynesian liberals or democratic socialists. The structuralists concentrated more sharply, however, than other liberals on what they perceived as the pronounced stratification of capitalist society. Aware that growth did not help many of the poor, they called for great increases in public assistance, as well as for major initiatives to counter low wages and underemployment. The most visible structuralists were not social workers or government bureaucrats looking for ways to improve the situation of individuals, but social scientists and left-wing writers who took a broad and reformist view of the functional relationship between inequality and the social system.

One structuralist was the sociologist Robert Merton, whose classic article on anomie in 1938 had stressed that lower-class Americans began with mainstream values but were set back by structural barriers blocking their economic opportunity. This approach greatly influenced later structuralist writings. In *An American Dilemma* (1944) the Swedish social scientist Gunnar Myrdal stressed the barriers to economic opportunity confronted by American Negroes. Myrdal emphasized that poverty was a "vicious cycle," which created a deprived "underclass." An optimist, he believed that public policy could break the vicious cycle at any of several points. Smash the structural barriers, and the underclass could rise above itself.[41]

This structuralist approach had little impact on public policy in the 1940s, but within a few years, the situation began to change slightly.[42] A long-lived congressional subcommittee headed by Senator John Sparkman of Alabama found that 25 percent of families were poor in 1948 and 22 percent in 1955. It highlighted demographic trends such as the aging of the population and the rise of broken families, documenting the high incidence of poverty among such groups. It emphasized also the prevalence of low-wage work. Staff reports of the committee stressed the concentration of income in the hands of a small percentage of families. These reports showed that millions of working families who were nonpoor in one year were poor in the next. Low income clearly plagued far more families than a one-year snapshot of poverty could expose.

The Sparkman committee's concern with low income was a significant step toward a no-nonsense, quantitative definition of poverty, which it set at around $2,000 for a family of four. Its definition, resolutely economic in emphasis, eschewed crude and subjective stereotypes; it linked poverty to flaws in the marketplace; it placed the poor within the context of what the committee perceived as a maldistributed income structure; above all it suggested the desirability of setting a floor under income. Its findings led states to develop their own objectively compiled subsistence budgets for various-sized families in need. If Congress as a whole had heeded the committee—which it did not—it would have been forced to promote not only Keynesian fiscal measures and post-Keynesian growth economics but also much-expanded social services. In the 1960s, indeed, experts on poverty developed "poverty lines" according to the subcommittee's objective measures of low income. And advocates of guaranteed minimum income in the 1960s and 1970s ultimately adopted the logic of its approach.[43]

The structuralist perspective gained some political force in the late 1950s, when legislators began to press for aid to "surplus labor markets" and "depressed areas." The argument here, championed by Senator Paul Douglas of Illinois, was simple enough: "pockets" of poverty and unemployment stemmed from structural flaws such as depletion of resources and technological change. In the recession of 1958-1959, which hiked the unemployment rate to 1940 levels (7.7 percent), Douglas succeeded in getting a depressed areas bill through Congress, only to see President Eisenhower veto it. If enacted, the legislation would not have worked wonders—only one in twelve unemployed workers actually lived in such areas. Still, the elevation of such legislation to the congressional agenda suggested that congressmen were prepared to attack some of the structural weaknesses in the economy.

In 1958 John Kenneth Galbraith published *The Affluent Society*, the liveliest summary of structuralist thinking to that time. Repeating Myrdal and others, Galbraith reminded readers that the country confronted a vicious cycle of poverty involving the insular poverty of depressed areas as well as case poverty affecting families without employable breadwinners. Galbraith went so far as to call attention to

the inequality of American society and to question absolute definitions of poverty. "People are poverty-stricken," he wrote, "when
their income, even if adequate for survival, falls radically behind that
of the community." This perspective took him beyond those liberals
who hoped that economic progress bestowed its blessings equitably.
He demanded great increases in social services to reduce the gap between the rich and the poor. Galbraith anticipated the concern with
egalitarianism that was to become a pronounced feature of social
thought in the late 1960s and 1970s.

Many reviewers noticed that Galbraith did not carry his arguments
about poverty very far. His poverty line for families was $1,000 per
year, a cutoff that placed only 8 percent of the population in poverty.
Activists complained that the line should have been at least as high as
the Sparkman committee's $2,000, at which point poverty would have
measured 25 percent. Other critics thought he should have stressed
even more the inequality of American society, instead of talking about
the affluence and materialism of the middle classes.[44]

Galbraith's structuralism was nonetheless ahead of the times, for
few people then considered poverty and unemployment permanent
problems or wanted to believe that the economy was structurally un-
sound. This continuing optimism ensured that structuralist thinking
had little impact on policy in the 1950s and early 1960s. One of President Kennedy's antipoverty warriors later regretted this: "I don't
think any of us were using the term 'a structural approach' . . . We
were not talking about changing the nature of the organization of
society . . . That's probably the Achilles heel of what we were attempting to do, in that we did not have a more solid structural framework
for what we were about."[45]

The cultural and liberal views of poverty also failed to awaken
much popular interest until the 1960s. Then the long-range economic
and demographic forces of the previous decades combined with a
more activist political climate in Washington to produce a new look at
poverty. Then, and only then, did the liberals and structuralists get
much of a hearing. Only then did a changed "social philosophy," in
R. H. Tawney's phrase, begin to appear in policy.

III
DOORS TO
OPPORTUNITY
1960-1965

6

THE REDISCOVERY
OF POVERTY

In 1962 THE ACTIVIST Michael Harrington catalyzed a rediscovery of poverty in America. His powerful, passionate book, *The Other America*, exposed the misery of a "new," specially deprived poor. This new poverty, he wrote, affected 40 to 50 million people. It was

> a system designed to be impervious to hope. The other America does not contain the adventurous seeking a new life and land. It is populated by failures, by those driven from the land and bewildered by the city, by old people suddenly confronted with the torments of loneliness and poverty, and by minorities facing a wall of prejudice . . . The entire invisible land of the other Americans became a ghetto, a modern poor farm for the rejects of society and of the economy.[1]

Harrington's book did not become a best-seller right away, but it challenged complacent assumptions about American affluence, and it focused movingly on poverty. Soon it attracted favorable notice from intellectuals, especially Dwight Macdonald, who reviewed it at great length in the *New Yorker* in January 1963. Within the next few years a virtual avalanche of books and articles on poverty rolled off the presses. President John F. Kennedy read both Harrington and Macdonald and set his advisers to study the problem. President Lyndon Johnson inherited the staff work, directed it forward at full speed, and in 1964 announced a "war on poverty." This dramatization of the issue then pushed Harrington's book onto the best-seller lists. For the first time since the 1930s, poverty was front-page news.[2]

As it turned out, the war on poverty eventually sputtered into a skirmish. But the attention given the poor by social scientists and publicists in the early 1960s was salutary. After many years of neglect, economists, sociologists, and anthropologists at last began to scrutinize poverty and to ask harder questions about its causes, effects, and cures. By 1966, when their largely academic debate began to move in new directions, they had not dispelled the fuzziness that had always enveloped the subject. But they had made a strong enough start that later analysts and policymakers could refine and implement their essentially structuralist insights. These years of rediscovery marked a modest turning point in academic and theoretical approaches to the problems of poverty and welfare.

It is much easier to observe that poverty became a subject of debate than to explain why. Destitution was nothing new, as America's 39 million poor people (by official definition) in 1960 could attest. Nor were writers like Harrington the first to announce their discovery of it. As early as the 1840s Dr. John Griscom, a leading sanitary reformer, had proclaimed, "One half the world does not know how the other half lives." Jacob Riis and Robert Hunter had discovered poverty again fifty years later. One bemused observer, noting the wonder with which American reformers discovered the poverty in their midst, perceived a "Columbus complex." Poverty, it seemed, was always being seen for the first time.[3]

According to one explanation of the rediscovery, people were finally beginning to worry about the apparently proliferating social problems of the late 1950s, including an apparent rise in juvenile delinquency. An exposé entitled *1,000,000 Delinquents* (1955) asserted that it was a "national epidemic . . . unless this cancer is checked early enough, it can go on spreading and contaminate many good cells in our society." Other books and articles, applying anthropological insights, concluded that delinquents inhabited a separate subculture. One study in 1955 argued that this subculture was a "normal, integral, and deeply rooted feature of the social life of the modern American city." Another scholar linked delinquency to the growing number of female-headed families; teen-aged boys joined gangs to find male models, seeking on the streets the excitement and toughness they missed in the home. Still others, like Harrington and Kenneth Clark, argued from a structuralist point of view that juvenile delinquents grew up holding mainstream values, but found their aspirations blocked by the larger society. Frustrated, they stumbled into the delinquent world.[4]

The Children's Bureau called a conference on delinquency as early as 1954, and a year later President Eisenhower requested $5 million in grants to states to study the problem. Though this request did not survive bureaucratic disputes and budgetary constraints, settlement house workers and community organizers continued to press for public funding. Leaders in this effort included Richard Cloward and Lloyd Ohlin, professors of social work at Columbia University. Their influential book, *Delinquency and Opportunity*, published in 1960, took the classic structuralist view, stressing the blockage of opportunity facing young people in the modern slums. Their arguments underlay a research proposal, funded in 1958 by the National Institute of Mental Health, for a community organization program in New York City known as Mobilization for Youth. Ohlin later became a top adviser to the Kennedy administration's efforts against juvenile delinquency.[5]

Cloward, Ohlin, and Harrington emphasized that juvenile delinquency reflected a broader deterioration in slum conditions. Their writings, in fact, helped rediscover urban poverty. The older ethnic slum, they said, had been crowded and unsanitary, but the people had had a vital community life and, most important, aspirations. By the 1950s, a few such areas, like Little Italy or Chinatown in New York, remained, but most modern slums were populated by "dregs" who could not get out and by ill-prepared migrants from the South, many of whom carried the added burden of racial discrimination. Unlike the ethnic poor in 1900, modern slum dwellers lived mainly in cities offering relatively few blue-collar jobs and in which the political machines—once havens for certain ethnic groups—were skeletal organizations run by professionals. Government urban renewal programs, although well intentioned, frequently disrupted old neighborhoods and compounded social problems. Harrington, like scholars of black life in the 1930s, worried especially about the breakdown of the family in the slums and the growing tendency of young adults to engage in "serial monogamy"—one mate after another.[6]

"Serial monogamy" was a fancy term for a deep concern about slum life at the time: illegitimacy. From 1940 to 1962 the illegitimacy rate (the ratio of illegitimate births per 1,000 live births among women between the ages of fifteen and forty-four) increased from 7.1 to 21.5. Rates for blacks alone, always much higher, jumped from 35.6 to 90.1. Given the increased availability of contraceptives in these years, the rise in illegitimacy was disturbing, especially to students of black family life. The black scholar E. Franklin Frazier regarded family disorganization and illegitimacy as the major cause of the "large number of criminals and juvenile delinquents" as well as of the "aimlessness and lack of ambition" of black youth.[7]

The escalating illegitimacy rates exposed the still broader problem of family breakup. Indeed, the increase in the number of female-headed households was one of the most striking demographic trends of the 1940s and 1950s. The number headed by women under fifty-five jumped from 2.5 million in 1940 to 4.4 million in 1962. Nearly half of these families were poor and many were black. Researchers showed that the proportions of white households headed by women rose from 3 percent in 1940 to 6 percent in 1960, and of black, from 7 to 20 percent. Assistant Labor Secretary Daniel Moynihan then wrote a report, *The Negro Family: The Case for National Action*, that summed up the alarm among those experts who studied black life. Perceiving a "tangle of pathology," he noted in 1965 that one-fourth of black marriages dissolved, that one-fourth of black babies were illegitimate, and that one-fourth of black families were headed by females. The result, he said, was a "startling increase in welfare dependency."[8]

There was little that was new in the Moynihan report. It recognized that the disruption of families was largely caused by racial discrimination, leading to low income and unemployment, rather than by cultural traits. But Moynihan, like Frazier and others, incautiously linked "pathology" to the heritage of slavery—a dubious point suggesting that black cultural traits led to family instability. Moreover, the civil rights movement was then moving toward its black power stage, so the report provoked outraged protests from many writers that Moynihan denigrated black culture. William Ryan, a Boston psychologist, complained in *The Nation* that the report was "irresponsible nonsense" and "damnably inaccurate simplicity." The black leader James Farmer termed it a "massive academic cop out for the white conscience." He added, "We are sick unto death of being analyzed, mesmerized, bought, sold, and slobbered over, while the same evils that are the ingredients of our oppression go unattended."[9]

Although critics like Farmer overreacted and obscured the issues, the controversy over illegitimacy and family life was salutary in the long run. It induced scholars in the next few years, drawing on already available sources, to bring out a number of important points about black families, juvenile delinquency, slums, and poor people generally. Though the debate forced Harrington, Moynihan, and others to qualify their views, it confirmed some of their fears and prompted a more solidly structuralist perspective on various aspects of lower-class life.

From this surge of interest came solid findings that helped destroy mistaken notions of sexual immorality among lower-class blacks. Studies showed that the white illegitimacy rate, although much lower than that for blacks, had increased faster in the 1950s: illegitimacy was a broad social phenomenon related in part to changing sexual attitudes that affected all races and classes. Scholars found also that the black illegitimacy rate had peaked around 1958 and then had stabilized.[10] They added that the statistics on illegitimacy were deceptive. White rates were lower in part because blacks were less informed about contraception (though poor whites, too, were relatively ignorant in such matters) and because whites had greater access to abortions. Findings such as these did not dismiss illegitimacy as an unimportant problem, but they set it in a broad social and demographic perspective.[11]

Other scholars contested Moynihan's stress on slavery. They argued that the two-parent family had been the norm for 65 to 80 percent of Afro-Americans during and after slavery; that high rates of mortality among black males accounted for some of the female-headed black families throughout American history; and that families headed by women, far from being "disorganized" or "pathological," often showed less competitiveness and sibling rivalry and more cooperation, informality, and humor than existed in two-parent families. Female-headed families developed networks of kin that took the place of the absent father. As one scholar put it, "The black urban family, embedded in cooperative domestic exchange, proves to be an organized, tenacious, active, lifelong network."[12]

To Kenneth Clark, who had preceded Moynihan into the field, the cause of illegitimacy and family instability among blacks was simple: low income, compounded by racial discrimination. Racial and economic forces accounted for the inability of black males to secure decent jobs—or any jobs. "The dark ghettos," Clark wrote, "are social, political, educational, and—above all—economic ghettos." Young black males, frustrated by failure after failure, felt defeated and useless. Some left home to find better opportunities; others pursued women to prove their masculinity or to establish some better human contact. Clark, like Moynihan, called for improved economic opportunities. Then, he observed wryly, there would be a " 'higher' level of behavior; then the Negro's sexual 'misbehavior' will be indistinguishable in all respects from that of the respectables—with full participation in divorce, abortions, adultery, and the various forms of jaded and fashionable middle- and upper-class sexual explorations."[13]

Other writers took issue with the fears about juvenile delinquency and "pathological" slums. By the mid-1960s it was becoming clearer that juvenile delinquency was neither rampant nor clearly correlated with poverty. Studies suggested that some juvenile crime reflected broader definitions of illegal activity and the fact that police were much more likely to arrest lower-class youth, especially blacks, than middle-class offenders. They revealed also that many of the very poor —those on welfare—were not likely to be delinquent. Crime and delinquency among young people on public assistance was far below the national average. Other studies, resurrecting the work of William F. Whyte, stressed that not all slums were "disorganized" or "jungles"; many were characterized by viable kin and community relationships. As one scholar had noted in 1955, most slums were "anything but the picture of chaos and heterogeneity which we find drawn in the older literature." Rather, they featured a "vast and ramifying network of informal associations among like-minded people, not a horde of anonymous families and individuals."[14]

Scholars suggested also that it was wrong to sensationalize the relationship between agricultural disruption in the South, mass migrations, and social disorganization in the slums. Temporarily, of course, migration separated families, just as it had done to immigrant families throughout world history. Moreover, it was true that economic and political opportunities were scarce in many northern cities in the 1950s and 1960s. But like the earlier immigrants, black migrants tended to be younger, more ambitious, and better educated than those who stayed behind. Most of them had some experience in city living before coming to the large northern ghettos. The migrants were not loafers or seekers after welfare, and they settled near friends or kin who helped them find employment. Their rates of delinquency, crime, and welfare dependency were lower than those of the more settled urban dwellers. The assumed connection between migration and social disorganization was accurate only in that economic opportunities in the cities could not accommodate the onslaught. Poverty thus shifted from the South to the North and from the countryside to the city. Otherwise, the belief in that connection rested on the dubious (and often racist) proposition that the new migrants were somehow culturally less able to cope with their new surroundings than the immigrants of 1880 to 1914.[15]

All these findings emphasized one overriding fact: social problems such as illegitimacy and family breakup correlated best with low income. For blacks, poverty stemmed in part from racial discrimination far more intense than the immigrants from Europe had faced. For able-bodied whites as well as blacks, it reflected mainly low-wage labor and underemployment. Compared to racial and economic problems, all the other presumed causes of social ills—slum location, family size, presumed cultural or personal attributes—were relatively insignificant.[16]

This emphasis on structural forces was not especially consoling, for it meant that any worsening of general economic conditions was likely to intensify poverty and social "pathology." Something of the sort was happening already in many black ghettos, where unemployment, criminal activity, and drug addiction increased so much in the 1960s that they dwarfed the ills of the 1950s. In this limited sense, the dire forecasts of Harrington, Cloward, and Ohlin in the late 1950s, and of Moynihan in the mid-1960s, were prophetic.

The middle classes, however, did not perceive a crisis of social pathology; rather, polls in the early 1960s revealed great optimism about the future. Although it is difficult to assess the level of popular interest in such social problems, it was not intense before 1965, when the Moynihan report set off an acrimonious debate. The rediscovery of poverty in the early 1960s, in short, did not take place because people detected a social crisis in the country. That perception occurred to some extent only amid the racial turmoil of the late 1960s.

A related explanation for the rediscovery of poverty stresses its tenacity combined with the rise in welfare costs. Harrington's insistence that the poverty of the 1950s and 1960s was deeper and more pathological than before was right in that higher percentages of the poor were sick, disabled, old, nonwhite, or members of female-headed families. These were the unfortunates left out of economic growth— the "new" poor in his terms. And these poor were captives of the media-based consumerism of the age. Studies at the time showed that 90 to 95 percent of poor families had TV sets, 50 percent had washing machines. In California 70 percent had cars. Those who purchased expensive goods had no choice but to buy them on the installment plan, leaving them with virtually no liquid assets.[17]

The situation of poor Americans worsened in the late 1950s and 1960s also in the important sense of relative deprivation. Although few experts paid much attention to this development until around 1964, it is clear in retrospect why it became a source of class tension. Income remained badly maldistributed. The lowest one-fifth of income earners got 5 percent of total income in 1947, 4.6 percent in 1962; the lowest two-fifths received 16 percent in 1947, 15.5 percent in 1962. The top fifth got about 46 percent throughout the period. In the 1960s, the percentage of people officially defined as poor dropped sharply, from 22 percent in 1959 to 11 percent in 1973, but the percentage who earned less than half the median income stayed the same, at around 20 percent. These statistics showed that while many Americans rose above the poverty line, those who were stranded struggled with incomes far below the levels deemed adequate in the contemporary culture. Unlike the ethnic poor in Hunter's day and the sharecroppers in the 1930s, who were not so aware of their relative deprivation, people living in a mass media age could not help knowing that fact.[18]

Even in an absolute sense, the poor of the early 1960s had very little. A survey of 13,000 families (81 percent black) on AFDC in Detroit in 1962-1963 made this clear. According to budgets there, a family of four was expected to get along on $160 a month, or $1,920 a year, far below the federal poverty line of $3,000 for such families. These poor people ordinarily did without fruit and vegetables, and their meat was canned or neck cuts. Half said they did without "adequate food." About half the families tried to better their situation by purchasing food stamps; the other half could not afford to go to the food stamp office or to buy the stamps. The families scrimped on clothes; three-fourths of the children had no raincoats, half had no rubbers or boots. Only one in nine of these families had phones, one in ten, money for recreation. Though one family in three had medical expenses, Detroit provided no health allowances.[19]

A survey of AFDC families by HEW in 1967 revealed other evidence of continuing deprivation. Of those surveyed, 11 percent did not have private use of a kitchen; 24 percent lived in flats or shacks without running water; 30 percent did not have enough beds for their family; 25 percent were without sufficient furniture to sit down for meals; 17 percent had children who sometimes did not attend school because they lacked decent clothing; and 46 percent had not had money to buy milk for their children at least once within the previous six months. Although these AFDC recipients, like the poor in general, on the average lived better than they had in the 1950s, such statistics exposed standards of living that would have been unenviable even in the 1930s. In the much more affluent 1960s they were galling.[20]

The persistence of poverty, especially in a rapidly growing population of female-headed families, inevitably increased the expense of AFDC. In 1950, that cost $864 per family, for a total bill of $565 million. Twelve years later, the average cost per family was $1,512, or $1.4 billion per year. AFDC, the most expensive of the federal public assistance plans, had evolved from a program to aid "deserving" widows with dependent children to one that supported all kinds of "misfits" and "undesirables."[21]

There were some signs that the AFDC program thoroughly irritated political leaders. A Senate committee report issued in 1961 by Senator Robert Byrd of West Virginia purported to show that 60 percent of AFDC cases in the District of Columbia were ineligible for aid under the law. Byrd's fellow senators, including the liberal Hubert Humphrey of Minnesota, leaped to praise the report. Despite Byrd's known hostility to the program and his disparaging remarks about people on welfare, he was treated as the Senate expert on the subject. The warm response he received on the Hill testified to enduring congressional coolness to welfare.[22]

Many were concerned that the AFDC program might grow out of hand, and scattered evidence appeared to support their case. Studies showed that about 40 percent of AFDC families remained on the rolls for three to five years, and 25 percent for five years or more; between 30 and 40 percent of recipient families included a parent who had been on welfare as a child. One Labor Department report resisted the conclusion that welfare was a "way of life" but ruefully conceded that "significant proportions of AFDC families do represent a second or third generation on welfare."[23]

Few people took the trouble to read statistical studies or government reports, but they could hardly ignore the debate over welfare that erupted in Newburgh, New York, in the summer of 1961. City manager Joseph Mitchell and his council, in an effort to cut back welfare costs, ordered thirteen changes in city welfare policy, chief among which were that all able-bodied adult males who refused to do city work must forfeit benefits; unwed mothers would lose benefits if they had another illegitimate child; new applicants must prove that they came to Newburgh with firm offers of employment in hand (if they could not prove, they were to get but one week's aid); and all recipients, save the aged and disabled, were to get only three months of aid per year. Mitchell's proposals, widely publicized, sparked what one person called the "biggest public discussion in welfare in the past quarter century."[24]

Amid this hullaballoo, careful observers noted that Mitchell's rhetoric obscured his performance. New York state law already required relief officials to investigate whether new applicants for welfare had migrated with the aim of getting public aid. That law, like many in the country, echoed the colonial settlement statutes that tried to curb welfare costs. Mitchell's proposals, if enacted, would not have saved the city much money or affected very many people; of Newburgh's 30,000 residents, only ten able-bodied males were on relief. Between 2 and 9 percent of the people collected welfare, which accounted for only 13 percent of city expenditures. Newburgh spent so little money on relief that it did not qualify as one of New York's forty-one districts entitled to extra state aid for welfare. Newburgh's mayor, who hotly opposed Mitchell, stated flatly, "We have no serious welfare problem here at all . . . We are just an ordinary city as far as welfare is concerned."[25]

Mitchell, a reactionary zealot, and his supporters ignored such fine points. "It is not moral," he said, "to appropriate public funds to finance crime, illegitimacy, disease, and other social evils." Ever since the Leopold-Loeb case, he said, "criminal lawyers and all the mushy rabble of do-gooders and bleeding hearts in society and politics have marched under the Freudian flag toward the omnipotent state of Karl

Marx.'' Senator Barry Goldwater endorsed Mitchell's efforts. ''I don't like to see my taxes paid,'' Goldwater announced, ''for children out of wedlock. I'm tired of professional chiselers walking up and down the streets who don't work and have no intention of working. I would like to see every city in the country adopt the plan.''[26]

Mitchell's proposals seemed to arouse widespread public sympathy. In Newburgh his support came from people who resented the black migrations of the 1950s. Blacks then made up one-sixth of the city's population—as opposed to one-sixteenth in 1950—and got two-thirds of the welfare money. A retired grocer commented, ''The Negroes who are moving up here these days, want everything for nothing; they have no respect for anybody; they knock you right off the street.'' A construction worker added, ''Mitchell is right in keeping the riffraff out. They come here by the truckload, get in a house, and have kids of all colors, and force all the decent people to move away.'' Mitchell pandered to such views by observing that Newburgh was attracting the ''dregs of humanity'' in a ''never-ending pilgrimage from North Carolina.''[27]

Outside Newburgh, Mitchell's supporters expressed all the standard arguments that had characterized hostile views toward welfare for decades. Such people readily assumed a connection among black migrations, illegitimacy, and welfare. One citizen wrote the New York World Telegram and Sun, ''Illegitimate children should not be bred at public expense. It makes no sense for state and Federal governments to spend millions in efforts to wipe out slums, while at the same time subsidizing the birth of the kind of mental and moral incompetence which makes slums.'' The conservative Saturday Evening Post editorialized, ''One of the announced purposes of the Newburgh plan is to discourage 'immigration' by those who are attracted to Newburgh as a soft touch for, among others, unmarried mothers, actual and putative. Surely a community should have some defense against Bankruptcy by Bastardy.''[28]

The controversy over welfare in Newburgh ultimately disappeared from the front pages and entered the domain of the courts, which ruled in December 1961 that most of Mitchell's proposals violated the law. But complaints about welfare persisted. Newspapers published stories on relief administration, some of which offered sensational accounts of fraud and mismanagement. One told of eighteen unmarried mothers in Albany, New York, whose applications for AFDC named the same man as father of their children. Another featured mothers spending relief checks in barrooms while their children grubbed for scraps in garbage cans outside. Many stories discovered a ''hard core'' of cheaters who gobbled up taxpayers' funds.[29]

The majority of middle-class Americans seemed to endorse these hostile views of welfare. A nationwide Gallup poll taken in August, 1961—in the middle of the Newburgh controversy—asked 1,681 adults if they would "give local communities more say as to which persons should get relief, and how much." Of the respondents, 55 percent favored more local discretion, 29 percent opposed it, and 16 percent had no opinion. Sentiment for local (and less generous) welfare administration was slightly higher (57 percent) in towns with populations of fewer than 10,000 and in farm regions. No regional differences surfaced. Some 56 percent of Republicans favored local control, as opposed to 51 percent of Democrats and 66 percent of those who called themselves independents.[30]

A Gallup poll in March 1964 revealed similar thinking among middle-class Americans. It asked respondents, "In your opinion, which is more often to blame if a person is poor—lack of effort on his own part, or circumstances beyond his control?" A third of the respondents cited lack of effort, 29 percent said circumstances. Of the rest, 32 percent thought both were equally important, and 6 percent had no opinion. Analysis of the data revealed what might have been true at any time in recent decades: the people most likely to blame "circumstances" were older, less well educated, and poorer. Only 18 percent of people earning less than $3,000 a year (roughly the poverty level) pointed to lack of effort.[31]

Another poll in January 1965 discovered a whole range of unfavorable attitudes toward welfare recipients. It revealed that 50 percent of respondents favored denying relief to unwed mothers who had further illegitimate children; 20 percent favored sterilizing the mothers. The poll showed that 84 percent wanted (11 percent opposed) to require able-bodied people on relief to take "any job offered which pays the going wage"; 73 percent favored (19 percent opposed) giving welfare clients food and clothing instead of cash; 58 percent approved (30 percent opposed) of sixty-day residence requirements; and 69 percent (22 percent opposed) said that people who migrated in order to get relief "should be required to prove they came to the area because they had a definite job offer." If these results were to be believed, Mitchell was a minor national hero.[32]

These findings, however, were ambiguous. Results of polls had always depended heavily on the wording of questions. Those that used scare words like "welfare" had always prompted conservative answers, while questions about helping the "needy" elicited favorable replies. One poll in 1961 asked respondents if the government should spend more, the same, or less on a specified list of public programs. A total of 60 percent supported more funds for the "needy." Only 47 percent wanted more for defense, 20 percent wanted more for farmers. A poll in October 1964 discovered that 68 percent of people wanted the government to "see to it that no one is without food or shelter." (As if defying the pollers, 64 percent at the same time said that "welfare and relief make people lazy.")[33]

The mixed results of polls suggested the difficulty of apprehending attitudes toward welfare per se. When thinking about welfare, Americans inevitably conjured up images of the potential recipients, and the unfavorable attitudes toward welfare in the 1960s in part reflected white hostility toward blacks, even though most recipients were white. Although white views of blacks in general became warmer in the early 1960s, concern about illegitimacy, female-headed black families, and the explosive growth of nonwhite populations in the poorest areas of large cities guaranteed that people would think of poor blacks and welfare together.[34]

This ethnic dimension to popular perceptions of poverty, broad even in a predominantly white city like Newburgh, resembled that of the progressive era. By contrast, the stereotype of the 1930s was often of a hard-luck, hard-working farmer or small-town resident, the white yeoman staggered by circumstances. In the 1940s and 1950s people thought of the poor—whites as well as blacks—as a dwindling minority that would soon wither away. But by the early 1960s the stereotype was likely to evoke visions of "hard core" black welfare mothers with hordes of illegitimate children. It was no wonder that people who in one breath favored aiding the "needy" gulped again and blamed "lack of effort" for welfare dependency.

This change aside, the ambiguities were not new. The philanthropic impulse had always coexisted uneasily with the work ethic, as had the vague distinctions between the deserving and the undeserving poor. The polls of the 1960s merely revealed the continuing power of these unquantifiable, often contradictory values. There was no reason to expect sudden changes in historically durable attitudes toward the poor.

Most important, in the early 1960s Americans did not consider poverty and welfare urgent or deeply troubling problems, the short-lived controversy in Newburgh aside. People were confident about the future of the economy, and with good reason, for those were years of great economic growth and prosperity. Economic progress forced down the percentages of poor Americans from around 22 percent in 1959 to 17 percent in 1965. The rediscovery of poverty occurred not in the trough of a depression, not at a time of social turmoil, but in the midst of the most sustained period of economic well-being in national history.

People therefore tended to discount pessimistic forecasts. Granted, automation was creating some unemployment, but a declining rate of joblessness tempered such fears. Granted, increasing educational requirements for jobs posed obstacles to occupational mobility, but the explosive increase in the percentages of young people in high school and college seemed to be keeping pace. Granted, the severe limits on immigration since 1924 left many nonwhites permanently at the bottom of the heap, but even in the automated age, most found jobs and bettered themselves. Poor urban blacks were absolutely wealthier than their fathers and mothers had been on the tenant farms of the rural South, as they had shown by voting with their feet. The early 1960s was in most ways a time for optimism, not gloom, about the future.[35]

There were also some optimistic ways of looking at trends in welfare spending. For one thing, the number of people receiving old age assistance declined steadily in the 1950s, and though still at 2 million in 1960, promised to decline even more. This was not because old people were relatively well off—they were not—but because increasing percentages of them were qualifying for Social Security. It was possible also to argue that the baby boom of the 1940s and early 1950s had temporarily increased the AFDC population; when the boom subsided, as it began to do in 1957, the need might abate. Even illegitimacy, although a real problem, was clearly not going to break the bank: only one-eighth of all children on AFDC in 1961 were illegitimate. Finally, the focus on a "hard core" welfare population of undeserving people was distorted. Many of the long-term relievers were in families with a disabled father or widowed mother, and 50 percent of families on welfare were off the rolls within two years. This was not grounds for self-congratulation, for it meant that a vast population staggered in and out of welfare, but at least it undercut simplistic notions about an enormous permanent class of deadbeats shuffling to the public till.[36]

Qualifications such as these did not get careful elaboration at the time. But that mattered little, for Americans did not perceive a welfare crisis in the early 1960s. Nor did the writers who rediscovered poverty reflect a popular fear of mass unrest. That developed later, during the social turmoil of the late 1960s. Before 1964, most civil rights leaders were still pursuing a nonviolent, integrationist path, and the ghettos appeared quiet. The poor, not yet an organized pressure group, were perceived as apathetic, not dangerous. Activist radicals, like community organizer Saul Alinsky in Chicago, thought they should organize to develop what they needed most of all: an awareness of their own political power.

The push to rediscover poverty came instead from other beliefs about contemporary conditions. Some experts began to recognize around

1960 that economic growth was slowing down, and that the withering away of poverty needed help. Liberal economists, including Gunnar Myrdal, Kenneth Boulding, and perhaps most insistently, Leon Keyserling, took the lead in making this case. For years Keyserling, who had been a member of President Truman's Council of Economic Advisers (CEA), had demanded a range of liberal government policies, especially public spending, to accelerate economic growth—his weapon against poverty. He stepped up the fight in the early 1960s. "The one universal characteristic of all the poor," he wrote in 1964, is "lack of money." He added that "nearly half of those in poverty [he set the number at 66 million in 1963, or 33 percent of the population] are direct or indirect victims of an economy operating at less than full capacity with excessive unemployment." He concluded,

> Any effort to draw a fundamental distinction between the unemployment and growth problem on one hand and the poverty problem on the other would be self-defeating on all scores. An assault upon poverty not interwoven with the attack on these other problems would focus excessively on a purely "case work" or "welfare" approach which ought to make poverty a bit less oppressive or lose itself in a few dramatic situations of no great nationwide import, instead of building an economic environment in which massive poverty would find no place.

But Keyserling believed that because poverty was an economic, not a cultural, problem, it could be controlled. If the government increased its budget from $98 billion in 1965 to $156 billion in 1975, it could work wonders. He concluded, "We can abolish poverty in America within ten years."[37]

Not all economists shared Keyserling's faith in growth. They pointed to what Myrdal and others still called a vicious circle that trapped an "underclass" that was too sick, too old, too black, too unemployable, or too unskilled to benefit much from economic growth. These poor people needed special help. As the Council of Economic Advisers stated in 1964 in the report that formed the intellectual foundation for Johnson's program against poverty, "In the future, economic growth alone will provide relatively fewer escapes from poverty. Policy will have to be more sharply focused on the handicaps that deny the poor fair access to the expanding incomes of a growing economy." Still, the differences between liberals like Keyserling and the CEA were essentially those of emphasis. They all thought that government must give a sharp boost to the economy.[38]

Most economists did share Keyserling's optimism that the government could direct the economy. At that time the economics profession was more confident, indeed more cocksure than at any time in American history. Having lived through twenty years of growth and prosperity, liberal economists had lauded the role of purposeful government fiscal policy—witness the impact of spending in World War II. Having developed sophisticated new tools for quantitative analysis, they found themselves in demand by both the public and private sectors. No one expressed this certitude better than George J. Stigler, president of the American Economic Association. In his presidential address in 1965 he asserted that "economics is finally at the threshold of its golden age—nay, we already have one foot through the door."[39]

Economists and social scientists at the influential Survey Research Center at the University of Michigan, who were engaged in a long-range study of the income of 5,000 American families, expressed the same certitude. Supported by the Ford Foundation, their research was published in many carefully written, if unread, volumes. In 1962 the authors asserted that Americans had only to make one big push to do away with destitution. "The elimination of poverty," they claimed, "is well within the means of Federal, state, and local governments." The "poverty gap," as economists called it, could be abolished "simply by a stroke of the pen. To raise every individual and family in the nation now below a subsistence income to the subsistence level would cost about $10 billion a year. That is less than 2 percent of the Gross National Product. It is less than 10 percent of tax revenues. It is about one-fifth of the cost of national defense."[40]

The Survey's attitude revealed two fundamental assumptions about poverty in the early 1960s that explained the readiness of activists to rediscover poverty. One was the faith that a wealthy country like the United States could afford to abolish destitution, a point that had been a major contribution of Galbraith's *Affluent Society*. Robert Hunter could never have imagined such a utopian development, nor could Harry Hopkins in the 1930s. But by the early 1960s it appeared to experts that the country possessed the means, and economists the tools, to do it. As in the progressive era, it was neither hard times nor even awareness of social problems but economic progress that excited the expectations of reformers and prompted a rediscovery of those in need.[41] Therein lay a limitation of the discovery: should the task of ending poverty prove more difficult than the optimists imagined, the disillusion could be strong and lasting. And it was.

The second assumption was that poverty was both anomalous and immoral in such an affluent society; indeed it was fundamentally un-American. This was Harrington's central theme, who was appalled at the coexistence of wealth and poverty, and it moved Galbraith, Myrdal, Keyserling, and the Council of Economic Advisers. By 1965 it agitated *Time* magazine, which echoed Harrington's horror about the "new" poverty amid middle-class prosperity. As stated in a special report on the subject,

> The reality of the new poverty lies in its contrast to U.S. afflu-
> ence, and it is heightened by the constant, often self-congratula-
> tory talk about that affluence. It is the poverty of a Harlem
> woman who says, 'I'm tired of 49¢ meat; I want some 89¢ meat
> just once.' It is the poverty of people who have a refrigerator,
> assert their right to own a TV set, may genuinely need a car,
> should visit a dentist. Even if this poverty is not like any earlier
> poverty or the poverty of much of the rest of the world, it is
> worth declaring a war on.[42]

7

A CULTURE
OF POVERTY?

To REDISCOVER POVERTY was not necessarily to agree on its nature, which gave experts in the field no end of trouble. Between 1958 and 1966, when they finally developed a rough consensus, they debated heatedly the very old question: was poverty a culture or an economic condition?

Structuralists naturally stressed that poverty was an economic condition stemming from blocked opportunities. Gunnar Myrdal, who had argued that point for years, used as his key word "exclusion." "Something like a caste line," he wrote in 1964, "is drawn between the people in the urban and rural slums, and the majority of Americans who live in a virtual full-employment economy . . . There is an under-class of people in the poverty pockets who live an ever more precarious life and are increasingly excluded from any jobs worth having, or who do not find any jobs at all."[1]

Writers with a more anthropological point of view tended to use terms like "lower-class culture" or "subculture." Like Whyte, whose work they reflected, they tried neither to romanticize nor to denigrate such cultures. They sought to clarify the distinction between lower-class cultures with positive ethnic or regional characteristics and a culture of poverty, a vague concept they deplored. They stressed nonetheless that poverty was more than lack of income, that various racial and ethnic groups responded differently to economic misfortune, that poor people did not necessarily want to act like the middle classes, and that policymakers must be sensitive to the cultural gulf that separated lower-class groups from each other and from the rest of society. The Council of Economic Advisers, borrowing from (and twisting) this perspective, said, "The poor inhabit a world scarcely recognizable, and rarely recognized by the majority of Americans. It is a world apart, whose inhabitants are isolated from the mainstream of American life and alienated from its values."[2]

The most discriminating of these observers tried hard to shatter the notion that America was a classless, homogenizing society, but they stopped short of claiming that there existed the "we-them" division that was characteristic of some other areas of the world. They stopped short also of claiming that poor people grew up with radically different values: in the mass media age, it was impossible to be wholly immune to mainstream middle-class attitudes. These writers insisted, however, that real class, racial, and ethnic divisions persisted and that the United States in the postindustrial age remained heterogeneous.

According to this perspective, the various subcultures developed their own functional values. Working-class people, for instance, knew they were supposed to succeed; like middle-class people, they were ambitious and hard-working. But a combination of forces—cultural traits instilled in the home, peer-group pressures, above all lack of opportunity—often altered the meaning of success from "getting ahead" to "getting by." If working-class people seemed crudely materialistic by middle-class standards, it was not because they were inherently different but because money, goods, and creature comforts were more realistic goals than occupational prestige or a "career." Recognizing the impossibility of rising very far, they were reluctant to defer gratifications in the present.[3]

Writers applied similar anthropological perspectives to lower-class black cultures, suggesting that blacks, including those who remained in the rural South, were well aware of prevailing middle-class norms. Many blacks, indeed, showed levels of aspiration higher than those of lower-class whites. Their goal was to transcend racial discrimination and the self-hate that they perceived in their fathers, but they soon recognized the barriers that held them back and adopted appropriate strategies for survival. As one scholar phrased it, "A depriving world is often all that the individual experiences in his life, and his whole life is taken up in perfecting his adaptation to it, in striving to protect himself in that world, and to squeeze out of it whatever gratification he can."[4]

By 1966 most leading social scientists in this area were focusing on the adaptability—the key word—of lower-class cultures. The sociologist Herbert Gans wrote that the poor were "an economically and politically deprived population whose behavior, values—and pathologies—are adaptations to their existential situation, just as the behavior, values, and pathologies of the affluent are adaptations to *their* existential situation." The sociologist Hyman Rodman said that the lower classes "share the general values of the society with members of the other classes, but in addition they have stretched these values, or developed alternative values, which help them adjust to their deprived circumstances." The anthropologist Elliot Liebow, citing Lloyd Ohlin and Richard Cloward, concluded that "lower class and delinquent cultures today are predictable responses to conditions in our society rather than persisting patterns."[5]

This was a sophisticated, nonjudgmental view of lower-class culture, sensitive both to structuralist emphases on class and to anthropological perspectives on the power of cultural traditions. It was neither romantic nor patronizing. Careful not to claim too much, this view conceded that there were many types of lower-class cultures—some stable, some coping, some skidding, some nearly pathologically disorganized: there was no such thing as an undifferentiated culture of poverty.

A few curious analysts poked tentatively into more dangerous waters. Alert to the pluralism of American life, they attempted to discover whether the cultural traditions of particular groups—blacks, for instance—helped explain their relatively low incomes. Their tentative conclusions did not satisfy many people—daring to ask such questions opened these investigators to charges of racial or cultural bias. But some writers persisted in stating that the cultural traditions of certain groups interacted dynamically with structural barriers such as racial prejudice to inhibit the entrepreneurial zeal that characterized the more economically successful middle classes. Some groups—notably blacks, Orientals, some Hispanics, and American Indians—obviously faced special barriers stemming from their color, and others carried the burden of ugly stereotypes (Italians were mobsters, Irish were drunks, Slavs were stupid). To the extent that these people internalized such images, they were marginal men and women. Sometimes they reacted by deliberately separating themselves from the mainstream middle-class culture. Mothers advised their young to "stay on your own block," and not to trust or mix with the wider world. That lesson learned, the young grew up with culturally transmitted feelings of distance from middle-class mores.

Other low-income groups, especially the "hard-living" Okies, Arkies, and hillbillies, faced no such racial barriers but were equally determined to cling to the distinctive traditions they had fashioned through generations of living apart geographically from modern urban life. So were American Indians, who stoutly sought to preserve their own ways of life. These groups resisted absorption into the routinized world of factory labor—the traditional first step up the occupational ladder. In these dynamic ways, discrimination, economic deprivation, and cultural heritage combined to hold back certain groups from economic progress. "Culture," though it never acted independently of other forces, was perhaps not so irrelevant to an understanding of the behavior of certain low-income groups as some optimistic liberals liked to think.[6]

If these carefully reasoned messages had transcended the bounds of academe, they might have swept away some tired stereotypes about the poor and sensitized policymakers to the durability of cultural traditions. Instead, the messages had to contest the more popular notion of a deviant culture of poverty. Ironically, it was Harrington, a determined structuralist, who unintentionally popularized this notion. Like other activists—both Hunter and Riis come to mind—Harrington wanted to dramatize his cause. Perhaps for that reason, he argued that poverty in the 1960s was not only new, not only a vicious cycle, but a "separate culture, another nation, with its own way of life." Citing F. Scott Fitzgerald's opinion that the rich were different, he applied it to the poor. The poor, he said, had their own language, their own psychology, their own world view. "To be impoverished is to be an internal alien, to grow up in a culture that is radically different from the one that dominates the society." He concluded, "The most important analytic point to have emerged in this description of the other America is the fact that poverty in America forms a culture, a way of life and feeling, that makes it a whole."[7]

In popularizing this view, Harrington sided with the anthropologist Oscar Lewis, whose name became virtually synonymous with the culture of poverty argument. Lewis, a Marxist, labored on occasion to align himself with social scientists who emphasized the adaptability of lower-class cultures. "The culture of poverty," he protested in 1966, "is not just a matter of deprivation or disorganization, a term signifying the absence of something. It is a culture in the traditional anthropological sense in that it provides human beings with a ready-made set of solutions for human problems, and so serves a significant adaptive function." He explained that he meant the term to apply to situations, as in Latin American slums, involving sudden and disruptive transitions from traditional to modern market societies. He added that few American poor people lived in a culture of poverty and that the civil rights movement, like socialism in Cuba or the independence movement in Algeria, could do much to "destroy the psychology and social core of the culture of poverty."[8]

But Lewis was not always so careful, and it was easy for people to see in his early writings an emphasis on the grim and obdurate nature of poverty as a culture. Lewis claimed that poverty affected the very personality of slum dwellers. People in the culture of poverty, he wrote in 1961, have a "strong present-time orientation with relatively little ability to defer gratification and plan for the future, a sense of resignation and fatalism based upon the realities of their different life situation, a belief in male superiority which reaches its crystallization in *machismo* or the culture of masculinity, a corresponding martyr complex among women, and finally, a high tolerance for psychological pathology of all sorts."[9] Nineteenth-century critics of paupers and the undeserving poor could hardly have improved on this description.

Lewis and other writers attributed to poor people a variety of unflattering, though not always compatible, traits. The poor were supposed at once to be apathetic yet alienated, happy-go-lucky yet miserable. They were lazy, unambitious and, especially, disorganized and fatalistic. Lewis explained that "it is the low level of organization which gives the culture of poverty its marginal and anarchic quality in our highly complex, specialized, organized society." Harrington added, "Like the Asian peasant, the impoverished American tends to see life as fate, an endless cycle from which there is no deliverance."[10]

Harrington and Lewis drove home two points about the poor. One was that the culture of poverty produced psychological consequences ranging from "present-mindedness" and inability to "defer gratification"—key terms—to mental illness. Lewis said that people in such cultures were "provincial and locally oriented and have very little sense of history." They showed a "high incidence of maternal deprivation, of orality, a lack of impulse control, a strong present-time orientation, with relatively little ability to defer gratification and to plan for the future." In reaching similar conclusions, Harrington relied on a study of mental illness in New Haven that purported to discover high rates of psychosis among the very poor. Harrington concluded, "There is . . . a personality of poverty, a type of human being produced by the grinding, wearing life of the slums. The other Americans feel differently than the rest of the nation. They tend to be hopeless and passive, yet prone to bursts of violence; they are lonely and isolated, yet often rigid and hostile. To be poor is not simply to be deprived of the material things of this world. It is to enter a fatal, futile universe, an America within an America, a twisted spirit."[11]

Their second point was that the culture of poverty was familial and intergenerational. As Lewis said, it was "not only an adaptation to a set of objective conditions of the larger society. Once it comes into existence, it tends to perpetuate itself from generation to generation because of its effect on the children." Harrington added, "There is a very real possibility that many, even most, of the children of the poor will become the fathers and mothers of the poor. If that were to take place, then America, for the first time in its history, would have a hereditary underclass." Lurid phrasing such as this came close to matching the quasi-hereditarian jeremiads of nineteenth-century writers who had perceived poverty as an infectious disease. Edward Dugdale, describing the deviant world of the Jukes family, could not have done much better.[12]

As Harrington's book attracted attention, others picked up this theme. In January 1964 the Council of Economic Advisers cited the study showing that 40 percent of AFDC parents had themselves been in welfare families, and concluded, "Poverty breeds poverty. A poor individual or family has a high probability of staying poor." Poverty's "ugly by-products include ignorance, disease, delinquency, crime, irresponsibility, immorality, indifference . . . Worst of all, the poverty of the fathers is visited upon the children." Eight months later, the *Saturday Evening Post* carried the intergenerational notion into popular discourse. The roots of poverty, its editorial read, "lie in the self-perpetuating 'culture of poverty'—of ignorance, apathy, resignation, defeat, and despair—by which one generation of the poor infects the next, until, among thousands of families now on the relief rolls across the country, poverty has been perpetuated into third and fourth generations." No piece of writing better manifested the persistent medical metaphor used to describe the poor.[13]

It was impossible to know how many Americans believed these ideas about a culture of poverty. It was also impossible to know exactly what the term meant. Was it supposed to signify an inescapable, virtually genetic phenomenon? Or did it mean that poverty, though a vicious circle, could be broken by wise public policy? Not even Lewis, the most articulate writer on the theme, dispelled the fuzziness that still enveloped the term.

But it was easy to understand why the general notion of a culture of poverty was somewhat fashionable. Although some who employed the term had in mind places like Appalachia, most people probably thought of the new poor of the ghettos. Not because the ghettos contained a majority of the poor—only one of seven poor people lived in central city slums—but because these people, contrary to Harrington's assumptions, were fairly visible, at least in contrast to the rural poor of past generations. Moreover, they seemed overwhelmingly black. Their comparative visibility, their geographical concentration, and their color made cultural interpretations of poverty more plausible than they might otherwise have been.[14]

But culture of poverty arguments did not go unchallenged. Even at that time some knowledgeable observers warned that talk about the present-mindedness of the poor played directly into the hands of those who wished to cut back on welfare programs. Elizabeth Wickenden, a veteran social worker, warned in 1964,

There is some danger in the current usage of the term "culture of poverty" because it suggests that something other than the absence of money distinguishes the poor as a *group* from the rest of us. It is true that poverty is discouraging, debilitating, and cuts people off from the mainstream of American life. But there is a danger in suggesting that these qualities are intrinsic to the poor themselves rather than the end-product of remediable social ills. The danger lies in the ease with which this assumption moves toward the charge that the poor are poor by their own fault.[15]

The ensuing counterattack against the concept of the culture of poverty arose on all fronts. Critics asked if it was a geographical, personal, or familial culture. Pointing to the eagerness of poor people to sign up for manpower training programs, they asserted the continuing power of the work ethic at all levels of the income pyramid. They showed that poor people, although disillusioned, were neither passive nor apathetic—only realistic. Within a few years, the protests and riots of poor people showed that passivity was about as inappropriate a label as could have been found.[16]

Simplistic notions about the "present-mindedness" of the poor, critics added, overlooked two basic points. First, middle-class people, who were buying every consumer good in sight, going deeper into debt, and saving proportionally less than in the past, were hardly deferring gratifications. The entire society, not just the poor, was in important ways more "present-minded" than ever before. Second, poor people could hardly be expected to develop long-range goals that were beyond their economic means. Planning for the future, the sociologist Lee Rainwater observed later, "requires a certain confidence in one's ability to control oneself and to be partly in control of the outside world. Lacking that control, poor people understandably tend to discourage planning and the hope that it implies, lest one court disappointment."[17]

Critics of the culture of poverty school heaped scorn on the view that the poor were psychologically different. They showed that no studies were really able to prove that whole groups of people—the poor? the rich? blacks? whites?—possessed recognizably distinctive psyches. Critics also exposed the fact that research linking low socioeconomic status and psychosis did not take into account class-based negligence that helped to increase the incidence of severe psychological problems among lower-class people. That research also failed sufficiently to point out the likelihood that psychologists, being middle class, looked at lower-class styles of expression and called them neurotic. Critics of such research concluded that most poor people displayed psychological strength, not deviancy. As Rainwater argued later in stressing the difficulties confronted by poor blacks, "The problems of lower-class persons make the soul-searching of middle-class adolescents seem like a kind of conspicuous consumption of psychic riches."[18]

Scholars questioned on three separate grounds the assertions that poverty was long-term or intergenerational. The first argument stressed that the main problem was not the longevity but the risk, or potential incidence, of poverty. The University of Michigan study, the first major survey of poverty over time, reinforced scattered findings that more than one-third of people who were poor in one year had been nonpoor the year before and became nonpoor the year afterward. More than two-thirds of poor people rose above the poverty line within two years. Emphasizing the high incidence of poverty, the researchers calculated that fully one-third of the population was poor in one or more of nine consecutive years of the study. But only 3 percent of the population and 22 percent of the poverty population were below the line all nine years.[19]

The finding that 22 percent of poor people in the affluent 1960s were impoverished for nine straight years was hardly grounds for applause, but it was clear that the long-term poor were a small minority of the poverty population in any one year. The majority suffered from particular circumstances lasting from a few months to two years. Many were low-wage workers who lived more or less regularly in straitened but not always destitute circumstances; under a higher poverty line they would have been poor most of the time. But they were not lost in a culture of poverty. Many of these short-term poor owed their plight to temporary unemployment, illness, or especially to the financial strain that hit all low-income families and individuals at various times in their lives.[20]

The second critique of the belief in a long-term culture of poverty more directly confronted the generational proposition. It cited studies of twentieth-century occupational mobility showing that only 21 percent of the sons of service workers, 22 percent of the sons of manufacturing laborers, and 17 percent of the sons of "other nonfarm laborers" ended up in any of these three low-status occupations; most of the rest moved up the ladder. A majority of the men listed in the census as "laborers" had fathers who had toiled in even lower-status jobs, mainly as farm laborers, poor farmers, or "operatives." These studies highlighted the harmful burden of race, not of personality or of a "culture of poverty."[21]

The Michigan researchers, approaching the question from a similar perspective, conceded that there was "some correlation between the poor earning power of the present generation and the earning power of the fathers.'' They highlighted the importance of education: low educational level of the fathers was the best predictor of low income for the sons, even after taking into account the mother's income, the father's income or occupation, the number of children in the family, the place of residence, and race. But the researchers emphasized that the "lack of education and skilled occupations among heads of poor families does not result solely from the unskilled and uneducated background of their parents. It also stems from the *failure* of these persons to improve their skills in the way that *typical* family heads have improved their skills over the past generation. Though no sweeping generalizations can be made . . . [statistics] offer little support for a theory of poverty that rests entirely on an intergenerational transmission.''[22]

The anthropologist Elliot Liebow, after studying black street-corner life in Washington, D.C., phrased a similar conclusion more clearly. The vicious cycle of poverty, he said, was not a "puncture-proof" culture. Rather, it stemmed from racial discrimination and lack of opportunity that affected individuals in each new generation. He concluded:

Many similarities between the lower-class Negro father and son (or mother and daughter) do not result from "cultural transmission" but from the fact that the son goes out and independently experiences the same failures, in the same areas, as his father. What appears as a dynamic, self-sustaining cultural process is, in part at least, a relatively simple piece of machinery which turns out, in rather mechanical fashion, independently produced look-a-likes.[23]

The third line of attack on the notion of a culture of poverty came from anthropologists who lamented the misuse of the concept of culture in that context. "Culture," they reminded readers, was not something in itself, an independent variable that could be isolated from the socioeconomic setting. The people of Appalachia, frequently identified as living in a culture of poverty, in fact belonged to and were exploited by the coal mining economy of the region. Blacks suffered from racial discrimination, not cultural deprivation. It was impossible, indeed, to rope off culture from the power relationships of society. Nor were those people who were seen as being in a culture of poverty—the long-term poor, people in the most destitute regions or ghettos—unchanging mirror images of some culture. As individuals, such people were never predictable; their values and behavior altered as they aged and as circumstances affected them. One scholar explained, "A subculture is not a consistent whole but an entity shot through with conflicting elements . . . What appear to be strong impulses to action under one set of circumstances may be severely weakened by a change in circumstances." Liebow said wryly, " 'Culture' and 'historical continuity' may not be the most useful constructs for dealing with lower class behavior."[24]

These conclusions were admittedly tentative; no studies had systematically related poverty to large numbers of individuals, let alone particular cultures, over generations. And what was known offered a crack in the door for cautious and sophisticated writers who emphasized the role of cultural transmission. It was clear that nearly 6 million Americans were poor every year during the most affluent decade in the country's history. The findings also showed the obvious: distinctions of class—as measured quantitatively by education, occupation, and income—persisted to some degree over more than one generation. In the face of such data, few social scientists in the mid-1960s displayed the fatuous optimism about the end of class distinctions that had characterized writings in the 1950s. Observers who recognized the distinctive traits of different groups were thus right to employ cultural perspectives. In this qualified (if obvious) sense, a cultural perspective was necessary.

But writers like Harrington and Lewis did not always qualify the culture of poverty argument. Some, including Harrington, used the term carelessly to promote active public measures against poverty. Others, such as the conservative *Saturday Evening Post*, employed it to confirm crude and unflattering stereotypes about the poor and to excuse a policy of neglect. The considerable attention given the notion —in scholarly debates, by the Council of Economic Advisers, by editorialists—suggested that many people wanted to believe the worst of the very poor. Like the metaphor of contagion as applied to the urban slums of 1900, the stereotype enabled more fortunate Americans to relieve themselves of guilt and anxiety.

Did these debates make any difference? In one sense, they did not. As late as 1966, a high-level seminar on problems of race and poverty sponsored by the American Academy of Arts and Sciences wrangled at very great length over the tired question of whether a culture of poverty existed. A decade later the most thoughtful authority on the subject, Henry Aaron, concluded that "the debate between the cultural and environmental view of poverty seems to have vanished without leaving significant intellectual residue." He pointed to the wasted effort involved in this argument and to its failure to stimulate, even in the 1970s, solid studies that could have answered empirically the large questions about the nature and causes of poverty. As a result, most authorities believed only what liberals and structuralists had always believed: poverty was less a cultural trait than an economic condition.[25]

Still, the debate served some useful purposes. Concerned writers like Lewis, Harrington, and (about blacks) Daniel Moynihan attempted to clarify what they meant by a culture of poverty, thereby allowing social scientists to cut the concept down to manageable size. If the largely structuralist consensus that emerged among experts by 1966 failed to affect popular opinions, it at least spared the experts from rehashing old arguments thereafter. Having delivered a scholarly coup de grâce to the notion that most poor people wallowed in a culture of poverty, they could go on to discuss economic remedies for poverty, notably income maintenace.

The debate also helped sustain poverty as an item on the agenda of public discussion. And it highlighted Harrington's most useful point: that an obdurate new poverty devastated certain deprived groups in American life. They were the aged, migrant workers, small farmers, nonwhites, people with little education, and children in female-headed families. Harrington, however, was a little unreliable historically; to begin with, this new poverty was old indeed. Furthermore, it was not at all clear that the poor of 1960 were more hopeless, invisible, or isolated than had been the poor of Robert Hunter's time. Events within a very few years, notably the angry protests of blacks and of advocates for "welfare rights," proved that the lower classes, too, participated in the revolution of expectations that gripped the nation. Still, Harrington's rage and concern seemed to touch a nerve of sympathy for the needy, tinged with shame that so un-American a condition could persist in an affluent age. Having been helped to rediscover poverty, Americans could not immediately shove it out of sight again.

8
GIRDING FOR WAR
ON POVERTY

THE RISING EXPECTATIONS of Americans in the 1960s virtually ensured that the rediscovery of poverty would have political repercussions. The liberal, activist presidential administrations of John F. Kennedy and Lyndon B. Johnson, who became personally engaged in the subject of poverty, gave it a new visibility. The combination of rising expectations and political involvement sparked significant developments, including an unanticipated consequence: the arousal of the poor themselves. The most immediate programmatic result, however, was the war on poverty of 1964. Like many social welfare proposals of the era, it aimed primarily at the age-old goal of preventing poverty, but it diminished destitution only marginally. By the time the war on poverty lost its political glamor, its limitations had intensified the country's doubts about the ability of experts to diagnose, much less cure, the ills of the poor.

When Kennedy reached the White House in 1961, he had already studied questions of social welfare. In 1958-1959 he had supported a range of programs for the poor—Medicare, federal aid to education, manpower training, and extension of public assistance. During his campaign for the presidency, he had been shaken by the misery he witnessed first hand in West Virginia. In August of that year, speaking on the twenty-fifth anniversary of the passage of Social Security, he praised the law for undertaking a "war on poverty." His inaugural address five months later referred three times to poverty. "If the free society cannot help the many who are poor," he said, "it cannot save the few who are rich."[1]

Before 1963 Kennedy and his top advisers were concerned mainly about sustaining economic growth and relieving unemployment. Aside from worrying about juvenile delinquency, they did not sense any social breakdown or believe in a culture of poverty. They employed what one important official later described as a "bricks and mortar kind of focus . . . with no real linkage to the human problems." He added, "The notion of declaring a war on poverty in 1960 just wouldn't have grabbed people."[2]

In pursuing economic expansion, the administration approached problems categorically. In May 1961 Kennedy established the President's Committee on Juvenile Delinquency and Youth Crime (PCJD), nominally headed by Attorney General Robert Kennedy; its organizer was Robert's friend and political aide, David Hackett, who picked Lloyd Ohlin as his technical director. Under Ohlin, the committee financed planning in a dozen cities, including comprehensive action programs in New Haven, Cleveland, and New York. The most visible of these, Mobilization for Youth in New York City, explicitly sought to vitalize all the resources of the Lower East Side. It sponsored employment programs, manpower training, remedial education, antidiscrimination activities, and neighborhood service centers, which later became features of the community action programs of the war on poverty. By 1963 the PCJD had become a "$30 million test of Ohlin's 'opportunity theory.' "[3]

Aid to depressed areas represented a second approach of the early Kennedy years. After the recession of the late 1950s, Congress proved receptive and passed the Area Redevelopment Act (ARA) in May 1961. By the end of 1964, some $300 million in federal money had flowed from the Area Redevelopment Administration to depressed regions. Some $170 million of this was in loans to private businesses. Another $90 million helped improve public facilities, while smaller sums went for technical assistance and retraining. Other legislation also helped depressed areas, notably the accelerated public works act of 1962, which provided $900 million in public funds, and the Appalachia Act of 1964, which allocated $1 billion.[4]

In 1962 Congress enacted the Manpower Development and Training Act (MDTA), the third element in Kennedy's categorical attack on poverty. This program operated on the structuralist premise that unemployment was not just a cyclical phenomenon. Sold as a way of helping people help themselves and thereby get off welfare, the program was popular with Congress, which also approved the Job Corps of 1964. By 1973 the MDTA program had enrolled 2.2 million people at a cost in federal money of $3.2 billion. The focus on job training showed that policymakers in the 1960s had greater ambitions than the New Dealers, who thought less about retraining people than about giving them money or public work.[5]

None of these programs amounted to a confrontation with, let alone a war on, poverty. The sums spent to alleviate juvenile delinquency were pitifully small. At Kennedy's death, the program was still largely experimental. The ARA and related efforts, though larger, barely dented the problem of depressed areas; its programs provided little meaningful job training and developed no more than 100,000 new jobs by 1965. Moreover, the idea grew increasingly unpopular: labor spokesmen resented granting loans to nonunion employers; local businesses complained when competitors got public aid; and many congressmen opposed sending money to areas other than their own. As early as 1963 Congress refused to renew the first ARA appropriations, and aid to depressed areas staggered on under renamed but ill-funded programs thereafter.

Although the MDTA program was the largest and most popular of the three, its limitations led to growing criticism. Many experts doubted the cost efficiency of the programs; some thought job training merely skimmed off the most highly motivated workers, who would ultimately have found satisfactory employment in any event. Some of the neediest poor, such as unskilled people in rural pockets, rarely found it possible to enroll in job training, and at least two-thirds of the hard-core unemployed (ghetto blacks and early school dropouts) failed to get stable work even if they completed the courses. Dropout rates were high—one-third of enrollees in early Job Corps centers. And the programs cost as much as $7,500 per enrollee per year; public employment programs, critics argued, required far less money per participant. In 1975 one assessment of job training was that the "effect has probably been, at least partly, to put newly trained workers into jobs previously filled by other workers, who were simply displaced."[6]

Some liberals were cool to manpower programs from the beginning. Hackett, pointing to Job Corps centers that emphasized conservation work in the countryside, dismissed that form of training as "outmoded," a "fresh air concept which really didn't make an awful lot of sense." Training for factory jobs, others added, was often just as irrelevant in an age of rampant technological change. "When the poverty money runs out," one observer wrote, "the indigenous worker finds that he has his foot firmly planted on the bottom rung of a career ladder with only one rung." Some critics concluded that the whole approach reflected nineteenth-century efforts to promote the work ethic. What defenders of the programs called "investment in human capital," these critics insisted, was really the creation of quasi-military training centers that tried to develop in trainees middle-class habits and lower-class skills.[7]

Not all observers were so harsh. Many emphasized that it was difficult to know the long-range impact of such programs. One evaluation concluded that at least some enrollees "seize the opportunity and benefit substantially." Job Corps director Otis Singletary maintained that a dropout rate of, say, 35 percent was not bad, considering that all of the enrollees had already dropped out of high school and that half of all college freshman did not finish their studies. Singletary was frank also in defending the ambitious effort of training centers to instill habits of industry, thrift, and reliability. "Instead of taking that as an accusation," he recalled, "I took that as a statement of fact. My answer was: 'Exactly. Precisely.' "[8]

Manpower training represented no more than a jab at the problem of poverty. During the mid- and late 1960s such programs enrolled an average of only 300,000 per year; from the beginning there were far more applicants than spaces. From the beginning, too, some Job Corps centers confronted unfavorable publicity because of some incidents of sex and violence. Singletary admitted that the early problems with the Job Corps "would make your hair stand on end." Though officials soon controlled most of the early difficulties, they never mounted a serious attack on poverty. Manpower training remained a potentially useful, though not fully tested, weapon in the war against poverty.[9]

All three programs of the Kennedy administration represented conservative applications of partially structuralist diagnoses. Except in New York City, the juvenile delinquency action plans focused on providing services—notably education and job training—that would help people help themselves. Most of the ARA money went to private businesses, and the public-works dollars went to construction projects long favored by legislators. Manpower training, although ambitious, aimed at preventing dependency—at saving on welfare—not at providing income maintenance for poor people. All three programs emphasized striking at the "roots" of poverty, that is, spending limited (and ultimately diminishing) amounts of money to aid the younger, more employable poor who, as always in modern America, were a minority of all the needy. Of the 34 million poor people in 1964, 5.4 million were over sixty-five, 5.7 million were preschool children, and 2.8 million were mothers who in effect were forced to stay home with these children. Three of five poor people were younger than eighteen or older than sixty-five.[10]

Kennedy knew little about the larger population that needed long-run public assistance and relied heavily on Social Security experts whom he had begun to cultivate in the late 1950s. Among them were activists in such organizations as the American Public Welfare Association, the National Association of Social Workers (NASW), and the National Social Welfare Assembly, a group embracing the NASW and many other social work organizations. The chief lobbyist for the assembly in Washington, the knowledgeable Elizabeth Wickenden, served as consultant to a postelection task force to study legislation in the field of health and Social Security.

Wilbur Cohen, who headed the task force, became assistant secretary for legislation of HEW. In the apt phrasing of one scholar, Cohen was "ubiquitous, inexhaustible, irrepressible." He had come to Washington in 1934 to serve on the staff of the Committee on Economic Security, then stayed as a top aide on the Social Security Board. During the Eisenhower years he had left to teach at the University of Michigan, but he had maintained his contacts in Washington. Informed, pragmatic, persuasive, he was a key formulator and implementer of legislation under both Kennedy and Johnson, who made him secretary of HEW in 1968.[11]

Led by Cohen, the task force emerged in late 1960 with a wide range of proposals to reform Social Security and welfare. None was new: all echoed the twenty-year consensus among liberal social workers and Social Security officials: broaden social insurance, provide federal support for general assistance, increase federal matching payments for categorical public aid, deny federal money to states that retained residence or citizenship requirements, move toward equalizing public assistance payments in the various states. These and other proposals stemmed from the awareness that poverty would never wither away.[12]

The network around Cohen pressed also for legislation to extend AFDC to needy two-parent families whose heads of household were out of work and had exhausted unemployment benefits. This purpose was at once liberal—to help families in need—and conservative—to keep such families together. Kennedy, tutored by Cohen, asked for congressional action on it in February 1961. Hoping to cut back on desertions by unemployed fathers, Congress in 1961 approved extension of AFDC to two-parent families for one year, then continued it several times thereafter. The legislation authorized federal matching grants under AFDC to families in which fathers were either out of work or employed for less than a hundred hours a month. The program was not mandatory on the states, and half, mostly rural and poor states, refused to provide for it throughout the 1960s and 1970s. In these states, families with unemployed fathers fit the age-old definition of "undeserving." Nor did AFDC-UP (for "Unemployed Parent") stem the tide of desertions, which increased even in states that availed themselves of the plan. Still, AFDC-UP marked a liberal step forward in the evolution of federal welfare, and making the program mandatory became one of the top items on agendas of welfare reform after 1962.[13]

The Kennedy administration's major accomplishment in the field was the Public Welfare Amendments of 1962, which extended AFDC-UP for five more years and granted federal funding for special training of social workers. Most important—or so it seemed at the time—the legislation authorized federal payment to the states of 75 percent of the cost of rehabilitative or preventive social services for the needy. Kennedy hailed the amendments as "the most far-reaching revision of our public welfare program since it was enacted in 1935 . . . and a turning point in this nation's efforts to cope realistically and helpfully with these pressing problems."[14]

One of the forces that hastened this legislation was the growing influence of social workers, who had historically emphasized that "cases" needed expert professional service as well as cash assistance. Officials in the Eisenhower administration, hoping that services would rehabilitate people and lower the long-range costs of assistance, had subscribed to this view. As HEW Secretary Marion Folsom had said in 1955, "All our policies and programs should have one emphasis: prevention and elimination of need rather than the mere relief of need after it develops." In 1956 Congress had authorized federal money, at the ratio of 50-50 with state funds, for such services, but in the next few years states did not take the hint. The amendments of 1962, by raising the federal ante to 75 percent, merely increased the inducement to states.[15]

A second force behind the 1962 amendments was the perception that "multiproblem families" posed an increasingly heavy burden on state and local budgets. This problem impressed Kennedy's secretary of HEW, Abraham Ribicoff, who as governor of Connecticut until 1961 had fretted over the rising cost of public welfare and worried that dependency was becoming chronic. "I have been appalled," he said in 1961, "at the thought of generation after generation on welfare. We must have a new direction." To prevent this calamity, he thought social work must concentrate on multiproblem families. The legislation he designed proposed to rename the Bureau of Public Assistance the Bureau of Family Services.[16]

Ribicoff especially promoted rehabilitation. America, he wrote Kennedy in 1961, must reorient "the whole approach to welfare from a straight cash hand-out operation to one in which the emphasis is on rehabilitation of those on relief and prevention ahead of time." This cry for rehabilitation also appealed to Kennedy. The needy, the president said, must get more than a "relief check . . . such a check must be supplemented, or in some cases made unnecessary, by positive services and solutions . . . emphasis must be directed increasingly toward prevention and rehabilitation—on reducing not only the long-range cost in budgetary terms but the long-range cost in human terms as well."[17]

The controversy over welfare in Newburgh during the summer of 1961 merely strengthened Ribicoff's hand. A services approach, he realized, appealed not only to professional social workers but also to conservatives who wanted to cut back on spending in the long run. Welfare reform, he told Kennedy, was becoming a "hot issue . . . conservatives are up in arms over the reports of welfare abuses—the ADC mother with a dozen illegitimate kids, the relief checks that buy liquor instead of food and rent, the able-bodied man who spurns a decent job to stay on relief." What better way to appease this sentiment, he argued, than to substitute (over time) services for cash?[18]

As Ribicoff had anticipated, Congress was quick to buy a program that might help welfare wither away. In reporting out the bill favorably, the House Ways and Means Committee explained that the legislation "places emphasis on the provision of services rather than depending on welfare checks. The bill would . . . provide incentives to recipients . . . to improve their condition so as to render continued public assistance . . . unnecessary." On the House floor, conservatives tried but failed to scuttle the provision extending AFDC-UP. The measure then passed the Senate with little debate and was signed in July 1962.[19]

In practice, the legislation fell far short of its sponsors' hopes. From the start the Bureau of Family Services (the new name for the Bureau of Public Assistance) had no end of trouble trying to define "services." Were states seeking federal money supposed to describe these according to the services provided or according to the "most common problems" (alcoholism? desertion?) of the families in need? Or did services simply mean an extension of the case work already provided by professional social workers? After going through thirty-eight drafts, the BFS finally defined services in effect as whatever case workers did to help make families self-sufficient. That vague endorsement of prevention was hardly a revolutionary development in the history of case work.[20]

The legislation did not even help conservatives achieve their goal of cutting costs. On the contrary, federal spending for welfare services escalated from $194 million in fiscal 1963 to $2.5 billion in 1972, partly because of a rise in the number of cases. More important, several provisions in the 1962 amendments proved too tempting for states to resist. One was the 3-1 formula, which was more generous than formulas then used for cash assistance. Another clause permitted such money to be spent on *potential* welfare recipients, and no clause limited the amount the federal government would match. As states scrambled for ways to pay their bills, they seized on these provisions to get money supposedly slated for services—still vaguely defined—and use it for a variety of programs they had had to pay for themselves in the past. Congress, appalled at what it had done in the name of promoting rehabilitation, finally (in 1972) set a limit on spending for services.[21]

Some reformers complained that the services approach did little anyway. The outcome in Massachusetts was a case in point. Thanks in part to federal funds, the number of case workers there increased from 22,000 to 33,000 between 1963 and 1967. But at the same time the number of applicants for aid increased, for a variety of reasons, so AFDC case loads stayed about the same—around sixty per worker. For these reasons, the service amendments made little difference—either in facilitating attention to cases or (as a few liberals feared) in creating nosier intrusions from case workers. One survey of AFDC recipients in 1967 concluded that "social service is little more than a relatively infrequent, pleasant chat. It is somewhat supportive. It is rarely threatening but also not too meaningful in the sense of either helping poor people get things they want or of changing their lives."[22]

Many activists had recognized that rehabilitation was part of the age-old, elusive goal of preventing dependency. It sought to change the poor, not to give them the employment and income they really needed. No one expressed this critique better than Leo Perlis, an AFL-CIO activist. Responding to Kennedy's proposals in early 1962, he wrote:

> The current somewhat apologetic emphasis on rehabilitation seems almost obscene—as if rehabilitation would not cost more (at first at least), as if rehabilitation is always possible (in the face of more than 4,000,000 jobless among other things), as if rehabilitation is a substitute for relief for everybody and at all times.
>
> I think we all need to make a forthright declaration that direct public assistance in our competitive society is unavoidable, necessary, and even socially useful.[23]

Fifteen months after passage of the public welfare amendments, Kennedy and his top advisers committed themselves to a broad attack on poverty in America. Why the change of focus?

It did not come from popular pressure. As late as March 1964, when President Johnson called for a "war on poverty," a Gallup poll showed that 83 percent of Americans thought poverty would never be done away with in the United States. Nor did it come from the civil rights movement and unrest among the black poor. In 1963 that movement remained largely integrationist, nonviolent, and confined to the South. Richard Cloward and Frances Fox Piven misread history in contending in 1971 that the war on poverty attempted to "reach, placate, and integrate a turbulent black community."[24]

Cloward and Piven also judged the Kennedy administration's belated concern about poverty as a political strategy aimed at cementing the allegiance of blacks to a faltering coalition within the Democratic party. That goal, they held, accounted for the concentration of the poverty program in the northern cities, where potentially valuable blocs of black voters lived, instead of in the South, where the incidence of poverty was highest. Their argument, however, assumes that the Kennedy people were essentially Machiavellian. They were liberals, anxious to improve economic conditions. Moreover, the civil rights bill proposed in June 1963 was enough to develop black political support.[25]

The political strategy argument also slights a key point: the Kennedy people did not consider poverty as a problem that primarily affected blacks. As Adam Yarmolinsky, a key planner, put it later, "The war on poverty was in no sense a help-the-blacks program . . . We felt it would do very little for the blacks. We said, 'Most poor people are not black, most black people are not poor.' " Yarmolinsky alluded to the timeliness of a newspaper exposé on poverty in eastern Kentucky in the New York *Herald Tribune* in 1963. Administration planners, he said, paid less attention in 1963 to the problems of the ghettos than to Appalachia. Yarmolinsky concluded, "Color it [the war on poverty] Appalachian [not black] if you are going to color it anything at all."[26]

One consideration was to do something for low-income people generally. In 1963 the Kennedy administration was working strenuously for a tax cut to stimulate spending and investment. That proposal promised to assist middle and upper-income groups. But as one antipoverty planner said later, the tax cut "didn't do a damn thing for poor people." A program to combat poverty, Kennedy's aides realized, might counter the accusation that they favored the middle classes. Walter Heller, chairman of the Council of Economic Advisers, and the most influential proponent of a poverty program in 1963, explained to Kennedy in October that "having mounted a dramatic program for one disadvantaged group [civil rights for blacks] it was both equitable and politically attractive to launch one specifically designed to aid other disadvantaged groups." The white poor, like blacks and the middle classes, should have something to cheer about on election day.[27]

More important than political considerations, however, were the ideas that made contemporary social scientists receptive to the rediscovery of poverty, especially Harrington's view of a new poor. Top advisers like Heller did not take this view directly from Harrington, who called for huge and politically unrealistic increases in federal spending. Rather, they confronted statistics compiled by the Wisconsin economist Robert Lampman that showed a slowing down between 1957 and 1962 of the rate at which economic growth was attacking poverty and an increase in the percentage of the poor who were aged, members of female-headed families, or minorities. There was a "dramatic slowdown in the rate at which the economy is taking people out of poverty," Heller told Kennedy in May 1963. Poverty could be—must be—attacked by the government.[28]

Some officials cherished the old preventive dream of making welfare virtually unnecessary. A program against poverty, they hoped, was a good investment. As the CEA explained in January 1964, "We pay twice for poverty: once in the production lost in wasted human potential, again in the resources diverted to coping with poverty's social by-products. Humanity compels our action, but it is sound economics as well." Sargent Shriver, who headed the task force that drew up the final plan, added a month later, "I'm not at all interested in running a hand-out program, or a 'something for nothing' program." President Johnson, in calling for a war on poverty in March, proclaimed, "Our fight against poverty will be an investment in the most valuable of our resources—the skills and strengths of our people. And in the future, as in the past, this investment will return its cost many-fold to our entire economy." Later he said, "We are not content to accept the endless growth of relief rolls or welfare rolls. We want to offer the forgotten fifth of our people opportunity, not doles." Johnson's rhetoric was politically necessary, but it was sincere. He looked upon his program as a way of lessening welfare dependency.[29]

The most fundamental faith of many of the planners was in opening up "opportunity," a goal that again emphasized helping the poor help themselves and offering services, not cash, much like the manpower training programs and the public welfare amendments. It aimed to get the poverty out of the people—and afterward the people out of poverty. New Deal programs, the CEA explained, did not go far enough: "A new federally led effort is needed, with special emphasis on prevention and rehabilitation." The council added, "Let us deny no one the chance to develop and use his native talents to the full. Let us, above all, open wide *the exits from poverty* to the children of the poor." Extolling the Office of Economic Opportunity (OEO), which was to run the poverty program, Shriver added, "Opportunity is our middle name."[30]

Opening up opportunity meant looking for ways to help young people, because they could still take advantage of such help. Heller confidently cited surveys that stressed the correlation between low educational levels and poverty. In December 1963 he advised Johnson to "emphasize that the major focus on the attack on poverty is on youth: to *prevent* entry into poverty." A month later he reiterated that "education is at the core of any successful sustained campaign against poverty. The preponderance of persons with little education in the ranks of the poor is striking." Heller's attitude reflected the enhanced importance that Americans in general attached to formal schooling. It was also characteristic of American reformers: from the times of Charles Loring Brace and Jacob Riis, antipoverty activists had proclaimed the necessity of promoting the work ethic in the young.[31]

It was in this way that the poverty program, like other government efforts of the early 1960s, reflected a conservative application of structuralist observations. The planners recognized that millions of the so-called new poor were not in the labor force, that they needed income maintenance more than opportunity. They knew that formidable structural forces like technological change, shortages of decent paying jobs, and racial discrimination, blocked the opportunities of many who were willing and able to work. They realized also that enhanced economic growth would not work miracles—welfare had to remain a central part of any comprehensive program against poverty. Yet in developing legislation, they drew back from these facts and placed their faith in extending opportunity. They tried to open up doors, not set down floors; to offer a hand up, not a handout. Their war on poverty extended the long tradition of quests for prevention and rehabilitation. It never seriously considered giving poor people what many of them needed most: jobs and income maintenance.

As Heller and others solicited advice at the end of 1963, some officials in the administration criticized various draft proposals. Labor Secretary Willard Wirtz demanded a large program of public employment. "Without question," he wrote in January 1964, "the biggest single immediate change which the poverty program could bring about in the lives of most of the poor would be to provide the family head with a regular, decently paid job." Wilbur Cohen at HEW wanted more done about racial discrimination and automation, and he urged especially the need for more welfare. Preliminary drafts, he wrote in December 1963, do "not do enough for children, broken families where the women have to support the family, minority groups, and special problem areas like alcoholics, delinquents, and the mentally ill." Aside from defending their bureaucratic interests, these officials were trying to augment the immediate income, as opposed to the long-range opportunity, of the poor.[32]

Other critics compared the war on poverty unfavorably to New Deal programs that pragmatically had offered cash and jobs. The war on poverty, they sneered, constituted another paternalistic effort to develop lower-class skills and middle-class values. The very term Job *Corps*, they charged, exposed the militaristic thrust of the program. Educational programs like Head Start and Upward Bound struck them as overbearing and patronizing. Critics suggested new titles: Head Shrink for Head Start, Uplift Bounce for Upward Bound, Office of Economical Orthopsychiatry for Office of Economic Opportunity. The whole effort amounted to a War on the Culture of the Poor.[33]

The war on poverty was indeed more ambitious in its long-range goals, and therefore more intrusive and paternalistic, than New Deal programs. But that contrast merely reflected the crucial difference between conditions in the 1930s and the 1960s. During the Depression the architects of the welfare state, struggling desperately to save the nation from disaster, fashioned new ideas and tools as they went along. By the 1960s the planners no longer perceived a Malthusian world. Despite some sluggishness in the late 1950s, continuing economic growth was assumed. This affluence made people confident, indeed cocky; they congratulated themselves on the professionalism of social science. The precision of modern economics (so it seemed) had resuscitated western Europe and was "modernizing" the "underdeveloped" countries. The tax cut was about to revive the American economy. The CEA at first named their proposals "Widening Participation in Prosperity." The advisers explained that "conquest of poverty is well within our power. About $11 billion a year would bring all poor families up to the $3,000 income level." That amount, they asserted, was less than one-fifth of the annual defense budget and less than 2 percent of the GNP.[34]

Just as in the progressive era, confidence in social science and in the economic future lay behind the rediscovery of poverty and fueled the activism of the liberals who developed the war on it. The planners, sure that they had the tools to do the job, plunged ahead with a program. Johnson, told by Heller of the planning, hardly paused to reflect—"Push ahead full-tilt on this project," he commanded. In this heady atmosphere it was not surprising that the framers made enthusiastic (and politically useful) predictions about the abolition of poverty, that they emphasized opportunity instead of equality, tinkered with existing institutions instead of embarking on hard-to-manage structural change, or that they dared to think, as Josephine Shaw Lowell had thought, of changing the habits and attitudes of the poor.[35]

The goal of opportunity, though dominant, was not the planners' only concern. While Heller and other economists on the CEA and the Bureau of the Budget were circulating memos and meeting with Kennedy and Johnson, others were toying with an idea that later became almost synonymous with the OEO—community action.

The earliest and most consistent advocates of community action were the officials and social scientists connected with the President's Committee on Juvenile Delinquency. Along with Robert Kennedy and David Hackett, they included Lloyd Ohlin, the technical adviser to PCJD, and Richard Boone, a top aide. They began by trying to bypass what they considered the dead hand of welfare bureaucracy—"professionalism run rampant," one said. "Our intention," Robert Kennedy said in December 1963, "is to avoid becoming entangled in the Federal government's system of vested interests," meaning the professional social workers, bureaucrats in existing federal agencies, and most city machines. Getting around them meant including poor people themselves in "comprehensive" community action along the lines of New York's Mobilization for Youth. Existing programs, Kennedy said, "are always planned for the poor—not *with* the poor." Government must "encourage local communities to coordinate their own public and private resources, and to plan and propose their own programs."[36]

Ohlin, the most articulate theorist of the group, insisted that community action must aim at broad and comprehensive changes in the institutional life of poor communities. Such comprehensive planning, he thought, would transcend the piecemeal approach then employed by city institutions. It was also the way to achieve the ultimate goal of opening opportunity. The "good society," he said, "is one in which access to opportunities and the organization of facilities and resources are so designed as to maximize each individual's chance to grow and achieve his greatest potential for constructive contribution to the cultural life of the social order." Ohlin admired the old ethnic neighborhood, where a vital community life had helped ambitious individuals to break through the structural barriers and move ahead in life. His approach reflected also the hostility of many American reformers, then and in the past, to large bureaucratic institutions. This anti-institutional strain influenced not only community action programs but many other areas of American life and thought in the 1960s.[37]

Some other planners operated from an ecological perspective on urban life. One sociologist heavily involved with Mobilization for Youth and discussions about community action in 1963 was Leonard Cottrell. In 1929 he had written parts of *Delinquency Areas*, a product of the so-called Chicago school of sociology that stressed the role of city neighborhoods. In the 1930s he had been involved in Chicago area projects, which had been inspired in part by the settlement house movement and in turn were direct forerunners of community action. Cottrell, in fact, worked for the Henry Street settlement house in New York, which helped operate MFY. Many of those who pushed for community action in the 1960s shared in some degree Cottrell's belief in reestablishing community life in the otherwise large, impersonal, and bureaucratic world of the modern city.[38]

Advocates of community action had many differences, however, including the question of means. Some officials had as models such existing operations as the Peace Corps or certain kinds of foreign aid which, they believed, spread out after starting at a community level. This sometimes elitist view imagined the community as the place where experts might plan a reinvigoration of the larger society. Ohlin tended to agree. Although he wished to involve the poor in community organization and was ready to confront City Hall if necessary, he also regarded many modern slums, unlike the older ethnic communities, as socially disorganized and leaderless. Experts therefore had to start the process of community action. Even Mobilization for Youth, which was then arousing the poor in direct action tactics, relied heavily on leadership and funding from middle-class professionals and planners.

Other planners were more distrustful of the role of experts; Cottrell maintained a Jeffersonian faith in individual initiative and self-reliance. Like others with a background in Chicago, he was familiar with (though not a disciple of) the work of Saul Alinsky, the veteran radical and community organizer. Alinsky had nothing but contempt for professionals and experts who presumed to tell the poor what to do. The role of organizers, he thought, was ideally both brief and simple. If invited, they should meet with community people, offer a few helpful hints about tactics and methods of protest, and retire to the sidelines.[39]

People who agreed with Alinsky's stress on self-direction by the poor usually asserted that poverty was a psychological as well as an economic condition. Poor people without independence were damaged. "Dependency," a psychologist engaged in community action explained, "erodes self-realization with the loss of self-responsibility." It followed that "rather than provide opportunities for the 'lower class,' the poor must as a group be helped to secure opportunities for themselves." Robert Kennedy stated this premise explicitly in testimony in 1964 before Congress. "Part of the sense of helplessness and futility," he said, "comes from the feeling of powerlessness to affect these [big city] organizations. The community action programs must basically change these organizations by providing real responsibility for the poor. This . . . calls for maximum feasible participation of residents." Kennedy's zeal to overcome "powerlessness" epitomized this psychologically based view of community action. "Maximum feasible participation" of the poor ultimately became a byword, though a most imprecise one, for the OEO program as a whole.[40]

Still another view of community action came from Ohlin's colleague at Columbia, Richard Cloward, who agreed with the "powerlessness" theory advanced by Alinsky and others, but split with Alinsky over the role of experts. A professional himself, Cloward was ready to assume sustained leadership of community groups and did so for Mobilization for Youth after 1960. At the same time, Cloward departed somewhat from Ohlin's perspective on tactics. Where Ohlin conceded the utility under certain circumstances of confronting City Hall, Cloward thought direct action and conflict necessary for progress. Conflict gave poor people a cause with which they might overcome their feelings of powerlessness. Using this conflict model of community action, Mobilization for Youth employed a variety of direct action tactics, including rent strikes and school boycotts. The predictable outcome was abrasive and sustained controversy.[41]

During the drafting process that began seriously in December 1963, few insiders tried seriously to resolve these differing theoretical perspectives. Few, in fact, expected community action to be at the core of a war on poverty. By then, John Kennedy's death had diminished Robert Kennedy and Hackett's access to power. The economists in the CEA and the Bureau of the Budget continued to argue for prevention and rehabilitation. The Budget Bureau people, wary of expensive experiments, recommended confining community action—or "development corporations" as they called them—to a few experimental situations. They imagined that community organization would involve demonstration programs, not action agencies.[42]

But policy formation rarely follows predictably from a single intellectual perspective, and the poverty program was no exception. The man whom Johnson placed in charge of the drafting, Sargent Shriver, above all wanted to get on with the task. Impatient with theory, he saw his job as securing agreement on a plan, chasing it through Congress, and implementing it. The first of these tasks he accomplished in less than two months, an incredibly rapid process for such a heralded piece of legislation. Johnson, restless, eager to prove himself, had gotten his start in politics as a protégé of Franklin Roosevelt. He thought of the New Deal as a kind of gigantic antipoverty program. Seeing himself as a populist, he wanted to carry on where FDR had left off and wipe out poverty from the land. Johnson's and Shriver's impatience helped to impel a vast and unanticipated expansion of community organizing, from research and demonstration to community action.

But the president shied from a program that would cost too much money or force a rise in taxes, the more so because he had just put through the tax cut. These political realities dictated a conservative approach to spending. At one stage in the drafting process, Labor Secretary Wirtz and others lobbied for a $1.25 billion program for public employment, perhaps to be financed by a cigarette tax. Though this proposal resembled the WPA, which Johnson had helped to administer in Texas, the president recoiled from the idea of a tax increase. When Shriver presented the plan at a Cabinet meeting, Johnson was stony. One participant recalled, "I have never seen a colder reception from the president. He just—absolute blank stare—implied without even opening his mouth that Shriver should move on to the next proposal." Thus ended the possibility that the war on poverty would do much to produce jobs (or enhance income) in the present.[43]

The outcome of this haste and disagreement was predictable: political compromise. One of the participants, Daniel Moynihan, remembered that "the resulting program sent to Congress March 16, 1964, thus represented not a choice among policies so much as a collection of them." To a bill that had toyed with one major new idea, community action, was added new sections, including one that set up the Jobs Corps. Another authorized the Neighborhood Youth Corps to provide local training and make-work jobs in public service. A third provided money for work study to assist needy college students. The drafters tacked on Volunteers in Service to America (VISTA), a domestic peace corps. To pacify rural interests, the Shriver task force included a title that called for loans to farmers and rural businessmen, and the drafters worked with the Small Business Administration to approve a loan program for low-income businessmen.[44]

Though the bill offered something for everybody, it did not offer much. Total funding was to be $962.5 million for the first year, $462.5 million of which was to come from elsewhere in the budget. Liberals complained that this was a piddling sum, but few heeded them. The framers, although anticipating the need for more money, hoped that their bill, along with existing welfare programs, could prevent poverty, that their proposals would help people to help themselves. It was entirely appropriate that they labeled their creation the Economic Opportunity Act, to be administered by an Office of Economic Opportunity.

9
OEO: A HAND UP, NOT A HANDOUT

ONCE SHRIVER'S TASK FORCE had completed its work, and Johnson had endorsed its product as the "center-piece" of his legislative program, it was highly likely that Congress would approve it. That they did, on partisan votes in the summer of 1964. Shriver, named to head the OEO, charged ahead with characteristic enthusiasm. An inspirational leader, he quickly attracted what one observer called "just an awful lot of good, bright, liberal, solid people." Shriver's qualities of energy and salesmanship adapted well to a new program that aimed to bypass existing governmental bureaucracies.[1]

But almost from the start, the OEO encountered administrative difficulties, most stemming from confusion over goals. When the bill passed in August, the economist Robert Theobald grumbled that it exposed a "lack of research. We don't know enough. We are flying blind." Shriver himself conceded later, "It's like we went down to Cape Kennedy and launched a half dozen rockets at once." Americans, he agreed, "are just plain confused about what the poverty program is all about. It's like giving an American sports page to an Englishman."[2]

Confusion resulted from the very structure of the package. Some framers had expected OEO to coordinate programs that would actually be administered by Cabinet departments, and this did happen to an extent: Labor ran the Neighborhood Youth Corps, HEW some provisions relating to higher education and training. But OEO operated the Job Corps, VISTA, and the community action programs. Assumption of these tasks enabled OEO to evade the incessant feuding that plagued HEW and Labor. But it saddled a new agency with formidable operating functions. No government agency can easily

142

wear two hats, and that was doubly true of OEO, which lacked experienced staff to administer action programs.[3]

OEO's dual role intensified the ever-present bureaucratic struggles between departments in Washington. From the start Labor Secretary Willard Wirtz proved hostile to the new agency. Wilbur Cohen went so far as to call Wirtz "constantly a pain in the neck." Although it ran the Neighborhood Youth Corps, the Labor Department supplied OEO with virtually no data on its programs. Bertrand Harding, who took over as deputy administrator of OEO in 1966, recalled that the old-line departments viewed the free-wheeling Shriver as antiestablishment. Many of OEO's difficulties, he said, were with the "other established agencies. They hated our guts, most of them."[4]

Some thought Shriver's presence exacerbated the problems. His strengths as an administrator lay in what Moynihan later called his "infectious energy" and in his tireless efforts to publicize the program and cultivate congressional contacts that prevented radical cuts in the OEO budget. But Johnson loyalists distrusted him, for he was a Kennedy brother-in-law. Some associates found him inattentive to orderly management and unwilling to share authority. "He runs his office like a big-business corporation," one aide complained. "Occasionally he may bestow lavish praise, more often he forgets who accomplished what." Another aide noted that Shriver "never readily agreed to delegate a damned thing." A third dismissed him as "a hundred per cent operator by temperament." These criticisms are one-sided and fail to mention the intellectual excitement that existed in OEO under Shriver's direction. Still, the poverty program suffered from considerable infighting and confusion.[5]

But administrative problems caused only some of OEO's early difficulties. Many contemporaries had other complaints. Some liberal social workers worried about what one aptly called the "severe dangers of over-sell." None of the OEO programs, he warned, "including the so-called new efforts, are sufficiently broad and comprehensive to make a major dent in the problem of economic poverty." Within six months of passage of the program, the National Association of Social Workers issued a position paper entitled "Poverty," a classic statement of activist social work philosophy that emphasized the limits of enhancing opportunity. Antipoverty programs, it said, "should be such as to assure income as a matter of right, in amounts sufficient to maintain all persons throughout the nation at a uniformly adequate level of living."[6]

Social workers objected especially to the bulldozing intervention of OEO bureaucrats. In March 1965, when the NASW sent a questionnaire to hundreds of social work organizations, some replies expressed hostility to the poverty program. "Neither the poor, nor anyone else except the 'inner circle' around the mayor and his appointees have been involved," one agency responded. Another shot back, "It is a politicians' program and social workers had to be asked to be involved." Other social workers independently complained about being excluded and insulted. The head of the Washington office of NASW grumbled about OEO's "pretty stiff hands-off attitude to what they call a 'handout' welfare program." He said, "We would like to demonstrate that they ought to start where they are and not go off in the wild blue yonder setting up some kind of high-powered community leadership group with business and labor and so forth that is going to solve the problem of poverty in a particular community."[7]

Because OEO was designed in part to cut through the allegedly tired welfare bureaucracy, it was not surprising that Shriver never developed amicable relations with the social workers, who understandably protected their turf. And hostility from radicals like Saul Alinsky, who demanded that the poor themselves confront the power structure, was equally predictable. Alinsky branded OEO as a paternalistic ally of a welfare establishment that had always coopted the poor. In 1965 he blasted OEO as "the worst political blunder and boomerang of the present administration," as a "huge political pork barrel," and as "history's greatest relief program for the benefit of the welfare industry." Denouncing social workers as "pimps of the poor," he concluded, "The poverty program as it stands today is a macabre masquerade and the mask is growing to fit the face, and the face is one of political pornography."[8]

Conservatives, too, predictably denounced OEO. Some Republicans grumbled, not without cause, that OEO jumbled together many old programs. In a searing minority report on the bill, senators Barry Goldwater of Arizona and John Tower of Texas called the bill a "Madison Avenue deal" and a "poverty grab bag." Community action programs, they charged (inaccurately), were "a sort of retread WPA." The Job Corps, like the old CCC, sought to give young men "sun tans and an appreciation for outdoor living." They objected especially to Shriver's "poverty czar powers," which would "dangerously centralize Federal controls."

Behind conservative arguments such as these lay two durable notions about poverty and welfare. First, poor people deserved their fate. "The fact is," Goldwater said, "that most people who have no skill have had no education for the same reason—low intelligence or low ambition." In the United States, people are rewarded by "merit and not by fiat." Goldwater asserted that the "mere fact of having little money does not entitle everybody, regardless of circumstances, to be permanently maintained by the taxpayers at a comfortable standard of living." The second notion followed from the first: welfare was wasteful. Conservatives pointed out that the nation had never been so affluent and that the economy would flourish if the government minded its own business. "The only solution to poverty," wrote the conservative columnist Henry Hazlitt, "is free enterprise and continued economic growth—those things which made America great."[9]

Once OEO started spending money, in October 1964, conservative critics pounced on it. Indeed, OEO confronted the same kind of sniping that had damaged the WPA in the 1930s. Why was OEO money going to support the antiwhite plays of LeRoi Jones and the Black Arts Theater of Harlem? Or to Job Corps centers like the one at Camp Breckinridge, Kentucky, where enrollees were rioting? Or to the Child Development Group in Mississippi, which senators James Eastland and John Stennis charged was being used to organize black voters? Or to the community action program in Syracuse, which was employing Alinsky-like tactics to confront local officials? Some of these complaints zeroed in on sloppy administration—the accounting procedures in Mississippi were open to criticism. Most reflected hostility from right-wing politicians who objected to leftists or blacks getting OEO money.[10]

An article in *U.S. News and World Report* in 1965 typified the scattershot approach of conservative opposition. Entitled "Poverty War out of Hand?" it featured two anti-OEO cartoons and a photograph of young blacks loafing about a Jobs Corps center. It hit OEO for "administrative chaos, bureaucratic bungling, waste, extravagance, costly duplication of existing services, internal squabbling." It exposed the excesses of the Syracuse community action program, the allegedly excessive salaries in the Head Start program, and the Job Corps generally. It concluded with quotes from a black educator who described OEO as a "slaphappy, sloppy, wasteful procedure," and from a Republican representative who said, "This program could become not just a national disgrace, but a national catastrophe."[11]

What hurt OEO most were grievances from state and local politicians who resented OEO's ideas of community action. The villains, as the politicos saw it, were Jack Conway, Shriver's deputy, and Conway's aide, Richard Boone. Conway had served on the task force since March 1964, when he had taken leave from the AFL-CIO. Boone, an activist who had worked with Hackett and the PCJD, had helped draft the sections of the antipoverty program that called for "maximum feasible participation" of the poor. During the drafting, most of the task force members had paid no attention to the phrase. Those who had, like Moynihan, had assumed it meant that southern communities should not exclude blacks. Or they saw it as a way of bypassing the bickering federal agencies and the social work establishment—what one planner called the "board ladies and bureaucrats." Few had anticipated that maximum feasible participation might lead to programs that placed the poor in power and challenged local authorities.[12]

Few people in early 1964 quite appreciated the accelerating militancy of the civil rights movement and especially the anger of blacks in the urban ghettos. In the summer of 1964 the first of many riots by blacks broke out in Harlem. There and elsewhere, these decisively refuted the old stereotype of the apathetic poor. By late 1964, when OEO began dispensing money to a thousand communities across the country, activists were determined to take charge of the funds. Conway often agreed that established urban officials were excluding the activists from community action. Early in 1965, OEO withheld funds from New York, Los Angeles, Philadelphia, San Francisco, and Chicago on the grounds that their community action plans did not give the poor maximum feasible participation. Activism at the top had coincided with unrest at the grass roots to confound the expectations of the framers.[13]

The protests from urban politicians ranged from reasoned discourses to screams of rage. Some officials merely pressed Shriver to define maximum feasible participation. Were the poor to dominate the community action boards? Must they be poor themselves or merely representatives of the poor? Did they have to be elected by the poor, or could they be appointed by city officials? Others openly opposed the notion of control by the poor. Mayor Robert Wagner of New York told a House subcommittee, "I feel very strongly that the sovereign part of each locality . . . should have the power of approval over the making of the planning group." The mayors of San Francisco and Los Angeles accused OEO of "fostering class struggle" and demanded that only elected officials be entrusted with antipoverty funds. Explaining this view, one city official grumbled, "You can't go to a street corner with a pad and pencil and tell the poor to write you a poverty program. They won't know how." Mayor Richard Daley of Chicago added that involving the poor as leaders "would be like telling the fellow who cleans up to be the city editor of a newspaper." Complaints such as these led the U.S. Conference of Mayors to pass a resolution in June 1965 urging OEO to recognize City Hall or existing relief agencies as the proper channels for antipoverty money.[14]

Some state politicians, such as New York Governor Nelson Rockefeller, protested that antipoverty money was going only to Democrats. Senator Robert Byrd of West Virginia, an influential Democrat, countered that the OEO officials were "offering employment to persons who will change their registration from Democrat to Republican."

Governor John Connally of Texas protested in 1965 to his friend Lyndon Johnson against a proposed amendment that would deprive governors of the right to veto antipoverty projects. The president assured his friend that the veto would remain, but governors remained unhappy. A top aide to Johnson, after attending the governors' conference in July 1965, reported, "I didn't talk with a single governor who approves of the way it is being handled in Washington and at the state level. Our closest friends are very much upset by the way it is being administered."[15]

Johnson, alarmed, had already dispatched Vice President Hubert Humphrey to reassure the politicians. OEO, meanwhile, attempted to clarify what it meant by maximum feasible participation. The poor, it explained in February 1965, were to participate "either on the governing body or on a policy advisory committee" or have "at least one representative selected from each of the neighborhoods" involved. At least one-third of the representatives on local boards should be poor people elected by the poor. Although the issue remained controversial, these guidelines clarified some of the confusion for a time.[16]

But giving the poor only one-third of the pie did not please activists. They feared that state and local politicians were winning the battle against Conway and Boone. Conway resigned in September 1965 and returned to the AFL-CIO. Congress, to ensure social peace in the cities, passed a series of amendments, removing the words maximum feasible participation and establishing procedures for poverty boards. Representation was to be one-third poor people, one-third local elected officials, and one-third local community groups. State or local governments were to design or approve of local poverty agencies, and increasingly large percentages of antipoverty money were earmarked for "safe" programs, such as Head Start, that were popular on Capitol Hill. A total of $846 million of the $1.17 billion OEO appropriation for fiscal 1967 was so earmarked. These actions effectively curbed community control. One scholar observed later, "Local initiative, which is presumed to rank just below motherhood on the political scale of values, was further circumscribed."[17]

By then Johnson, who had stood by OEO in some of these fights, was losing heart. When he instructed Walter Heller to go "full tilt" in late 1963, he had seen himself as another FDR and the program as a popular monument to his humanitarian instincts. Instead, it had embroiled him in conflict with his own political allies. He wondered how Shriver had allowed himself to be surrounded by so many "kooks and sociologists." Increasingly absorbed in the Vietnam war, disillusioned by his venture into economic uplift, Johnson gave the OEO little presidential support after 1965.[18]

The disaffection of politicians and the pressing fiscal demands of the war guaranteed that OEO would henceforth get low priority in Washington. Congress passed the Model Cities program in 1966, which competed openly with OEO by funneling funds for urban needs through existing city political organizations. Congress ultimately deprived OEO of its operating functions: Head Start went to HEW, the Job Corps to Labor, manpower training ultimately to local governments under the Comprehensive Employment and Training Act (CETA) of 1973. Community action programs survived until going to a new Community Services Administration in the 1970s. In 1974 OEO was dead, and the poverty war, such as it was, moved on from beachheads scattered through the federal bureaucracy.[19]

Evaluating the war on poverty confronts manifold difficulties. First is the virtual impossibility of singling out the effect of OEO during a time of phenomenal economic progress and equally phenomenal growth in other public services. Between 1965 and 1970, OEO's peak years, the number of Americans defined as poor fell from 33 to 25 million. During these same years total federal spending for social welfare—including education, Social Security, health, and welfare—more than doubled. The war on poverty presumably contributed something to this broad fight against poverty, but how much was impossible to tell. As one scholar said in 1970, "The only strong statements that can be made are that poverty has dropped sharply since 1964, that the War on Poverty was associated with that drop, and that the extent of causation cannot at present be known."[20]

Experts have also had trouble evaluating particular OEO programs. Despite its administrative problems, its record in delivering services under the auspices of community action was generally well regarded. The Head Start and Follow Through education programs reached more than two million young children during the late 1960s. The Neighborhood Youth Corps gave low-paying, make-work jobs to perhaps two million young people aged sixteen to twenty-one. Legal services provided under community action programs were estimated to serve almost 500,000 poor people in 1969, a peak year.

Whether these services enhanced the opportunity of the poor, however, was difficult to say; the answer depended heavily on the observer's expectations, political orientation, and standards of cost effectiveness. Early reports, for instance, suggested (probably wrongly) that Head Start did not improve the long-range educational performance of poor children who participated in it. Despite that unflattering reputation, Head Start continued to command support in Congress, which regarded it as an investment in long-range prevention of social deviancy and illiteracy. The Job Corps, which did help some young people find permanent employment, and which may therefore have been more cost effective, had a much cooler reception on the Hill.[21]

It was particularly hard to evaluate the community action programs. With a thousand in operation at the peak of OEO, there were wide variations that defied easy generalizations. Some, as in Syracuse, excited conflict and controversy that led to counterattack from existing authorities. Others, as in Newark, paved the way for the rise of black political leaders and a shift in local leadership. The majority worked more or less harmoniously with existing institutions and concentrated on delivering educational, legal, and family planning services. In these places community action personnel augmented existing social service agencies and did not make dramatic changes in what had long been done.[22]

These more-or-less traditional programs rarely paid more than lip service to the ideal of maximum feasible participation, but not because the organizers were cynical or engaged in a charade to pacify the poor. Rather, it was because MFP was as difficult to practice as it was to define. Some of the truly poor residents of a given area were, in Moynihan's words, "inarticulate, irresponsible, and relatively unsuccessful," and others were transients who did not identify with the "community." In areas divided by racial or ethnic tensions it was hard to mobilize the whole community as a group. For all these reasons, it was frequently difficult to involve the poorest members of a given neighborhood. The organizers of community action tended instead to be the more upwardly mobile near-poor, some of whom might have risen out of poverty without federal intervention; many wanted to escape the neighborhood, not to mobilize it. Some organizers were middle-class professionals who imposed structure from above. Although this sort of elitism sometimes worked fairly well to bring communities together and identify their problems, direction from above hardly approximated maximum feasible participation of the poor.[23]

The results achieved by the relatively few community action agencies that were run by militants were dubious. The agency in Syracuse succeeded in rousing the poor but outraged public officials, who mobilized their formidable economic and political resources, fought back, and reestablished control. Militants did not always stop to ask: conflict for what? When it involved the poor, conflict perhaps lessened feelings of powerlessness, but did it promote community cohesion? And what was the point of arousing the poor, perhaps stimulating riotous behavior, if you could not gratify them? Of what use was power if it did not bring tangible economic rewards? A leftist critic of Alinskyism identified this dilemma as early as 1964. Organizers who attempted to challenge the power structure, he said, were like "unions who fight the boss at the shop level but fail to transform the fight into its political expression."[24]

Some experts thought that the most promising community action programs were those in which determined reformers employed confrontational but nonviolent tactics. They were able to force authorities to grant poor people fairly broad participation in antipoverty boards. Evaluators believed that nonextreme forms of confrontation paid off in that poor people developed greater self-respect, and their feelings of powerlessness dissipated. One expert concluded later that community action programs of this type "changed the institutional structure in city slums and ghettos drastically and favorably." But evidence for such a judgment was short-run and anecdotal. What worked in one community did not work in another. And feelings like "self-respect" and "power" are not subject to very solid measurement. It remains unclear whether this sort of community action did more than more traditional efforts to change the opportunity, incomes, or psychological well-being of the poor.[25]

It is possible to reach a few negative conclusions about community action. One refutes the notion that activity at the community level could ever accomplish very much. As one scholar commented, "The liveliest local participation . . . is futile without the resources and co-ordination appropriate to the problem." Another critic, Elizabeth Wickenden, emphasized that the "problems of poverty are only in limited instances localized in character. They are for the most part widely distributed, related to economic and social factors that operate nationwide, and would require more than local action for solution." In the absence of a very heavy financial commitment from federal funds, gaining control of a community was often a hollow victory. Community solutions to poverty, indeed, frequently represented romantic dreams reminiscent of the settlement house workers' faith in "neighborhood" at the turn of the century. It was not surprising, therefore, that conservatives during the Nixon years continued to support, though at modest levels of funding, the by then nonthreatening community action programs, which constituted a safe and inexpensive alternative to massive commitments of federal funds.[26]

Another conceptual limitation of OEO was its almost exclusively urban cast. Like Riis and Hunter, like most people who rediscovered poverty in the 1960s, the OEO planners were virtually mesmerized by a vision of poverty in the cities and paid little attention to area redevelopment. Although the Appalachian program was part of the overall fight against destitution, it did not figure largely in the thinking of the task force that designed OEO. Aside from OEO's ill-financed rural loan program, the war on poverty did virtually nothing to alleviate destitution in the countryside, where almost 40 percent of the poor still lived in 1965, or to stem the South-to-North migrations that magnified the problems of the northern cities. Whether any program could have slowed these migrations is almost beside the point: no one much tried to develop one. James Sundquist concluded accurately that "when it comes to the solution of the poverty problem, a good many of the urban poverty thinkers have written off the rural areas and have concluded that the only way to deal with rural poverty is to let the people move and then handle them in the cities."[27]

The greatest conceptual fuzziness concerned OEO's diagnosis of poverty. The program, like the contemporary rediscovery of the poor, depended at first on the structuralist insight that economic growth, however beneficial, could not pull all people out of poverty. Government transfer payments were therefore essential. But OEO then stressed the need to enhance opportunity. The contradiction is clear. If the poor included many who did not gain from economic growth— mostly people outside the labor market—then they probably needed handouts of some sort. The reluctance of planners to face that fact, and the refusal of Congress seriously to consider it, exposed again the resistance in America to costly programs that might sustain a permanent class of dependents on welfare.[28]

Other negative conclusions concern the operation of OEO. Conceptual flaws aside, it never got much money to do what it proposed to do. Funding was low from the start, when Leon Keyserling had snorted, "It will hardly scratch the surface." After 1965 money became ever harder to get, and Shriver spent most of his time tramping the halls of congressional office buildings to preserve what funds he could. From 1965 until 1970 (after which time it no longer controlled most of the programs), OEO scrambled for an average of about $1.7 billion per year. The amounts never amounted to more than around 1.5 percent of the federal budget, or one-third of one percent of the gross national product. During these years the number of people officially regarded as poor never fell below 25 million. If all the OEO money had gone directly to the poor as income—and most of it did not—each poor person in America would have received around $50 to $70 per year.[29]

Of course, OEO funds never went equally to every poor person. Most of the money went to community action areas or to Job Corps centers. Of the 600 poorest counties in the United States (one-fifth of all counties), 215 were not covered at all by a community action agency. And the war on poverty was never intended to reach those people who were not likely targets for greater opportunity: the aged, dependent children in female-headed families, the welfare poor. One expert, formerly an assistant director of OEO, concluded in a study for the Brookings Institution in 1970, "More than five years after the passage of the Economic Opportunity Act the war on poverty has barely scratched the surface. Most poor people have had no contact with it, except perhaps to hear the promises of a better life to come."[30]

These serious limitations stood in cruel contrast to what had been promised. Johnson had foreseen a war against poverty; Shriver had assured everyone that he would abolish destitution in ten years. But Congress did not give him the tools. Perhaps no government program in modern American history promised so much more than it delivered. The contrast chastened theorists, who began to reconsider their utopian notions about the potential for social science and to lead a surge of neoconservative thinking in influential journals like *The Public Interest*. The sociologist Nathan Glazer concluded as early as 1966, "There are limits to the desirable reach of social engineering." Moynihan added that social scientists "have no business prescribing. They don't know enough even to seriously consider attempting that." Wilbur Cohen, who remained eager for more reform, concluded in 1968 that OEO "tried to do too much at one time." More than any other program of Johnson's so-called Great Society, the war on poverty accentuated doubts about the capacity of social science to plan, and government to deliver, ambitious programs for social betterment.[31]

The contrast between promise and performance infuriated some of the poor. This was perhaps the cruelest cut. The rhetoric of OEO in a mass media age did reach some poor people, especially the activist leaders. Some, notably blacks, were militant anyway for racial justice. When they got little in the way of tangible, secure benefits, they were disappointed, frustrated, outraged. One planner noted, "There was the assumption of regularly increased funding. Promises were made that way . . . the result was a trail of broken promises. No wonder everybody got mad and rioted." While such riots had deeper causes, notably racial discrimination, the most angry urban blacks tended to be those who raged at the gulf that separated reality from expanded expectations, which the poverty programs had helped to whet. When rioting hit Detroit, Mayor Jerome Cavanaugh blamed OEO and other federal programs. "What we've been doing, at the level we've been doing it, is almost worse than nothing at all . . . We've raised expectations, but we haven't been able to deliver all we should have."[32]

In spite of these negative consequences of the war on poverty, in the longer run it is possible to conclude that some benefits, mostly unanticipated, came of it. One was the lessons experts learned from its failings. If some grew despondent about the potential of government and inclined toward a new policy of benign neglect, others reconsidered and recognized, first, that it was wrong to emphasize the apathy or even the powerlessness of the poor. Events of the late 1960s proved that needy people, far from being apathetic denizens of a culture of poverty, were capable of rage. Second, experts recognized the limited potential for rehabilitating the poor by opening up opportunity. The key was augmenting people's income by finding work for the employable, and giving welfare to the dependent poor. Beginning in 1965, these insights prompted a rapidly growing sentiment among experts for some form of guaranteed income maintenance for all Americans.[33]

The war on poverty also had the unanticipated consequence of helping to arouse the poor. To some extent, that was happening anyway, thanks to the civil rights movement and to the general rise in expectations in the affluent 1960s. But the war on poverty, by promising government help, gave these expectations a shove in the same direction. Sundquist observed in 1969, "Out of the community action milieu are rising political candidates, public office holders, and entrepreneurs as well as agitators and prophets." The "most common phrase" of local authorities, he said, was, "This town will never be the same again."[34]

The legal services programs, which employed 1,800 lawyers in 850 law offices by 1969, probably did more than any other OEO service to encourage this change. The lawyers worked closely with community spokesmen to challenge discriminatory and stigmatizing aspects of welfare administration. In the long run, they contributed to the faith, widespread by the mid-1970s, in legal attacks on old practices. They also sharpened the political awareness of poor people. As early as 1966, they helped George Wiley, an activist, form the National Welfare Rights Organization, which stridently publicized the cause of the welfare poor. They aided in suits, ultimately supported by the Supreme Court, to overturn residency requirements and the absent father rule of AFDC. With such institutionalized support, previously poor Americans at last knew where to turn for help. If the militancy of these poor people was more unpredictable and short-lived than radical organizers wished, it was nonetheless more articulate and rights-conscious than at any time in the past. It was no longer easy to think that the poor were content to suffer.

The war on poverty, finally, dramatized the contemporary rediscovery of poverty, which might not have happened so rapidly without the involvement of Heller, of Kennedy, of Johnson. The result was to lift poverty from benign neglect to a place on the public agenda. That prominence prepared Congress to accept other programs helping the poor, notably federal aid to education and health insurance for the indigent, or Medicaid, in 1965. Those landmarks safely passed, the way lay open for Cohen and others to urge further liberalization of Social Security—on the somewhat novel basis that it would aid the poor. More directly, the focus on poverty was one of many elements that made public officials a little more responsive to the newly articulated demands of the poor. In this entirely unanticipated way, the rediscovery of poverty, and the OEO that institutionalized that discovery, contributed to one of the most astonishing developments of the 1960s: the explosion in welfare.[35]

IV
THE UNSUNG
REVOLUTION
1965-1973

10
THE REVOLUTION
IN SOCIAL WELFARE

Two DRAMATIC DEVELOPMENTS changed the face of American poverty and welfare between the mid-1960s and the early 1970s: a fantastic drop in the number of poor and a stunning enlargement of social welfare programs, especially Social Security. These developments did not occur because of changed popular attitudes toward poverty and welfare. Insofar as these attitudes were measurable, they revealed that most middle-class Americans continued to stereotype the poor disparagingly and to recoil at the thought of expanding welfare. Their social philosophy, in Tawney's term, had not changed. The developments also owed little to careful planning by reformers. On the contrary, these were years of social turbulence, when many experts took stock of the situation. Although some activists continued to plan new and better wars on poverty, others doubted the capacity of government to accomplish much on the domestic front. Far from being planned, these turning points were neither popular nor anticipated.

Underlying these transformations were broad social changes, notably unprecedented economic growth. Demographic changes, especially the aging of the population, together with the inexorable expansion of existing programs worked along with that growth. And well-organized pressure groups provided much of the political thrust for them. The result was a virtual revolution.

Some studies of poverty in the late 1960s and early 1970s scarcely suggested changes of such magnitude. Instead they revealed poverty that continued to select out specially deprived groups for lives of deprivation.[1] As ever, people living in the South were more likely to be poor, although by the mid-1970s economic growth in the Sun Belt, combined with massive migrations of poor southerners to the North, dramatically reduced the numbers of poor people below the Mason-Dixon line. Indeed, most of the officially defined reduction in poverty between 1959 and 1975—11 million of 13 million—was in the South. But the average southerner was still almost twice as likely to be poor as were people living in other sections. The South in the early 1970s still contained around 12 million poor people, or nearly half the official poverty population of 25 million. Of these, around 70 percent were white. All suffered from an "old" poverty rooted in low wages and underemployment.[2]

This southern poverty was a measure of the continuing problems of rural areas. Not that the rural poor were a majority—around 65 percent of the nation's poor lived in cities in 1970, and the percentage was increasing slowly. But the incidence of poverty among rural Americans was 19 percent in 1966, as opposed to 14 percent for those in the cities. And many of the urban poor had fled the even deeper poverty of the farm.[3]

Nonwhites, as always, were especially hard hit by poverty. Though nearly 70 percent of the nation's poor were white in the late 1960s, the nation as a whole was more than 85 percent white. The incidence of poverty among nonwhites remained staggeringly high—41 percent in 1966, as opposed to 12 percent for whites—and was falling more slowly than the white incidence. In 1959 it had been three times that of whites; by the mid-1970s, it was three and a half times as high.[4] More and more of this nonwhite poverty reflected the newer urban poverty of the North. Despite economic progress, there were more poor blacks in the North and West in the early 1970s than there had been in 1959. The scarcity of decent jobs in the city especially afflicted urban blacks aged sixteen to nineteen, whose unemployment rate approximated 30 percent—two to three times that of young urban whites—by the early 1970s.[5]

Low-paying employment remained a key source of poverty. In 1967, 32 percent of the poor, 8.2 million people, lived in households whose head worked full time. Another 25 percent, or 6.5 million, lived in families whose head worked part time. These statistics merely echoed the litany sung by structuralists from Hunter on: badly paid work—on the farm, in the factory, and increasingly in the service sectors of a postindustrial economy—continued to swell the poverty population.[6]

The aged, historically susceptible to poverty, dramatically improved their status by 1970. About 25 percent of old people were then poor, as opposed to 40 percent in 1959. Thanks to huge increases in Social Security benefits, only 16 percent were poor by 1974. Still, about one in nine Americans under age sixty-five was then officially poor; for the aged the number was closer to one in six. And the aging of the population meant that increasing numbers of old people might slip into poverty.

People living in female-headed families, on the other hand, stayed poor. Economic progress between 1963 and 1969 pulled 12 million people in male-headed families out of poverty but stranded 11 million in female-headed families, the same number as in 1963. This group made up more than 40 percent of the poverty population. Most of these people were children; in the early 1970s around 40 percent of poor Americans were under sixteen. By 1974, 6 percent of white male-headed and 17 percent of nonwhite male-headed families were poor. By contrast, 27 percent of female-headed white families and 55 percent of female-headed nonwhite families were in poverty.[7]

For all these people, poverty officially meant living below the income line set by the Social Security Administration. Reflecting the rising cost of living, this amount rose from $3,000 for an urban family of four in the early 1960s to around $4,200 in 1972 and to $5,500 in 1976. Farm families were supposed to get along on 85 percent of that, or $3,570 in 1972. Certain advantages of these poverty lines sustained their use by public officials. The income standards were objective, not culturally vague definitions subject to subjective stereotyping. But the official line was low for the 1960s, an affluent age of rising expectations. Originally it allotted people only seventy cents per day for food prepared at home, and it allowed nothing for transportation costs to and from work, for taxes paid, for new furnishings or utensils, or for food eaten out. Well before 1970, many experts called for higher poverty lines, such as those used by the Bureau of Labor Statistics, whose "low" budget for a family of four was $6,960 in 1969, almost twice the official level. Such a line would have shown that 33 percent of the population lived in poverty—not the 12-14 percent estimated by the government.[8]

Other critics complained that the official poverty line measured only absolute poverty and thus presented a falsely bright picture of progress in the late 1960s and early 1970s. The government, they said, ought to calculate relative poverty, the relationship of low to median family incomes. Measured by that standard, the median income in that affluent age rose faster than the poverty line, based on the more slowly increasing cost of living. The poverty line was one-half of median family income in 1959, one-third of it in 1974. This development, hardly progressive at any time, was galling in the age of mass communications and expanded expectations. The poor could not help but know how much they were missing. As Dwight Macdonald expressed it, "Not to be able to afford a movie or a glass of beer is a kind of starvation—if everybody else can."[9]

Macdonald and others stressed that the distribution of income had not changed much in the postwar years, when families in the lowest fifth of income earners got between 4.5 and 5.6 percent of the national income. Indeed, the overall income deficit—defined as the total dollars needed to bring all poor Americans up to the poverty line— seemed to increase slightly in the otherwise affluent late 1960s and early 1970s. Because the total number of poor people declined in those years, the people who remained below the line were not just poor, but on the average even poorer. Clearly, the country's economic growth was highly selective.[10]

The limitations of the official, absolute poverty line were perhaps of more than academic importance. In affecting impressions of the size and character of poverty, the line had the potential to influence policy. Use of the official low line tended to identify as poor those at the very bottom of the heap and to magnify the visibility of nonworking people, including the hard-core unemployed and female heads of household. Casual observers, confronting these "facts," could logically conclude that the government ought to respond by developing jobs, manpower training, or "opportunity." Use of a higher poverty line would have identified many more millions of working poor, and encouraged support for measures, such as wage supplements, guaranteeing better pay. A measurement highlighting relative poverty might have encouraged a few idealistic (and politically unrealistic) planners to stress the redistribution of income.

These grim features—the concentration of poverty among particularly disadvantaged groups, the stringency of budgets set at the official poverty line, the persistence of relative poverty in an age of galloping expectations—understandably worried some experts, although none of the trends was altogether new. Knowledgeable writers had long recognized that poverty afflicted certain groups; social workers for years had bemoaned the budgetary standards used in measuring need; Galbraith and a few others had drawn some attention to the problem of relative deprivation. In part for these reasons, few people paid very much attention to the Cassandras.

Instead, they clapped their hands with pride at what was in truth a phenomenal reduction of absolute poverty. According to the official, absolute definitions, the number of poor Americans decreased from 39 million (22 percent of the population) in 1959, to 32 million (17 percent) in 1965, to 25 million (13 percent) in 1968, to 23 million (11 percent) in 1973. The vast majority of those who climbed over the line were previously poor workers and their families, who profited from the astonishing overall growth of the economy during those years.

From this perspective, the fact that higher percentages of the poor were "hard-to-reach," such as members of female-headed families, was cause for gratification not despair. It meant that the economy was coming closer to the goal of wiping out all but the "residual" poverty concentrated among those outside the labor force. These people, it followed, could get welfare.[11]

Optimists also stressed that the official poverty line was set at a level that enabled people to live much better than poor people ever had before. It allowed for far better diets and shelter than had been the case in Hunter's time or in 1929, and it offered more than the measures used by liberals in the 1940s and 1950s. By 1977 the line for an urban family of four was almost $6,600, 23 percent higher in purchasing power, in constant 1977 dollars, than the $2,000 used by the Sparkman committee in the 1950s. This upgrading of the line of course reflected the rising expectations of an affluent society. "As time passed," one observer explained, "society agreed that the minimum should increasingly involve more than filling a belly and obtaining a roof."[12]

Studies that began to appear in the mid-1970s also showed that most people did not stay poor for long. The University of Michigan's investigation of "income dynamics" between 1967 and 1975 concluded that about a third of all those in the study fell below the official poverty line in at least one year out of the nine. That was around 70 million Americans, most of whom were near the margin most of the time. Around 50 percent of the poor in 1975, some 13 million, had been poor more than half the time in those nine years. But the study also showed that only 22 percent of the poverty population, 3 percent of American society, was poor all the time. That was less than 6 million people in 1973. If that number still seemed high to some observers —and it is indeed a stern test of poverty—it was nonetheless far smaller than pictured by some contemporaries who imagined millions wallowing forever in a culture of poverty.[13]

The optimists later showed that poverty statistics in some ways grossly overestimated the number who were officially designated as poor in the early 1970s. They pointed in particular to the vitally helpful role of in-kind benefits, including Medicaid, public housing, and food stamps, that proliferated after 1965 but that did not figure in the official measures of income. Writers noted also that poor people (like many Americans) systematically underreported their varied sources of income and property. If the in-kind benefits and unreported money were added to cash incomes, some experts concluded later, the official percentages of those in absolute poverty would have been as low as 6.5 percent by 1972.[14]

But it was not necessary to talk about in-kind benefits and under-reporting to sing "Hallelujah" by 1973. Save for the World War II years that ended the Depression, no comparable period in American history witnessed such progress in diminishing poverty as did the 1960s and early 1970s. The percentage that was poor—whether 6 or 12 percent—was so low as to be virtually unbelievable. Hunter, living at a time when perhaps 40 percent of Americans were poor by a lower standard, would have been amazed that capitalism, sustained by government spending, could do so much in seventy years. By any standard, the progress by 1973 was astonishing.

An overview of social welfare policy during these years reveals many of the flaws that had plagued the jerry-built system since its origins in the 1930s. Harrington, ignoring political realities, maintained that the "welfare state benefits those least who need help most" and that it offered "socialism for the rich and free enterprise for the poor." The head of New York City's welfare department said in 1967, "The welfare system is designed to save money instead of people and tragically ends up doing neither." Another expert concluded in 1970, "The current public assistance system of the United States, particularly AFDC, deserves to go down in history with the British poor laws of the early Industrial Revolution."[15]

The AFDC program, by far the largest welfare plan, seemed most open to criticism. Reformers complained that states and localities still managed to avoid federal regulations aimed at humanizing the application of aid. Until the late 1960s, administrators continued the old practices designed either to humiliate recipients or to keep them off the rolls altogether. Midnight raids to detect men in the home, new twists on supposedly outlawed "suitable home" rules, tough residency requirements—all stigmatized or excluded poor people. Until 1967, any earnings were substracted from welfare checks, thus eliminating all incentive to work. Patronizing social workers were especially resented. One AFDC mother said, "The worst thing is they just make you feel no good at all. They tell you they want to make you into them, and leave you without a cent of yourself to hang on to. I keep asking myself, why don't they fix the country up, so that people can *work*, instead of patching up with this and that."[16]

The continuing variation from state to state in the size of AFDC payments further enraged reformers. By 1970 these variations had actually increased, mainly because the richer states provided more. Payments for old-age assistance, generally higher per individual, ranged equally widely. So did general assistance, which was usually lower than other forms of relief. Despite federal prohibitions, payments within states even varied, with rural areas generally paying less per recipient than the cities.

The grossest flaw in the categorical assistance programs continued to be the low level of payments. All but six states set their standards for AFDC below the federal definitions of poverty, and all but sixteen states failed to appropriate the money necessary to meet their own low standards. In 1966 the average national payment per recipient of AFDC was $36 per month, so a family of four received $144 per month, or $1,728 per year. The official poverty line in that year for a nonfarm family of four was $3,355.[17]

Some people argued that "individualism" and the "work ethic" accounted for America's stinginess in welfare. Some blamed the decentralized political system, which gave local elites wide discretion. Others claimed that keeping welfare low was above all a way of subjugating blacks. Richard Cloward and Frances Fox Piven insisted that welfare had a functional role within the capitalist system, that except when scared by social unrest, elites deliberately kept welfare payments as low as possible to ensure abundant supplies of cheap labor.[18]

Such broad explanations were as difficult to document as they had been in earlier periods. Individualism and the work ethic were virtually unmeasurable, and similar values appeared to be just as widespread in other western nations, most of which had more extensive welfare programs. Decentralization certainly played into the hands of local elites and accounted for some of the meanness in application of aid. But decentralization was more an institutional manifestation of such meanness than a cause of it. The racial interpretation relied in part on findings that showed eligibility requirements to be stiffest, and average AFDC payments lowest, in states with large percentages of blacks in the population. But these states, mostly in the South, were also the poorest and least prepared to advocate generous public aid. It was therefore difficult to prove that racial attitudes toward blacks—which grew more liberal in the 1960s—independently accounted for the illiberal nature of public welfare.[19]

To a limited degree, the Cloward-Piven critique appears correct. Low welfare levels were clearly functional, particularly for employers of poorly paid farm labor. In agricultural areas, especially in the South, harsh application of welfare coexisted with low wages. But Cloward and Piven were more successful in showing the coexistence of welfare and low wages than in proving a causal connection. Many forces, including the work ethic, hostile attitudes toward blacks, and historically disparaging views of poor people helped account for the low levels of public aid in the South.

Cloward and Piven's argument tends also to slight perhaps the most reliable predictor of welfare standards: the state's ability to pay. In the 1960s, as throughout the recent American past, per capita income provided as good a guide as any to state-by-state differentials in standards and requirements. Northern states, wealthier per capita, were better able than southern states to take advantage of matching-grant provisions of the categorical assistance plans. Although never a simple one-to-one proposition, the relationship between state per capita income and welfare standards was too powerful to be dismissed.[20]

But public assistance is only one, narrow way of measuring the role of social welfare. In fact, means-tested programs targeted at the poor, such as AFDC, old-age assistance, general assistance, public housing, and food stamps, made up only 10 to 19 percent of social welfare expenditures between 1965 and 1975. Other programs—especially old age pensions, unemployment compensation, and Medicare—affected roughly four times as many nonpoor as poor, but their impact on the poor was enormous. These programs, in fact, proved that "throwing money at problems" works.

The growth in all social welfare programs was staggering. Expenditures rose between 1965 and 1976 at an annual rate of 7.2 percent in constant dollars, compared to 4.6 percent annually between 1950 and 1965. In 1960 such spending was 7.7 percent of the GNP; in 1965, 10.5 percent; in 1974, 16 percent. By far the largest sums went for non-means-tested programs like Social Security, unemployment compensation, and Medicare. But public aid also rose during these years, accounting for 1.3 percent of the GNP in 1950, 1.9 percent in 1968, 2.8 percent in 1974. Public assistance payments per recipient increased both in constant dollars and in comparison to average wage rates. These figures reveal that the war in Vietnam, however draining, did not prevent vast increases in domestic spending. On the contrary, social welfare expanded to dimensions that would have been unimaginable in 1960 and continued to do so during the early Nixon years. One careful overview concluded that the nation had a "system within sight of assuring at least a poverty threshold standard of living for all citizens."[21]

In-kind welfare payments (as opposed to cash) jumped especially during these years. Medicaid, a federal-state health program targeted mainly at the welfare poor in 1965, provided $9 billion in benefits to 23 million recipients by 1974. The value of public housing during those same ten years rose from $236 million to $1.2 billion. Food stamps, which in 1965 was a small, virtually unnoticed program that spent $36 million on 633,000 people, was by 1975 outlaying $4.3 billion to 17.1 million recipients. Unlike Social Security, which helped the nonpoor as well as the poor, Medicaid, public housing, and food stamps went almost exclusively to the poverty population. Other in-kind benefits, notably Medicare, raised the total spent for such purposes even more astronomically. The sum doled out in in-kind benefits leaped from $1.2 billion in 1965 to $10.8 billion in 1969 to $26.6 billion in 1974.[22]

A RAND study of AFDC recipients in New York City during 1974 demonstrated the vital help that in-kind benefits gave to people on welfare. It estimated that the average family on AFDC received the equivalent of $6,088, of which only 38 percent was cash, the rest in food stamps, Medicaid, public housing, and social services. Even discounting a little the actual cash value of such benefits, the income of these families was well above the $4,160 that a person could earn laboring full time at the minimum wage of $2 per hour. No wonder conservatives believed there was no work incentive for the welfare poor.[23]

No program, however, expanded so much absolutely as the old age and survivors' insurance plan set in motion by the New Deal. In 1965 this provided $16.6 billion to 20.8 million recipients. Nine years later it cost $54 billion and went to 29.9 million beneficiaries. During those years benefits went up almost twice as fast as personal incomes on the whole. With other insurance programs, such as unemployment compensation and Medicare, Social Security accounted for more than four-fifths of public income maintenance in the United States in 1974. Though much of this money went to people above the poverty line, Social Security programs had a moderately equalizing effect on income distribution and a decisive role in shifting income from the young to the aged, historically one of the most deprived groups of the population.[24]

This growth of social welfare expenditures, broadly defined, was effective in reducing poverty in the United States. Experts who attempted to isolate the impact of social welfare laws distinguished between the "pretransfer" poor (the number left in poverty by the market) and the "posttransfer" poor (those who remained poor after social insurance, public assistance, and in-kind benefits were added to incomes). The impact of such programs was considerable in the mid-1960s and grew dramatically in the next ten years. Cash payments alone pulled about 33 percent of the pretransfer poor, or 5.1 million households, out of poverty in 1965. By 1972 the number of households was 7.7 million, 44 percent. If the impact of in-kind benefits is added, 60 percent or more of the pretransfer poor were removed from poverty.

The decisive role of social welfare in reducing poverty is clear from a snapshot of pre- and posttransfer poverty in 1974. Without any public programs, 20.2 million American families, more than one-quarter of the total population, would have been poor. With social insurance and public aid added to their incomes, 9.1 million remained poor. Adding Medicaid, food stamps, and the other in-kind benefits, the number fell to 5.4 million, or 6.9 percent of all families. Moreover, despite the regressive taxes that supported Social Security and other insurance plans, public programs overall, combined with the moderately progressive income taxes that financed some of them, had what one careful scholar called a "highly egalitarian effect on income distribution." When Harrington blasted welfare as "socialism for the rich, free enterprise for the poor" in 1962, he was already exaggerating. By 1975 such a statement was downright misleading.[25]

These gains managed to bring the United States a little closer into line with other industrialized nations in the field of social welfare. This had not seemed to be the case in 1965, when one expert concluded that America was "more reluctant than any rich democratic country to make a welfare effort appropriate to its affluence." The United States spent a smaller percentage of its GNP on social welfare, broadly defined, than did other comparably advanced countries. Indeed, the nation ranked twentieth (ahead only of Japan) of twenty-one industrial nations in this respect during the mid-1960s. Other critics emphasized the unusually harsh and stigmatizing quality of American public aid, in part resulting from the categorical nature of American legislation, which singled out specially needy groups. In part, critics argued, it stemmed from the power of a poor-law philosophy rampant in a country that glorified success.[26]

By 1975 the American way of public assistance still seemed especially harsh. Where countries such as Sweden—the most advanced welfare state in the West—looked for ways to bring the needy under the umbrella of social welfare, Americans tried to keep them off the public payroll. Where western European nations moved in the direction of placing a floor under income, the United States adhered officially to the war-on-poverty idea of opening up doors. Americans steadfastly rejected the view that all citizens had a right to a minimum income. As ever, prevention remained the highest priority.

But in strictly monetary terms, the United States moved slightly ahead between 1965 and 1974, to a point where its spending for social insurance plus welfare as a percentage of GNP was close to that of other western countries. By 1974 it still ranked only seventeenth (ahead of Japan, Australia, New Zealand, and Switzerland), but that was progress of a sort. Moreover, in nations with comprehensive systems, the percentages of people officially defined as poor were probably as high, or higher than, in the United States. England, for instance, had a poverty population that ranged between 4 and 14 percent (depending on placement of the poverty line) in the early 1970s.

America's overall system also came more and more to resemble those of other nations. Until the 1960s, some pioneering countries, such as England and Sweden, had featured collectivist, egalitarian social insurance programs that used general revenue funds to pay equal benefits to all recipients. America, by contrast, relied heavily on wage-based Social Security: the more paid in, the higher the benefits. By the late 1970s Sweden and England were adding wage-based programs to their existing plans, while the United States—thanks in part to the spread of in-kind benefits—moved further away from strictly insurance principles. As one scholar put it, a key development throughout the West was the "progressive blurring of the line between social insurance and public assistance." He added, "Entitlement to income security has become less individually earned and more a social right of citizenship."[27]

One of the many forces that prompted this revolution in social welfare was demographic. By far the largest increases in social spending between 1965 and 1975 occurred in old age insurance; America's population was aging, and ever higher percentages of old people had been in the program long enough to qualify for coverage. By 1975, 93 percent of elderly Americans got Social Security, as opposed to but 20 percent in 1940. Old people as a group also commanded more political respect than they had in the 1930s. At that time, old age lobbies such as the Townsendites had seemed a little zany to younger Americans. By the late 1960s, old people began to be called senior citizens. Their "gray lobbies," increasingly well organized and financed, reflected "senior power." Without the force of such lobbies, Medicare, the other area of great increases in social spending, would not have been passed in 1965. Nor would a range of subsequent amendments have passed that dramatically liberalized benefits—20 percent in the election year of 1972 alone—and that in 1974 indexed them so that they kept pace with the inflation of the 1970s. The leap in spending for Social Security and Medicare continued to depend on the faith among experts as well as in Congress that "insurance" would "prevent" poverty and put a lid on the outpouring of money for welfare.

The maturing of the social welfare system also abetted the increases in spending of the late 1960s and early 1970s. Before then in the United States, a Johnny-come-lately to the field, many old people lacked the required amount of covered time under Social Security to qualify for pensions. No wonder that the most generous countries in the early

1960s were those, like Germany and Austria, that had pioneered in old age insurance and that had high percentages of old people in their populations. By the mid-1960s, America had been expanding its social insurance for thirty years—long enough to move closer at last to the leaders in the field.[28]

Political forces further contributed to the rise in social welfare spending. Passage of Medicare revealed the role of these forces in the area of aid to the aged. They accounted also for the unheralded but vitally important liberalization of food stamp legislation, a liberalization that began in 1968, when a TV documentary on hunger in America dramatized the problem of malnutrition. The following year Senator George McGovern of South Dakota picked up the attack in an investigation of hunger and malnutrition. President Nixon, anxious not to be outflanked, in August 1969 called for a vast expansion of the food stamp program, a change that appealed not only to liberals but also to conservatives, who preferred to give food instead of cash to the poor and who recognized that the program could be administered locally, thus simplifying and decentralizing welfare administration. The food stamp program also received important political support from well-organized producers and retailers. For all these reasons it developed great momentum in both parties, and Congress gave Nixon what he wanted in December 1970. Its response showed that certain kinds of welfare spending had become part of a bipartisan consensus, in spite of the rhetorical flourishes of conservatives. By 1974 food stamps were available to all poor families that passed certain means tests, not just to those on welfare. Without exaggeration, one expert later hailed the expansion of food stamps as "the most important change in public welfare policy since the passage of the Social Security Act."[29]

Bureaucratic pressures added to these demographic and political imperatives. By the 1960s Social Security officials were experienced, self-assured, anxious to enlarge their domain. As one study said, "With the passage of time, administrative routines become established, consensus grows on what has already been accomplished, and administrators acquire an interest in further piecemeal expansion." Another expert observed, "Expansion of the program appears to occur independently of change in social conditions . . . or of party regimes . . . Policy making and program extension have a continuity, momentum, and political logic of their own . . . aggrandizement is inherent in the modern welfare state."[30]

A partial case in point was Medicaid. In other advanced nations, there was widespread popular consensus that health care for the poor was a fundamental right of citizenship. But that consensus did not exist in America. Rather, Medicaid grew quietly and incrementally out of existing programs that were not working very well. Chief among these was the Kerr-Mills Act of 1960, which set up a matching grant program of medical care to the aged. By 1965, when Congress took up the legislation that resulted in Medicare, the deficiencies of Kerr-Mills were obvious. Reformers complained that it did nothing for people under sixty-five and that the matching grant method resulted in wide state-by-state variations, with the poorer states ignoring the program altogether. Governors and lobbyists for the wealthier northern states, meanwhile, grumbled about its escalating costs.

In the course of passing Medicare, Congress paid special heed to these governors and state lobbyists. It approved Medicaid, which eased the burden on states by obligating the federal government to provide between 50 and 85 percent (for the poorest states) of funding for medical care to the needy blind, disabled, and aged, and to members of poor families with dependent children. States were also permitted to use Medicaid funds to help the "medically indigent"—certain people who did not technically qualify for public assistance but who faced impoverishing medical bills.

The passage of Medicaid, like that of food stamps, testified to three important aspects of welfare legislation since 1960. The first was the role of pressure groups, including state and local officials seeking federal aid. These pressures contributed to the gradual nationalizing process that had characterized the welfare state since the 1930s. The second aspect may be stated as a kind of dictum about welfare bills: the less heralded they are at the time, the fewer potential opponents they arouse, and the more likely they are to slip through Congress. The third follows from the second: such legislation may have totally unforeseen consequences. Few people at the time thought that Medicaid, a sleeper, would become such an expensive program. They expected only that it would offer some fiscal relief to states or that by dealing with illness it would actually help keep people off the welfare rolls. So did preventive thinking lead unexpectedly to largess.[31]

The jump in welfare spending resulted finally from the nation's increased ability to pay. Until the 1960s the United States was the richest nation in the world per capita, but the economic growth of the 1960s and early 1970s was impressive. So was the all-important belief held by many people that America could afford increased social spending, that poverty could be abolished without depriving the middle classes. The rediscovery of poverty, and the war against it that began early in the decade, were but early manifestations of these perceptions. In 1966 Shriver said that in ten years the United States "virtually could eliminate" poverty. His faith reflected a great underlying change that had developed slowly but powerfully over a generation of prosperity: the widespread conviction that the age of Malthusian scarcity had vanished forever.

A pervasive egalitarian ideology accompanied this perception of abundance. As people reached the stage where absolute need was rare, they grew hungry to share what the better half had. They felt deprived relatively, and they grew restless. In the United States, the civil rights revolution first exposed this egalitarian longing. Indians, ethnics, the aged, women, the handicapped—practically all groups that felt deprived—later joined in the demand for rights. Poor people inevitably benefited when public officials responded to the clamor of such groups. The revolution in social welfare in the United States depended finally on the revolution of expectations that was gathering momentum throughout the western world.

11

THE WELFARE
EXPLOSION

THE DIMINUTION OF POVERTY between 1965 and 1975 and the revolution in social spending were startling, but more amazing still was the explosive growth of the welfare rolls, of AFDC, during those years. More than any other development of the decade, that growth revealed the subversive force of egalitarianism and the enhanced sense of entitlement that pervaded those turbulent times. For the first time in American history, many of the poor themselves stood up and demanded attention.

A few statistics outline this change. The number of Americans on public assistance grew from 7.1 million in 1960 to 7.8 million in 1965 to 11.1 million in 1969 to 14.4 million in 1974. All of this growth came in the numbers on AFDC, which increased from 3.1 million in 1960 to 4.3 million in 1965 to 6.1 million in 1969 to 10.8 million by 1974. These increases meant striking improvements in coverage.[1]

What caused this surge in the size of the welfare rolls? Idealistic reformers might suggest that it represented the working out of the democratic process—that an informed, altruistic populace perceived the need and opened up the gates for the poor. But there is scant evidence to support such an argument.

Such evidence as there is appeared in findings from occasional public opinion polls. A Gallup poll in 1965 found 67 percent opposed to the idea of legislating a guaranteed annual income for all Americans, but by 1968 the percentage had dropped to 58, by 1972 to 50 percent. A poll in 1969 found only 35 percent favoring a guaranteed jobs program if that meant increasing taxes; by 1972, 42 percent favored it under those conditions. Revealingly, heavy majorities (around 80 percent) of blacks and people with poor educations favored such plans throughout the period.[2]

Additional evidence for a softening of views toward the poor came from popular magazines, which in the 1950s had paid little attention to the poor, save to confirm old stereotypes. After the rediscovery of poverty, however, the subject became a salable commodity. *The Saturday Evening Post*, which had previously shown scant interest in the needy, in the mid-1960s published sympathetic portrayals of the poor. *Look* opened its pages to Michael Harrington in 1964, and *Time* magazine devoted two extensive, balanced cover stories to the subject in 1968 and in 1971. While denouncing flaws in the welfare system, *Time* also attempted to destroy old, damning views of the poor. It reported that very few AFDC families were on the rolls illegally, that the United States spent a smaller percentage of its wealth on welfare than did many other countries, that most poor people were trapped by circumstances, that AFDC clients above all wanted work, not welfare.[3]

The bulk of the evidence about popular opinion, however, suggests that historically unflattering views of poor people persisted amid the dramatic changes of the late 1960s and early 1970s. A survey in 1967 revealed that 42 percent of Americans thought poverty resulted from "lack of effort"; only 19 percent blamed "circumstances beyond control." A poll two years later found that 58 percent of respondents thought poverty was caused by a "lack of thrift and proper money management by poor people"; 55 percent said it was the result of "lack of effort by the poor." A total of 84 percent agreed with the statement: "There are too many people receiving welfare who ought to be working," and 71 percent said "Many people getting welfare are not honest about their need." Only 34 percent agreed with the statement, "Generally speaking, we are spending too *little* money on welfare in this country."[4]

Even those who dismissed such negative views wondered if the welfare system was somehow to blame for the sins of the poor. *Time*'s essay in 1971, for instance, was entitled "Welfare: Trying to End the Nightmare." The administration of public assistance, *Time* said, "might have been designed in a demented collaboration between Franz Kafka and Rube Goldberg." It cited approvingly President Nixon, who had announced in his State of the Union address that welfare was a "monstrous, consuming outrage." Far from drawing attention to the benefits accrued from the expansion of welfare, the magazine article groped rather desperately for ways to cut it back. The increase in the rolls, it said, "stretched some cities to the verge of bankruptcy." *Time* concluded by saying, "The failure of the United States welfare system is in large measure a defeat for liberalism."[5]

Leading politicians joined in condemning the evils of welfare. The system, they said, was a "mess." Governor Ronald Reagan of California announced in his first inaugural address in 1967, "We are not going to perpetuate poverty by substituting a permanent dole for a paycheck. There is no humanity or charity in destroying self-reliance, dignity, and self-respect . . . the very substance of moral fiber." And Senator Russell Long of Louisiana, chairman of the influential Finance Committee studying welfare reform, concluded in 1972: "The welfare system as we know it today is being manipulated and abused by malingerers, cheaters, and outright frauds to the detriment not only of the American taxpayers whose dollars support the poor but also to the detriment of the truly needy . . . There is no question in anybody's mind that the present welfare system is a mess."[6]

When pressed to explain why welfare was a mess, critics like Long singled out three supposed flaws: it enticed lazy migrants from the rural South to northern cities, where welfare was more generous and more readily available; it disrupted families and encouraged illegitimacy; it undercut the work ethic. A poll in 1972 suggested that such views were widespread. In that year 41 percent of respondents agreed (and only 28 percent disagreed) with the statement: "A lot of people are moving . . . just to get welfare." A total of 61 percent believed (only 23 percent disagreed) that "many women getting welfare money are having illegitimate babies to increase the money they get." Only 43 percent supported the statement (49 percent dissented) that "most people on welfare who can work try to find jobs so they can support themselves." These questions concerning attitudes toward people on welfare, not toward poor people in general, revealed that the explosion of case loads did not result from the development of a new, liberal social philosophy among the middle class.[7]

These stereotypes of the welfare poor were as one-sided as they always had been. Any number of studies showed that migrants came north in search of jobs and to escape racial discrimination, not to sit around on welfare. Migrations, indeed, were heaviest in the 1940s and 1950s, when the welfare rolls were growing slowly, not during the explosive growth in public aid of the late 1960s. A study of New York City welfare mothers in 1966 revealed that three-fourths had either been born there or had lived there for ten or more years. A survey of AFDC recipients in Illinois after the residency requirement ended in 1968 showed that 95 percent had lived there a year or more, and 75 percent at least five years, before receiving welfare. It was of course possible, though impossible to prove, that the higher welfare payments of cities like New York kept recipients from moving back to where they had come from.[8]

The critics who blamed AFDC for contributing to illegitimacy and family breakup based their case in part on the effects of the so-called absent father rule that supposedly encouraged fathers to leave home so that their wives and children could get aid. Left to their own devices, such women—racists called them "black brood mares"—supposedly cohabited with men in the neighborhood and produced hordes of illegitimate offspring. Reformers who denounced the absent father rule campaigned for extending AFDC-UP to all states, partly on the grounds that it would encourage poor families to stay together. Conservatives tended rather to demand tighter supervision of welfare families—including "midnight raids"—to find out whether a man was in fact at home. Both liberals and conservatives assumed that the absent father rules encouraged the breakup of marriages.

They probably assumed incorrectly. Studies suggested that the rule helped to break up perhaps 1 to 5 percent of AFDC families at the time. They suggested also that the availability of welfare (but not the size of benefits), induced some nonwhite mothers not to remarry so quickly. But there was no correlation between state benefit levels and illegitimacy rates or the average number of children per welfare family. The main reason for family breakup among the poor, all the studies showed, was not welfare but poverty itself, as well as the more specific causes that also divided families of the nonpoor, such as alcoholism, drug abuse, infidelity, sexual and physical violence, simple incompatibility. The conclusion was clear: AFDC-UP ended much of the snooping into their lives, and if extended, the program would have made AFDC more uniform across the nation. But the absent father rule was not the cause of family disorganization which, like migration, stemmed from much wider social and economic causes. Welfare was not the root of the family's problems.[9]

The third main criticism, that welfare damaged the work ethic, flowed from two assumptions. One was the old belief that anyone on welfare was by definition lazy and improvident. The other, shared by some liberals, was that the categorical assistance programs destroyed people's incentive to work because prior to 1967 any earnings had to be subtracted from welfare checks. If people on welfare were given some financial incentive to work, they would do so, critics said.

When Congress reconsidered the assistance programs in 1967, it seized on this argument as a way of controlling the already rising numbers on welfare. Led by Congressman Wilbur Mills, the influential chairman of the House Ways and Means Committee, it passed a series of amendments to existing laws. One, reflecting the view that welfare spawned immorality, froze at existing levels the amount of federal matching money available for AFDC cases caused by illegitimacy or desertion. Hotly resisted by the hard-pressed states, this provision never went into effect and was repealed in 1969. More important were amendments that established the WIN, or Work Incentive program, which employed both the carrot and the stick. The carrot was the "thirty plus one-third" rule, which authorized recipients of categorical assistance to keep, without subtractions from their welfare checks, the first $30 per month from work, plus one-third of amounts above $30. To assist welfare mothers who wanted to work, Congress also increased funding for day care. The stick, what liberal critics called the "workfare" provision, allowed states to drop from the AFDC rolls those "appropriate persons"—parents and children over sixteen—who declined "without good cause" to participate in work or training programs.[10]

This emphasis on workfare betrayed an ironic shift from the goals of ADC as framed in 1935. The original legislation aimed to help deserving mothers to care for their children at home—to keep them out of the labor force. By contrast, WIN sought to get these mothers to work. WIN reflected the continuing power of the work ethic, especially in economically prosperous times when jobs appeared easy to get. It reflected also the sense, widespread in Congress as well as in the country at large, that many "welfare mothers" were "undeserving." That feeling remained as consistent a force in the evolution of American welfare programs as faith in the work ethic.

The stress on workfare, however, had no more effect in the 1960s and 1970s than it had had for the Charity Organization Societies of the late nineteenth century. First of all, the money for day care fell far short of establishing the needed numbers of such centers. And welfare mothers did not show much interest in leaving their children with strangers while being forced to undergo job training. In practice, therefore, workfare did not amount to much. As interpreted by HEW officials, only AFDC-UP fathers, dropouts over sixteen, and a few mothers of school-age children who had access to free day care ever had to register for work.

Advocates of WIN were even more misguided in thinking that work training could accomplish wonders. Of the 2.8 million welfare recipients eligible for WIN in 1967, only about 700,000 were deemed by local authorities to be "appropriate for referral." The rest were ill, needed at home, considered untrainable, or without access to day care. Of the 700,000, only 400,000 were actually enrolled in WIN as of mid-1972, four years after the program got under way. Around a quarter of these completed training, and only 52,000, or less than 2 percent of the total pool, actually were employed—at an average wage of around $2 an hour.[11]

This experience highlighted two major points that liberals and structuralists had made for years: first, most of the welfare poor were in no position to work; and second, those who were could not find decent-paying jobs when they tried. Responses of welfare mothers also revealed that many of them cherished culturally inherited values and resisted leaving the home for the work-place. For them, welfare was grim, but preferable to leaving their children with strangers. The women who actually enrolled in WIN initially welcomed the opportunity to get off welfare, but before long were frustrated by the irrelevancy of their training, the inadequacy of day care for their children, or the poor jobs that awaited them when they got out. Welfare was in no sense a satisfying condition for most of these people. They were willing to undergo training for decent-paying jobs, but they could not get them.

Ignoring these facts, Congress pressed ahead in its tireless quest for prevention. In December 1971 it approved unanimously the so-called Talmadge amendments to the WIN program, which expanded the categories of welfare recipients required to register for work or training, including mothers of school-age children. The amendments also penalized states that by mid-1974 did not refer at least 15 percent of their adult AFDC recipients to WIN. Thanks mainly to passage of a bill appropriating money for emergency "public service" employment, the record of the WIN-cum-Talmadge amendments was slightly better than WIN alone. But only slightly—perhaps 80,000 people found jobs, or about 8 percent of the eligible pool. Their work, paid at wage levels that were not to exceed welfare payments, did little to enhance their skills or to alleviate the much larger problem of welfare dependency.[12]

After 1974 the thirty plus one-third rule remained as an apparently lasting feature of American welfare. But WIN funds were frozen, and Congress assessed other ways to encourage work. It studied data amassed from experiments concerning the impact of guaranteed incomes on work incentives. The researchers examined experimental groups, all of which were guaranteed minimum incomes of varying levels and taxed at a range of rates for work they managed to find. The work behavior of the experimental subjects was compared to that of a control group to infer the programs' impact. Although contrived, this was the kind of research that advocates of WIN might have started before plunging ahead with workfare in 1967.

The results suggested again what structuralists had always argued: tax rates on wages performed under guaranteed income did at some point become punitive enough to cut back on the work incentives of wives. To that extent, the basic idea of WIN was valid. Men, however, seemed little affected by the tax rates. For them, having regular employment remained a vitally important value, and they worked (or did not work) without much regard for the income plan or tax rate that they were a part of. The experiments suggested generally that welfare per se had little to do with inhibiting work incentives. WIN was an overly simple approach that failed to grapple with the fundamental need: decent-paying, steady work for all able-bodied people.[13]

Focusing on efforts such as WIN in some ways distorts the views of Congress during this period of growth in welfare. During the same time that it tried to champion the work ethic, it was also appropriating much-increased sums to support the new millions on the categorical assistance programs, liberalizing Social Security, and expanding the in-kind programs that had such a major impact on reducing poverty in the 1970s. Still, workfare, along with polls showing continuing antipathy to welfare, revealed the central point about American attitudes at the time: far from recognizing that welfare would always be with us, most people continued to hope that the problem would wither away. A durable social philosophy featuring prevention and the work ethic continued to flourish.

Underlying these beliefs was the fundamental idea that America had a "welfare crisis." Despite rising case loads, this was not altogether so. If one excluded Medicaid, which went to medical establishments, the costs of public assistance in the United States represented a fairly stable percentage of the federal budget. Even in New York City, thought to be going broke because of welfare, the percentage of the city budget spent on public assistance rose from 3 percent in 1963-1964 to only 7 percent in 1968 and then dropped to 6 percent in 1972-1973. In both England and Sweden, where no sense of crisis existed, the percentage of the population getting cash relief was about as high as in the United States and rising more rapidly. The sense of crisis lent to the issue of welfare a new urgency that existed nowhere else in the world to such an extent.[14]

The sources of this crisis mentality intrigued commentators then and later. Many stressed the obvious fact that Americans did not know, or much care, what was happening in England or Sweden. They cared what was taking place at home—rising case loads. Others noted that state officials took the lead in talking about crisis. Facing budgetary problems because of rising educational and health costs, the states suddenly had to cope with unexpectedly large case loads, so they tried to squeeze more money out of Washington. Still other observers emphasized the disillusion resulting from the war on poverty—disillusion people expressed by projecting their frustrations on the poor. Why, they asked, was it not possible to settle this aggravating problem of poverty once and for all? Yet another explanation maintained that Americans, especially after the urban riots, perceived poverty and welfare as preeminently ghetto and black problems, and the AFDC crisis as a manifestation of black immorality. Enraged and offended, they looked for ways to penalize the perpetrators.[15]

The scattered quantitative evidence on the subject, mainly from poll data, suggests that all these elements contributed to the sense of crisis, but it is not possible to single out an overriding cause. The sense of crisis, however, was undoubted. It showed that historically cold attitudes toward the welfare poor had not changed very much since the 1940s and 1950s. In this sense, too, the growth of the welfare rolls cannot be traced to the rise of a more liberal public opinion about the poor or welfare. Or to an enlightened Congress, which was in fact frustrated by its inability to stop the explosion.

The sources of that explosion, from 3.1 million to 10.8 million in 1971, lay rather in the impact of socioeconomic forces on the expectations of the poor. Some observers thought that one such force was the "tangle of pathology" in lower-class families, especially among urban blacks and Puerto Ricans, that Moynihan dramatized in his report of 1965. This instability increased the percentage of AFDC families who were on the rolls because of desertion, separation or divorce (as opposed to widowhood) from two-thirds in 1961 to three-fourths in 1967. There was no doubting the problems leading to instability among lower-class families, especially among nonwhites and in the large northern cities, in the 1950s and 1960s. AFDC case loads were 32 percent nonwhite in 1950, 41 percent in 1960, and 46 percent in 1967.

Though this explanation commanded much credibility at the time, it was not in fact the major source of the welfare explosion. Statistically measurable family instability had been increasing well before the 1960s and could not account for the suddenness and size of the jump in the rolls after 1965. Moreover, to be on AFDC a family had to be poor, and the absolute number of female-headed families that were poor remained stable throughout the period of explosive growth in the rolls.

But the "tangle of pathology" explanation was helpful in two qualified respects. First, thanks in part to improvements in medical care, a higher percentage of these poor female-headed families was large. The number of children potentially eligible for AFDC benefits increased by nearly 20 percent between 1960 and 1967. Second, the mass migrations of the 1940s and 1950s left many such families in the more liberal northern states by the 1960s. Though the migrants had not gone north to get on welfare, the economic difficulties that trapped them in the ghettos rendered some of them in great need over the long run. Around three-fourths of the rise in case loads in the 1960s occurred in nine northern, urban states. California and New York alone accounted for more than 40 percent of the increase.[16]

Five other developments, especially in these liberal northern states, were more important in explaining the rise in case loads. One, of least significance, was the approval of AFDC-UP in the northern states. A second was the tendency of these relatively wealthy states to hike the income levels at which people could become eligible for AFDC. This tendency of states, especially in the North, to raise income levels lifted the number of people eligible for aid by perhaps 35 percent during the years of most rapid growth between 1967 and 1971.[17]

Changes in the law represented a third reason. Thanks in part to the civil rights movement, in part to the role of OEO legal services, in part to the egalitarian temper of the times, public interest lawyers at last mounted serious challenges to some of the hoary practices of state and local welfare officials. These challenges ultimately reached the Supreme Court, which acted to support the poor. Between 1968 and 1971 the Court struck down the absent father rule, residency requirements, and regulations that had denied aid to families with so-called "employable mothers." The Court also required welfare agencies to give fair hearings and proper notice to recipients threatened with termination. These decisions improved the quality of treatment accorded the poor and diminished the stigma attached to applying for welfare. They increased slightly the number eligible for benefits.[18]

The other two developments, the most important of all, vastly accentuated the significance of this rise in the pool of eligibles. One was a big jump in the percentage of eligible families that applied for aid, reflecting potential clients' much heightened awareness of their rights under the law. The second development was a sharp rise in the percentage of eligible applicants who were in fact assisted. Together, these forces resulted in a fantastic jump in the participation of eligible families in AFDC, from perhaps 33 percent in the early 1960s to more than 90 percent in 1971. For the first time in American history, the largest category of people eligible for assistance—AFDC families— was taking virtually full advantage of its opportunities.

What prompted this dramatic, historic development? The source of it most obvious to contemporaries was changing attitudes of poor people themselves. Despite the hostility of the middle classes to increases in welfare, poor Americans refused at last to be cowed from applying for aid. Despite the continuing stigma attached to living on welfare, they stood firm in their determination to stay on the rolls as long as they were in need. Welfare was not a privilege; it was a right, as was health care through Medicaid, the availability of which under AFDC clearly quickened the desire of poor people to apply for aid. Compared to the past, when poor people—harassed and stigmatized by public authorities—were slow to claim their rights, this was a fundamental change.[19]

In accounting for these new attitudes, some observers, notably Frances Fox Piven and Richard Cloward, again employed a conflict model. The civil rights revolution, they said, aroused blacks and prompted direct action tactics, such as the mobilization of poor people by the National Welfare Rights Organization, beginning in 1966. The NWRO, indeed, became a vocal, highly political lobby for welfare reform between 1967 and 1972, the years of greatest growth in the rolls. The social unrest that ensued, Cloward and Piven argued, worried Democratic politicians, who feared for the safety of the black vote. Unrest also worried public authorities, who reacted by easing eligibility requirements and responding more kindly to the rise in applications. "Expansion of the welfare rolls," Piven and Cloward concluded, "was a political response to political disorder."[20]

The role of the civil rights movement was undoubtedly vital. It enlisted militant leaders who campaigned to improve the legal and then the socioeconomic situation of the poor. It trained a cadre of activists who apprised poor people of their rights. Most important, though hardest to pinpoint, the civil rights movement quickened the sense of inequality and relative deprivation that affected all low-income people, whether black or white. No explanation of the welfare explosion can slight its significance.[21]

Sometimes the civil rights laws themselves facilitated the liberalization of public welfare. A case in point involved a Springfield, Massachusetts, lawyer, who filed a formal complaint in 1965 based on the 1964 civil rights act. His challenge attempted to stop police detectives from grilling black mothers applying for AFDC about their sexual activities. The complaint succeeded; state and local authorities ruled that no police should be assigned to welfare agencies or be given any information about welfare cases save what was necessary to locate absent fathers. The state also repealed its rule that mothers swear out warrants against fathers in order to get benefits. This was but one of many instances of the impact of civil rights activities on the welfare poor.[22]

It is less clear that the NWRO had much to do with the welfare explosion. Applications for AFDC and rates of acceptance began to grow dramatically well before 1967, when the NWRO became visible. The NWRO, indeed, never had more than 22,000 members—or around 2 percent of adult recipients of public assistance. It is equally doubtful that urban disorders, including riots in the mid- and late 1960s, did much to liberalize welfare. Some evidence suggests that welfare rolls and expenditures did rise more rapidly in cities hit by disturbances than elsewhere, but the need tended to be greatest there, especially in areas literally burned to the ground by rioters. And did the riots, as well as the militant rhetoric of the NWRO, create a backlash that did more harm than good? One careful study concluded, "The import of the rioting was probably to stimulate 'law and order,' not welfare benevolence."[23]

The focus on conflict as a cause of the welfare explosion is also one-sided in that it leaves the impression that the only impetus for change came from the poor themselves. Great though that force was, especially in contrast to what had been, it was accompanied by pressure from the federal welfare bureaucracy. Federal officials not only responded to agitation from below, they also encouraged and abetted it, in a dynamic relationship that maximized the thrust from the grass roots. Their important role in the expansion of welfare showed that the federal government did indeed make a difference, that post-New Deal liberalism, for all its limitations, could promote social justice, and that the nationalization of policies and politics mattered in enlarging and humanizing the welfare state.

Some of this action at the top began as early as 1961, when the Bureau of Public Assistance issued a directive against the "suitable home" rules that had traditionally served to keep families with illegitimate children off the rolls. Though evaded in places, the directive was rigorously enforced in many states and localities. In 1966 the Bureau of Family Services, which had replaced the BPA in 1962, ordered that state plans for eligibility "respect the rights of individuals . . . and not result in practices that violate the individual's privacy or personal dignity, or harass him, or violate his constitutional rights." These directives unambiguously reminded local agencies, and the poor, that a more resolutely liberal, rights-conscious administration was operating in Washington. States that wanted to get the all-important matching grants had no choice but to take notice.[24]

Federal officials became still more aggressive and innovative during the turbulent late 1960s. In part, they were continuing to respond to pressures unleashed by the civil rights movement, but their eagerness to aid the poor was also a force in itself. Until the mid-1960s social workers had dominated the Bureau of Public Assistance and its successor, the Bureau of Family Services. Veterans of acrimonious struggles against parsimonious state and local welfare agencies, they had concentrated on developing careful procedures and ironclad rules. They had focused especially on developing higher standards of case work: setting maximum case loads per worker, establishing the frequency of home visits, improving the training of professional workers. These worthy goals inevitably engaged the welfare bureaucrats in endless struggles with conservative local officials and resulted in thick volumes of rules and regulations, just the sort of red tape the designers of the war on poverty had tried to bypass by placing the locus of decisionmaking in the communities.

In the late 1960s, a new emphasis developed in Washington. By then, many of the first generation of Social Security professionals were retiring, and some very aggressive liberals were taking their place. Especially under HEW Secretary John Gardner, who reorganized the department in 1967-1968, top federal officials concentrated less on the old social work goals and more on finding ways to cut through the red tape so as to maximize benefits and services. To an extent, that meant divesting HEW of the social worker mentality. One rule in 1968 required "nonprofessional" people to "assist in the provision of services" and added that "recipients of assistance or other low income persons must be given preference for such positions." This was maximum feasible participation, HEW-style.[25]

The arrival of a presumably more cost-conscious Republican administration in 1969 made no difference. On the contrary, the Community Services Administration, which was created in 1969 to distribute funds for services, was headed by James Bax, whose motto was "You hatch it, we match it." Tom Joe, special assistant to the undersecretary of HEW, joined the administration after writing a paper for the American Public Welfare Association entitled "Finding Welfare Dollars." The aim, Joe explained, was "to maximize the total resources available to the poorest segment of our society." Joe, who was blind, had been on welfare as a child; he spoke persuasively for liberal welfare in the Nixon years. So did other Nixon officials, who in 1969 proposed a dramatic Family Assistance Plan. Attitudes such as these suggested that the NWRO was misguided in thinking that the "welfare establishment" was the enemy. HEW, rather, was a liberal bureaucracy with every reason to aggrandize itself.[26]

In doing so, HEW reacted to resourceful pressure groups that during the 1960s had grown steadily more expert at finding ways to tap the federal government. These included not only the American Public Welfare Association, from which Joe had moved to HEW, but a formidable network of consultants who made it their business to help state and local officials apply to Washington for fiscal relief. Their combined efforts scored a breakthrough in 1971, when state social service agencies were authorized to use federal welfare funds to underwrite a range of traditionally state-financed activities, including services dealing with drug abuse, alcoholism, mental illness, and mental retardation. This authorization vastly expanded the outpouring of federal monies for services, from $354 million in 1969 to $1.7 billion in 1972. It also construed the meaning of services in ways that Congress had never intended when passing the Public Welfare Amendments of 1962. Appalled, Congress stemmed the flow of funds in 1972.

Though it plugged the loophole, Congress could not destroy the network of bureaucrats and lobbyists who had opened it up in the first place. Indeed, the activism of that network was merely one manifestation, though a very important one, of the rise in expectations that affected Americans in the 1960s. The network reflected also the nationalization of politics that had accelerated since World War II. Thanks in part to economic growth, which stimulated wants, and to the New Frontier and Great Society, which promised the moon, Americans looked more and more to Washington for redress of their problems. There they found bureaucrats who needed little pressure from below to act. If this reliance on federal largess was not in fact a "new liberalism," or a "creative federalism," it was still a vital force in the explosion of public welfare in the 1960s and early 1970s.[27]

By 1980 it was fashionable among some observers to fret over the revolution in social welfare and the explosion in public assistance. Though these conservative observers rarely came right out and said it, they seemed to yearn for the good old days when the poor had minded their own business, and the government had plodded along doing only those things it always had done. The explosion in welfare rolls, far from being welcomed, continued to be perceived as a crisis.

Other observers wondered if the rise in welfare represented a democratic force. Granted, there was grass roots pressure from the poor and organized pressure from lobbies. But few elected political leaders carefully mapped out the new policies in advance. And Congress resisted liberal developments. Changes of vast moment, like Medicaid or the spread of food stamps, developed with little public attention or understanding of consequences. Americans still thought there was a large undeserving poor and that welfare should aim at prevention, not income maintenance. How much neater it would have been if the revolution in social welfare and the rise in rolls had occurred amid extensive, reasoned public debate, careful planning, and the ringing endorsement of representative bodies of government![28]

But these observers might have been less gloomy in describing what happened. Accompanying the rise in expectations was a broadened, if unforeseen, definition of the rights of citizenship. Long apparent in the political domain, this concept had manifested itself in expanding eligibility to vote (for women, blacks, eighteen-year-olds), and in heightening efforts to improve civil rights and civil liberties. In part because of dramatic improvements in educational levels and mass communications, definitions of citizenship by the early 1970s were also coming to include certain basic social and economic rights, such as the right to a secure income.[29]

Economic growth and social change were the most fundamental sources, and indicators, of this broadening of citizenship, which affected all western industrial nations. In America, developments in welfare administration within the various states revealed this connection. Between 1960 and 1970, the most developed states—those with the highest per capita incomes, the largest percentages of white collar workers, the highest educational levels—were also those that most extended public assistance policies. Those were the states in which the biggest percentages of poor people applied for aid, in which payments per recipient were most generous, and in which eligibility requirements and acceptance rates were the most liberalized. Changes in the extent of need or in levels of social unrest were by contrast much less important in predicting state-by-state variations in welfare policies throughout the decade.[30]

Progress in social welfare had not conquered all by the early 1970s, nor was that progress necessarily to continue. In the economically unstable 1970s it did not. But there has historically been a dynamic link between socioeconomic progress, expectations, and conceptions of the rights of citizenship. Like the progressive era, when Hunter and his contemporaries discovered the poor, the economically affluent 1960s and early 1970s were years that facilitated aid to those in need. Those were years of peaceful revolution in welfare.[31]

12

FLOORS
AND DOORS

For at least a hundred years prior to the 1960s, the gospel of prevention had possessed antipoverty reformers. That quest had assumed many forms, ranging from the harsh prescriptions of the eugenicists and the Charity Organization Societies to the more benign paternalism of those in the 1950s who wished to rehabilitate the poor. The war on poverty, preaching the same idea, aimed at opening doors to opportunity and preventing poverty at the same time.

The gospel of prevention did not die in the late 1960s and 1970s, but for most experts who explored ways of ending poverty, it did not stand alone. Preventive measures, they agreed, must still be pursued, but so must short-range efforts to augment income. Henceforth these experts stressed income maintenance for all—floors under income as well as doors to self-help.[1]

The aim of setting a floor under every American's income was in some ways—especially politically—ambitious. It reflected a new flowering of the apparently inexhaustible optimism of twentieth-century social science. Even so, compared to the gospel of prevention, the quest for floors was in a way modest in its aspirations. It set aside for a while the goal of welfare reformers who had tried to change human nature, and it accepted matter-of-factly that government must always engage in heavy spending for welfare. It conceded that the poor must always be with us. The sobered sights of these advocates, Robert Heilbroner observed as early as 1950, represented the "last resort of a society that has given up the ghost of progress."[2]

The idea of establishing a floor was an old one of liberal social workers, but its wider appeal to planners in the 1960s and 1970s was really

185

rather abrupt. William Capron, a top antipoverty planner, recalled talking with economists in 1963 about proposing a "negative income tax," only to conclude that "politically and budgetarily this was not something that was going to fly at all." Labor Secretary Willard Wirtz declared himself against the idea in 1964. "I don't believe that the world owes me a living," he said, "and I don't believe it owes anybody else a living."[3]

By the late 1960s the emphasis of many experts changed. This did not mean that they readily agreed on one answer; they squabbled over the best ways to achieve income maintenance. Some, drawing on the experience of the other industrialized nations, called for children's allowances to aid families when they most needed help. Because the allowances would go to all families with children, whether or not they were poor, they would involve no means tests, no stigma, no cumbersome new bureaucracy. Some who supported family allowances hoped to prod the American welfare system away from what they thought was an excessive emphasis on rehabilitating individuals. Like Daniel Moynihan, they expected their plans to arrest the alarming deterioration in family life and preserve the home as the foundation of social stability. "What strengthens the family," one writer explained, "strengthens society . . . If things go well with family, life is worth living; when the family falters, life falls apart."[4]

Other advocates of income maintenance emphasized the need to create jobs for people. In 1966 the National Commission on Technology reported that the federal government ought to be the "employer of last resort," and some liberals and unionists in the late 1960s and 1970s picked up this old refrain. Though they offered different proposals, most began with the unquestionable assertions that unemployment and low wages remained key causes of poverty and that a jobs program would command more political support than a dole. Advocates called on the government to subsidize low-wage employment and to create new "public service" jobs. These might range from low-skill work on sewers or in refuse collection to jobs in hospitals, clinics, schools, and day care centers. Ideally, such jobs would offer training and develop self-discipline and good work habits. But the key was not so much to rehabilitate workers as to pay them cash for working on projects that would benefit society. Those who were unable to work were to receive income maintenance in other ways. Broadly speaking, advocates of public employment were recommending a renewal of New Deal work relief programs such as the WPA—without its attendant problems.[5]

Many experts, however, doubted the magic of children's allowances or public employment. Allowances, they pointed out, usually stopped abruptly when children reached eighteen, and they did nothing for the childless poor. If they were to aid all families—and thus eliminate stigma—they would be paid to the nonpoor as well as the poor, raising costs and posing political obstacles.

Critics of the jobs approach insisted that many poor people were unable to work. They argued that government employment rarely provided skills or training, that it did nothing about technological unemployment. They recalled the dubious results of past government make-work programs, including the WPA: the possibility that such jobs would depress wage rates or compete with the private market, the stigma that necessarily attached to such employment, the tendency of conservative administrators to force workfare on people who were really unable to hold a regular job. They ridiculed especially the notion that needy persons could be lumped together in particular kinds of unskilled work. Poor people were not robots that could be programmed into slots. For these reasons, most experts regarded a jobs strategy as but a part of a much broader plan of income maintenance.[6]

Many authorities turned instead to some form of guaranteed cash income, not just for families with children or people who worked, but for all the poor. Preeminent among such thinkers was the conservative economist Milton Friedman, who had worked out a plan as early as the mid-1950s and explained it briefly in a book, *Capitalism and Freedom*, published in 1962. A staunch believer in the virtues of a free market economy, Friedman wanted to maximize the choices open to Americans. He was appalled by the bureaucratic excess in the "present rag-bag of measures" then providing welfare in America. A "negative income tax," he said, would accomplish the goal of alleviating poverty much more cheaply and efficiently and allow other programs to be abolished.

In Friedman's opinion such a plan could be run by the Internal Revenue Service, which could pay poor people a subsidy equal to 50 percent of the difference between the sum of income and allowed tax exemptions and deductions. A family of four with no income and $3,000 in exemptions and deductions might get 50 percent of $3,000 minus 0, or $1,500 (half the poverty line used by the government at the time). A family of four earning $1,000 and entitled to $3,000 in deductions could get half of the difference, $1,000. Its total income would be $2,000—$1,000 from earnings and $1,000 from the government. In this way, the plan protected the incentive to work; higher earnings would not be completely offset by cuts in benefits. The result, Friedman claimed, would be a "floor below which no man's net income [defined now to include the subsidy] could fall."[7]

If Friedman was the guru for conservatives, Robert Theobald, an

English economist, was a patron saint for some liberals. In his book *Free Men and Free Markets* (1963), Theobald agreed with the "necessity for free markets." But he rejected an "extreme, Adam Smith version of the free-market mechanism." He stressed instead the baneful effects of technological unemployment and the need for government to protect against it. Where Friedman spoke of giving "benefits" to the poor, Theobald talked about their "entitlements." "All western societies," he wrote, "should ensure that each individual obtains sufficient resources to allow him freedom in his choice of actions." He explained that "the initial step on the way to eliminate poverty is to supply money rather than moral uplift, cultural refinements, extended education, retraining programs, or makework jobs." His remedy was a guaranteed minimum income for all Americans equal to $1,000 a year for adults, $600 for children. A two-parent family of four would be entitled to $3,200. Unlike Friedman, Theobald did not expect such payments to replace all other forms of welfare. He favored a publicly financed health care program for old people. His emphasis reflected the expanded definition of citizenship that was spreading through the western world in the 1960s. He said,

> We all need to adopt the concept of an absolute constitutional right to an income. This would guarantee to every citizen of the United States, and to every person who has resided in the United States for a period of five consecutive years, the right to an income from the federal government sufficient to enable him to live with dignity.[8]

American economists took the lead during the mid-1960s in attempting to explain and popularize the general idea of income maintenance. The two most influential were perhaps James Tobin of Kennedy's Council of Economic Advisers and (cautiously) Robert Lampman, whose studies had formed the basis for the CEA's war against poverty in 1963-1964. Galbraith went so far as to hail Friedman's plan as "one of the two or three new ideas in economics in twenty-five years." Among economists the proselytizers had remarkable success. While most were cautious about endorsing the technical aspects of any particular plan, many agreed that the present welfare system needed radical overhaul and that the government should help all poor people get a guaranteed annual income. In 1968, 1,300 economists at almost 150 institutions signed a petition urging Congress to adopt a "national system of income guarantees and supplements."[9]

The idea of a guaranteed income appealed also to most liberal social workers. A workshop sponsored in 1964 by the National Association of Social Work attracted activists who demanded a "federally

guaranteed minimum for all families in the United States." The conference issued a position paper calling for "income as a matter of right
. . . at a uniformly adequate standard of living." The social workers
did not recommend scrapping all existing programs, which after all
gave them employment, nor were they ready necessarily to endorse a
negative income tax. But they insisted that public assistance be nation-
alized and thus made uniform across the country, and that payments
be raised so welfare families could come up to the official poverty
line. In 1967 the National Social Welfare Assembly demanded "minimum standards of assistance for all persons in actual need regardless
of their age, family situation, or length of residence in a state where
they are living." In this way, long-time advocates of welfare reform
made common cause, though uneasily, with economists, some of
whom proposed to scrap the existing welfare system. [10]

The seductive appeal of floors in the 1960s attracted government
officials as well. As early as 1964 President Johnson named the first of
many task forces to study income maintenance plans. His third task
force, in 1966, endorsed the idea of a negative income tax on a limited
basis and recommended creation of a presidential commission to
study the matter further. Meanwhile, the OEO was developing "Five
Year Plans." The second of these, drafted in 1966, stressed the need
for income maintenance. "The time is coming," it said, "when the
American people will accept a guaranteed minimum income at the
poverty level as a right in a wealthy country, and we propose to start
moving in this direction now." Wilbur Cohen, then undersecretary of
HEW, seemed cautiously to agree. Spelling out his ideas for welfare
reform, he urged the liberalization of existing programs, and "some
new program like the 'negative income tax,' to reduce the need for
welfare payments." In 1968 Shriver endorsed a "gradual work incentives program—a more descriptive term for what is frequently called
the Negative Income Tax." OEO-sponsored researchers tried out
incentive programs in parts of New Jersey and Pennsylvania which
suggested at the time that guaranteed income plans would not ad-
versely affect work incentives. [11]

The culmination of this thinking came in the report in 1969 of the
so-called Heineman Commission, the presidential body recommended
by the 1966 task force. Its head, Ben W. Heineman, was president of
North West Industries. Other members included top economists, businessmen, and political activists. The report took off from the consensus established in mid-decade as a result of the rediscovery of poverty:
destitution was an economic, not a cultural phenomenon. "The
poor," it said, "inhabit a different world than the non-poor, primarily because they lack money." It added, "Most of the poor want to

work. They want to improve their potential and to be trained for better jobs." It followed that they should be treated like the nonpoor, that they should have a secure income. "Only when the poor are assured a minimum stable income," the report said, "can the other mechanisms in our fight against poverty—education, training, health, and employment—begin to function adequately."[12]

The commission considered placing a jobs strategy first on the agenda of reform, but it concluded that the government would have to create 9 million jobs at a total annual cost of around $16 billion. It judged that "employment approaches alone cannot provide a satisfactory sole basis for a general economic security system and are not fundamental alternatives to income supplement proposals." Noting that there were approximately 10 million workers getting less than the minimum wage, it urged instead a "universal income supplement program . . . making cash payments to all members of the population with income needs." It recommended a low floor of $2,400 for a family of four.[13]

Endorsement by a presidential commission did not mean that Americans would buy the product. Congress, led by Representative Wilbur Mills, the acknowledged expert on Social Security and welfare, at first showed little interest in such proposals. So did the American public: polls showed 60 percent opposed to plans that guaranteed everyone a minimum income. Those were the years, after all, of the "welfare crisis," and of continuing stereotypes about the undeserving poor:

> I know the place ain't much, but I sure don't pay much rent
> I get a check the first of every month, from this here Federal
>   Government.
> Every Wednesday I get commodities, sometimes four or five
>   sacks
> Pick 'em up down at the welfare office driving that new Cadil-
>   lac.[14]

Not all social scientists subscribed to the "floors" approach. Edward Banfield, a professor and urbanologist teaching at Harvard, was the most outspoken of the articulate and increasingly influential writers who worried that the government simply did not know enough to undertake broad programs of social action. He insisted that poverty was more than lack of money. "Lower class forms of all problems," he wrote in 1968, "are at bottom a single problem: the existence of an outlook and style of life which therefore attaches no value to work, sacrifice, self-improvement, or service to family, friends, or community." Although few writers went so far as Banfield in repeating tired notions about a culture of poverty, others (mainly conservatives) shared his doubts about the capacity of public policy, in part because of the oversell of the war on poverty.[15]

Some liberal experts, too, were dubious about income maintenance proposals. Advocates of children's allowances still insisted that their idea was less stigmatizing, and politically more feasible, than maintenance programs aimed primarily at the poor. Social workers wondered how the IRS or any other Washington agency could bring to people's special needs the personal, decentralized attention offered by the welfare establishment. Economists raised technical objections: how would annual payments, à la the IRS, take care of the poor? How would the IRS compensate for regional variations in the cost of living? How could computers spewing out subsidies distinguish between the truly needy and those who were not, such as temporarily broke college students? Political observers argued that no sweeping plan stood a chance against the nexus of bureaucrats and clients who wished to preserve familiar existing programs. Union leaders feared that such a plan would merely institutionalize a low income standard, to which already inadequate wage rates would tumble.[16]

The experts' most telling objections centered on the so-called marginal tax rates, or benefit reduction rates. These were the "taxes" (actually money subtracted from transfer payments of various kinds) on money earned by the welfare poor who worked. If these rates were set high—say above 50 percent—they threatened, experts thought, to impede work incentives. A welfare family with some outside earned income might discover that the cumulative loss from such taxes was nearly as great as the money earned. Worst of all, a family on Medicaid could find itself facing the "notch" effect that occurred when the family earned almost enough to get off welfare. At that point, its cash subsidies would dwindle almost to zero, but its right to receive health care under Medicaid, a benefit worth many hundreds of dollars, would still be respected. If it earned slightly more, the cash welfare would end, but the family would also abruptly lose all its valuable health benefits. It was clearly better for such families not to work their way completely off welfare.[17]

The alternative, keeping marginal taxes low, posed equally difficult problems. Every dollar that was not subtracted from subsidies to those who had some income was a dollar that the government was losing, which would result in escalating costs and political opposition. Moreover, any income maintenance program that attempted to encourage work in this way inevitably ended up paying benefits to large numbers of people whose income (from work plus subsidies) exceeded the poverty line. To many Americans, that was illogical and indefensible.

Many of these objections, however, were to one or more specific proposals, such as Friedman's. The faith that there should be a floor under income was (among experts) an idea whose time had come by 1969. Its popularity among experts depended in part on the same disenchantment with the existing welfare bureaucracy that had prompted community action. It also exposed widespread disgust with the welfare state. Many supporters of a floor were conservatives who, like Friedman, hoped that some such plan could at once cut costs, enhance work incentives, and abolish the welfare bureaucracy. For such people, income maintenance promised a quick, cheap solution to the "crisis" of welfare.

But the sentiment in favor of income floors embraced many nonconservatives who had learned the structuralist lesson preached during the rediscovery of poverty in the early 1960s: poverty was an economic problem best attacked by economic measures. Their belief reflected also the lessons learned from unsatisfying flirtations with rehabilitation and with OEO: doors were not enough. Those who supported floors reflected especially the rising expectations that pervaded the society. Where reformers in the 1930s had been concerned with equity —hence the insurance principles that underlay Social Security—the experts of the late 1960s spoke about "entitlements" and "basic minimums." They sought not only equality of opportunity but also equality of result. In this way, as in so many others, the 1960s represented a sharp break with the past.

Much to the surprise of almost everyone, it was not a Democratic reformer, but President Richard Nixon who first tried to put the rough new consensus of experts into practice. He did so not because he was a political liberal, but because he wished to do something about the welfare "mess" and because northern governors were clamoring for federal help in combating the rise in case loads. Their complaints, indeed, again revealed the force of pressure groups in affecting the welfare state in America. Nixon responded by calling in August 1969 for a Family Assistance Plan that would have guaranteed all families with children a minimum of $500 per adult and $300 per child per year, or $1,600 for a two-parent family of four. FAP promised especially to sustain the incentive to work and supplant welfare dependency. A poor family could keep the first $60 per month of income without losing any government aid, and half of income above that, up to specified maximums, at which points benefits would vanish.[18]

Some contemporary commentators applauded the plan. The *Economist* asserted, "It may rank in importance with President Roosevelt's first proposal for a social security system in the mid-1930s." The main benefits of FAP, as supporters saw it, were first, that it would address the needs of children under eighteen, who made up 43 percent of the poverty population, and second, that it would give federal aid to the more than 10 million people in poor working families with children. Because FAP was not limited to families on categorical assistance, it promised to extend to the working poor and their children aid similar to that already received by clients in two-parent AFDC-UP families and female-headed AFDC families. In its goal of including the working poor, FAP was a modified and disguised version of a negative income tax, for families with children only. Some proponents could foresee the day when FAP could be extended as well to individuals and families without children and be administered by the IRS. At that point, the whole complex business of categorical assistance and matching grants might be abolished. [19]

FAP promised especially to help the poorest of the poor—those in the South, where welfare payments had historically lagged far behind those of the North and West. The proposed floor of $1,600 was higher than the AFDC levels in eight states, all southern, so the southern poor stood to gain by far the most from the plan. Some of Nixon's advisers even hoped FAP would slow down the northward migrations that created welfare problems in the North—and cries for relief from northern governors. Though this was a rather forlorn hope—few people migrated in order to go on relief—the goal of assisting the deprived southern masses was widely applauded.

But not everyone welcomed FAP. Few observers anticipated that it would do much for the welfare poor in the North, which supported around 80 percent of welfare clients. Critics added that advisers like Moynihan, partial to children's allowances, had sold Nixon a plan that excluded poor people without children, perhaps 20 percent of the poverty population. While welcoming the effort to reduce state variations in payments, critics pointed out that the legislation did not jettison matching grants used in categorical assistance. FAP might bring payments in southern states up to a minimum level, but it would not reform the wide variations in benefits that existed in the majority of states that paid above that level. [20]

Critics especially deplored the workfare aspects of the bill. In order to sell it to Congress, Nixon included a provision that closely resembled the WIN program passed two years earlier. It required adult recipients (save the aged, disabled, or mothers with preschool children) to accept "suitable" training or work or forfeit their subsidies. (Children would keep theirs.) It was estimated that perhaps 1.1 million people would have to register for such work or training. But Nixon planned to set aside only $600 million for such purposes, which experts expected would provide training for only 150,000 and day care for 450,000 children. No matter: workfare had a timeless political appeal.

Many people also worried about the tone of Nixon's message,

which rang with the conservative rhetoric that lay behind some of the contemporary thrust for income maintenance. Like many Americans, Nixon perceived a welfare crisis, and like Friedman, he lamented the bureaucratic excess and high cost of welfare. "Whether measured by the anguish of the poor themselves," he said, "or by the drastically mounting burden on the taxpayer, the present welfare system has to be judged a colossal failure." FAP, he stated inaccurately, would reform the hated AFDC program and bring to an end the "monster," the "welfare quagmire" that demoralized the nation.[21]

Still, the plan received a generally favorable reception in 1969, especially the attempt to raise levels in the poorest areas of the South. State officials welcomed the financial relief that the program might give to their welfare budgets. Liberals hoped that the workfare proposals were more symbolic than substantive, and most experts applauded the effort to assist the working poor with children. If FAP was not the "extraordinary, discontinuous, forward movement in social policy" that Moynihan said it was, it nonetheless promised to set up a national floor under income for such families. In 1969 that goal seemed to many experts a step in the right direction and a cause worth fighting for.[22]

Three years later the fight was lost. For the major contestants, it proved the most vicious war they would remember. Senator Abraham Ribicoff complained in 1973, "At times I felt like Ahab chasing the whale. This is the most long-running, most arduous single political issue I have ever been connected with in a long political life, and the most disappointing." A scholar described the skirmishing as "ugly, mean affairs marked by special interest group and constituency politics, congressional posturing and moralism, and the sad spectacle of the near-poor pitted against the more poor."[23]

Defeat of the bill stemmed partly from particular circumstances at the time. As the fight developed, neither liberals nor conservatives could work up great enthusiasm for FAP. Some Democratic liberals gagged at the thought of helping the hated President Nixon get credit for "reform" of anything. Other liberals demanded a higher floor and hotly opposed the vague workfare provisions. Conservatives, including the influential Senator Russell Long of Louisiana, balked at spending so much government money and fretted that FAP would magnify the welfare explosion. The Chamber of Commerce took out full-page newspaper ads that proclaimed, "FAP would triple our welfare rolls. Double our welfare costs." Conservatives worried especially about the impact of the plan on the supply of cheap labor. "I can't get anybody to iron my shirts," Long exploded at one point. Nixon himself quickly

tired of the struggle and refused to exert the pressure that might have
helped secure passage of a modified bill in 1971-1972.[24]

Advocates for the welfare poor, notably the National Welfare
Rights Organization headed by George Wiley, proved equally hostile
to the plan. They believed that the existing federal programs, while
bewildering and ungenerous, offered diverse ways of securing aid—
"different strokes for different folks." It was risky, they argued, to
tamper with the welfare apparatus as it stood. The NWRO, representing primarily the ghetto poor, also insisted that the proposal offered
relatively little to the North. The floor there, Wiley said, should be
$5,500, not $1,600. Failing in that quest, which was politically impossible, the NWRO set out to "ZAP FAP." With characteristic hyper-
bole, the NWRO asserted that the plan was an "act of political repres-
sion. Welfare for state and local governments, and illfare for poor
people." It was a "Family Annihilation Plan." In October 1971, the
NWRO's paper, *The Welfare Fighter*, printed a cartoon showing two
tattered charwomen. One asked the other, "What's that FAP mean?"
Her co-worker replied, "Fuck America's Poor."

NWRO speakers objected especially to the workfare provisions.
During congressional hearings in November 1970, black welfare
mothers, who had come to Washington to testify, angrily berated supporters of the plan. "You can't force me to work," one exclaimed to
shouts of applause in the hearing room. "You better give me something better than I'm getting on welfare. I ain't takin' it . . . I heard
that Senator Long said as long as he can't get his laundry done he's
going to put welfare recipients to work . . . Those days are gone forever . . . We ain't gonna clean it!" A few months later Nixon defended
the workfare provisions by explaining that "scrubbing floors or
emptying bedpans" was necessary and useful work. Wiley shot back,
"You don't promote family life by forcing women out of their homes
to empty bedpans. When Richard Nixon is ready to give up his
$200,000 a year salary to scrub floors and empty bedpans in the inter-
est of his family, then we'll take him seriously."[25]

The loud protests of the NWRO marked a historic point in the
annals of American poverty and welfare. Rarely had a group of poor
people spoken so forcefully before Congress. Their presence testified
again to the proliferation of pressure groups, and to the national revolution of expectations, which so often centered on getting money out
of Washington. But their efforts were possibly counterproductive.
Congressmen did not relish the "invasion," as they saw it, of black
welfare clients, and they resented the rhetorical excesses. One contemporary complained bitterly of Wiley's "diverse Mau Mau tactics."
Most important, the stand of the NWRO divided liberals. Some con-

tinued to defend FAP as the only politically salable welfare reform at the time. Others, however, could not stomach the idea of supporting Richard Nixon and opposing the black poor, especially those from their own urban constituencies. It was FAP's misfortune to run the congressional gauntlet just when social turbulence was rending a once biracial liberal coalition.[26]

Americans generally seemed cool to the idea of a national floor under income. "If it had been put to a referendum," one proponent of the plan admitted, "the public would have murdered it."[27] While that conclusion about popular opinion may exaggerate the negative, it corresponded well to polls at the time and merely expressed what was well known: few middle-class Americans wanted to spend very much time or money on a largely "undeserving" poor. Indeed, any attempt to place a floor under income (then and later) clashed with durable beliefs, especially self-help and the work ethic, and with the faith in prevention—in doors, not floors. In questioning FAP, these Americans reaffirmed the familiar, and Congress naturally listened.

These obstacles, serious enough in themselves, were perhaps not so formidable as two other difficulties that plagued efforts at welfare reform throughout the 1970s. One was political: the tendency of Congress, which relied heavily on specialized subcommittees, to approach welfare reform on a piecemeal, program-by-program basis. It was always difficult to promote wholesale changes within such a setting. Moreover, no interest groups with power applied pressure on these committees. Outside of the working poor, who were not well organized, no groups offered it much support, and some considered it a threat to established programs that with fine tuning could be made to work better. Many social workers, for instance, were lukewarm, for FAP might pose a long-range threat to their positions. Neither then nor later did such wholesale welfare reform have a potent constituency.

The other difficulty, technical on the surface, that stood in the way of welfare reform not only in 1969-1972 but throughout the 1970s, was the ever-vexatious problem of work incentives. Hostile conservatives, led by Senator John Williams of Delaware, subjected FAP to close examination that exposed unforeseen consequences of the plan. Williams showed that most of the welfare poor in the North also received vitally important in-kind benefits such as food stamps and Medicaid. If they worked, however, cumulative reductions in benefits meant that they would lose some, if not all, of the value of these in-kind benefits, and they would have to pay income and Social Security taxes. Any plan that hoped to induce the welfare poor to go to work, therefore, had to offer high floors and low marginal taxes on benefits (including in-kind benefits). Nixon's fiscally prudent FAP, like many later proposals, did not appear to do that. On the contrary, Williams and his allies showed that under FAP many poor people would do better to stay on welfare than to work.

Williams, an opponent of the whole concept, had a "solution": improve the incentive to work. One way to do that, perhaps, was to lower the marginal taxes, but that meant vastly escalating the cost of the plan, thus ensuring the wrath of conservatives. Nixon lacked the heart to try that, and the program ultimately floundered. Its defeat marked the end of the most ambitious effort for welfare reform in the forty years since creation of the welfare state in 1935.[28]

Instead, Congress, adhering to its habit of gradual and piecemeal change, settled at the last minute on a much less controversial form of welfare reform. At the same time that it scuttled FAP, in October 1972, it approved passage of the Supplemental Security Income program. SSI, as it was known, established an income floor under benefits paid to the less controversial adult categories of public assistance —the aged, blind, and disabled. These previously separate programs were henceforth administered as one and funded entirely by the federal government. Reflecting the design of FAP, SSI included a complicated formula that permitted recipients to keep all of the first $20 per month of unearned income and the first $65 of earned income, with further earnings taxed at the rate of 50 percent. For most people who were able to qualify, this was a more generous formula than that for recipients of AFDC.[29]

SSI struck two authorities on the subject as a "revolutionary right to cash income" for the aged, blind, and disabled. They were right in the sense that SSI established the precedent of a national floor under income, paid for by federal funds. That floor, $140 per month for aged individuals, $210 for aged couples, was higher than benefits then paid in twenty-six states under the federal-state categorical assistance programs. Mississippi at the time offered old people $75 per month! Moreover, SSI developed eligibility standards more generous than those in many states. It was established that 2.8 million people who had been previously ineligible for aid to the aged, blind, or disabled now received coverage under SSI, almost a 50 percent increase; the program covered 6.2 million people in 1974.[30]

Why did Congress approve SSI and jettison FAP? The reasons were most instructive—and not altogether reassuring to advocates of income floors. It did so first because of the influence of pressure groups, especially the aged and lobbyists working on behalf of fiscal relief for the states. Conservatives, for all their rhetoric about preserving states' rights and cutting federal spending, listened attentively to pressures from such influential constituents. Second, the aged, disabled, and blind were "deserving" in ways that black welfare mothers were not. Third, some advocates of welfare reform settled for SSI because they began to hope that existing programs, though flawed in many respects, might ultimately prove adequate. The food stamp program, then growing rapidly, seemed an especially promising approach to developing a floor under the incomes of all. Fourth, the provisions setting up SSI received little publicity and therefore aroused none of the fears stirred up during the years of debate over FAP. As with food stamps, Medicaid, and increases in Social Security, passage of SSI suggested that the best way of getting social welfare measures through Congress was to sell them as modest, incremental improvements. Grandiloquent talk about welfare "reform" or "floors for all" only raised objections that overcame the best of intentions.[31]

Advocates of floors under income for all therefore were not much gladdened by the way that SSI passed. Clearly, its success in Congress did not demonstrate that there was a broad consensus for the general principle of floors, or even that crusaders for more generous social policies counted for very much politically: demography and organized pressure groups mattered more. Nor did SSI help the masses of working families that had stood to gain from FAP. The 11 million AFDC recipients also had to continue under a system that no one seemed to like but that no one could change.

That did not stop the advocates of a guaranteed minimum income from trying to press their claims in the next few years. But it became apparent, from failure after failure, that instituting dramatic reform such as a negative income tax was difficult if not impossible within the bounds of a welfare system that had grown large and complex over the years. By the 1970s a host of programs—AFDC, SSI, food stamps, Medicaid, Social Security, general assistance—had developed helter skelter and overlapped in ways that few people had foreseen and fewer yet could untangle. And this tangle commanded bureaucratic and political loyalties that were very hard to overcome.[32]

Finding floors, not doors, still remained an important goal of many experts. But it was clear by 1973 that these floors would be very hard to construct.

13
STALEMATE

1976: There is practically no poverty—statistically speaking—in the United States today, and indeed, there has not been for several years. It only remains for our accounting procedures to be modified to record this achievement.

1977: The day of income poverty as a major public issue would appear to be past.

1977: If poverty is defined as a lack of basic needs, it's almost been eliminated.[1]

These three statements, by experts on the subject, repeated what observers had begun to perceive in the early 1970s: the explosive increase in social welfare payments, the quiet expansion of in-kind benefits, and general economic growth had greatly cut back absolute poverty. Some estimates placed the number of poor people in the late 1970s at around 13 million, or as little as 6 percent of the population. The great majority of them were the stubborn residue of unemployables for whom economic growth could do little, but who could presumably be sustained by improvements in the existing welfare system.[2]

The optimism of these observers was in large part justified, if one recalls how extensive welfare had become since the days of Robert Hunter. There *had* been great changes in poverty and welfare, especially after 1940 and again after 1963. No account of the story can fairly ignore these changes over time. The gains, moreover, placed the United States—ever a rich country—in an incredibly wealthy position vis à vis much of the world. In 1980 the World Bank estimated that altogether 780 million people suffered from "absolute poverty"—

199

living in a condition "beneath any reasonable definition of human decency."[3]

Even the much maligned welfare system in America seemed to cope fairly well in the late 1970s. By 1977 federal-state-local social welfare spending amounted to $362 billion (including $95 billion for education and $19 billion for veterans' benefits). That sum compared, in constant 1977 dollars, to $58 billion in 1950, $102 billion in 1960, and $223 billion in 1970. Of this money, $161 billion went to recipients of social insurance ($83 billion for old age insurance, $22 billion for Medicare, $26 billion for retirement of public employees, $15 billion for unemployment insurance, $9 billion for workers' compensation). A worker who retired at sixty-five could receive as much as $660 per month in 1980. Social insurance remained the bulwark of America's income support system.

But public aid, too, was an important part of the overall system. In 1977 the government spent $52 billion for AFDC, Medicaid, general assistance, SSI, food stamps, and work training and public employment under CETA. Together with social insurance, these expenditures approximated 20 percent of the GNP—the highest in American history. (They had been only 7 percent in 1939, 9 percent in 1950, 15 percent in 1970). They made up 60 percent of federal, state, and local spending—again a historic high (27 percent in 1939, 37 percent in 1950, 48 percent in 1970). Private expenditures—pension plans and private health insurance—of course continued to be necessary additions to America's mixed system of social welfare. But these private efforts did relatively little for the poor. And philanthropy for welfare purposes totaled only $3.7 billion in 1977. Ever since 1933 public programs had carried the giant share of the burden of alleviating poverty.[4]

Even AFDC, though its benefits fell in real terms in the late 1970s, did not seem so inadequate as some reformers claimed. Observe how it worked for a mother with three dependent children in Alameda County, California. There, as elsewhere in the United States, she was virtually certain to be aware of the program and to apply for help; the momentous changes of the late 1960s had dispelled much of the old stigma attached to seeking public aid. When she could cope on her own no longer, she went to the local welfare office (the county had seven—no problem finding one), where she picked up a twelve-page form for AFDC and a five-page questionnaire for food stamps. At home she filled them out, answering simple questions mainly about her sources of income. The next day she brought to the welfare office her birth certificate, driver's license, and identification for family members. Welfare officials interviewed her, explained her obligation to report any changes in her status, and advised her of her legal rights.

The waiting period was fifteen days, although emergencies could be processed more quickly. During that time the office checked out her answers and visited her home.

The woman qualified if her income did not exceed the county's needs standard of $420 month for a family of four and if she did not have too many assets. Limits for these were $1,500 for a car, $1,000 for personal property, and $20,000 for real estate. The vast majority of applicants easily met these standards. Having qualified, she then got her first biweekly check for $174. Any outside earned income fell under the still operative provisions of WIN: the first $30 per month was hers to keep, the rest was "taxed" at 67 percent. Unearned income (such as child support) was subtracted from the welfare check. The woman was authorized to use food stamps worth $166 per month, for which she paid $95. She got a Medicaid card. Her total from AFDC and stamps, but excluding Medicaid and outside income, was roughly the needs standard of $420 per month, or $5,040 per year. The value including Medicaid obviously varied according to the health of her family but could easily add greatly to her benefits.

While on welfare she did not find the bureaucracy especially paternalistic or intrusive. If all her children were older than six, she was required by the Talmadge amendment of 1971 to register at a state employment office for job training and placement. But for more than 90 percent of such women, that visit was a formality: thanks to poor funding for day care and for training, less than 10 percent of AFDC mothers ever entered the program. Otherwise she only had to fill out a two-page form once a month apprising the authorities of her economic situation and to reapply fully after one year on the rolls. Two-parent families getting aid in the twenty-five-odd states that participated in AFDC-UP did much the same, save that the man of the family was required to register for WIN regardless of the age of his children. If he worked more than one hundred hours a month, he lost his (but not his family's) benefits. All families, whether one or two parent, did not have to fear further visits to their homes. Unless they asked for special services or were investigated for fraud, they ordinarily had very little contact with social workers after their first application.

Whether this system encouraged "long-term welfare dependency" still depended on one's definition of long-term. But no evidence supported the tired notion that AFDC was creating a "welfare class" in the late 1970s. Rather, AFDC primarily served families that suffered from acute lack of income at certain stages in their life. Of the 2.7 million women on welfare in a given year, 20 percent—around 540,000—stayed on the rolls for nine straight years and got at least half of their income from public aid. These people, about one quarter of one percent of the population, were the closest to being a welfare class. More than 90 percent of all women who ever accepted welfare in the late 1960s and 1970s were in need for much shorter periods of time and supplemented their earnings from work or other sources. The average time on the rolls was forty-four months; the average for AFDC-UP families was twelve months. Obviously, the system abetted dependency in the narrow sense that these families stayed on welfare if they had no other way to survive. But they did not connive to get on AFDC or cling to it if they could better their conditions in other ways. Studies found that "welfare chiseling" was minimal—most of the ineligibles on welfare were there because of poor administration, not fraud.[5]

With such cheery statistics on income and a functioning system of public assistance, it was not surprising that poverty and welfare were less often in the headlines after the early 1970s. Even the "welfare crisis," once the growth in the rolls leveled off around 1973, seemed irritating but tolerable. One poll in 1976 asked people to list thirty-one national issues in order of importance; "reducing poverty" ranked fifteenth. Other polls revealed majority support for helping people in need, but also the same implacable hostility to the "undeserving" poor that had persisted in the United States (and Europe) since the seventeenth century. A *New York Times*-CBS survey in 1977 found that 54 percent of Americans thought "most people who receive money from welfare could get along without it if they tried." Only 31 percent disagreed. A total of 58 percent disapproved of "most Government-sponsored welfare programs." Half of those responding opposed a guaranteed annual income, with 44 percent in favor.

Straws in the wind perhaps revealed more than the ever-ambiguous polls. One such straw was an ad that ran regularly in the *New Republic*. Appealing to what were apparently widespread feelings, it urged readers to buy the Welfare Game: "An exciting new board game that is based on more than twenty actual government programs! Bankrupt the U.S. Treasury and the taxpayers and you'll earn the right to live off welfare forever. A riotous parody on 'The Welfare System.' "[6] Another straw was the popularity among some conservatives of the board game called Public Assistance. Invented by two libertarians in 1980, it stood Monopoly on its head. Players gained when they landed on squares that gave them illegitimate children and lost when they drew a "working person's burden" card. One such card read, "Your son is beat up by ethnic gang while being bused across town to school. Pay hospital bill, $200." Health and Human Services Secretary Patricia Roberts Harris branded the game "racist" and "sexist," but the inventors replied, "We didn't invent this game, government liberals did. We just put it in a box." In 1980, 10,000 copies of the game sold quickly; another 50,000 were quickly readied for sale.[7]

Breasting this tide of criticism, reformers persisted in trying to make the existing system more equitable, adequate, and efficient. Their litany of criticisms was as familiar as it was valid: half of the states did not offer AFDC-UP or give Medicaid to the "medically indigent"—people who were poor but did not automatically qualify for the program. Urban liberals reiterated that state-by-state variations in benefits grew ever larger—from $3,071 per year in AFDC and food stamps for a family of four in Mississippi to $7,354 in New York in 1978. (Alameda County's poor were comparatively well off.) These critics argued above all that social welfare programs were inadequate. Almost 20 percent of all poor people (mostly in families headed by a male under sixty-five) still got no transfer payments in 1979; 15 percent of workers were still ineligible for coverage under unemployment compensation. Poverty was more than ever concentrated among the hard-to-reach; two-thirds of the poor were in families headed by women, old people, and the disabled. And relative poverty remained as troubling a problem as in the late 1960s.[8]

Advocates of better welfare pointed to demographic and economic forces that appeared to portend some kind of doom. Chief among these forces was the growth in broken families, among which both the incidence of poverty and the numbers of needy were highest. The relatively higher birthrate among blacks also promised economic trouble in the future. The unemployment rate among teen-aged blacks, 1.3 times that of whites in 1950, jumped to 2.6 times that of whites by 1979. Observers worried also about the mass migrations of poor Latin Americans into the South and to the cities, which had to struggle to pay their welfare bills. And they were concerned about the great increases in the labor force caused by women and teenagers seeking jobs. That competition for employment existed at a time when other economic problems, including energy shortages and troubled industries like steel and autos, were helping to drive the level of unemployment higher after each recession.

Some reformers prescribed more federal medicine to cure such economic maladies. In October 1980 the National Advisory Council on Economic Opportunity, whose task it was to advise the Community Services Administration on issues surrounding poverty policy, reported to President Carter that a "politics of negativism," if unchecked, would soon abandon millions to destitution. Ignoring inkind payments, it said that 25 million Americans lived in families with incomes below the poverty line ($7,450 for nonfarm families of four), and another 40 million were near-poor. Only government transfer payments, which had accounted for "virtually all of the reduction of poverty since the mid-1960s" (11 million people), could turn the tide— economic developments in the private sector had done practically nothing since 1965. The council professed to be appalled by the contemporary "way of life that worships wealth and power" and by the "rise of a national pattern of brutal social inequality." It called for a "political debate—one that goes far beyond partisan politics—on how we can create an ethic of fairness and compassion in America."[9]

To activists, no development appeared more threatening than the economic deterioration of central cities in the North. This deterioration made very clear the major demographic change in poverty since World War II: its migration from country to city. A study in 1980, by President Carter's National Urban Policy group, revealed that during the 1970s real income rose in rural regions, suburbs, and small cities but dropped sharply in the cores of large metropolitan areas. There the incidence of poverty actually increased—in New York City from 14.6 percent in 1969 to 18.2 percent in 1978. Blacks were hardest hit. Alarmed, the experts who compiled the report recommended cost-of-living allowances to poor people in central cities and urged policies to help such people migrate to areas of economic expansion.

Two months later the Commission for a National Agenda for the 1980s also recommended helping migrants. "Industrial cities such as Boston, Cleveland, and Detroit," it concluded, "stand as brick-and-mortar snapshots of a bygone era." Explicitly rejecting an incremental approach, it urged a guaranteed "minimum security income" set initially at three-fourths of the official poverty line, with a 50 percent tax on earnings; the cost of such a negative income tax program was estimated at $15 to $20 billion per year. The commission also called for policies to assist "underemployed and displaced workers who wish to migrate to locations of long-term economic growth." This policy, if implemented, would drastically have reversed the decades-old efforts to give aid to the urban poor where they lived and to resist supplying relief to people who moved.[10]

Amid all these economic difficulties, bewildered public officials were buffeted by demands from all quarters. Looking for ways to economize, they tried, as in the past, to cut back on welfare costs— these, at least, might not arouse any potent interest groups. So it was that the rate of increase in public spending against poverty began to slip. While federal expenditures for all kinds of social welfare—including health, education, and Social Security—continued to climb as a percentage of GNP, the percentage spent for welfare alone dropped a bit after 1973.

Some experts sought to change what appeared to be an overemphasis on floors rather than doors. Although they granted the limits of prevention strategies, they wondered, like Hopkins and other New Dealers in the 1930s, if it made much sense in the long run merely to hand out income. Many social workers continued to believe that their expertise in offering services did more to help the poor than did "throwing money at problems." Henry Aaron, an authoritative writer on the subject, added in 1978 that federal funds to help the poor rose in the mid-1970s but that "efforts to transform the poor by education or training them did not increase." Instead, he wrote, "Aid to the poor was conveyed increasingly through transfers in kind that alleviated the symptoms of poverty but did not deal with its causes." How to fight those causes remained in 1980 about as nettlesome a dilemma as ever.[11]

Other pessimistic writers doubted if public policy could ever "deal with causes" in the fundamental sense of taking the "poverty out of people." They rejected the notion that welfare sustained or created a culture of poverty—a view that enlisted few serious scholars in the 1970s. But after witnessing so many false starts in the long struggle against poverty and after living through the resurgence of ethnic and racial consciousness in the 1960s, they were more sensitive to the ways in which various groups clung to inherited cultural patterns. Some poor Americans, in short, were different from the middle classes in ways that transcended income. It was therefore uncertain whether changes in their income could transform their values or those of their children. These writers had abandoned much of their progressive grandparents' faith in prevention. They were highly skeptical of the ability of government to change people.

Advocates of welfare reform were therefore not so sure of themselves after 1972 as they had been a few years earlier. While many in HEW and elsewhere continued to call for negative income tax schemes, other experts favored a more incremental fine-tuning of the existing system. They demanded especially extension of AFDC-UP to all states and federal subsidization of minimum levels of welfare near the poverty line. They urged the federal government to assume the costs of general assistance and Congress to repeal the rule denying benefits to welfare fathers who worked more than one hundred hours a month. Although they discounted the popular cries about fraud in the system, these experts agreed that administration of welfare was sloppy. (A study by HEW found an error rate of 10 percent in determining eligibility in 1973). The net effect of these recommended reforms would have been to increase the welfare bill; proponents gladly admitted that "throwing money at problems" was humane as well as effective. But they pointed out that incremental changes often did not require the highly politicized debate that always stymied more grandiose efforts for comprehensive reform. If stimulated further by short-run programs of public employment targeted mainly at unemployed young people, by wage supplements, and by imaginative federal programs to accelerate economic growth, such incremental changes promised—these writers believed—to approach the age-old goal of abolishing destitution in America.[12]

This trend toward incremental reform, although dominant among liberals as of 1980, did not convert all writers on poverty. Other liberals demanded larger reforms, including national health insurance, housing allowances, steeply progressive income taxes, increased funding for day care, and higher mandated minimum wage levels. Advocates on the right, like Milton Friedman, wanted to sweep the whole welfare "mess" into the ashcan and rely on negative income taxes. Other conservatives insisted, more self-assuredly than at any time since the 1950s, that welfare should aid only those unable to help themselves, that all others must be forced to work, that guaranteed income programs discouraged work and broke up marriages, that welfare fraud required tough responses. For such conservatives, the bottom line still was to cut costs and reduce welfare dependency.[13]

The Carter administration struggled to find an approach that could accommodate liberals and mollify conservatives. It responded in 1977 by proposing a two-track system, one for poor people able to work, including welfare mothers with children over fourteen, the second for those who could not work. In general, this was an old distinction—the New Deal, in advocating separate programs for employables and unemployables, had already tried to institutionalize it. In Carter's plan, those who could work were to receive wage supplements, federal help in finding employment, or one of 1.4 million public jobs to be created at slightly more than the minimum wage. People in this category who refused to work would get no welfare, although their children would. For the second group Carter offered streamlining of the existing bureaucracy. SSI, AFDC, state-local general assistance, and food stamps were to be combined into one program with one eligibility standard. All poor people (except those who refused to work) were to be given a floor under income of $4,200 (for a family of four) and were to have only half of earnings subtracted from their benefits. That marginal tax meant that many families of four earning up to $8,400 a year would receive some federal assistance.[14]

To no one's surprise, Carter's proposals ran into the same kind of opposition that had defeated the similar Family Assistance Plan in 1972. Conservatives doubted that the government could create efficiently 1.4 million public service jobs or that it could find enough good workers to fill them. They railed at the cost, which they said would add $18 to $20 billion (not the $2.8 billion that Carter claimed) to the existing welfare budget. Liberals complained that the minimum floor was too low and that public service workers should get more than the inadequate minimum wage. They objected especially to the linking of work and welfare, which they found reminiscent of the workfare proposals of WIN and FAP.

Many commentators accepted the broad goals of the plan to establish a national floor and to simplify welfare administration. Although worried about classifying the disabled, they tended also to favor the attempt to divide the needy into the employable and unemployable poor—an advance, they thought, over historic categories of "deserving" and "undeserving." But they raised two major doubts. The first was the old concern about work incentives. The poor who worked, they said, faced not only a 50 percent tax on income but also state and federal taxes. These, along with the fear of losing in-kind benefits like Medicaid, might discourage people from leaving welfare and going to work. The second doubt was perhaps more fundamental. By the late 1970s even activists began to wonder if wholesale "welfare reform" was either necessary or wise. Having lived through the utopian 1960s, they were leery of such grand efforts. Welfare reform on that scale might create more unforeseen inequities and loopholes than it would stop. These doubters, the incrementalists, believed that modest changes were politically more realistic and perhaps as beneficial as fundamental revision of a system that was far too complicated and bureaucratically entrenched to replace. (Indeed, sixty congressional committees and subcommittees considered income maintenance plans).

For all these reasons, Carter's welfare program bogged down in Congress. In 1979 the House finally passed a much diluted version that set a floor under AFDC payments, which was to be 65 percent of the poverty line by 1981. As in Nixon's FAP, that floor would have helped poor people mainly in the southern states. The plan also increased federal aid to northern states and mandated AFDC-UP throughout the country. But this modest effort stalled in the Senate, as did proposals for public service jobs. In 1980 thoroughgoing welfare reform, let alone a war on poverty or a floor under income, failed to pass.[15]

By that time, advocates of help for the poor worried deeply about inflation. That problem did not terrify all the needy: the benefits received by the aged, blind, or disabled on SSI and by retirees and survivors on Social Security were indexed to keep pace with the cost of living. But this was not the case for AFDC and general assistance clients;

states and localities in the economically shaky 1970s tried to cut back wherever they could on welfare costs.

The *New York Times* showed what inflation meant to Dorothy Johnson, the fictitious name it gave to a welfare mother of three living in Connecticut. In March 1980 she was entitled to a monthly AFDC grant of $445.92 ($5,301 per year). This was 44 percent higher than in 1972 and very high by national standards. But in those eight years the cost of living had risen by 76 percent. So Mrs. Johnson took a part-time job at the minimum wage that paid $300 a month. Under the provisions of WIN, the first $30 was hers to keep. But the rest, roughly $270, was "taxable" at 67 percent, resulting in the subtraction of $180 from her monthly grant of $445.92. That left her with a subsidy of around $265, plus the $300 from the job, plus $90 in food stamps, for a total of around $665 a month. Her income was $7,860 a year, slightly higher than the poverty line for an urban family of four.[16]

That amount, though $10,000 less than the median family income, seemed more than adequate to many Americans, who remembered earning much less in their youth. But expectations had exploded in the 1960s, and Mrs. Johnson found the quality of her life galling indeed. To manage, she spent all of her food stamp money the first week and used what she could spare from AFDC on food for the rest of the month. Near the end of the month, she had three packages of frozen vegetables and a tray of ice cubes left in her refrigerator. New clothes were a luxury. "The only time I buy clothes," she said, "is September, when school starts. I put them on layaway over the summer." She added, "Last year the kids needed shoes badly, and the state didn't do nothing about it, so I took a little job." That wore her out. "Half the time, I'd be shot. But I'd explain to the kids that's the only way we could get by."

The *New York Times* implied that the Mrs. Johnsons of this world deserved more help, but some readers surely disagreed with the newspaper's liberal intent. As the article pointed out, many Americans thought people like Mrs. Johnson received more than they deserved. Reflecting a general lack of concern about poverty, they argued that price indexes exaggerated inflation and that few poor people had to spend much for two of the fastest rising items: medical care and home mortgages. With Medicaid and food stamps added to basic grants, these critics added, an AFDC mother of four received more than the $124 a week earned by workers employed forty hours a week at the $3.10 per hour minimum wage. Women like Mrs. Johnson may have been poor relatively speaking, but with additional aid from divorced husbands and relatives—much of it unreported—they were able to get by. For all their privations many "welfare mothers" had standards of living that would have made middle-income Americans in 1900 or 1929 wildly jealous.

This lack of popular concern for women like Mrs. Johnson did not much surprise poor people. Inhospitable opinions about the poor, after all, were among the most durable features of America's experience with poverty and welfare since 1900. The persistence of such views testified to the power of historically important attitudes, among them the work ethic, amid the otherwise dramatic socioeconomic changes since the late nineteenth century. In the post-Malthusian world of 1980, middle-class Americans continued to denigrate many of the poor and to hope that the need for welfare might soon wither away. On this level of popular opinion, the "social philosophy" of Americans had not changed much in eighty years.

Popular coolness toward the poor did not necessarily signify much, moreover, about the prospects for public policy in the 1980s. Changes in welfare programs—in the government's social philosophy—had historically depended less on general attitudes toward the poor than on other social, economic, and political realities. Depression had promoted the welfare state in the 1930s. Demographic change, the nationalization of politics, the bureaucratic growth of existing programs, and the power of organized pressure groups had prompted the astonishing progress of the late 1960s and early 1970s. Catastrophes aside, these realities could be expected to sustain the American welfare state, which for all its limitations had grown enormously since 1930, although popular attitudes toward the poor changed very little.

Still, popular perceptions about poverty and welfare mirrored in part people's expectations of the economy. The stagflation of the late 1970s propped up attitudes that made dramatic welfare reform unlikely in the early 1980s. For the major "discoveries" of poverty in America had occurred either in times of great depression, as in the 1930s, or in boom times that generated great confidence about the future—times like the progressive era or the early 1960s. During the economically uncertain 1970s that all-important confidence was lacking. So were potent influence groups anxious to do battle for the poor. Because absolute poverty seemed a thing of the past, because the Mrs. Johnsons were coping, it was easy for middle-class Americans to put the poor out of sight. In 1980 no "rediscovery" of poverty seemed in sight.[17]

14

REGRESSION
IN THE EARLY 1980s

From many perspectives, the world of poverty and welfare seemed much the same in the early and mid-1980s as it had been five or ten years earlier. The welfare system revealed the same limitations and anomalies as it had for decades. The AFDC program still lacked a national minimum benefit, and state-by-state variations in the size of payments continued to be large. In many states the benefits remained far below most definitions of "need" and below the official federal poverty line. AFDC benefits, which were not indexed for inflation, fell nationally by almost one-third in real terms between 1976 and 1985. Half the states still refused to commit themselves to the AFDC-UP program, which enabled poor, two-parent families in which both parents were unemployed to qualify for benefits. These state-by-state variations testified to the enduring power of federalism in American life and more specifically to the continuing refusal of most of the poorer states (mainly in the South) to spend more public tax dollars for welfare expenses.

These problems were galling to liberals. But they were by no means the only matters reformers complained about. Recognizing that cash assistance constituted a decreasing part of the overall welfare effort, liberals lamented that appropriations for food stamp payments—which were available not only to AFDC families but also to childless poor people and to the working poor—were being cut back. These reformers also called for changes in the Medicaid program so that it would include all poor families with children. This fine tuning would increase work incentives for AFDC families by permitting them to keep Medicaid even after becoming ineligible for AFDC benefits. The importance of these goals in the liberal agenda of the 1980s revealed the great role of in-kind benefits, especially Medicaid, in the overall structure of American public assistance. In-kind benefits constituted more than three-fourths of total public spending on public assistance by 1984.

Advocates of improving the lot of the poor worried especially about the uncertain economy of the early 1980s. The recession that began in the late 1970s grew serious and sharp between 1980 and 1982, leaving 10 percent of the work force unemployed. High interest rates imposed by the Federal Reserve system further impeded economic growth. Although the economy surged upward again after that, the social damage was severe and lasting. The number of people defined as poor by the government's official poverty line increased from around 11 percent of the population in 1979 to more than 15 percent in 1983. This was the highest percentage since 1966-67. Despite a rebound of the economy thereafter, the number of poor was still at 14.4 percent in 1984. The result was a poverty population of between 33.7 and 35.5 million Americans at any given time, which was 9 to 10 million more people than in 1979.[1]

These statistics continued to be based on the government's official definition of the poverty line, which in 1985 was more than $10,600 for a family of four. This amount appeared to mark a striking increase over the $3,000 deemed necessary for such a family in the early 1960s, the starting point for such definitions. But the increase merely reflected the rising cost of living in those years — the poverty line did not really rise. And families at or below the line were continuing to slip farther away from the middle-class mainstream. The median family income by 1984 was $26,430. Liberals complained bitterly that relative poverty, which measured the distance from the poverty line to the median income line, grew in the 1980s, thus exposing the large gulf separating the poor from the rest of American society.[2] They added that historically deprived groups continued to experience widespread poverty: 33.8 percent of blacks and 28.4 percent of Hispanics were poor in 1984, compared to 11.5 percent of whites.

To many liberals the villain of the piece was Ronald Reagan. Their accusations were in some ways unfair, for the Carter administration, facing a frightening inflationary spiral as well as rising budgetary deficits, in 1978 had begun trying to stem the large increases in social welfare spending that had developed during the previous decade. Poverty increased to 13 percent by the time Reagan entered the White House. Reagan was far too shrewd a politician to attempt a wholesale disman-tling of the welfare state, especially the all-important insurance programs of Social Security and Medicare. Federal expenditures for social insurance (much of which went to people who were not poor) continued to grow during the Reagan years, thereby offsetting cuts in means-tested welfare programs and maintaining overall social spending at around 11 percent of GNP.

But critics were correct in perceiving the president as no friend of a generous public assistance state. He pared expenditures for food stamps, unemployment insurance, child nutrition, vocational education, the Job Corps, and AFDC, and he terminated public service employment. In general, his administration rejected the approach of liberal policymakers in the 1960s and 1970s, including the goal of a guaranteed minimum income. His proposed cuts in social programs were roughly twice as large as those ultimately accepted by Congress. As many liberals pointed out, the goal of social policy in the Johnson (and even the Nixon) years had started with the question, "How can we help the poor?" Reagan, in contrast, tended to ask, "How can we cut costs, and how can we get people to work?"

One sign of Reagan's determined conservatism was his effort to reduce federal disability benefits. This tightening had begun during the Carter years, but it accelerated under Reagan. By 1984 some 500,000 people had lost disability benefits following governmental decisions that they were well enough to work. Lawyers helped some of these people fight the decisions in the courts, and by 1985 they had scored some notable victories. Federal officials retreated, and many of the disabled again began receiving their benefits.[3] The struggle revealed anew the important role of the federal judiciary, which since the 1960s had frequently come to the rescue of the poor and the powerless.

Reagan's central thrust against liberal welfare began early in his administration and culminated in the Omnibus Budget Reconciliation Act of 1981. OBRA, as it became known, broke decisively with liberal efforts in the 1970s to move closer to the goal of a negative income tax. Instead, OBRA took aim at those AFDC recipients—a small minority of the total—who had substantial earnings. Its most important title eliminated the so-called thirty plus a third rule by which welfare recipients (after four months of consecutive employment) had been able to keep the first $30 per month of earnings as well as one-third of the rest, without having these amounts subtracted from their benefits. Other parts of the legislation cut monthly allowable deductions for work-related expenses and child care expenditures. Somewhat surprisingly, OBRA did not do much damage to the work incentives of the people affected, but it did drive some recipients deeper into need and made it harder for other poor families to get on AFDC in the first place. Estimates were that in two years OBRA increased poverty by roughly 2 percent—a significant figure. The savings by 1983 totaled some $1.1 billion in federal and state expenditures for public assistance. Approximately 408,000 families had by then lost eligibility; 300,000 lost some benefits.[4]

Liberals who opposed these conservative policies did not receive much of a hearing in the early 1980s. Indeed, Reagan's political popularity carried him to a smashing triumph in his quest for reelection in 1984. His continuing political strength derived from many sources, including his attractive personality and his tough-minded foreign policy. It derived also from his ability to tap a growing popular resentment of higher taxes (which increased from 26.5 percent to 30.7 percent of the Gross Domestic Product between 1965 and 1980).[5] Reagan's appeal rested ultimately on his celebration of time-honored American values – the work ethic, rugged individualism, and hostility to public "handouts." To him, as to many who supported him, poverty was un-American, welfare wasteful and counterproductive. His "social philosophy," like that of many Americans throughout the twentieth century, was profoundly hostile to all but the "deserving" poor.

Reagan's conservative views, moreover, seemed part of a broader trend that affected many Western nations in the early 1980s. Some of the most advanced social democratic states, such as those in Scandinavia, took stock of their generous programs and decided either to trim them back or to stop their spread. Work incentives, it seemed, were suffering as a result of expensive social programs. In England the conservative Margaret Thatcher became prime minister in 1979. Though she did not request large cuts in social programs, she regularly denounced what she considered the excesses of the welfare state – or "nanny state," as some of her supporters derisively called it. "To be blunt," her government said, "the British social security system has lost its way."[6]

At home Reagan's social philosophy received impressive backing from several articulate and aggressive neoconservatives. Chief among them by mid-decade was Charles Murray, whose book *Losing Ground* (1984) attracted considerable attention. Like many others of his persuasion, Murray argued vigorously that the social programs of the 1960s had long since become not only fruitless but also counterproductive. He insisted that handouts had demoralized the urban ghettos, leading young blacks to cling to welfare rather than work for a living. His view of these people reflected an ironic departure from nineteenth-century visions of the downtrodden in the slums. Then conservatives had often depicted slum dwellers as intemperate, shiftless, and immoral. To Murray these poor people were crassly rational calculators of their own self-interest: the benefits of welfare, Murray thought, induced them to quit work and live off the public trough.[7]

What were liberals to do in this conservative milieu? Many came close to despair or hoped wistfully for some political sea change in the presidential election of 1988. Liberalism, indeed, remained on the defensive during this period and seemed to have few fresh ideas — or at least few that captured the imagination of most Americans.

Some experts, however, were not quite so pessimistic. Many observed that the welfare state, for all its anomalies, nevertheless continued to make a very great difference in the lives of millions of Americans. As in the 1970s, the combined effect of social insurance (huge) and welfare (much smaller) greatly reduced the pretransfer poverty population. Most of the much-maligned social programs of the 1960s remained on the books, and some of them — notably food stamps, Medicaid, and Medicare — rescued millions from want. Old OEO ideas, such as Head Start, were shown to have some beneficial impact on the education and training of the needy.[8] Medicare and Social Security brought poverty among the elderly to 12.4 percent in 1984, two percentage points below the poverty rate of the entire population. Medicaid, though widely criticized as wasteful and costly, at last gave many poor people ready access to medical care. Prior to passage of this program, the middle classes saw doctors more frequently than did the poor, even though the poor needed more care. By the early 1980s the poor were seeing doctors more often than the middle classes. The large decrease in mortality rates after the 1950s may have followed from this fundamentally important advance. Cassandras like Murray, it was clear, underestimated the beneficial impact of certain of the Great Society programs.[9]

A few liberals actually ventured optimistic predictions. One was Eugene Smolensky, a scholar at the OEO-inspired Institute for Research on Poverty at the University of Wisconsin. Smolensky asked, "Is a golden age in poverty policy right around the corner?" and concluded that it might be, perhaps. The reason was demographic, specifically the end of the baby boom in the 1960s. By the late 1980s, he argued, the number of new entrants into the job market was likely to be half what it had been in the late 1970s — when President Carter's job creation initiatives foundered (in part) because of political reaction against the anticipated cost of trying to place millions of new, young workers on the government payroll. It would be comparatively inexpensive, Smolensky maintained, for a liberal government in the late 1980s to administer public employment and job training programs.

Was such a policy change likely, especially with the astronomically large federal budget deficits that all but stifled talk of increases in social spending in the early and mid-1980s? Most liberals in the early 1980s recognized that these deficits — seemingly anomalous in a "conservative" administration — effectively killed enactment of national health insurance, which many reformers in 1979-80 had assumed was next on the social policy agenda. Few liberals, therefore, had great expectations in the early 1980s. Still, demographic changes had often had more to do with shaping policy possibilities than had attitudes of the people or social philosophies of presidents. In any event, Smolensky and others were surely correct in calling attention to the continuing successes of many welfare programs and to the possibility of incremental changes in policy by the late 1980s.[10]

Liberals, finally, could perhaps derive some grim satisfaction from the likelihood that in the long run the combined impact of the recession and of Reagan's policies might prompt a reformist reaction. For the startling increase in the numbers of poor people naturally stimulated new debate over poverty in the early 1980s. Though conservatives dominated these debates, they could not claim that the 9 to 10 million new poor people in the 1980s were "undeserving." On the contrary, most of these needy Americans were white, working-class citizens living in male-headed households. Many, indeed, worked regularly, but at low-paying jobs that failed to rescue them from need: full-time employment at the minimum wage left family heads well below the poverty line. When this kind of destitution had developed on a large scale before, in the 1930s, the result had been agitation for creation of a welfare state. Should this situation develop again, as trends before 1984 appeared to suggest, it could begin to afflict not only blue-collar workers but also segments of the middle classes. In such circumstances the political pressure for expansion of the welfare state might prove irresistible.

One of the most hotly debated aspects of poverty in the 1980s, however, was neither the recession nor Reagan's policies. Rather, it was the mounting, indeed sometimes near-hysterical, alarm over the specter of what many contemporaries termed an "underclass." More than worries over the statistical increase in the numbers of poor people, this concern brought poverty back to the front pages, where it had not been since the 1960s. To many Americans, the underclass — an unflattering euphemism for the most deprived black masses in the ghetto — threatened to undermine all that was good and promising in national life. As one frightened liberal exclaimed in 1985, "An American version of a *lumpenproletariat* (the so-called underclass), without work and without hope, existing at the margins of society, could bring down the great cities, sap resources and strength from the entire society and, lacking the usual means to survive, prey upon those who possess them."[11]

One cannot pinpoint the year when these concerns about the underclass began to receive widespread expression. Indeed, neither the term, which had been used by Gunnar Myrdal and others in the 1940s, nor the concern, which had captured writers as diverse as Jacob Riis in the 1890s and Daniel Moynihan in the 1960s, was new to the 1980s. Gloomy exponents of the "culture of poverty" school had regularly assumed that black ghetto dwellers were a more or less permanent, intergenerational lower class that social policy was helpless to improve. The views of such observers had regularly clashed with more dominant opinions — that either the market or social policy (or some combination of both) could and did help virtually all poor people, given enough time and effort and economic growth.

But if talk about an underclass was not new in the 1980s, it clearly struck a more sensitive nerve. And it was expressed with a special sense of urgency. Mitchell Sviridoff, vice-president of the Ford Foundation, lamented,

> There is a segment of the nation's poor, small and sometimes invisible, that does not seem to be touched by. . .any traditional sort of outreach. For all our best efforts, this sector of the population is just about where we found them twenty years ago. . .Their isolation and concentration has only exacerbated the frustration and hopelessness of their life and made their condition the most dangerous and intractable problem facing the cities in which they live. Numerically this group is relatively small, but it is extraordinarily destructive, and its behavior reflects intense anger, with consequences on a scale that mocks its size. [12]

Senator Edward Kennedy agreed, and with comparable alarm. Speaking to a convention of the NAACP, he warned of

> the great unmentioned problem of America today — the growth, rapid and insidious, of a group in our midst, perhaps more dangerous, more bereft of hope, more difficult to confront, than any for which our history has prepared us. It is a group that threatens to become what America has never known — a permanent underclass in our society. [13]

These statements were made in 1979 and 1978, respectively — years that featured great economic uncertainty in the United States. Worries about the economy, combined with continuing skepticism — not to say cynicism — about the "failures" of liberal welfare policy in the 1960s, seemed to turn people's attention to the grimmer aspects of society. Perhaps for these reasons, this period also produced a crescendo of warnings about the "underclass." In 1981 the journalist Kenneth Auletta wrote a much-noticed series of articles on the subject in the *New Yorker* magazine, a collection published later as a book entitled *The Underclass*. Auletta, too, thought the situation of ghetto blacks was both frightful and frightening. His focus was on some 18,000 young people who had enrolled through 1980 in a New York City "supported-work" program. These people fell into four groups: welfare mothers, ex-criminal offenders, regular heroin users, and school dropouts. The incomes of almost all (save a few hustlers) were far below the poverty level; 30 percent had never worked, three-quarters had not finished high school, and 90 percent were black or Hispanic. The average mother in the group had been on welfare more than eight years; the ex-offenders had been arrested an average of nine times. This was an angry, unruly substratum of a poverty-stricken ghetto population. To Auletta, as well as to many reviewers, the underclass way of life was poisoning American cities in the 1980s.

Auletta was careful to distinguish these people from the general poverty population. The underclass, he said, included these groups, as well as miscellaneous others, such as the long-term unemployed, young people who had simply dropped out of sight, bag ladies, and "discouraged workers" who had given up on the job market. Altogether, he guessed, there were some 9 million of these people—about 4 percent of the total population, and at least 25 percent of the total poverty population of approximately 35 million. Most of the nation's needy were not members of this underclass; rather, they were, as always, people who had been poor for a year or two or less, and who fell below the poverty line because they lost their jobs, got sick, were divorced or widowed, or could not earn enough to support their families. Those in the underclass, by contrast, were poor for long stretches of time (Auletta's rule of thumb was five or more years out of the previous seven).

If the underclass was not numerous, it was, alarmists thought, growing in size. Whether this assertion was true, however, was in fact impossible to prove: no useful historical statistics existed to define the rather fuzzy concept of the underclass. Indeed, to read Jacob Riis on slums in the 1890s, one might well surmise that the percentage of very poor New Yorkers (even by the harsh standards of that day) was considerably higher then than at any later time in American history. The intergenerational poverty and degradation that afflicted the rural South well into the twentieth century represented a mass destitution of almost epic proportions in the American context. And Michael Harrington (among many) had pointed in the 1960s to the existence of millions of "new" poor, whose characteristics resembled those of the underclass in the 1980s. The alarm of Auletta and others was directed at a real problem, but it also marked the latest of periodic American expressions of cultural crisis—expressions stemming in part from the apparently intractable racial and cultural divisions that characterized the society.

The alarmists of the 1980s did not focus primarily on numbers; they concentrated, rather, on two aspects of lower-class ghetto life: crime and broken families. Sviridoff had said the underclass was "extraordinarily destructive," Kennedy that it was "dangerous." Many other writers recited statistics on crime in American cities. While these statistics were subject to varying interpretations, few readers doubted the essence of the numbers: violent crime—rape, murder, robbery, assault—was increasing in the United States; it was centered in ghetto areas and involved ghetto dwellers as both victims and offenders; it was a staggeringly more serious problem in the United States than in any other part of the urban, industrialized world. Criminals and hustlers, indeed, seemed to dominate many aspects of ghetto life in American cities.

Concern over crime in the ghettos, great though it was, seemed relatively controlled compared to the other big fear about the underclass in the 1980s: the deterioration of family life. This fear focused on the huge growth in the percentage of children growing up in households headed by unmarried women, especially in the ghettos. The problems of these families, wrote Eleanor Holmes Norton, who had been chairwoman of the Equal Employment Opportunity Commission during the Carter administration, "must be regarded as a natural catastrophe in our midst—a threat to the future of black people without equal."[14] Pierre deVise, a Roosevelt University urbanologist, added, "This disintegration is the most important and alarming demographic development in our time."[15]

Equally distressed cries arose from many other writers in the 1980s, including Murray, who blamed Great Society programs for making AFDC too attractive and for seducing young blacks into welfare. Moynihan was another. In the Godkin Lectures given at Harvard University in April 1985, Moynihan, by then a senator from New York, more carefully reiterated the warnings he had first uttered publicly twenty years earlier in his "Report on the Negro Family." At that time his statements had unleashed a storm of protest from blacks, who accused him of racism. Not so in the 1980s. By then blacks like Norton, the columnist William Raspberry, and many others conceded the "pathology" of family life in the ghetto. Like Moynihan (and unlike Murray) they demanded federal action.

Given the cold statistics, black reformers like Norton had little choice but to join the chorus of concerns. As recently as the early 1960s, some 80 percent of black households had been husband-and-wife families. This percentage represented considerable continuity with statistics going back to the late nineteenth-century. But in the 1960s many black marriages began to fall apart, and by the mid-1980s 45 percent of black families were headed by women. By contrast, the percentage of female-headed white families rose from 6 percent to 14 percent during the same period. The figures concerning illegitimacy among blacks were stunning: by 1982, 57 percent of all births to black women were out of wedlock.

These developments accentuated the already widespread poverty among female-headed families and led more specifically to two of the most talked-about social concerns of the era: the impoverishment of children and the "feminization of poverty." By early 1985 nearly 14 million children (22 percent of all American children) lived in families with incomes below the poverty line. They made up nearly 40 percent of the total poverty population. More than half of these poor children lived in families headed by women. They were disproportionally black and Hispanic: 47 percent of all black children and 39 percent of all Hispanic children under eighteen were poor in 1984. Experts calculated that the average black child would spend more than five years of his or her childhood in poverty; the average for a white child would be less than 10 months. [16]

While most observers agreed about the statistics, they divided over explanations of the trends and over remedies. Neoconservatives tended to blame either the welfare system (the numbers on AFDC, of course, had skyrocketed in the late 1960s and early 1970s), or cultural traits among minority groups, especially blacks. They stressed that interventionist public policies would make matters worse. It was best, they said, to hope that blacks, like other deprived groups in the cities at the turn of the century, would ultimately acclimate themselves to their surroundings, assimilate into the mainstream, and pull themselves up by their own bootstraps. Time, not social policy, was the preferred remedy for social pathology.

By the mid-1980s a few observers even wondered if some unanticipated consequences of the civil rights movement might have accentuated social problems in the ghettos. The movement, they emphasized, was altruistic and egalitarian. But in some cities it also had the unintended effect of propelling upwardly mobile black community leaders out of the ghettos and into a more racially desegregated world. Statistics on the incomes of middle-class blacks in the 1980s, and on educational achievement, revealed truly impressive improvements. Many blue-collar blacks also gained in these years — the conservative fixation on the ghetto exposed a racist stereotype. But if these blacks gained as a result of the civil rights revolution, some blacks farther down the social scale did not. On the contrary, according to this argument, many poor blacks now enjoyed less economic and moral support from their middle-class leaders, who were busy struggling to get ahead in a white-dominated environment. Nor could the lower classes depend so much on historically stabilizing black institutions — the church, local black businesses and schools, community centers. Cut adrift, many poor blacks found themselves less able to cope in the economically harsh ghetto environment.

Structuralists disagreed emphatically with most of these arguments. Instead they pointed to deeply imbedded demographic and economic problems leading to job competition, low wages, and rising unemployment. This was Moynihan's view, as it had been in 1964. It was also Harrington's in *The New American Poverty,* published in 1984. Like *The Other America,* it painted a deeply depressing picture of poverty in America, blamed the capitalistic system for the prevalence of need, and demanded that the government spend many more billions on social programs to alleviate destitution. [17]

Norton also took a structuralist view. Like Moynihan and others, she stressed the growing unemployment rates among young black men in ghetto areas. These rates had approximated those of whites in the 1940s and 1950s, but then escalated, so that by 1985 some 40 percent of teen-aged blacks were unemployed. This was two and a half times the rate among teen-aged whites. Lacking job prospects, young blacks were in no position to consider long-term personal relationships such as marriage. Women in the ghetto, similarly, did not see much to be gained from marrying men with little hope of getting a job. Given this situation, lower marriage rates and, later, family tensions were predictable consequences.

But why such increases in black unemployment? On this crucial point, theories proliferated. Some conservatives suggested that blacks (like others in the affluent society of post-1960s America) simply expected too much. Entry-level, low-paying jobs existed, these writers said, but many blacks (as well as whites) refused to demean themselves by taking them. Or ghetto dwellers would sign on for work, but would quickly tire of hard or ill-paid labor and turn to hustling on the street for a living. A variant on this argument blamed the low educational levels of blacks, many of whom were functionally illiterate and without the appropriate organizational skills or personal habits (such as punctuality) to hold even beginning-level jobs. Liberal policy makers who stressed these educational problems tended to offer solutions calling for new or better public programs to improve literacy and personal habits; one such effort was the supported-work program that Auletta described in his book. But many liberals came close to agreeing with the neoconservatives in stressing the personal limitations of young ghetto blacks. Shedding the liberal optimism of the 1960s, they conceded that existing job training programs were not getting to the deep behavioral roots of the problems.

The structuralists, needless to say, wanted to do more. They focused on the technological revolution in agriculture that had uprooted blacks from the southern countryside in the 1940s and 1950s and had flung them into the cities. Unlike the booming industrial cities of 1900 or the commercial metropolises of the 1920s, many northern and eastern urban areas in the 1970s and the early 1980s were stagnant economically. These contemporary cities did not offer much in the way of well-paying jobs for people — indeed, the stagnation often intensified the poverty that was afflicting the new working-class poor. It followed that these cities promised even less for newcomers, especially blacks pent up in the ghettos, which were often geographically removed from growth areas developing on the suburban fringes.

These writers also suggested that many of the black migrants of the 1950s and 1960s were different from the blacks who had come north in manageably smaller numbers in the 1910s and 1920s. Those earlier migrants, the argument went, had been pulled north by promises of better economic opportunities and less racial violence: they were enterprising, daring, an elite of sorts. By contrast, the masses who migrated after World War II had been pushed from their small plots of land or from their tenant holdings by the agricultural revolution of the 1940s that mechanized cotton farming. Driven north, they lacked the skills and the resources to cope with the more hostile city life of postwar America. Their families often broke under these strains, further handicapping their children, the generation of the 1970s and 1980s. Hispanics, arriving in the millions in the 1970s and early 1980s, had the additional burden of learning a new language. The answer to these problems, such writers argued, was not benign neglect — or the passage of time. It was more and better educational and job training programs, combined perhaps with imaginative government employment opportunities. Meanwhile, public assistance had to be increased, ideally with a guaranteed national minimum benefit level. [18]

A few antipoverty warriors urged adoption of a national Child Support Assurance System. They argued that some 60 percent of women with children who were eligible for child support did not get such an award and that only half of those who had an award got the full amount due. They called for a "child support tax" to be levied on all parents who lived apart from their children. This tax, to be collected like a payroll tax, was to be used for child support, in most cases for female-headed families. Such a plan, proponents maintained, would promote equity, increase the economic well-being of children, and ultimately reduce welfare costs and case loads. [19]

But proponents recognized that the tax would not do much for mothers whose former husbands were poor or unemployed; the levy was more a moral statement than an antipoverty weapon. No one, moreover, had a ready solution to the problems of family breakup and illegitimacy. Indeed, experts on the subject prophesied that less than half of the families to be formed between 1985 and 2000 would still be headed by a husband-wife couple, and that almost one child in three born during this time would end up on welfare. They also pointed to the ever more active sexuality of young people: in 1980, 55 percent of black girls aged fifteen to seventeen and 29 percent of white girls in this age group were sexually active, as opposed to percentages of 44 percent and 15 percent in 1971. Statistics such as these made it clear that family problems were not limited to the ghetto. These problems stemmed at least in part from broader trends in sexual behavior and values that affected all races and classes in the United States, especially after 1960.[20]

To look at the sources of family instability in the 1980s from this broad societal perspective is to understand better why the subject of poverty returned to the front pages, and why so much ink was spilled on the familial and criminal behavior of the "underclass." For while this group constituted only a small minority of the nation's poor, they did behave in ways that profoundly disturbed liberals and conservatives alike. Barring some unforeseen revival of economic vitality in the central cities and some reversal of the sexual revolution, it hardly seemed likely as of the mid-1980s that the deep-seated weaknesses of the ghettos could be easily addressed, much less solved.

Still, careful observers reminded Americans that all was not lost. They pointed out that the ghetto poor were hardly new to the American scene. Nor were they totally immune to public intervention, ranging from older approaches such as public employment, job training, and welfare to slightly newer ideas such as the Child Support Assurance System and innovative supported-work plans. The very attention that the underclass was getting, while sometimes near-hysterical, was probably salutary in that black leaders as well as whites were forced to focus on problems that had often been swept under the rug at earlier times in American history. Reflecting this renewed attention, the Ford Foundation in 1985 announced a major, three-year project to fund research into future directions for social welfare policy in the United States.

Liberals also emphasized a final, important point: the so-called underclass still made up only a fourth of the nation's needy. The other three-quarters, while less concentrated geographically and less alarming behaviorally, suffered from economic deprivation that was also severe. Their poverty most often derived from economic realities — unemployment, low wages, costly illness, cutbacks of social programs — that they could not control. But their need could be alleviated by social policies that either had started or had grown astronomically in the 1960s and early 1970s, such as food stamps, Medicaid, Medicare, Head Start, AFDC-UP, and Supplemental Security Income for the aged, and by older programs — AFDC in particular — that continued as bulwarks of the public assistance system. This system continued in the early 1980s to lift nearly half of the "pretransfer" poor over the poverty line, and to bring many of the rest closer to it. For these poor people, far more numerous than the "underclass," liberal social policy had a demonstrable track record.

Perhaps the late 1980s would witness another "golden age" of poverty policy—or perhaps not. But two things seemed as clear in the early 1980s as they had been since the 1930s. First, no substantial improvements in welfare or social insurance benefits were likely to be legislated unless a severe depression threatened the middle classes, as it had in the 1930s, or unless policy makers again summoned great confidence in the capacity of liberal social programs, as they had in the early 1960s. These very different preconditions—one rooted in the desperation of hard times, the other in the optimism of affluence—had historically done much to set the parameters of America's twentieth-century struggle against poverty. They would probably continue to do so in the late 1980s and 1990s.

Second, the jerry-built welfare state of America was vitally important to recipients and beneficiaries. So although social programs might undergo assaults from the right, as they did under Reagan, it seemed most unlikely that they would be substantially dismantled. As in the past, the American welfare state offered vital support to millions in need. Its considerable flaws notwithstanding, it will necessarily survive.

15
WELFARE REFORM:
NO CONSENSUS

"WE FOUGHT A WAR on poverty," Ronald Reagan once said, "and poverty won."[1] This comment, like many by the former President, was at best a half-truth—a jab that ignored the lasting and beneficial efforts advanced by Great Society programs of the 1960s. These programs included Medicare for the elderly, Medicaid for the welfare poor, and increased funding for food stamps. Aid to Families of Dependent Children (AFDC) was extended to millions of people who had previously been eligible but who had been denied benefits under the conservative management of public assistance before the 1960s. Reagan's remark also ignored important social welfare programs approved during the Nixon years, such as Supplemental Security Income (SSI) for the aged, blind, and disabled, the extension of Social Security, and the indexing of both programs in 1972.[2] These programs combined with substantial economic growth up to the mid-1970s to reduce poverty—as officially defined by government measures—from around 21 percent of the population in 1962 to all-time lows of approximately 11 percent in the early 1970s.

Reagan's doubts about social welfare programs, however, reflected the attitudes of millions of Americans from the mid-1980s into the mid-1990s. For anti-poverty reformers, this was a decade of continued stalemate and frustration. Liberal welfare reform policies remained under siege from conservatives whose ideas of reform focused on cutting costs and making "reliefers" work. Others, including William Clinton, elected President in 1992, were not sure what to do. Though Clinton was slightly to the left of his opponents in the 1992 election, President George Bush and independent H. Ross Perot, he shared their aversion to long-term, costly public assistance. If elected, Clinton promised, he would "scrap the current welfare system and make welfare a second chance, not a way of life."

Liberal reformers, surveying the uneven performance of the American economy, shook their heads in dismay over the durability of these conservative attitudes. Serious social and economic problems, these liberals complained, demanded public attention. The economic recovery of the mid-1980s was heartening, and the 1980s were more prosperous for most people than the late 1970s had been: most Americans had slightly more real income by 1988 than they had had early in the decade. But recession descended again between late 1989 and 1991, and labor markets recovered only in late 1992. Although not as sharp a slump as the recession of 1978–1982, it was nonetheless serious. Unemployment, measured at 5.3 percent in 1989, increased to an average of 7.4 percent three years later, leaving 9 million people out of work.[3]

Harder times caused the number of people living in poverty to rise sharply between 1989 and 1992. In 1992 the government's poverty line was $7,143 for a single person, $11,186 for a family of three, and $14,335 for a family of four. (Median family income was then $34,293.) These figures, adjusted upward according to changes in the consumer price index, were around four and a half times the dollar amount of early 1960s figures. By these standards, the number of people defined as poor by the Census Bureau increased for three years in a row beginning in 1990, climbing to 36.9 million people in 1992, 10 million more than had been poor during the postwar low in 1971 and the highest total since 1962. The poor in 1992 constituted 14.5 percent of the total population, up from 12.8 percent in 1989. The poverty rate in 1992 was higher than in any year since 1983, when it had been 15.2 percent.[4]

As in the past, aggregate figures concerning unemployment and poverty concealed wide variations. Unemployment in late 1993 ranged from 8.6 percent in California to around 4 percent in North Carolina. In New York City the rate exceeded 10 percent.[5] The South remained the nation's poorest section, with 14.8 million poor people (16.9 percent of the southern population and 40 percent of all poor Americans).[6] Poverty rates also varied by age. The poverty rate for people over the age of 65, though increasing in the early 1990s, continued to average slightly below the overall rate. It was 12.9 percent in 1992, affecting approximately 4 million people, compared to the overall poverty rate of 14.5 percent. By contrast 21.9 percent of Americans below the age of eighteen—14.6 million children—were poor at that time. (Fewer than 10 million children had been poor in the late 1970s, when the rate of child poverty had been around 14 percent.) In 1992, 25 percent of children under six were poor.

Race and ethnicity also continued to matter. While most poor people were white, certain minority groups continued to be at the bottom of the income pyramid.[7] In 1992 the poor included 33.3 percent of African-Americans (10.6 million people); 29.3 percent of Hispanics (6.7 million); and 9.6 percent of non-Hispanic whites (18.3 million).[8] Poverty rates among recent immigrants were much higher than among natives, with the exception of Native Americans.[9] The rate on certain Native American reservations was as high as 60 percent.[10]

The rising poverty rate among children—twice as high as Canada's and 10 times higher than Sweden's—owed much to the acceleration of trends in family composition that Daniel Patrick Moynihan and others had lamented as early as the 1960s. In 1993 approximately 25 percent of all families were headed by a single parent, usually a woman, as opposed to 9 percent in 1960. Nearly one-third of all children born in 1993 had unmarried parents. Figures for African-Americans were even higher: two-thirds of black children were born out of wedlock in 1993. Among black children in some central city areas, this figure exceeded 80 percent. In large part because of these developments, 47 percent of black children under eighteen lived in poverty, as did 50 percent of black female-headed households, involving 1.8 million mothers and children.[11]

In some ways, experts cautioned, these were misleading statistics. Smaller percentages of African-American women were getting married, and those who did had fewer children. These trends, not higher fertility among unmarried blacks (their fertility was in fact declining, thanks in part to greater availability of birth control and access to abortion), led to decreases in the *percentage* of African-American babies born to married couples. These caveats, however, did not affect public perceptions of rising illegitimacy, some of which rested on historically deep-seated assumptions about black sexuality and "immorality." Moreover, it was obvious that family life in America's ghettos was often deeply troubled, and that poverty especially plagued female-headed households. Since the Moynihan Report, African-American scholars and activists had dismissed talk about the "pathology" of lower-class black life as racist, but they now began writing books and making speeches demanding that the problems of the African-American family return to the agenda of public action. Some of these activists, the Reverend Jesse Jackson included, sounded almost as alarmist as people like the former Education Secretary, William Bennett, a vociferous conservative voice on the subject.[12]

Alarm over illegitimacy and family life fueled broader fears that "underclasses," as Americans called the most disadvantaged blacks in central cities, would grow even more dangerous to the rest of society than they had been in the 1980s.[13] This alarm, too, was sometimes misfocused. Statistics from the Federal Bureau of Investigation, for instance, showed that while the rates of many violent crimes had increased greatly in the 1960s, they had stabilized at those levels in the 1970s and the 1980s, and had decreased slightly from 1991 through mid-1993, possibly because the percentage of young men in the population—the group most likely to be violent— declined after 1970.[14] Those who focused on the "pathology" of the black underclasses also slighted the substantial economic progress made by the majority of African-Americans in the wake of the civil rights movement. Blacks made unprecedented economic progress in the 1960s and early 1970s.[15] Moreover, the number of African-Americans who fit common definitions of the underclasses—people who were persistently poor, on long-term welfare, members of female-headed households, inner city lawbreakers, or school dropouts—was relatively small. Some estimates ran as low as one or two million people, or a very small proportion of the overall poverty population of 36.9 million, not to mention of the total United States population in the early 1990s of around 250 million.[16] Poverty extended well beyond the ghettos; most poor Americans, as always, were white, and almost 50 percent of poverty in the United States afflicted rural, small town, or suburban areas of the country.[17]

Still, the underclasses attracted reams of attention from scholars and other worried contemporaries in the late 1980s and early 1990s.[18] And many of these worries were understandable. One study estimated that the number of African-Americans who lived in areas of concentrated poverty (40 percent or more poor) in central cities grew substantially during the 1980s, from 5.6 million people in 1980 to 10.4 million in 1990.[19] Some of these areas, because of substantial out-migrations by middle-class blacks, were left with few middle-class role models or stable social institutions such as churches or neighborhood organizations. Many young men from families trying to survive in what the sociologist William Julius Wilson called "social isolation" drifted into drug addiction and crime.[20] The result, Wilson added, was a falling off in the number of "marriageable males." Young African-American women, recognizing this, were more likely to have children out of wedlock, and the cycle repeated itself.[21]

Wilson focused especially on the barriers keeping young African-Americans from stable employment. These barriers, he said, were rooted less in racial discrimination, which while omnipresent was probably less vicious than in the past, than in structural-economic problems. One of these problems was the accelerating flight of business to suburban areas, some of them far from the central city. The resulting "spatial mismatch" made it difficult for African-Americans to find work. Wilson also stressed the general sluggishness of the American economy. Manufacturing, which had been the ladder to success in many northern industrial cities, laid off millions of workers. Unemployment rates among young black men rose to unprecedented postwar highs—sometimes more than 40 percent in central city areas.

Not all observers entirely agreed with such structural-economic analyses of the underclass problem. Some scholars used broader cultural forces to explain what they considered to be dysfunctional behavioral patterns among the poor (and to a lesser extent among Americans generally). One of these forces was the rapid growth of sexual permissiveness—a trend affecting people of all classes and colors. Another was the contagious allure of the consumer culture, which promoted unreal expectations. These expectations, it was said, gave the poor (and many others) a "gimme" mentality and sabotaged the work ethic.[22] Unemployment among African-Americans, for instance, was rising rapidly, but did not account for the much faster growth of female-headed families, which escalated among the employed as well as the unemployed. There is more to family instability, critics said, than a dearth of "marriageable males." Scholars also argued that increases in unemployment in the 1970s were about the same for black males living in suburban areas as for those trapped in poor central areas. The "spatial mismatch" theory, they concluded, explains only some of African-American joblessness. The rest, some scholars thought, might require some attention to racial discrimination and cultural change as well as to economic forces.[23]

Whatever explanation was offered for the rise of the underclasses, life in the ghettos was grim. It was hardly surprising that some young people turned to the peddling of drugs and to violent crime to protect their turf. In 1990 nearly a fourth of all African-American men in their twenties spent time in jail, on probation, or on parole. More were in jail than in colleges or universities.[24] The

Children's Defense Fund reported that homicides involving firearms claimed 24,000 children and teen-agers between 1979 and 1991.[25] Millions of Americans, reading about such killings in their daily papers, ignored FBI statistics and concluded that violent crime was the single most serious social problem facing the country.[26] Racial tensions in the early 1990s seemed sharper than ever before, especially in the wake of rioting in poverty-stricken areas of Los Angeles in April 1992.[27]

Many Americans worried especially about what they considered to be the increasing tendency of the urban poor to cling to welfare instead of working for a living. As in the past, this tendency was not so widespread in the late 1980s as conservative opponents of welfare imagined: depending on the state of the economy, between 50 and 70 percent of entrants to AFDC left the rolls within 2 years. Still, the problem of long-term welfare dependency was increasing. Similar proportions (50 to 70 percent) of these same people returned to the rolls within 5 years. Perhaps 30 percent of entrants to AFDC became long-term users (5 years or more) of assistance. It was estimated in 1993 that three-quarters of black children would spend a year or more on welfare before reaching the age of eighteen.[28] The number of welfare recipients increased dramatically following the recession of 1989–1991, during which AFDC rolls jumped by 25 percent to a record 14 million people.

Another widely noted aspect of the poverty problem was the growth of homelessness in the late 1980s and early 1990s. Students of this discouraging development argued hotly with one another over its scope, some setting the numbers of homeless in the late 1980s and early 1990s as low as 250,000, others as high as 3 million. Scholars and activists also debated the major causes of homelessness. Some blamed the deinstitutionalization of mentally ill people who were released from hospitals without receiving decent alternative care in the community. This was clearly a significant part of the problem, accounting for perhaps a third of the total number of homeless persons, but experts cited additional causes: rising substance abuse, cutbacks in selected welfare and social services during the Reagan and Bush administrations, and a substantial decline in inexpensive housing in urban areas. Homelessness upset citizens who encountered scenes of public destitution and desperation that had supposedly disappeared after the Great Depression of the 1930s.[29] It also taxed the budgets of many municipalities: New York City's outlays for shelters increased from $6.8 million in 1978 to $320 million in 1989.[30]

The deepest structural problem of the late 1980s and early 1990s, most experts agreed, was the sluggishness of the American economy, which was growing slowly only in terms of real per capita income. Even in relatively good times, macroeconomic forces retarded the expansion of secure, skilled, and well-paying jobs available in the United States. Among these forces were the flight of manufacturing out of the United States to countries with low wage scales; the crowding of some labor markets by millions of immigrants, especially from Mexico, the Caribbean, and Asia; ever higher percentages of women and baby boomers seeking work; and the ongoing effects of automation and technological change. Foreign competition seemed a special concern in the wake of the Cold War.[31]

For all these reasons, ever smaller percentages of jobs in the United States were in the better-paid, higher-skilled sectors of the economy. Larger percentages were in the lower reaches of the service sector, where work was often ill paid, part-time, and without benefits.[32] Americans employed full-time at the minimum wage ($4.25 per hour in 1993) earned around $8,500 a year. This was a little above the poverty line for a single person ($7,143), below the line for a couple ($9,100), and entirely inadequate for heads of families without other workers. In 1992, 18 percent of full-time workers (14 percent of men and 24 percent of women) received less than $13,091, an adjusted poverty line for families of four for that year. That means they earned no more than $6.50 per hour if they worked the entire year. In 1979, by contrast, only 12 percent of full-time workers fell under the line for that year.[33] Many of those eligible for welfare calculated correctly that they were better off on welfare than working (and paying for child care, transportation, and other work-related expenses). Many others resided in intact two-parent families that were ineligible for categorical federal aid such as AFDC or Medicaid—nearly 10 million of the nation's 36.9 million poor received no means-tested aid in 1992.

A disturbing corollary of these trends was the rising inequality of income and wealth in the 1980s and early 1990s. Some liberals blamed this development on conservative tax laws and spending priorities set in place during the Reagan-Bush years. Other critics maintained that federal fiscal policies had caused little change in the distribution of income and that there continued to be potential for individuals to rise (or fall) on the occupational or income scale. The economy, they reminded pessimists, had been stronger in the mid-1980s than it had been between 1975 and 1982. But most experts agreed that the distribution of income had become more unequal. Between 1973 and 1990 the income share going to the most affluent fifth of Americans increased by 7.8 percent (to 44.3 percent of total income) while the share received by the lowest fifth declined by 16.4 percent (to 4.6 percent of total income).[34] Economists also pointed with alarm at long-term structural realities that threatened to entrench or even widen these gaps. Barring government policies or market developments that would improve the competitive position of the United States in the international economy, it seemed likely that smaller numbers of Americans would be able to compete for high-tech or high-skill openings, and that larger numbers of others, including growing percentages of blacks and other minorities, would have to settle for low-paid work in the service sector.[35]

If the social safety net in the United States had been firmly in place, many of these problems might not have seemed so alarming. But the net continued to have some dangerous holes in it. The United States taxed less and spent less per capita on social welfare, broadly defined, than did other industrialized nations of the West (though these nations began to cut back on their services in the 1990s). As of late 1994, the United States remained the only industrialized nation, aside from South Africa, with no comprehensive system of publicly managed national health insurance. The number of Americans without medical insurance at some time during a year increased by 4.2 million between 1989 and 1992, to a total of 38.9 million. Of these, 22 million were without insurance for all of 1992.[36]

In 1988 Congress made a determined pass at filling holes in the social safety net by approving the Family Support Act.[37] The law mandated that all states participate by late 1990 in the AFDC-UP program aiding two-parent families who were needy because of the temporary unemployment of one parent.[38] The act also called for 15 percent of single-parent adult AFDC recipients (except those with children under three years of age) to be enrolled by 1993 in "job opportunities and basic skills" (JOBS) programs.[39] These were to be designed by the states and financed by federal and state money, and to consist of training or work. Other provisions of the Family Support Act made AFDC recipients automatically eligible for Medicaid, required states to provide transitional Medicaid and child-care benefits for people who lost AFDC eligibility, offered child-care support for JOBS parents who could not otherwise participate in the training programs, and outlined stronger measures aimed at forcing absent fathers to make child support payments.[40] Senator Moynihan, chief author of the act, proclaimed it a major addition to the American social welfare network.

Although the Family Support Act was well-intended, state officials were slow to develop JOBS plans or to set aside matching money for child care, thanks in part to the recession, which created huge deficits in state budgets. Congress, too, appropriated far smaller sums than advocates had expected. For these reasons very few adult recipients of AFDC were receiving training or education six years later. Some conservative critics, moreover, doubted the premise of the JOBS idea, a timeless American reliance on education, training, and work as the keys to economic opportunity. The act assumed that large numbers of welfare parents could be trained or educated for good jobs. But how, critics asked, were poor, mostly ill-educated people with heavy family responsibilities to be trained for remunerative employment? Could people in the under-classes, trapped in what *The New Republic* called a "ferociously entrenched culture of poverty," readily develop a work ethic?[41]

The philosophy behind the Family Support Act raised other familiar objections to job training. Where were the jobs at the end of the training? How could an economy with so many structural weaknesses be expected to generate new openings? Why should people on welfare get government-financed training when most of the non-welfare unemployed—more than 8 million strong in 1993—had to shift for themselves once their unemployment benefits ran out? Why should taxpayers support job training programs that might enable welfare recipients to take the place of already employed workers? Most Americans continued to believe that "reliefers" were less deserving than the working poor. Some of those who doubted the effectiveness of JOBS complained of the "notch" effect that continued to discourage welfare clients from taking their chances in the private sector. Why, they said, would women heading families make the effort to find work when the sum total of their wages (minus work-related child-care and transportation expenses) might leave them worse off than they were with public assistance, which sometimes included Medicaid, food stamps, and housing allowances in addition to cash assistance through AFDC?

A program like JOBS, other critics pointed out, would not only have to train and find employment for as many as 5 million adult recipients of AFDC but (if it hoped to raise their standard of living to near the poverty line), would also have to supplement wages with free medical care and up to $5,000 per year in additional resources. All these expenditures could cost as much as $50 billion.[42] Adequate day care, estimated to cost at least $3,000 per child per year for as many as 5.2 million pre-schoolers in poverty, could cost up to $15.6 billion more, which Congress showed no interest in spending. Liberal activists complained that JOBS was not only ill funded but also was intended to become compulsory for many. It would thus be an entering wedge for "workfare," a harsher alternative being enacted in some states. Workfare plans varied, but generally aimed to force people on public assistance to take often low-paying jobs or face the loss of some of their benefits.[43]

Teresa McCrary, one of the 5 million mothers receiving AFDC in 1993, bewailed some of these realities in a *Newsweek* column at the time. Struggling to become self-sufficient, McCrary was trying to finish college and wanted to work. But her road was bumpy. "If the unemployed can't find work," she wrote, "where are we moms supposed to look? The only jobs open to us are maid work, fast-food service and other low-paying drudgery with no benefits. How are we supposed to support our children? Minimum wage will not pay for housing costs, health care, child care, transportation and work clothes that an untrained, uneducated woman needs to support even one child."[44]

Other critics, including liberals who had supported AFDC in the past, joined the chorus of Americans who lamented flaws in the nation's public welfare system in the 1990s. An increase in AFDC recipients during the recession of 1989–1991 caused the total spent for AFDC to reach record levels—$23 billion in federal and state money by 1992. But because AFDC, unlike Social Security or SSI, was still not indexed to keep pace with inflation, the real value of benefits declined by 30 percent between the mid-1970s and the early 1990s, mostly between 1975 and 1990. Smaller proportions of poor children received AFDC benefits in 1993 than in the past (around three in five as opposed to four in five in 1973). Although expansion of the food stamp program cushioned these losses, the real value of AFDC plus food stamps decreased by 25 percent between the early 1970s and the early 1990s. Together, these programs brought typical families of three up to only 72 percent of the federal poverty line in 1992.

These stringencies provoked widespread violation of regulations by recipients. The majority of adults of AFDC failed to report savings, earnings, or other sources of income, much of which would have been deducted, in accordance with AFDC rules, from their welfare checks. The system encouraged these types of illegal behavior. One liberal critic concluded that AFDC remained an "outdated, administratively burdensome, stigma-laden, initiative-depressing program designed to remedy adverse outcomes, not to enhance personal opportunities. It does not bring the poor into mainstream society. And it is very unpopular—among the poor and even among those who want to spend more to help the poor."[45]

The AFDC program also continued to rely on state money to

trigger federal grants. As in the past, this bow to federalism resulted in wide variations in benefits. In early 1992 maximum benefits for a family of three ranged from $680 per month in Connecticut to $120 in Mississippi. Average grants nationally were around $370 for families of three in 1992. Medicaid, a much bigger program, was another federal-state collaboration. In 1993 the federal government paid out nearly $76 billion for Medicaid (more than six times its spending on AFDC), with states adding $56 billion. Medicaid recipients in Mississippi received an average of $1,067 per year in state money; Connecticut allotted its recipients an average of $5,994.[46]

Provisions of the Social Security and Medicare system also sparked criticism among advocates of change in the American social welfare system. These contributory programs continued to be much the largest of the nation's entitlements—at $320 billion for Social Security and $140 billion for Medicare in 1993 they were far costlier than AFDC ($23 billion in federal and state funds) or food stamps ($26 billion). The spending of such vast sums mainly accounted for the greatest success of social policy in modern United States history: the alleviation of poverty among the elderly.[47] Social Security has been among the most prudently run of America's social support programs,[48] but it was hardly immune to criticism. Most Social Security and Medicare benefits, like many other federal entitlements, went to people who were not poor. Only one-tenth of all federal entitlements (including farm subsidies) in 1993 was spent on poor people.[49]

These and other aspects of Social Security prompted both liberal and moderate reformers to demand that these entitlements be taxed for wealthy recipients on a sliding, progressive basis. Some suggested that the savings go toward reducing the large federal deficit; others wanted some of the new revenue spent on the needy. Other critics worried about demographic forces (including greater longevity and the retirement of the baby boomers in the 2000s) that were rapidly increasing the number and proportion of elderly people in the United States. Seeking to avoid deficits in the Social Security fund, these critics urged that the retirement age be raised from 65 to 67 by the early 2000s, instead of in 2022 as currently anticipated. Most of these proposals for change, however, encountered stiff resistance from the elderly. The "Gray Lobby," as it was called, was perhaps the most powerful in Washington.[50]

Some reformers of America's safety net also demanded changes in a fundamental underpinning of social welfare thinking: the measurement of poverty.[51] Official government measures, which rose with the consumer price index, were the source of most stories in newspapers and magazines that counted the number of people who were poor. Census reports used the same figures to determine poverty lines. But these measures, critics charged, increasingly underestimated the real living costs incurred by the poor, and greatly undercounted the number of Americans who were defined as living in poverty. Some critics said the number of poor people in the early 1990s was as high as 60 million, instead of the 35 to 36 million counted by the federal government. These lower government figures left the impression that poverty mainly affected the long-term welfare poor, including the underclasses, thereby enabling Americans to imagine that all poor people belonged to a special class of the "undeserving." If higher income levels had been set including a percentage of the working poor among those defined as living in poverty, Americans might have better appreciated the magnitude of the poverty problem, and public officials might have been pushed into expanding social and economic programs.

The undercount, these critics said, stemmed mainly from reliance on the consumer price index (CPI), which included in its composite "non-essential" items whose costs had risen relatively slowly and which most poor people could not buy. But the cost of "basic necessities"—things everyone had to have—rose more rapidly over time than did the CPI as a whole. Rents had skyrocketed for many poor people. In 1991, when the government poverty line for a family of four was $13,920, one estimate of needs concluded that such families had to have at least $20,600 for basic necessities. These included food, rent, medical care, taxes, clothing and shoes, transportation, household products, appliance repairs, and furnishings. Spending $20,600, the family would have to do without child care, toys, books, entertainment, pets, or even haircuts. The budget had no room for savings, higher education, emergencies, retirement, or care of ill or elderly parents.[52]

Conservatives countered these arguments by replying that many of the poor received "in-kind" government aid, notably food stamps, housing allowances, and Medicaid. These benefits were not counted in family income when the government measured poverty; the value of some, such as food stamps and Medicaid, had been rapidly increasing. Many poor people also had unreported sources of income, such as undeclared wages, alimony or child support, savings, gifts, or inheritances. If in-kind benefits and unreported income were added to family budgets, critics said, many poor people would have assets that were close to twice as high as their cash income from work or AFDC, making America's poor population much smaller than the numbers reported by the government.[53]

Poverty, these critics added, was a relative concept: most people defined as poor in the 1980s and 1990s in fact lived very well by the standards of the American past—or by the standards of most societies in world history. Some 40 percent of people defined as poor in 1992 owned their own homes, 64 percent had cars, and 91 percent owned a color TV.[54] Throwing more money at such people, the critics said, would feed the unreal expectations that were damaging American society. Moreover, the country could not afford further spending. The already capacious safety net, which cost $770 billion in federal money alone in 1993, amounted to more than half the federal budget.[55] Conservatives (and many moderates) said that if liberal reformers succeeded in spending more money on social welfare, the already enormous federal deficit (around $300 billion in 1993) would spin out of control.[56]

Liberals scored several points in this renewed debate over the measurement of poverty. The total cost of basic necessities was indeed higher for many poor people than official poverty lines. Moreover, poverty lines after the early 1970s fell relative to median family incomes in the United States. In the early 1960s the line for a family of four (roughly $3,000) had been 49 percent of the median, but by 1988 it had dropped to 37 percent.[57] This meant that officially poor Americans (as well as many "near-poor") in the 1990s were *relatively* poorer than they used to be. Some felt increasingly isolated and angry. As Christopher Jencks put it, "when you can't have or can't do something that 95 percent of the population has or does, you are in some sense a nonparticipant in society."[58]

But as of the mid-1990s the liberals had not yet persuaded Congress or the American people. In-kind benefits indeed made a big difference in the lives of many Americans in the 1980s and 1990s. Federal deficits, moreover, had grown so much during the Reagan-Bush years that almost everyone, including liberals, demanded fiscal prudence. Few politicians dared suggest spending large new sums on the poor. Most remained ready to protect contributory programs such as Social Security and Medicare, but were highly skeptical of expanding means-tested welfare. For many, Reagan's quip, "We fought a war on poverty—and poverty won," did not seem far from the truth.

When Clinton entered the White House in 1993, he brought with him mixed messages about welfare and poverty. One of his campaign promises, "to end welfare as we know it," sought to get many AFDC recipients off the welfare rolls and into work after two years.

Conservatives were encouraged. On the other hand, he called for enactment of a potentially very expensive national health insurance program, and he surrounded himself with advisers on social welfare problems who seemed eager to alleviate poverty. Most liberals hoped that the Clinton administration would explore solutions in a more aggressive way than had the Bush administration.

Clinton's first year and a half did little to clarify his message. Many liberals were pleased with his efforts to raise public consciousness about the problem of homelessness and with his requests for better funding for Head Start and public housing. They applauded his quest for reform of the health care system, to further extend emergency unemployment benefits, and to create a National Service program, which promised to put 20,000 young people to work in distressed areas. Above all, they celebrated passage of an act in 1993 that considerably expanded the existing Earned Income Tax Credit for low-income workers with children. This plan, started in the 1970s, enabled such workers to deduct job-related credits from income tax obligations. If the credits exceeded taxes paid, employees got refunds. These credits had totalled $11 billion for 13 million American workers in 1992. The expansion in 1993 promised to more than double that amount within the next few years and to make the program as large—in terms of public dollars—as AFDC or food stamps.[59]

These legislative initiatives generally favored helping *working* people and their families. The politically weak welfare poor, by contrast, received a more cautious hearing. In dealing with the deep-seated problems of these people, Clinton's advisers struggled to resolve chronic difficulties that had confronted earlier generations of policymakers. These problems were ideological as well as political: how to devise anti-poverty policies that would at once help the needy, reduce dependency, promote work incentives, and keep federal expenditures under control; how to help the welfare poor without antagonizing the working poor—and labor unions representing them; and how to get anything substantial through Congress. Clinton's advisers especially disagreed about how to expand the economy to create well-paying *work*—the key, they believed, to controlling the spread of dependency. Some liberals in his administration privately suggested WPA- or CCC-style public employment. Public employment, however, was expensive and did not—many critics thought—accomplish much of lasting value to the country. Opponents of such programs pointed to previous efforts, such as the WPA in the 1930s and CETA in the 1970s, to maintain that setting up such jobs was more costly than administering welfare and that most people who wanted work could find jobs in the more efficient private sector.

Other advisers considered measures, including special tax incentives, to create "empowerment zones" that would entice businesses to operate in poverty-stricken areas. But advocates of empowerment zones, including many conservatives seeking market-based approaches to poverty, also confronted cogent opponents. Most poor people, these critics rejoined, wanted to get *out* of the ghetto, not find work within it. Such zones flew in the face of market realities and had a poor track record.[60] For these reasons support for empowerment zones, like public employment, did not find consensus.

Uncertain how to proceed in 1993 and early 1994, Clinton's advisers suggested a child support insurance program, with federal tax dollars to be used whenever noncustodial parents could not pay or be located. Cautiously endorsing the Family Support Act, they focused mainly on expanding job training and education for the poor, perhaps including noncustodial fathers, and on extending Head Start and child care benefits to some of the working poor.[61] Their primary goal, like that of so many planners in modern United States history, was to find work for the welfare poor.

Clinton's advisers faced considerable constraints, among them the President's centrist opposition to additional net spending on social welfare. Any new outlays for public employment, job training, or child care, he made clear, would have to come from money allotted to existing means-tested programs, such as AFDC, SSI, or Medicaid.[62] Executive frugality was a familiar theme in America's struggle against poverty. Moreover, Clinton's first priority was to reform health care—an extraordinarily complicated and time-consuming effort that was expected to place a drain on governmental funds. Welfare reform would have to wait its turn on the administration's agenda.

The President finally gave clues of what he would do in his State of the Union message of January 1994. Congress, he said, would be asked to expand training opportunities for welfare recipients, thereby helping them to find work. Those who remained on the rolls after two years would be expected to enter community service. The government would either subsidize private employment for these people or perhaps set up public jobs in community service projects. These jobs would likely be at the minimum wage.[63]

Clinton more or less reaffirmed these guidelines during the next few months. But the guidelines left important questions unanswered and provoked familiar doubts. Was it likely, as he seemed to assume, that job training would get many people off the rolls?[64] Many welfare recipients were either disabled, ill, or extraordinarily difficult to train. Other were mothers with very young children. Others might be trainable, but for unsatisfactory jobs: millions of would-be workers remained unemployed. Would welfare recipients be willing to take jobs at the minimum wage, and if not, would they be forced to? Union leaders heatedly opposed any large-scale program that might drive down wages in the private sector or destroy existing jobs. Finally, what would happen to the people who used up their two years on welfare but could not find work? Would they stay on the rolls, or would they be expected to shift for themselves? If they were placed in community service, how long would public funding support them?

Exacerbating these difficulties was the problem of cost. Because it was assumed that training would not find jobs for everyone, some of Clinton's advisers seemed prepared to consider providing public employment. But for how many people? Early estimates of the number of public sector jobs that would have to be created differed widely, from 500,000 to more than 2 million. (The WPA at its peak had provided 3.3 million jobs; CETA, 750,000.) The cost of such programs, even at the minimum wage, was expected to range between $7 billion and $14.5 billion per year.[65] If the jobs paid above the minimum wage, as some advocates insisted would be necessary, the costs would be still higher. Even funding at $7 billion to support 500,000 jobs, the lowest estimate, had very doubtful congressional prospects. Estimates of other possible changes, such as expansion of publicly supported job training and child care support, were also so high (ranging from $10 billion to $18.4 billion for the next five years) that they provoked widespread unease on Capitol Hill.[66]

Meanwhile, states were jumping in with anti-poverty approaches of their own, many of which required and received federal waivers permitting experimentation.[67] Popular opinion seemed to support these government waivers. Most of the approaches reflected a time-worn hope that public assistance policies could decisively alter human behavior. Maryland enacted a "healthfare" plan that reduced AFDC benefits to welfare mothers who did not ensure that their children received health checkups or immunizations. New Jersey approved a "wedfare" program that offered bonuses to welfare mothers who married and lowered grants to children conceived while the mother was on the rolls.[68] The governor of New York, Mario Cuomo, considered expanding a program that authorized electronic fingerprinting of certain welfare recipients as a way of detecting fraud.[69] Ohio tried to keep teen-aged welfare mothers in school by giving them a bonus when they attended and cutting their benefits when they did not. Other political leaders talked favorably about making Norplant, a contraceptive implant, a condition for receiving benefits under AFDC.[70] The most common approach of states was simply to cut or freeze benefits in order to control their deficits: more than forty states did so in 1992.[71]

In 1993 the Clinton administration waived AFDC rules to permit Wisconsin to develop a bipartisan "work not welfare" initiative that the *New York Times* called potentially "the most radical experiment in the welfare program's history."[72] This initiative proposed to set a two-year time limit on welfare benefits for families with children in two low-unemployment counties, beginning in 1995. At first, adult recipients would be required to work full-time or to participate in 40-hour-a-week training programs. After a year, to continue receiving benefits they would have to take 40-hour-a-week private sector or community service jobs at the minimum wage. At the end of two years, these families, if still eligible, could continue to receive food stamps (and in some cases vouchers to help with housing costs), but they would no longer have guaranteed jobs or get AFDC or other cash assistance, except perhaps in dreadful local job markets. Although proponents of "work not welfare" emphasized that it was an experiment, liberals perceived it as "workfare" and worried that it was a sign of the future. "Children will be hurt by the Wisconsin waiver," said a spokesman for the Children's Defense Fund. "It violates the most basic standards of fairness and decency."[73]

As many of these state initiatives indicated, the statistics concerning female-headed families and out-of-wedlock childbearing provoked some of the most anguished debates of the early 1990s. In 1993, the conservative Charles Murray again jumped into the center of these debates. He insisted that the escalating rates of illegitimacy, which had risen from 20 percent to 67 percent for African-Americans and from 2 percent to 22 percent for whites since 1960, were creating a "white underclass" as well as a black one.[74] "European-American whites," he said, were the ethnic group with "the most people in poverty, most illegitimate children, most women on welfare, most unemployed men, and most arrests for serious crimes." These problems, Murray emphasized, were class-based, with rates of illegitimacy soaring among women under the poverty line (44 percent of births to poor white women) and among women with less than a high school education. Murray's answer to these alarming trends was to end all public support (save health insurance) for single mothers. This change in welfare policy, together with the stigma attached to unwed parenthood, would deter out-of-wedlock births. Women who nonetheless had illegitimate children would have to rely on relatives for support, put their babies up for adoption, or turn to orphanages.

Murray's extreme proposals stood very little chance of securing significant political support. But it was a sign of popular concern about family decay in the 1990s that they attracted considerable attention. To many Americans the decline of "traditional family values" threatened to unravel the very fabric of the social order: some way, they thought, must be found to arrest the spread of illegitimacy, especially among teen-agers, and to stem the expanding cost of the welfare that supported them. Perhaps, some experts said, these teen-agers could be required (as they were in Ohio) to live at home and finish school as a condition of receiving most of their cash benefits.[75]

Liberal policy-makers continued to struggle in the mid-1990s, as they had for many years, to reach the elusive goal of ensuring more substantial economic opportunity and security for all citizens. They insisted that government had an important role: anti-poverty programs had cushioned the ill effects of hard times for millions of people, especially since the 1960s. President Clinton, by reasserting the liberal potential of government, encouraged some reformers.[76] But conservatives continued to command the high ground in debates, while liberals lacked consensus and were stymied by fiscal realities blocking bold new ventures.[77] Larger ideological and political realities posed especially daunting barriers to change. These were rooted in one of the most durable aspects of America's long struggle against poverty: popular reluctance to spend substantial tax dollars on the "undeserving" poor. Congress, unwilling to offend politically dominant middle-class constituencies, shared this reluctance. Political realities such as these made it doubtful that the Clinton administration would summon the will—or get the backing—to implement very liberal versions of welfare reform. Barring substantial improvement in the economy, poverty seemed likely to persist as one of the ugliest blights on American society.

NOTES

1. Snapshots of the Poor

1. Quotations, in order, are from Jacob Riis, *How the Other Half Lives* (New York, 1890), 36; Riis, 179; Anne J. Daniel, "The Wreck of the Home," *Charities*, 14 (April 1, 1905), 624-628; National Federation of Settlements, *Case Studies of Unemployment* (Philadelphia, 1931), 121-123; Clinch Calkins, *Some Folks Won't Work* (New York, 1930), 40-42; ibid., 28-29.

2. Robert Hunter, *Poverty* (New York, 1904), 56-65. See also Richard T. Ely, "Pauperism in the United States," *North American Review*, 152 (April 1891), 395-409.

3. Hunter, *Poverty*, 5-7 (italics in original). For changes in poverty lines over time, and their effect on estimates of the numbers of poor, see Asa Briggs, *Social Thought and Social Action: A Study of the Work of Seebohm Rowntree* (London, 1961), esp. 283-286. Rowntree studied poverty in York, England, in 1899 and again in 1936.

4. For poverty in Europe at the time, see C. L. Mowat, "Charity and Casework in Late Victorian London: The Work of the Charity Organization Society," *Social Service Review*, 31 (Sept. 1957), 258-270; Albert Fried and Richard M. Elman, eds., *Charles Booth's London* (New York, 1968); Gertrude Himmelfarb, "The Culture of Poverty," in H. J. Dyos and Michael Wolff, eds., *Victorian Cities: Images and Reality*, II (London, 1973), 707-738; G. S. Jones, *Outcast London: A Study in the Relationship Between Classes in Victorian Society* (Oxford, 1972); and Robert Roberts, *The Classic Slum: Salford Life in the First Quarter of the Century* (Manchester, England, 1971). Major works that trace changes over time in western Europe are Karl Polanyi, *The Great Transformation* (New York, 1964); and Peter Laslett, *The World We Have Lost: England Before the Industrial Age* (New York, 1971).

5. Hunter, *Poverty*, 3-4.

6. Edward Devine, *Misery and Its Causes* (New York, 1920), 200; Amos Warner, *American Charities* (New York, 1894), 134; Charles Booth, *Life and*

Labour of the People of London (London, 1899-1903), I, 167-169; Hunter, *Poverty*, 56-65.

7. Devine, *Misery*, 182-191, 224-226.

8. Hunter, *Poverty*, 29.

9. Briggs, *Social Thought*, 283-286; Devine, *Misery*, 204. For a broad study of unemployment over time, see John Garraty, *Unemployment in History: Economic Thought and Public Policy* (New York, 1978). See also Abraham Epstein's classic account, *Insecurity: A Challenge to America* (New York, 1933), esp. 191-193.

10. Hunter, *Poverty*, 331.

11. Laslett, *World We Have Lost*, 32-33; Keith Thomas, *Religion and the Decline of Magic: Studies of Popular Beliefs in 16th and 17th Century England* (London, 1971), 4-19. Quote, p. 19.

12. Olwen Huften, *The Poor of 18th Century France, 1750-1789* (Oxford, 1974), 13-63, 331-367; Louis Chevalier, *Laboring and Dangerous Classes in Paris during the First Part of the 19th Century* (Paris, 1958; trans. 1973).

13. Wayne Flynt, *Dixie's Forgotten People: The South's Poor Whites* (Bloomington, Ind., 1979), 6-7. See also Marcus W. Jernegan, *Laboring and Dependent Classes in Colonial America, 1607-1783* (Chicago, 1931); Jackson Turner Main, *The Social Structure of Revolutionary America* (Princeton, 1965); Edward Pessen, *Riches, Class, and Power Before the Civil War* (Lexington, Mass., 1973); M. J. Heale, "From City Fathers to Social Critics: Humanitarianism and Government in New York, 1790-1860," *Journal of American History*, 63 (June 1976), 21-41.

14. James A. Henretta, "Economic Development and Social Structure in Colonial Boston," *William and Mary Quarterly*, 22 (Jan. 1965), 75-92; Douglas Lamar Jones, "The Strolling Poor: Transiency in 18th Century Massachusetts," *Journal of Social History*, 8 (1975), 28-54; James T. Lemon and Gary E. Nash, "The Distribution of Wealth in 18th Century America: A Century of Change in Chester County, Pennsylvania," ibid., 2 (1968), 1-24; Gloria L. Main, "Inequality in Early America: The Evidence from Probate Records of Massachusetts and Maryland," *Journal of Interdisciplinary History*, 7 (Spring 1977), 559-581; Gary E. Nash, "Urban Wealth and Poverty in Prerevolutionary America," ibid., 6 (Spring 1976), 545-584; Nash, "Poverty and Poor Relief in Pre-revolutionary Philadelphia," *William and Mary Quarterly*, 33 (Jan. 1976), 3-30; and esp. G. B. Warden, "Inequality and Instability in 18th Century Boston: A Reappraisal," *Journal of Interdisciplinary History*, 6 (Spring 1976), 585-620; and Raymond Mohl, *Poverty in New York, 1783-1825* (New York, 1971).

15. Flynt, *Dixie's Forgotten People*. See also Margaret F. Byington, *Homestead: The Households of a Mill Town* (New York, 1910); Paul E. Mertz, *New Deal Policy and Southern Rural Poverty* (Baton Rouge, La., 1978).

16. Ryan, *A Living Wage* (New York, 1906). See also Jacob H. Hollander, *Abolition of Poverty* (Cambridge, Mass., 1914); National Industrial Conference Board, *The Cost of Living in the United States* (New York, 1925); Paul Douglas, *Wages and the Family* (Chicago, 1925); and Bureau of Applied Eco-

nomics, *Standards of Living: A Compilation of Budgetary Studies*, bulletin no. 7 (Washington, 1920).

17. Scholarly studies that touch on these issues include Kirsten A. Grønbjerg, *Mass Society and the Extension of Welfare, 1960-1970* (Chicago, 1977), 66; Harold Wilensky and C. N. Lebeaux, *Industrial Society and Social Welfare* (New York, 1958), 105; Diana Karter Appelbaum, "The Level of the Poverty Line: A Historical Survey," *Social Service Review*, 51 (Sept. 1977), 514-523; Herman P. Miller, "The Dimensions of Poverty," in Ben B. Seligman, ed., *Poverty as a Public Issue* (New York, 1965), 20-51; Kirsten A. Grønbjerg, David Street, and Gerald D. Suttles, *Poverty and Social Change* (Chicago, 1978), 66-67.

18. Quote from Peter d'A. Jones, in introduction to Hunter, *Poverty* (1965 ed.), xxiii. Michael Harrington's influential work was *The Other America: Poverty in the United States* (New York, 1962).

19. Quote from Nathan I. Huggins, *Protestants against Poverty: Boston's Charities, 1870-1900* (Westport, Conn., 1971), 177-183. Other scholars who emphasize the extent of poverty around 1900 include Allen Davis, *Spearheads for Reform: The Social Settlements and the Progressive Movement* (New York, 1967), xv; and esp. Stephan Thernstrom, "Poverty in Historical Perspective," in Daniel Moynihan, ed., *On Understanding Poverty: Perspectives from the Social Sciences* (New York, 1968), 160-186; and Thernstrom, "Is There Really a New Poor?" *Dissent*, 15 (Jan.-Feb. 1968), 59-64. A useful article is David Matza, "The Disreputable Poor," in Reinhard Bendix and Seymour Martin Lipset, eds., *Class, Status, and Power: Social Stratification in Comparative Perspective*, 2nd ed. (New York, 1966), 289-302. A heroic but not altogether convincing effort to see the poor "from the bottom up" is Eric H. Monkkonen, *The Dangerous Class: Crime and Poverty in Columbus, Ohio, 1860-1885* (Cambridge, Mass., 1975), 4-5, 136-137, 153.

20. The quote is from Hunter, *Poverty*, p. 65. For one description of lower-class culture in early American history, see Eric Foner, *Tom Paine and Revolutionary America* (New York, 1976), chap. 2. A first-rate study of urban life and urban reform is Paul Boyer, *Urban Masses and Moral Order in America, 1820-1920* (Cambridge, Mass., 1978). An influential nineteenth-century view of the urban poor was Charles Loring Brace, *The Dangerous Classes of New York* (New York, 1872). The "culture of poverty" view relied especially on R. L. Dugdale, *"The Jukes": A Study in Crime, Pauperism, Disease, and Heredity* (New York, 1877). Relevant articles include Francesco Cordasco, "Charles Loring Brace and the Dangerous Classes: Historical Analogies of the Urban Black Poor," *Journal of Human Resources*, 20 (Nov. 1972), 379-386; W. D. P. Bliss, "Poverty," *Encyclopedia of Social Reform* (New York, 1897), 1071-1079; Helen Campbell, "Certain Convictions as to Poverty," *Arena*, 1 (1889-1890), 101-113; Washington Gladden, "The Problem of Poverty," *Century*, 45 (1892-1893), 245-256; and Oscar Handlin, "Poverty from the Civil War to World War II," in Leo Fishman, ed., *Poverty Amid Affluence* (New Haven, 1966), 3-17. Easily the most comprehensive study of attitudes toward the poor in this period is Robert Bremner, *From the Depths: The Discovery of Poverty in the United States* (New York, 1956).

21. Stephan Thernstrom, *The Other Bostonians: Poverty and Progress in the American Metropolis, 1880-1970* (Cambridge, Mass., 1973), 243-244. Other studies that stress the spirit and drive of working-class Americans include David Montgomery, *Workers' Control in America: Studies in the History of Work, Technology, and Labor Struggles* (Cambridge, Mass., 1978); Herbert Gutman, *Work, Culture, and Society in Industrializing America* (New York, 1977); and Thomas Kessner, *The Golden Door: Italian and Jewish Immigrant Mobility in New York City, 1880-1915* (New York, 1977). Relevant articles include Alvin B. Kogut, "The Negro and the Charity Organization Society in the Progressive Era," *Social Service Review*, 44 (March 1970), 11-21; and Steven J. Diner, "Chicago Social Workers and Blacks in the Progressive Era," ibid., 44 (Dec. 1970), 393-410. A sympathetic contemporary study of New York Jews is Hutchins Hapgood, *Spirit of the Ghetto* (New York, 1902). A good recent synthesis focusing on the family is Carl N. Degler, *At Odds: Women and the Family from the Revolution to the Present* (New York, 1980), 111-143.

22. Scholarly studies that reveal the optimism of social scientists in the 1920s—and the difficulties encountered by reformers—include Roy Lubove, *The Struggle for Social Security, 1900-1935* (Cambridge, Mass., 1968); Lubove, *The Professional Altruist: The Emergence of Social Work as a Career, 1880-1930* (Cambridge, Mass., 1965); Daniel Nelson, *Unemployment Insurance: The American Experience, 1915-1935* (Madison, Wis., 1969); Charles Hunt Page, *Class and American Sociology: From Ward to Ross* (New York, 1940); and Clarke H. Chambers, *Paul U. Kellogg and the Survey: Voices for Social Welfare and Social Justice* (Minneapolis, 1971). For contemporary assessments, see Howard Odum, "Newer Ideals of Public Welfare," *Annals*, 105 (Jan. 1923), 1-6; "Where Are the Social Engineers?" *Survey*, 52 (Aug. 14, 1924), 524-543; and esp. Odum, "Public Welfare Activities," in President's Research Committee on Social Trends, *Recent Social Trends in the United States* (New York, 1933), 1224-1273. Articles focusing on social science in the 1920s include Barry Karl, "Presidential Planning and Social Research: Mr. Hoover's Experts," *Perspectives in American History*, 3 (1969), 347-409; and Wesley C. Mitchell, "The Social Sciences and National Planning," *Science*, 81 (Jan. 18, 1935), 55-62.

I rely for statistics on Census Bureau data, especially as reported in *Historical Statistics of the United States* (Washington, 1961), hereafter referred to as *Historical Statistics*.

23. See note 16. Also Robert Kelso, *Poverty* (New York, 1929).

24. Maurice Leven, Harold G. Moulton, and Clark Warburton, *America's Capacity to Consume* (Washington, 1934).

25. *Historical Statistics*, 72-76; Montgomery, *Workers Control*, passim.

26. Nels Anderson, *The Hobo* (Chicago, 1923): Edwin H. Sutherland and Harvey J. Locke, *Twenty Thousand Homeless Men: A Study of Unemployed Men in the Chicago Shelters* (Chicago, 1936), 178-181.

27. Gilbert Osofsky, *Harlem: The Making of a Ghetto: Negro New York, 1890-1920* (New York, 1963), 149.

28. Calkins, *Some Folks*, 12-13. See also Corrington Gill, *Wasted Man-*

power: The Challenge of Unemployment (New York, 1939), 19-22; Epstein, *Insecurity*, 191-193.

29. See notes 16 and 17.

30. Federal Writers' Project, *These Are Our Lives* (Chapel Hill, N.C., 1939), 365-371.

2. The Gospel of Prevention, Progressive Style

1. Daniel M. Fox, *The Discovery of Abundance: Simon N. Patten and the Transformation of Social Theory* (Ithaca, N.Y., 1967), 160; Daniel T. Rodgers, *The Work Ethic in Industrial America, 1850-1920* (Chicago, 1978), 94-96.

2. Robert Bremner, *From the Depths: The Discovery of Poverty in the United States* (New York, 1956), emphasizes the connection among economic growth, optimism, and reform during the progressive era. Roy Lubove, *The Struggle for Social Security, 1900-1935* (Cambridge, Mass., 1968), makes prevention the central theme of social reformers at the time.

3. Quote from Cardinal Gibbons, "Wealth and its Obligations," *North American Review*, 152 (April 1891), 385-394; see also Clifford E. Clark, Jr., "Religious Beliefs and Social Reforms in the Gilded Age: The Case of Henry Whitney Bellows," *New England Quarterly*, 43 (March 1970), 59-78. Also Oscar Craig, "The Prevention of Pauperism," *Scribner's Magazine*, 14 (1893), 121-128; John Hope Franklin, "Public Welfare in the South during the Reconstruction Era, 1865-80," *Social Service Review*, 44 (Dec. 1970), 379-392; and Andrew Carnegie, "The Advantages of Poverty," *19th Century Magazine*, 29 (1891), 367-385. Relevant scholarly books include George Fredrickson, *The Inner Civil War: Northern Intellectuals and the Crisis of the Union* (New York, 1965), chaps. 7, 13; Nathan I. Huggins, *Protestants Against Poverty: Boston's Charities, 1870-1900* (Westport, Conn., 1971); and Paul T. Ringenbach, *Tramps and Reformers, 1873-1916* (Westport, Conn., 1973), 13-18.

4. Maurice Bruce, *The Coming of the Welfare State* (London, 1961); Derek Fraser, ed., *The New Poor Law in the 19th Century* (New York, 1976); J. R. Poynter, *Society and Pauperism: English Ideas on Poor Relief, 1795-1834* (London, 1969); and David Roberts, *Victorian Origins of the British Welfare State* (New Haven, 1960), all concern themselves with the institutionalization of this attitude in England during the nineteenth century.

5. Quotes are from Helen Campbell, "Certain Convictions as to Poverty," *Arena*, 1 (1889-1890), 101-113; and Josephine S. Lowell, "The Economic and Moral Effects of Public Outdoor Relief," National Conference of Charities and Corrections, *Proceedings* (1890), 91. See also Barry J. Kaplan, "Reformers and Charity: The Abolition of Public Outdoor Relief in New York City, 1870-1898," *Social Service Review*, 52 (June 1978), 202-214; and Josephine S. Lowell, "The True Aim of Charity Organization Societies," *Forum*, 21 (1896), 494-500. An authoritative treatment of American welfare is Blanche D. Coll, *Perspectives in Public Welfare* (Washington, 1970), 44 ff.

6. Amos Warner, *American Charities: A Study in Philanthropy and Eco-*

nomics (New York, 1894), 87-117; Robert Hunter, *Poverty* (New York, 1904), 75-76. See also Raymond Mohl, "Three Centuries of Public Welfare: 1600-1932," *Current History*, 65 (July 1973), 6-10; and James Leiby, "Amos Warner's *American Charities*, 1894-1930," *Social Service Review*, 37 (Dec. 1963), 441-455.

7. Francis Walker, "The Causes of Poverty," *Century*, 55 (1897-1898), 210-216. Scholarly treatments of this view include Roy Lubove, *The Professional Altruist: The Emergence of Social Work as a Career, 1880-1930* (Cambrige, Mass., 1965), 68-71; John S. Haller, Jr., *Outcasts from Evolution: Scientific Attitudes of Racial Inferiority, 1859-1900* (Urbana, Ill., 1971); and Mark Haller, *Eugenics: Hereditarian Attitudes in American Thought* (New Brunswick, N.J., 1963).

8. Joseph Lee, *Constructive and Preventive Philanthropy* (New York, 1902), 8-9; Robert Kelso, *Poverty* (New York, 1929), 338. Also Kenneth Kusmer, "The Functions of Organized Charity in the Progressive Era: Chicago as a Case Study," *Journal of American History*, 60 (Dec. 1973), 657-678.

9. Jamieson B. Hurry, *Poverty and Its Vicious Circles* (London, 1921), 1-3. Also Gustav Keene, "The Statistical Study of Causes of Destitution," in James Ford, ed., *Social Problems and Social Policy: Principles Underlying Treatment and Prevention of Poverty, Defectiveness, and Criminality* (Boston, 1923), 273-285.

10. Kelso, *Poverty*, passim. Quote from *Charities* cited in Clarke A. Chambers and Andrea Hinding, "Charity Workers, the Settlements, and the Poor," *Social Casework*, 49 (Feb. 1968), 96-101. Edward Devine's views are in his *Misery and Its Causes* (New York, 1920), 11. Key articles suggesting the modern outlook of progressives before 1930 are Robert L. Buroker, "From Voluntary Association to Welfare State: The Illinois Immigrants Protective League, 1908-26," *Journal of American History*, 58 (Dec. 1971), 643-660; Clarke A. Chambers, "Creative Effort in an Age of Normalcy, 1918-33," *Social Welfare Forum*, 1961, 252-271; and Allen Davis, "Welfare, Reform, and World War I," *American Quarterly*, 19 (Fall 1967), 516-533.

11. Jacob Hollander, *Abolition of Poverty* (Cambridge, Mass., 1914), 5, 16. On Hollander, see H. M. Douty, "Poverty Programs: The View from 1914," *Monthly Labor Review*, 93 (April 1970), 69-71. For comparable structuralist views see Lilian Brandt, "The Causes of Poverty," *Political Science Quarterly*, 23 (Dec. 1908), 637-656.

12. Jacob Riis, introduction to Lee, *Philanthropy*, 123.

13. Lee, *Philanthropy*, 211. Also Homer Folks, *The Care of Destitute, Neglected, and Delinquent Children* (New York, 1902), 72-81, 188, 288; Jack M. Holl, *Juvenile Reform in the Progressive Era: William R. George and the Junior Republic Movement* (Ithaca, N.Y., 1971); and Ellen Ryerson, *The Best-Laid Plans: America's Juvenile Court Experiment* (New York, 1978), 47-48. Among Walter I. Trattner's many books in the field of social welfare history is a useful biography of Folks, *Homer Folks: Pioneer in Social Welfare* (New York, 1968).

14. Allen Davis, *Spearheads for Reform: The Social Settlements and the Progressive Movement* (New York, 1967), passim. Also Dorothy G. Becker,

"Exit Lady Bountiful: The Volunteer and the Professional Social Worker," *Social Service Review*, 38 (March 1964), 57-72.

15. Robert Woods, "Universal Settlements: Their Point and Drift," *Quarterly Journal of Economics* (Nov. 1899), 67-86. See also Edward S. Shapiro, "Robert A. Woods and the Settlement House Impulse," *Social Service Review*, 52 (June 1978), 215-226; James Leiby, "State Welfare Institutions and the Poor," *Social Casework*, 49 (Feb. 1968), 90-95; Marvin E. Gettleman, "Charity and Social Classes in the United States, 1874-1900," *American Journal of Economics and Sociology*, 22 (April 1963), 313-330, and ibid. (July 1963), 417-426; Samuel Mencher, "The Influence of Romanticism on 19th Century British Social Work," *Social Service Review*, 38 (June 1964), 174-190; and John F. McClymer, "The Emergence of Social Engineering in America, 1890-1925: An Essay in the History of the 'New' Middle Class," PhD. dissertation, State University of New York at Stony Brook (1973), 21-32.

16. Thorstein Veblen cited in Davis, *Spearheads*, 17. A thoughtful retrospect on settlements in Herbert Gans, "Redefining the Settlements' Function for War on Poverty," *Social Work*, 9 (Oct. 1964), 3-12.

17. Edwin H. Sutherland and Harvey J. Locke, *Twenty Thousand Homeless Men: A Study of Unemployed Men in the Chicago Shelters* (Chicago, 1936).

18. Other evaluations of settlements, and of the bureaucratization of social work by 1930, include Paul Boyer, *Urban Masses and Moral Order in America, 1820-1920* (Cambridge, Mass., 1978), 155-157; Frank J. Bruno, *Trends in Social Work, 1874-1956*, 2nd ed. (New York, 1957), 119, 186; Lubove, *Professional Altruist*, 157-178; Michael J. Austin and Neil Betten, "Intellectual Origins of Community Organizing, 1920-1939," *Social Service Review*, 51 (March 1977), 155-170; and Robert Fisher, "Community Organizing and Citizen Participation: The Efforts of the People's Institute in New York City, 1910-1920," ibid., 51 (Sept. 1977), 474-490.

19. Virginia Robinson, cited in Lubove, *Professional Altruist*, 113.

20. Kellogg and Muste cited in Chambers, "Creative Effort."

21. My analysis relies on Gaston Rimlinger, "American Social Security in European Perspective," in William Bowen et al., eds., *The American System of Social Insurance* (New York, 1968), 213-232; Rimlinger, *Welfare Policy and Industrialization in Europe, America, and Russia* (New York, 1971); Rimlinger, "Welfare Policy and Economic Development: A Comparative Historical Perspective," *Journal of Economic History*, 26 (Dec. 1966), 556-571; Daniel Nelson, *Unemployment Insurance: The American Experience, 1915-1935* (Madison, Wis., 1969), 11-46; Roy Lubove, "Economic Security and Social Conflict in America," *Journal of Social History*, 1 (Fall 1967), 61-87, and ibid. (Summer 1968), 325-350; and Irwin Yellowitz, "The Origins of Unemployment Reform in the United States," *Labor History*, 9 (Fall 1968), 338-360.

22. Folks cited in Winifred Bell, *Aid to Dependent Children* (New York, 1965), 7. Basic sources on the mothers' aid movement are Grace Abbott, *From Relief to Social Security: The Development of the New Public Welfare Services and their Administration* (Chicago, 1941), 230-233, 262-279; U.S.

Children's Bureau, *Mothers Aid*, publication 220 (1931); Bruno, *Trends in Social Work*, 208-210; and Coll, *Perspectives*, 76-77. See also David Rothman, "The State as Parent," in Willard Gaylin et al., *Doing Good: The Limits of Benevolence* (New York, 1978); Edward Berkowitz and Kim McQuaid, *Creating the Welfare State: The Political Economy of 20th Century Reform, 1900's-1950's* (New York, 1980).

23. Howard Odum, "Public Welfare Activities," in President's Research Committee on Social Trends, *Recent Social Trends in the United States* (New York, 1933), 1224-1273; Robert Kelso, "The Transition from Charities and Correction to Public Welfare," *Annals*, 105 (Jan. 1923), 21-25.

24. Mitchell, introduction to Report of Committee on Recent Economic Change in the United States of the President's Conference on Unemployment, *Recent Economic Changes in the United States* (New York, 1929), xx. For statistics, see *Historical Statistics*, 193; Coll, *Perspectives*, 80-82.

25. *Statistical History of the United States, from Colonial Times to the Present* (Washington, 1976), 340, 359. A key source for statistics on poverty in the 1920s is Isaac Rubinow, "Poverty," *Encyclopedia for the Social Sciences*, 12 (1934), 284-332. Also Joanna C. Colcord, *Cash Relief* (New York, 1936); Odum, "Public Welfare"; and Josephine C. Brown, *Public Relief, 1929-1939* (New York, 1940), 56-62.

26. Major sources are Lubove, "Economic Security"; Bell, *Aid to Dependent Children*, 13-15; Coll, *Perspectives*, 77-80; Brown, *Public Relief*, 380.

27. Edith Abbott, *Public Assistance*, I (Chicago, 1940), 127.

28. Abbott, *Public Assistance*, I, 35, 125-136, 157-162, 174-175, 190, 220-223. Also Martha Derthick, *The Influence of Federal Grants: Public Assistance in Massachusetts* (Cambridge, Mass., 1970), 28; and Sophonisba Breckenridge, *Public Welfare Administration in the United States* (Chicago, 1927), 708-709.

29. Helen Hall, "English Dole and American Charity," *Atlantic Monthly*, 151 (May 1933), 538-549; Paul H. Douglas, *Wages and the Family* (Chicago, 1925), 47-49.

30. Relevant sources include Gunnar Myrdal, *Beyond the Welfare State: Economic Planning and Its International Implications* (New Haven, 1960); Asa Briggs, "The Welfare State in Historical Perspective," *Archives Européenes de Sociologie*, 2 (1961), 221-258; Nathan Glazer, "The Limits of Social Policy," *Commentary*, 52 (Sept. 1971), 51-58. Myrdal and Glazer especially stress the unique ethnicity of the United States. See also Arthur Mawick, "The Labor Party and the Welfare State in Britain, 1900-1948," *American Historical Review*, 73, (Dec. 1967), 380-403; Paul Addison, *The Road to 1945: British Politics and the Second World War* (London, 1977); and the works by Rimlinger (see note 21).

31. See Boyer, *Urban Masses*, 60-64; M. J. Heale, "From City Fathers to Social Critics: Humanitarianism and Government in New York, 1792-1860," *Journal of American History*, 63 (June 1976), 21-41; David Rothman, *The Discovery of the Asylum: Social Order and Disorder in the New Republic* (Boston, 1971); Marvin Meyers, "The Jacksonian Persuasion," *American*

Quarterly, 5 (Spring 1953), 3-15; R. Richard Wohl, "The 'Country Boy' Myth and Its Place in American Urban Culture: The 19th Century Contribution," *Perspectives in American History*, 3 (1969), 77-158; Clifford Griffin, "Religious Beneficence as Social Control, 1815-1860," *Mississippi Valley Historical Review*, 44 (Dec. 1957), 423-444; and especially Frances Fox Piven and Richard A. Cloward, *Regulating the Poor: The Functions of Public Welfare* (New York, 1971).

32. Quotes in Carroll Smith Rosenberg, *Religion and the Rise of the American City: The New York City Mission Movement, 1812-1870* (Ithaca, N.Y., 1971), 156; Roy Lubove, "The New York Association for Improving the Condition of the Poor: The Formative Years," *New York Historical Quarterly*, 43 (July 1959), 307-327.

33. Psychological interpretations include William Ryan, *Blaming the Victim*, rev. ed. (New York, 1976); and Kai Erikson, *Wayward Puritans: A Study in the Sociology of Deviance* (New York, 1966).

34. Sources that criticize "social control" interpretations include Eugene Durman, "Have the Poor Been Regulated? Toward a Multivariate Understanding of Welfare Growth," *Social Service Review*, 47 (Sept. 1973), 339-350; Gerald Grob, "Reflections on the History of Social Policy in America," *Reviews in American History*, 7 (Sept. 1979), 293-308; William A. Muraskin, "The Social Control Theory in American History: A Critique," *Journal of Social History*, 9 (Summer 1976), 559-568; Lois Banner, "Religious Benevolence as Social Control: A Critique of an Interpretation," *Journal of American History*, 60 (June 1973), 23-41; Timothy L. Smith, *Revivalism and Social Reform in mid-19th Century America* (New York, 1957), 1-10; and Smith Rosenberg, *Religion*, 59, 186-187, 260-261.

35. Theodore Roosevelt cited in Rodgers, *Work Ethic*. See also Benjamin J. Klebaner, "Poverty and Its Relief in American Thought, 1815-1861," *Social Service Review*, 38 (Dec. 1964), 382-399; and R. Richard Wohl, "The 'Rags to Riches Story': An Episode of Secular Idealism," in Reinhard Bendix and S. M. Lipset, eds., *Class, Status, and Power* (Glencoe, Ill., 1953), 388-395.

36. Hugh Heclo, *Modern Social Politics in Britain and Sweden: From Relief to Income Maintenance* (New Haven, 1974), 296-301; Arnold J. Heidenheimer, "The Politics of Public Education, Health, and Welfare in the United States of America and Western Europe: How Growth and Reform Potentials Have Differed," *British Journal of Political Science*, 3 (July 1973), 315-340. See also the authoritative historical account of José Harris, *Unemployment and Politics: A Study in English Social Policy, 1886-1914* (Oxford, 1972); and Bentley Gilbert, "Winston Churchill versus the Webbs: The Origins of British Unemployment Insurance," *American Historical Review*, 71 (April 1966), 846-862.

37. Quotes from Heidenheimer, "Politics." See also Heclo, *Modern Social Politics*, 312.

38. Rimlinger, *Welfare Policy*, 75-80. See also Richard M. Titmuss, *Commitment to Welfare* (New York, 1968), 188-199.

39. Edward D. Berkowitz and Kim McQuaid, "Bureaucrats as 'Social Engineers': Federal Welfare Programs in Herbert Hoover's America," *The American Journal of Economics and Sociology*, 39 (Oct. 1980), 321-325.

3. The Poor in the Depression

1. Quotations, in order: Martha Gellhorn to Harry Hopkins, Dec. 10, 1934, Hopkins papers, box 66, Franklin D. Roosevelt Library, Hyde Park, N.Y.; Hazel Reavis to Hopkins, Nov. 4, 1934, ibid.; "Survey of Current Relief Situation," p. 18, March 21, 1938, American Association of Social Workers papers, box 19, Social Welfare History Archives, University of Minnesota; ibid., p. 18; "Survey of Immediate Relief Situation in Illinois," July 31, 1936, ibid., box 20; "Survey of Current Relief Situation," p. 14.
2. Paul E. Mertz, *New Deal Policy and Southern Rural Poverty* (Baton Rouge, La., 1978), 5-13; See also *Low Income Families and Economic Stability: Materials on the Problem of Low Income Families*, Sen. Doc. 231, 81st Cong., 2d Sess. (1950), 111-138.
3. Charles Johnson, *Shadow of the Plantation* (Chicago, 1934), 100. Also pp. 29, 119, 125, 208. See also Arthur Raper, *Preface to Peasantry: A Tale of Two Black Belt Counties* (Chapel Hill, N.C., 1939).
4. Allison Davis and John Dollard, *Children of Bondage: The Personality Development of Negro Youth in the Urban South* (Washington, 1940), xxi-xxii; Hortense Powdermaker, *After Freedom: A Cultural Study of the Deep South* (New York, 1939), 143; John Dollard, *Caste and Class in a Southern Town* (New Haven, 1937), 414.
5. E. W. Burgess, introduction to E. Franklin Frazier, *The Negro Family in the United States* (Chicago, 1939), ix-xii; Frazier, *The Negro Family in the United States*, rev. ed. (Chicago, 1957), 367-368; Gunnar Myrdal, *An American Dilemma: The Negro Problem and Modern Democracy* (New York, 1944), 928-929; Daniel Moynihan, *The Negro Family: The Case for National Action* (Washington, 1965).
6. Relevant studies include Herbert Gutman, *The Black Family in Slavery and Freedom, 1750-1925* (New York, 1976), xix, chap. 10; Lawrence Levine, *Black Culture and Black Consciousness: Afro-American Folk Thought from Slavery to Freedom* (New York, 1977), 442; Robert Blauner, "Black Culture: Lower Class Result or Ethnic Creation?" in Lee Rainwater, ed., *Black Experience: Soul* (New Brunswick, N.J., 1973), 143-180; Dorothy K. Newman, et al., *Protest, Politics, and Prosperity: Black Americans and White Institutions, 1940-1975* (New York, 1978); Carol Stack, *All Our Kin: Strategies for Survival in a Black Community* (New York, 1971); Crandall A. Shifflet, "The Household Composition of Rural Black Families: Louisa County, Virginia, 1880," *Journal of Interdisciplinary History*, 6 (Autumn 1975), 235-260; and Frank Furstenberg, Jr., Theodore Hershberg, and John Modell, "The Origins of the Female-Headed Black Family: The Impact of the Urban Experience," ibid., 211-233. For rural whites, see J. Wayne Flynt, *Dixie's Forgotten People: The South's Poor Whites* (Bloomington, Ind., 1979); Mar-

garet J. Hagood, *Women of the South: Portraiture of the White Tenant Farmer Woman* (Chapel Hill, N.C., 1939); and Mildred Rutherford Mell, "Poor Whites of the South," *Social Forces*, 17 (Dec. 1938), 153-167.

7. Works Progress Administration, *Urban Workers on Relief*, pt. I (Washington, 1936), xxiii ff., 50-52.

8. Statistics from *Historical Statistics of the United States: Colonial Times to 1957* (Washington, 1961). See also Edwin H. Sutherland and Harvey J. Locke, *Twenty Thousand Homeless Men: A Study of Unemployed Men in the Chicago Shelters* (Chicago, 1936), 32-49; and Corrington Gill, "How Many Are Unemployable," *Survey*, 71 (Jan. 1935), 3; *Low Income Families*, 7-8, 99-106, 138.

9. National Resources Planning Board, *Security, Work, and Relief Policies* (Washington, 1942), 24, 130-133, 445-449. For Roosevelt, see Samuel Rosenman, comp., *Public Papers and Addresses of Franklin D. Roosevelt*, vol. 6 (New York, 1941), 4.

10. Unemployment Census File, Official File 2948, Roosevelt Library; Bernard Sternsher, "Counting the Unemployed and Recent Economic Developments," in Sternsher, ed., *The New Deal* (New York., 1979), 101-103; John Garraty, *Unemployment in History: Economic Thought and Public Policy* (New York, 1978), 174; Paul Webbink, "Unemployment, 1930-40," *American Economic Review, Proceedings*, 30 (Feb. 1941), 248-272.

11. Herman Miller, "The Dimensions of Poverty," in Ben B. Seligman, ed., *Poverty as a Public Issue* (New York, 1965), 20-51; Mayer N. Zald, "Demographics, Politics, and the Future of the Welfare State," *Social Service Review*, 51 (March 1977), 110-124.

12. Hopkins speech, April 9, 1934, box 9, Hopkins papers; Hopkins, *Spending to Save* (New York, 1936), 111. See also Hopkins's testimony to the Special Committee Investigating Unemployment and Relief, April 8, 1938, box 11, Hopkins papers.

13. Unemployment Committee, National Federation of Settlements, *Case Studies of Unemployment* (Philadelphia, 1931); Clinch Calkins, *Some Folks Won't Work* (New York, 1930).

14. See Hopkins papers, esp. boxes 61 and 66; and papers of the National Association of Social Workers (NASW) and of Survey Associates, Social Welfare History Archives.

15. Harry Lurie, "Future Coordination of Federal Dependency Relief Program," Feb. 16-17, 1934, NASW papers, folder 210; Ewan Clague, "The Fundamental Principles Governing a Social Welfare Program," Nov. 20, 1934, ibid., folder 201.

16. Committee on Current Relief Problems, "The Work and Relief Program," February 1935, NASW papers, folder 210; William Hodson, "Current Problems of Government and Social Work," March 1937, ibid., folder 231. See also Kenneth L. M. Pray, "A Plan for the Treatment of Unemployment," *Survey*, 69 (March 1933), 135.

17. "Poverty," *Encyclopedia for the Social Sciences*, 12 (1934), 284-292.

18. See Robert H. Bremner, "Poverty in Perspective," in John Braeman, Robert H. Bremner, and Everett Walters, eds., *Change and Continuity in*

20th Century America (New York, 1966), 262-280. Relevant contemporary sources reflecting structural views of poverty include Josephine Brown, *Public Relief, 1929-1939* (New York, 1940); William Haber, "Relief: A Permanent Program," *Survey Graphic*, 27 (Dec. 1938), 591-594; Ewan Clague and Webster Powell, *Ten Thousand Out of Work* (Philadelphia, 1937); and Elizabeth W. Gilboy, *Applicants for Work Relief: A Study of Massachusetts Families Under the FERA and WPA* (Cambridge, Mass., 1940), 146-147, 233.

19. Charles H. Trout, "Welfare in the New Deal Era," *Current History*, 65 (July 1973), 11-15 ff; Neil Betten, "American Attitudes toward the Poor: A Historical Overview," ibid., 1-5; Michael E. Schiltz, *Public Attitudes Toward Social Security, 1935-1965* (Washington, 1970), 35-37, 114, 155.

20. See Robert McElvaine, "One-third of a Nation: Working Class Thought in the Great Depression," unpublished manuscript, p. 4.

21. Hopkins speeches, May 10, 1935, and March 14, 1936, box 9, Hopkins papers.

22. Cited in Tom E. Terrill and Jerrold Hirsch, *Such as Us: Southern Voices of the Thirties* (Chapel Hill, N.C., 1978), xxi.

23. Erskine Caldwell and Margaret Bourke-White, *You Have Seen Their Faces* (New York, 1937), 12, 165. An excellent evaluation of this and other such efforts is William Stott, *Documentary Expression and Thirties America* (New York, 1973), 141-170. See also Ann Banks, ed., *First-Person America* (New York, 1980), a collection of interviews from 1938-1942 of mostly working-class people.

24. Federal Writers Project, *These Are Our Lives* (Chapel Hill, N.C., 1939), 17, 371, 30. See also Leonard Rapport, "How Valid Are the Federal Writers' Project Life Stories: An Iconoclast among the True Believers," *Oral History Review* (1979), 6-17.

25. Caldwell and Bourke-White, *You Have Seen*, 25, 52.

26. Judith Mara Gutman, *Lewis W. Hine and the American Social Conscience* (New York, 1967); Kirsten A. Grønbjerg, *Mass Society and the Extension of Welfare, 1960-1970* (Chicago, 1977), 97-103; Stott, *Documentary Expression*, 145-146, 156-158, 220-221. Some people in contemporary documentaries did criticize the system. One farmer told WPA interviewers, "I'm not sayin' that the capitalistic system shouldn't be maintained, but it should be maintained with a more equitable distribution of wealth." (*These Are Our Lives*, 407).

27. Orwell, *The Road to Wigan Pier* (London, 1937), 51. A relevant recollection of European approaches is Paul F. Lazarsfeld, "An Episode in the History of Social Research," in Donald Fleming and Bernard Bailyn, eds., *Intellectual Migration, Europe and America, 1930-1960* (Cambridge, Mass., 1969), 270-337.

28. See Stott, *Documentary Expression*, 58, for Lange quote and for arguments along these lines.

29. Abraham Epstein, *Insecurity: A Challenge to America* (New York, 1933), 214; August B. Hollingshead, "Selected Characteristics of Classes in a Mid West Community," in Reinhold Bendix and S. M. Lipset, eds., *Class,*

Status, and Power: A Reader in Social Stratification (Glencoe, Ill., 1953), 213-224.

30. Wayne Parris to Hopkins, Nov. 17, 1934, box 66, Hopkins papers; Martha Gellhorn to Hopkins, Nov. 9, 1934, ibid.; Lazarsfeld, "An Episode," 227-278; Gellhorn to Hopkins, April 25, 1935, box 66, Hopkins papers.

31. Martha Gellhorn to Hopkins, Nov. 9, 1934, box 66, Hopkins papers; Lorena Hickok to Hopkins, Sept. 9, 1934, Federal Emergency Relief Administration papers, OF-444, box 3, Roosevelt Library; John Garraty, "To Be Jobless in America," *American Heritage*, 30 (Dec. 1978), 65-68. See also Philip Eisenberg and Paul F. Lazarsfeld, "The Psychological Effects of Unemployment," *Psychological Bulletin*, 35 (June 1938), 358-390; National Federation of Settlements, *Case Studies*, xxxvi, 385-400 ("How Unemployment Looks to the Unemployed"); and Bernard Sternsher, "Depression and New Deal in Ohio: Lorena A. Hickok's Reports to Harry Hopkins, 1934-1936," *Ohio History*, 86 (Autumn 1977), 258-277.

32. Thad Holt to Hopkins, Nov. 15, 1934, box 61, Hopkins papers; Wayne Parrish to Hopkins, Dec. 8, 1934, and Nov. 11, 1934, ibid.

33. A useful article that stresses the concern of contemporaries for the "morale" of the poor is William W. Bremer, "Along the 'American Way'; The New Deal's Work Relief Programs for the Unemployed," *Journal of American History*, 62 (Dec. 1975), 636-652. For Gellhorn's comment, see Gellhorn to Hopkins, Dec. 10, 1934, box 66, Hopkins papers.

34. These paragraphs owe their argument to McElvaine, "One Third of a Nation," and McElvaine, "Down and Out: The 'Forgotten Man' in the Great Depression." For quotes from the latter, in order, see pp. 36, 341, 291, 388. Poll data from Hadley Cantril and Mildred Strunk, *Public Opinion, 1935-1946* (Princeton, 1951), 893.

35. Hickok to Hopkins, April 2, 1934, box 61, Hopkins papers; McElvaine, "One Third of a Nation."

36. William Matthews to Fiorello La Guardia, Nov. 16, 1934, folder 730, Survey Associates papers; E. Wright Bakke, *The Unemployed Worker: A Study of the Task of Making a Living without a Job* (New Haven, 1940), 362-366.

37. Gellhorn to Hopkins, Dec. 10, 1934, and Dec. 19, 1934, box 66, Hopkins papers. Also Gellhorn, *The Trouble I've Seen* (New York, 1936) and Glen H. Elder, Jr., *Children of the Great Depression* (Chicago, 1974).

38. Bernard Sternsher, "Victims of the Great Depression: Self Blame/Non-Self-Blame, Radicalism, and Pre-1929 Experiences," *Social Science History*, 1 (Winter 1977), 137-177. Two scholars who emphasize the potential radicalism of the poor in the 1930s are Frances Fox Piven and Richard A. Cloward, *Poor People's Movements: Why They Succeed, How They Fail* (New York, 1977), 43, 56.

39. Bakke, *Unemployed Worker*, 315-316; Orwell, *Road to Wigan Pier*, 90. See also Jacqueline D. Goodchilds and Ewart E. Smith, "The Effects of Unemployment as Mediated by Social Status," *Sociometry*, 26 (Sept. 1963), 287-293.

40. E. Wight Bakke, *Citizens without Work: A Study of the Effects of Unemployment upon the Workers' Social Relations and Practices* (New Haven, 1940), 226-242, 277, 303-304; Bakke, *Unemployed Worker*, 371-372. See also Zavada D. Blum and Peter H. Rossi, eds., "Social Class Research and Images of the Poor: A Bibliographic Review," in Daniel Moynihan, ed., *On Understanding Poverty: Perspectives from the Social Sciences* (New York, 1968), 343-397. Also Glen H. Elder, Jr., and Richard C. Rockwell, "The Depression Experience in Men's Lives," in Allan J. Lichtman and Joan R. Challinor, eds., *Kin and Communities: Families in America* (Washington, 1979), 95-118; and Robert C. Angell, *The Family Encounters the Depression* (New York, 1936).

4. The Early Welfare State

1. Josephine C. Brown, *Public Relief, 1929-1939* (New York, 1940), ix.
2. National Resources Planning Board (NRPB), *Security, Work, and Relief Policies* (Washington, 1942), 291; Brown, *Public Relief*, 73; Joanna C. Colcord, *Cash Relief* (New York, 1936), 28 ff.
3. Bonnie R. Fox, "Unemployment Relief in Philadelphia, 1930-1932: A Study of the Depression's Impact on Voluntarism," *Pennsylvania Magazine of History and Biography*, 93 (Jan. 1969), 86-108. For other examples, see Raymond L. Koch, "Politics and Relief in Minneapolis during the 1930's," *Minnesota·History*, 41 (Winter 1968), 153-170; Richard T. Ortquist, "Unemployment and Relief: Michigan's Response to the Depression During the Hoover Years," *Michigan History*, 57 (Fall 1973), 209-236; and especially Barbara Blumberg, *The New Deal and the Unemployed: The View from New York City* (Lewisburg, Pa., 1979).
4. NRPB, *Security*, 99, 291; Edith Abbott, *Public Assistance*, vol. 2 (Chicago, 1940), 680-682, 763-764; R. Clyde White and Mary K. White, *Research Memorandum on Social Aspects of Relief Policies in the Depression*, Social Science Research Council Bulletin no. 38 (New York, 1937), 13-14. The most valuable general work on New Deal welfare policy is William E. Leuchtenburg, *Franklin D. Roosevelt and the New Deal, 1932-1940* (New York, 1963), esp. chap. 6.
5. Minutes, Board of Directors meeting, National Federation of Settlements, Jan. 29-30, 1932, folder 587, Survey Associates papers, Social Welfare History Archives, University of Minnesota; Gertrude Springer memo (Oct. 1933), folder 487, ibid. Others sources dealing with private charity in the 1930s are Clarke A. Chambers, "Social Service and Social Reform: A Historical Essay," *Social Service Review*, 37 (March 1963), 76-90; John Finbar Jones and John Middlemist Herrick, *Citizens in Service: Volunteers in Social Welfare During the Depression, 1929-1941* (East Lansing, Mich., 1976); Judith Ann Trolander, *Settlement Houses and the Great Depression* (Detroit, 1975); Eveline Burns, oral history interview, 68, Columbia University Oral History Office; and Elizabeth Wickenden, "Social Security and Voluntary Social Welfare," *Industrial and Labor Relations Review*, 14 (Oct. 1960), 94-106.
6. Sherrard Ewing to FERA, June 23, 1933, box 58, Harry Hopkins

papers, Franklin D. Roosevelt Library; Field Reports of FERA, box 56, ibid. See also James T. Patterson, *The New Deal and the States: Federalism in Transition* (Princeton, 1969).

7. Hazel Reavis to Hopkins, Nov. 18, 1934, box 66, Hopkins papers; Hickok to Hopkins, Sept. 9, 1934, box 3, FERA papers, OF-444, Roosevelt Library; Pierce Williams to Hopkins, Aug. 31, 1933, box 56, Hopkins papers. See also Eileen Blackey, "Paternalism Bewilders Poor Farmers," *Survey*, 71 (Sept. 1935), 264.

8. Harry Hopkins, *Spending to Save* (New York, 1936), 99. Statistics from NRPB, *Security*, 99.

9. Leuchtenburg, *Franklin D. Roosevelt*, 122-123.

10. Roger Daniels, ed., introduction to Hopkins, *Spending to Save* (Seattle, 1972 ed.), 8; Hopkins speech, March 14, 1936, box 9, Hopkins papers; Samuel Rosenman, comp., *Public Papers and Addresses of Franklin D. Roosevelt* (New York, 1938-1950), 5:19-21.

11. Hopkins, *Spending*, 142. See also Arthur J. Altmeyer, *The Formative Years of Social Security* (Madison, Wis., 1966); Charles McKinley and Robert W. Frase, *Launching Social Security: A Capture and Record Account, 1935-1937* (Madison, 1970); Theron F. Schlabach, *Edwin E. Witte, Cautious Reformer* (Madison, 1969); and Edwin E. Witte, *The Development of the Social Security Act* (Madison, 1963).

12. The focus here is on the major welfare programs of the New Deal. Many other programs, of course, such as the Civilian Conservation Corps, the Farm Security Administration, the Public Works Administration, and the United States Housing Administration included relief and welfare in their activities.

13. Ellen C. Potter to Roosevelt, Jan. 15, 1935, Jan. 29, 1935, OF 727, Roosevelt papers; Gov. Herbert Lehman to Roosevelt, March 16, 1936, OF 2037, ibid.; Roosevelt to Lehman, March 30, 1936, ibid.

14. Eric Beecroft and Seymour Janow, "Toward a National Policy for Migration," *Social Forces*, 16 (May 1938), 475-492.

15. "Survey of Immediate Relief Situation in Illinois," July 31, 1936, box 20, American Association of Social Workers Papers, Social Welfare History Archives.

16. Edith Abbott, "Federal Relief—Sold Down the River," *Nation*, 142 (March 18, 1936), 346-347; American Association of Social Workers, "Survey of the Current Relief Situation," March 21, 1938, box 19, AASW papers.

17. Brown, *Public Relief*, 386-389.

18. Abbott, *Public Assistance*, 2:763-764; AASW, "Survey of Current Relief Situation."

19. Hopkins speeches, May 10, 1935, Dec. 15, 1935, box 9, Hopkins papers; Hopkins, *Spending to Save*, 114.

20. Leuchtenburg, *Franklin D. Roosevelt*, 124-130; Donald S. Howard, *The WPA and Federal Relief Policy* (New York, 1943), 381-394, 794 ff.

21. Brown, *Public Relief*, 444-446; Howard, *WPA*, 819-821, 854-857; NRPB, *Security*, 236.

22. Congressman Walter Pierce (Oregon) to Marvin McIntyre, Aug. 24,

1935, box 21, OF 444, Roosevelt papers; AASW, "Proposed Outline for Federal Work and Relief Program," Jan. 1936, National Association for Social Work papers, Social Welfare History Archives; Blumberg, *New Deal and Unemployed*, 54, 72, 138-139; Susan Wolfe Ware, "Political Sisterhood in the New Deal: Women in Politics and Government, 1935-1940," PhD. dissertation, Harvard University, 1978, 144-160.

23. E. Wight Bakke, *The Unemployed Worker: A Study of the Task of Making a Living without a Job* (New Haven, 1940), 386-425; Lewis Meriam, *Relief and Social Security* (Washington, 1946), 415-425; William W. Bremer, "Along the 'American Way': The New Deal's Work Relief Programs for the Unemployed," *Journal of American History*, 42 (Dec. 1975), 636-652; Wayne Parris to Hopkins, Nov. 17, 1934, and Martha Gellhorn to Hopkins, Dec. 13, 1934, box 66, Hopkins papers.

24. Howard, *WPA*, 812-815; Bakke, *Unemployed Worker*, 396-397.

25. Grace Abbott, *From Relief to Social Security: The Development of the New Public Welfare Services and their Administration* (Chicago, 1941), 38-40.

26. Howard, *WPA*, 824-828; Blumberg, *New Deal and Unemployed*, 223-224.

27. Useful accounts are Jay L. Roney, "Twenty Years of Public Assistance," *Social Security Bulletin*, 18 (Aug. 1955), 17 ff; Brown, *Public Relief*, 373-374; Grace Abbott, *From Relief*, 209-211; Arthur J. Altmeyer, "The New Social Security Program," *School Life*, 25 (Jan. 1940), 103-104; Wilbur J. Cohen, "Factors Influencing the Content of Federal Public Welfare Legislation," *Social Welfare Forum*, 81 (1954), 199-215; Jules Berman, "Public Assistance under the Social Security Act," *Industrial and Labor Relations Review*, 14 (Oct. 1960), 83-93; and Ellen J. Perkins, "AFDC in Review," *Welfare in Review*, 1 (Nov. 1963), 1-16.

28. See Martha Derthick, *Uncontrollable Spending for Social Service Grants* (Washington, 1975), 20-22; Derthick, *The Influence of Federal Grants: Public Assistance in Massachusetts* (Cambridge, Mass., 1970), 60-62, 130, 230-232; McKinley and Frase, *Launching Social Security*, 138-217, 473-492; Arthur J. Altmeyer statement to Committee on Economic Security, Nov. 16, 1939, box 9, Chairman's Files, Social Security Administration, Record Group 47, National Archives, Washington.

29. Department of Health, Education, and Welfare, *Characteristics of State Public Assistance Plan under the Social Security Act*, Public Assistance Report no. 50 (1962); Social Security Board, "Proposed Changes in the Social Security Act," Jan. 1939, OF 1710, box 2, Roosevelt papers; Winifred Bell, *Aid to Dependent Children* (New York, 1965), 206.

30. Criticisms include Eveline M. Burns, "Where Welfare Falls Short," *Public Interest*, 1 (Fall 1965), 82-95; Gilbert Y. Steiner, "Reform Follows Reality: The Growth of Welfare," ibid., 34 (Winter 1974), 47-65; Grace Abbott, *From Relief*, 280-281.

31. Quote is by Joseph Harris in letter to Jane Perry Clark, April 2, 1935, box 13, Committee on Economic Security Files, Social Security Administration papers. See also Derthick, *Influence*, 43-44; Cohen, "Factors"; Witte, *Development of Social Security Act*, 143-144.

32. Dorothy K. Newman et al., *Protest, Politics, and Prosperity: Black Americans and White Institutions, 1940-1975* (New York, 1978), 256-257; Jane Hoey interview, 42-47, Columbia Oral History Project; Bell, *Aid*, chap. 1.

33. Brown, *Public Relief*, 383; Joe R. Feagin, *Subordinating the Poor: Welfare and American Beliefs* (Englewood Cliffs, N.J., 1975), 71; Bell, *Aid*, 203.

34. Frances Fox Piven and Richard A. Cloward, *Regulating the Poor: Functions of Public Welfare* (New York, 1971).

35. Witte's remarks are in letters to Harry Hopkins, Feb. 26, 1935, box 57, and to Raymond Moley, March 6, 1935, box 15, Committee on Economic Security Files, Social Security Administration papers. See also Altmeyer, *Formative Years*, 260-261; Gilbert Y. Steiner, *Social Insecurity: The Politics of Welfare* (Chicago, 1966), 22-26; Witte, *Development of Social Security Act*, 163-164; Steiner, *The Children's Cause* (Washington, 1976), 38-39; Charles E. Gilbert, "Policy-Making in Public Welfare: The 1962 Amendments," *Political Science Quarterly*, 81 (June 1966), 196-224.

36. Witte to Harry Hopkins, Feb. 26, 1935, box 57, Committee on Economic Security Files, Social Security Administration papers.

37. See Witte to Raymond Moley, May 10, 1935, box 15, Committee on Economic Security Files, Social Security Administration papers, for the role of the Court.

38. Witte, *Development of Social Security Act*, 78-79; Witte, "What to Expect of Social Security," *American Economic Review*, 34 (March 1944), 212-221; Andrew Achenbaum, *Old Age in the New Land: The American Experiment since 1790* (Baltimore, 1978); Arnold J. Heidenheimer, Hugh Heclo, and Carolyn Teich Adams, *Comparative Public Policy: The Politics of Social Choice in Europe and America* (New York, 1975), 195-196.

39. Daniel Nelson, *Unemployment Insurance: The American Experience, 1915-1935* (Madison, Wis., 1969), 120-128, 183-197; Roy Lubove, "Economic Security and Social Conflict in America," *Journal of Social History*, 1 (Fall 1967), 61-87, ibid. (Summer 1968), 325-350; Witte, *Development of Social Security Act*, 130, 140-142.

40. Gaston V. Rimlinger, *Welfare Policy and Industrialization in Europe, America, and Russia* (New York, 1971), 229-231; William Graebner, "Retirement and the Corporate State, 1885-1935: A New Context for Social Security," paper delivered at Organization of American Historians convention, New York, April 1978. Also Graebner, *A History of Retirement: The Meaning and Functions of an American Institution* (New Haven, 1980).

41. Witte to Raymond Moley, May 10, 1935, box 15, Committee on Economic Security Files, Social Security Administration. Important sources are Henry J. Aaron, "Social Security: International Comparisons," in Otto Eckstein, ed., *Studies in the Economics of Income Maintenance* (Washington, 1967), 13-48; Edward Berkowitz and Kim McQuaid, "Businessman and Bureaucrat: The Evolution of the American Social Welfare System, 1900-1940," *Journal of Economic History*, 38 (March 1978), 120-142; and Eveline M. Burns interview, 146-147, Columbia Oral History Project.

42. Quote by Eveline M. Burns, "Social Insurance in Evolution," *American Economic Review*, 34 (March 1944), 199-211. See also Achenbaum, *Old Age*, 131-138; Berkowitz and McQuaid, "Businessman and Bureaucrat."

43. Graebner, "Retirement and the Corporate State"; Michael K. Taussig, "Long-Run Consequences of Income Maintenance," in Kenneth Boulding and Martin Pfaff, eds., *Redistribution to the Rich and the Poor: The Grants Economics of Income Distribution* (Belmont, Calif., 1972), 376-386.

44. Frank J. Bruno, *Trends in Social Work, 1874-1956* (New York, 1957), 309-310; Witte, *Development of Social Security Act*, 130; Nelson, *Unemployment Insurance*, 208.

45. Edwin Witte, "Twenty Years of Social Security," *Social Security Bulletin*, 18 (Oct. 1955), 15-21; Altmeyer, *Formative Years*, 12-13; Frances Perkins, introduction to Witte, *Development of Social Security Act*, vi; Burns interview, 40-50; Nelson, *Unemployment Insurance*, 213-220.

46. Wilbur Cohen interview, 10, Lyndon B. Johnson Library, Austin, Texas. See also Cohen, "The First 25 Years of the Social Security Act, 1935-1960," *Social Work Year Book* (New York, 1960), 49-61.

47. For criticisms, see Howard, *WPA*, 831-832; Hugh Heclo, "The Welfare State: The Costs of American Self-Sufficiency," in Richard Rose, ed., *Lessons from America* (New York, 1974), 253-262; Taussig, "Long-Run Consequences"; and Abraham Epstein, *Insecurity*, rev. ed. (New York, 1936), 669-759.

48. Comparative studies include Aaron, "Social Security"; Otto Eckstein, "Financing the Social Security System," and Gaston Rimlinger, "American Social Security in European Perspective," in William Bowen et al., eds., *The American System of Social Insurance* (New York, 1968), 47-66, 213-232; and Harold Wilensky, *The Welfare State and Equality: Structural and Ideological Roots of Public Expenditures* (Berkeley, 1975), 105-106.

49. NRPB, *Security*, 99-100, 161, 291; Stephan Thernstrom, "Poverty in Historical Perspective," in Daniel Moynihan, ed., *On Understanding Poverty* (New York, 1968), 160-186.

5. Withering Away

1. For Boulding, see Herman P. Miller, ed. *Poverty, American Style* (Belmont, Calif., 1968), 49; for Miller, "Changes in the Number and Composition of the Poor," in Margaret S. Gordon, ed., *Poverty in America* (Berkeley, 1965), 81; for Bell, "Relevant Aspects of the Social Scene and Social Policy," in Eveline Burns, ed., *Children's Allowances and the Economic Welfare of Children* (New York, 1968), 163-171. Similar judgments are expressed by Robert J. Lampman, the economist whose studies of income distribution provided a data base for the war on poverty, in "Ends and Means in the War Against Poverty," Leo Fishman, ed., *Poverty Amid Affluence* (New Haven, 1966), 18-42; Herbert Gans, "Culture and Class in the Study of Poverty," in Daniel Moynihan, ed., *On Understanding Poverty: Perspectives from the Social Sciences* (New York, 1968), 201-228; and Henry J. Aaron in his authorita-

tive *Politics and the Professors: The Great Society in Perspective* (Washington, 1978), 17.

2. Gilbert Y. Steiner, *Social Insecurity: The Politics of Welfare* (Chicago, 1966), 190; Frederick Hayes, in "Poverty and Urban Policy: Conference Transcript of 1973 Group Discussion of the Kennedy Administration Urban Poverty Programs and Policies," 67, John F. Kennedy Library, Boston; Jack K. Roach and Janet K. Roach, eds., *Poverty* (London, 1972), 9; M. Elaine Burgess and Daniel O. Price, *An American Dependency Challenge* (Chicago, 1963), 156-157. Also Elizabeth Wickenden to Alvin Schorr, June 11, 1959, National Social Welfare Assembly papers, box 61, Social Welfare History Archives (SWHA), University of Minnesota. She wrote, "Social work does not attract or produce many individuals who are gifted at the objective analysis and clear exposition of the social implications of the programs that determine and support the ultimate tasks of social work."

3. Important comparative perspectives are Henry J. Aaron, "Social Security: International Comparisons," in Otto Eckstein, ed., *Studies in the Economics of Income Maintenance* (Washington, 1967); Hugh Heclo, "Income Maintenance Patterns," in Arnold J. Heidenheimer, Hugh Heclo, and Carolyn Teich Adams, *Comparative Public Policy: The Politics of Social Choice in Europe and America* (New York, 1975), 187-226; Gaston Rimlinger, *Welfare Policy and Industrialization in Europe, America, and Russia* (New York, 1971); Morris Janowitz, *Social Control of the Welfare State* (Chicago, 1976); and esp. Harold Wilensky, *The Welfare State and Equality: Structural and Ideological Roots of Public Expenditures* (Berkeley, 1975). See also Jacqueline R. Kasun, "United States Poverty in World Perspective," *Current History*, 64 (June 1973), 247 ff; Martin Rein and Hugh Heclo, "What Welfare Crisis? A Comparison among the United States, Britain, and Sweden," *Public Interest*, 33-36 (Fall 1973), 61-83; and Sidney E. Zimbalist, "Recent British and American Poverty Trends: Conceptual and Policy Contrasts," *Social Service Review*, 51 (Sept. 1977), 419-433.

4. Miller, "Changes," 81-101. The following pages depend heavily on this article and on Miller, *Rich Man Poor Man* (New York, 1964), 56-83; Miller, "The Dimensions of Poverty," in Ben B. Seligman, ed., *Poverty as a Public Issue* (New York, 1965), 20-51; James N. Morgan et al., *Income and Welfare in the United States* (New York, 1962); Oscar Ornati, *Poverty Amid Affluence* (New York, 1966), esp. chap. 3; and Council of Economic Advisers, "The Problem of Poverty in America," in *Economic Report of the President* (Washington, 1964), 55-83. Other relevant sources include Christopher Green, *Negative Taxes and the Poverty Problem* (Washington, 1967); Peter Townsend, "The Meaning of Poverty," *British Journal of Sociology*, 13 (Sept. 1962), 210-227; and Diana Karter Appelbaum, "The Level of the Poverty Line: A Historical Survey," *Social Service Review*, 51 (Sept. 1977), 514-523. All statistics used here concern the number who remained poor after public transfer payments. For Tobin, see "It Can Be Done," *New Republic*, 156 (June 3, 1967), 14-18.

5. Wilson C. McWilliams, "Poverty: Public Enemy Number One,"

Saturday Review, 49 (Dec. 10, 1066), 48 ff.; Miller, *Rich Man*, 57-58.

6. J. Wayne Flynt, *Dixie's Forgotten People: The South's Poor Whites* (Bloomington, Ind., 1979), 96-97; Miller, "Changes," 81-101; Larry Long, *Interregional Migration of the Poor: Some Recent Changes*, Current Population Report, Census Bureau (Nov. 1978).

7. *Low Income Families and Economic Stability: Materials on the Problem of Low Income Families*, Senate Document 231, 81st Congress, 2d Session, 1950; and Report of the Subcommittee on Low Income Families of the Joint Committee on the Economic Report, Sen. Doc. 146, 81 Cong., 1st Sess., March 1950. Figures used are those developed by the Council of Economic Advisers and pulled together conveniently in Mollie Orshansky, "Counting the Poor: Another Look at the Poverty Profile," *Social Security Bulletin*, 28 (Jan 1965), 3-29. Orshansky's figures are widely used. Unless otherwise noted, figures deal with poverty in families and do not include poverty of individuals not in families. Orshansky also reported statistics on poverty based on the Social Security Administration's so-called "economy budget." These differ only slightly from those used here.

8. Michael Harrington, *The Other America: Poverty in the United States* (New York, 1962).

9. Ornati, *Poverty*, 158.

10. For official methods, see Orshansky, "Counting the Poor"; and Orshansky, "Who Was Poor in 1966?" in Burns, *Children's Allowances*, 19-57; for debates over measures, see Orshansky, "Recounting the Poor—A Five Year Review," *Social Security Bulletin*, 29 (April 1966), 2-19; Orshansky, "How Poverty is Measured," *Monthly Labor Review*, 92 (Feb. 1969), 37-41; Morton Paglin, "The Measurement and Trend of Inequality: A Basic Revision," *American Economic Review*, 65 (Sept. 1975), 598-609; Mayer N. Zald, "Demographics, Politics, and the Future of the Welfare State," *Social Service Review*, 51 (March 1977), 110-124. See esp. John B. Williamson and Kathryn M. Hyer, "The Measurement and Meaning of Poverty," *Social Problems*, 22 (June 1975), 652-662; Joseph A. Kershaw, *Government Against Poverty* (Washington, 1970), chap. 1; and Robert D. Plotnick and Felicity Skidmore, *Progress Against Poverty: A Review of the 1964-1974 Decade* (New York, 1975), 30-40.

11. M. Elaine Burgess, "Poverty and Dependency: Some Selected Characteristics," *Journal of Social Issues*, 21 (Jan. 1965), 79-97. See also Joint Committee on the Economic Report, Subcommittee on Low Income Families, *Characteristics of the Low Income Population and Related Federal Programs*, 84th Cong., 1st Sess. (1955), 1-5, 43-50; Morgan, *Income and Welfare*, 216-227; and Robert H. Mugge, "Aid to Families with Dependent Children: Initial Findings of the 1961 Report on the Characteristics of AFDC Recipients," *Social Security Bulletin*, 26 (March 1963), 3-15.

12. Stephan Thernstrom "Is There Really a New Poor?" *Dissent*, 15 (Jan.-Feb. 1968), 59-64.

13. Aaron, *Politics and the Professors*, 17.

14. T. H. Marshall, *Class, Citizenship, and Social Development* (Garden City, N.Y., 1964), 267-268, 293; J. F. Sleeman, *The Welfare State: Its Aims,*

Benefits, and Costs (London, 1973), 41-43; Norman Furniss and Timothy Tilton, *The Case for the Welfare State* (Bloomington, Ind., 1977), 104-107; Angus Calder, *The People's War* (London, 1959). In practice, the Beveridge plan, hampered by fiscal constraints and by inflation, fell short of its goals.

15. John Kenneth Galbraith, *The Affluent Society* (Boston, 1958).

16. Richard Polenberg, *One Nation Divisible: Class, Race, and Ethnicity in the United States Since 1938* (New York, 1980).

17. For functionalism, see Kingsley Davis and Wilbert E. Moore, "Some Principles of Stratification," *American Sociological Review*, 10 (April 1945), 242-249, the major statement of this kind of functionalism. Criticisms are John Pease et al., "Ideological Currents in American Stratification Literature," *American Sociologist*, 5 (May 1970), 127-137; George Huaco, "The Functionalist Theory of Stratification: Two Decades of Controversy," *Inquiry*, 9 (1966), 215-240; Curt Tausky, "Parsons on Stratification: An Analysis and Critique," *Sociological Quarterly*, 6 (Spring 1955), 128-138; Dennis Wrong, "The Functionalist Theory of Stratification: Some Neglected Considerations," *American Sociological Review*, 24 (Dec. 1959), 772-782. For psychologically oriented views see Arnold Green, "The Middle Class Male Child and Neurosis," *American Sociological Review*, 9 (Feb. 1946), 31-41. A useful critique is Frank Riessman and Seymour M. Miller, "Social Class versus the 'Psychiatric World View,' " *American Journal of Orthopsychiatry*, 34 (Jan. 1964), 29-38.

18. Robert Nisbet, "The Decline and Fall of Social Class," *Pacific Historical Review*, 2 (Spring 1959), 11-17.

19. "A Sociologist Looks at an American Community," *Life*, 27 (Sept. 9, 1949), 108-118.

20. A useful look at economic writing of the time is Margaret S. Gordon, *The Economics of Welfare Policies* (New York, 1962), esp. 46-50, 117-119.

21. Martha Derthick, *Policymaking for Social Security* (Washington, 1979), 160, 216; Gilbert Y. Steiner, "Reform Follows Reality: The Growth of Welfare," *Public Interest*, 33-36 (Winter 1974), 47-65.

22. Figures from U.S. Department of Commerce, Bureau of the Census, *Historical Statistics of the United States, Colonial Times to 1957* (Washington, 1961), 193-201, and ibid., *Continuation to 1962* (Washington, 1965), 28-31. See also Council of Economic Advisers, "Problems of Poverty," 68. The number receiving old age assistance ranged between 2 and 2.8 million between 1945 and 1960, and the number getting unemployment insurance between 1 and 1.5 million. Another 430,000 to 1.1 million got state-local general assistance in those years. Private spending against poverty was around $3 billion in 1960, compared to $49 billion in public funds. See Ornati, *Poverty*, 100, 105.

23. For a characteristic liberal critique, see Eveline Burns, *Social Security and Public Policy* (New York, 1956). Charles I. Schottland, *The Social Security Program in the United States* (New York, 1963), is factual. Derthick, *Policymaking*, is authoritative and absorbing.

24. Morgan, *Income and Welfare*, 216; Burgess and Price, *American Dependency Challenge*, xii, 182; Winifred Bell, *Aid to Dependent Children* (New

York, 1965), 204. ADC became AFDC (aid to families of dependent children) in 1950 when grants were added for mothers as well as children.

25. Ornati, *Poverty*, 21-22; Charles Lebeaux, "Life on A.D.C.: Budgets of Despair," in Louis Ferman et al., *Poverty in America* (Ann Arbor, 1965), 401-411; Mary Wright, "Public Assistance in the Appalachian South," *Journal of Marriage and the Family*, 26 (Nov. 1964), 406-409.

26. Gordon, *Economics of Welfare Policies*, chap. 2; Harold Wilensky and C. N. Lebeaux, *Industrial Society and Social Welfare* (New York, 1965), 157-159; Ida Merriam, "Social Welfare in the United States, 1934-54," *Social Security Bulletin*, 18 (Oct. 1955), 3-14; Kathleen Woodroofe, "The Making of the Welfare State in England: A Summary of Its Origin and Development," *Journal of Social History*, 1 (Summer 1968), 303-324. Such studies did not ordinarily compare the extent of need. The assumption—supported by the high percentages of poor people in America—was that need in the United States was as great as it was in Western Europe.

27. Martha Derthick, *The Influence of Federal Grants: Public Assistance in Massachusetts* (Cambridge, Mass., 1970), 79-80. An exceptionally solid comparison of the American, English, and Swedish welfare states during this period and later is Furniss and Tilton, *Case for the Welfare State*, esp. 94-183.

28. Derthick, *Influence*, 23, 87-89, 269; Ellen J. Perkins, "AFDC in Review, 1936-62," *Welfare in Review*, 1 (Nov. 1963), 1-16; U.S. Bureau of Public Assistance, *Families Receiving Aid to Dependent Children, Oct., 1942:* pt. I, *Race, Size, and Composition of Families and Reasons for Dependency*, Public Assistance Report no. 7 (Washington, 1945); Department of Health, Education and Welfare, *Characteristics of State Public Assistance Plans under the Social Security Act*, Public Assistance Report no. 50 (Washington, 1962).

29. Bell, *Aid*, 47-48, 77-87; Joel F. Handler and Ellen Jane Hollingsworth, "The Administration of Social Services and the Structure of Dependency: The Views of AFDC Recipients," *Social Service Review*, 43 (Dec. 1969), 406-420. It is worth noting that AFDC's denial of aid to families in which an unemployed parent lived in the house probably contributed only slightly to separations. See Heather L. Ross and Isabel V. Sawhill, *Time of Transition: The Growth of Families Headed By Women* (Washington, 1975), 177.

30. Titles from regional conference of American Public Welfare Association, Charleston, S.C., Sept. 25, 1957, in box 2, APWA papers, SWHA.

31. Quote from editorial in *Social Work*, 1962, cited in Steiner, *Social Insecurity*, 188. See also Derthick, *Influence*, 135; Ernest Greenwood, "Social Science and Social Work: A Theory of Their Relationship," *Social Service Review*, 29 (March 1955), 20-33; Roy Lubove, "The Welfare Industry: Social Work and the Life of the Poor," *Nation*, 202 (May 23, 1966), 609-611; Charles O'Reilly, "Sociological Concepts and Social Work Theory," *American Catholic Historical Review*, 21 (Fall 1960), 194-200; and esp. Clarke A. Chambers, "Social Service and Social Reform: A Historical Essay," *Social Service Review*, 37 (March 1963), 76-90; and Elizabeth Wickenden, "Social Security and Voluntary Social Welfare," *Industrial and Labor Relations Review*, 14 (Oct. 1960), 94-106.

32. Loula Dunn, speech, March 4, 1957, APWA papers, box 2, SWHA.

For the work of the Committee on Social Issues and Policies, see National Association of Social Workers papers, box 45, SWHA. These files, and those in boxes 1-5 of the APWA, reveal the network of activists who intensified efforts for welfare reform after 1957. Important among them were Elizabeth Wickenden, the chief Washington lobbyist, and Wilbur Cohen, then teaching at the University of Michigan and shortly to return to HEW in the Kennedy administration. Their efforts spearheaded the public welfare amendments of 1962.

33. Jacob Panken, "I Say Relief is Ruining Families," *Saturday Evening Post*, 223 (Sept. 30, 1950), 25 ff.; Fletcher Knebel, "Welfare: Has It Become a Scandal?" *Look*, 25 (Nov. 7, 1961), 31-33 ff.; Rufus Jarman, "Detroit Cracks Down on Welfare Chiselers," *Saturday Evening Post*, 222 (Dec. 10, 1949), 19 ff. See also "Slums: An Encroaching Menace," *Life*, 38 (April 11, 1955), 125-134; Raymond Moley, "Vanishing Proletariat," *Newsweek*, 53 (Jan. 19, 1959), 92; Albert N. Votaw, "The Hillbillies Invade Chicago," *Harper's*, 216 (Feb. 1958), 64-67; Charles Stevenson, "When It Pays to Play Pauper," *Nation's Business*, 38 (Sept. 1950), 29 ff.; Edgar May, *The Wasted Americans* (New York, 1965), 18, 170.

34. Sources that attempt to quantify and discriminate among attitudes are Michael E. Schiltz, *Public Attitudes Toward Social Security, 1935-1965* (Washington, 1970); Gilbert Y. Steiner, *The State of Welfare* (New York, 1971); Joe R. Feagin, *Subordinating the Poor: Welfare and American Beliefs* (Englewood Cliffs, N.J., 1975); and Leonard Goodwin, *Do the Poor Want to Work? A Social-Psychological Study of Work Orientations* (Washington, 1972). Important articles include Zavada D. Blum and Peter H. Rossi, "Social Class Research and Images of the Poor: A Bibliographic View," in Moynihan, *Understanding Poverty*, 343-397; David J. Kallen and Dorothy Miller, "Public Attitudes Toward Welfare," *Social Work*, 16 (July 1971), 83-90; John B. Williamson, "Beliefs about the Motivation of the Poor and Attitudes toward Poverty Policy," *Social Problems*, 21 (June 1974), 635-648; and Williamson, "The Stigma of Public Dependency: A Comparison of Alternative Forms of Public Aid to the Poor," ibid., 22 (Dec. 1974), 213-223. Also Gallup polls of Aug. 11, 1961, and Dec. 15, 1964.

35. William F. Whyte, *Street Corner Society: The Social Structure of an Italian Slum* (Chicago, 1943); E. Wight Bakke, *The Unemployed Worker: A Study of the Task of Making a Living without a Job* (New Haven, 1940). Regionalism, especially as explored by sociologists such as Howard Odum, was also sensitive to cultural and subcultural forces. See Mildred Mell, "Poor Whites of the South," *Social Forces*, 17 (Dec., 1938), 153-167; Odum, "The Way of the South," *Social Forces*, 23 (March 1945), 258-268. The work of Robert Coles stressed the importance of culture. For a sample, see "The Poor Don't Want To Be Middle Class," *New York Times Magazine* (Dec. 19, 1975), 7 ff. See also W. Lloyd Warner and P. S. Lunt, *The Social Life of a Modern Community* (New Haven, 1941).

36. Allison Davis, "Ability and Survival," *Survey*, 87 (Feb. 1951), 60-63. See also Davis and Havighurst, "Social Class and Color Differences"; and Davis, "The Motivation of the Underprivileged Worker," in W. F. Whyte, ed., *Individualism and Society* (New York, 1946).

37. Ruth Rosner Kornhauser, "The Warner Approach to Social Stratification," in Reinhard Bendix and Seymour M. Lipset, eds., *Class, Status, and Power* (Glencoe, Ill., 1953), 224-255; C. Wright Mills, "The Professional Ideology of Social Pathologists," *American Journal of Sociology*, 49 (Sept. 1943), 165-180; Harold W. Pfautz and Otis Dudley Duncan, "A Critical Evaluation of Warner's Work in Community Stratification," *American Sociological Review*, 15 (April 1950), 205-216; Dennis Wrong, "The Failure of American Sociology," *Commentary*, 28 (Nov. 1959), 375-380; and esp. Pease et al., "Ideological Currents in American Stratification Literature."

38. NRPB, *Security, Work, and Relief Policies* (Washington, 1942), 24, 42, 130-133, 446-447, 518; Howard, *WPA*, passim; Joanna C. Colcord, *Cash Relief* (New York, 1936); F. Stuart Chapin and Stuart A. Queen, *Research Memorandum on Social Work in the Depression* (New York, 1937); WPA, *Urban Workers on Relief* (Washington, 1936); Barry D. Karl, *Charles E. Merriam and the Study of Politics* (Chicago, 1974), 276-277. See also "American Assn. for Social Workers Platform on the Public Social Activities," May 1944, NASW papers, folder 238, SWHA; and Social Security Board, "An Expanded Social Security Program," Sept. 29, 1941, OF 1710, box 3, Franklin D. Roosevelt Library. For FDR's speech, see Samuel Rosenman, comp., *Public Papers and Addresses of Franklin D. Roosevelt* 12 (New York, 1950), 40-41.

39. Edward D. Berkowitz, "The American Disability System in Historical Perspective," in Berkowitz, ed., *Disability Politics and Government Programs* (New York, 1979), 16-74. Quote by I. S. Falk, p. 34.

40. Eveline Burns, *Social Security and Public Policy* (New York, 1956); Daniel S. Sanders, *The Impact of Reform Movements on Social Policy Change: The Case of Social Insurance* (Fair Lawn, N.J., 1973); Schottland, *The Social Security Program*; Edward D. Berkowitz and Kim McQuaid, "Welfare Reform in the 1950s," *Social Service Review*, 54 (March 1980), 45-58.

41. Robert Merton, "Social Structure and Anomie," in Merton, *Social Theory and Social Structure*, rev. ed. (Glencoe, Ill., 1957), 131-160; Gunnar Myrdal, *An American Dilemma: The Negro Problem and Modern Democracy* (New York, 1944). See also Robert Heilbroner, "Who Are the American Poor?" *Harper's*, 200 (June 1950), 27 ff.

42. James L. Sundquist, *Politics and Polity: The Eisenhower, Kennedy, and Johnson Administrations* (Washington, 1968), 57-110; Ornati, *Poverty*, 82-84.

43. See note 7. Also *Characteristics of the Low Income Population*.

44. Galbraith's papers, box 123, Kennedy Library, conveniently collect reviews of the book. See especially the exchange of letters between Galbraith and the economist Leon Keyserling, box 38.

45. Sanford Kravitz, "Policy and Urban Policy," 56-57, Kennedy Library.

6. The Rediscovery of Poverty

1. Michael Harrington, *The Other America: Poverty in the United States* (New York, 1962), 10.

2. Overall views of the contributions made by writers in the early 1960s include Henry Aaron, *Politics and the Professors: The Great Society in Perspective* (Washington, 1968), chap. 2; and Peter H. Rossi and Zavada D. Blum, "Class, Status, and Poverty," in Daniel Moynihan, ed., *On Understanding Poverty: Perspectives from the Social Sciences* (New York, 1968), 36-63. Dwight Macdonald's review, "The Invisible Poor," appeared in *The New Yorker*, 38 (Jan. 19, 1963), 130 ff.

3. For Griscom, see Robert Bremner, *From the Depths: The Discovery of Poverty in the United States* (New York, 1956), 5-6. "Columbus complex" is from David Matza, "The Disreputable Poor," in Reinhard Bendix and Seymour Martin Lipset, eds., *Class, Status, and Power: Social Stratification in Comparative Perspective*, 2d ed. (New York, 1966), 289-302.

4. The "national epidemic" argument is in Benjamin Fine, *1,000,000 Delinquents* (Cleveland, 1955), 25-26. Approaches emphasizing cultural forces include Allison Davis, *Social Class Influence Upon Learning* (Cambridge, Mass., 1952); and Walter B. Miller, "Focal Concerns of Lower Class Culture," in Louis A. Ferman et al., *Poverty in America* (Ann Arbor, 1965), 261-270. For balanced views, see Lee Rainwater, "The Lower Class Culture and Poverty-War Strategy," in Moynihan, *On Understanding Poverty*, 229-259; and Albert K. Cohen, *Delinquent Boys: The Culture of the Gang* (Glencoe, Ill., 1955), chaps. 1, 2. For Kenneth Clark, see *Dark Ghetto: Dilemmas of Social Power* (New York, 1965).

5. Cloward and Ohlin, *Delinquency and Opportunity: A Theory of Delinquent Gangs* (New York, 1960).

6. For sources comparing the "new" with the old ethnic poor, see Harrington, "Slums, Old and New," *Commentary*, 30 (Aug. 1960), 118-124; Herman Miller, "The Dimensions of Poverty," in Ben B. Seligman, ed., *Poverty as a Public Issue* (New York, 1965), 20-51; Ben B. Bagdikian, *In the Midst of Plenty: The Poor in America* (Boston, 1964), 6-18; and Walter B. Miller, "Implications of Lower Class Culture for Social Work," *Social Service Review*, 33 (Sept. 1959), 219-236. See also Cloward and Ohlin, *Delinquency*, 207-210.

7. Kingsley Davis, "Some Demographic Aspects of Poverty in the United States," in Margaret Gordon, ed., *Poverty in America* (Berkeley, 1965), 299-320; Daniel P. Moynihan, "The Crises in Welfare," *Public Interest*, 10 (Winter 1968), 3-29; U.S. Children's Bureau, material prepared for House Appropriations Committee for the Record, April 1961, reprinted in Robert Bremner et al., eds., *Children and Youth in America: A Documentary History* (Cambridge, Mass., 1970-1974), 3:822-823; M. Elaine Burgess and Daniel O. Price, *An American Dependency Challenge* (Chicago, 1963), 94-95; and Winifred Bell, *Aid to Dependent Children* (New York, 1965), 211. For Frazier, see his *The Negro Family in the United States*, rev. ed. (New York, 1957), 636-637.

8. Clark, *Dark Ghetto*, 47; Phillips Cutright, "Components of Change in the Number of Female Family Heads Aged 15-44: United States, 1940-1970," *Journal of Marriage and the Family*, 36 (Nov. 1974), 716; Daniel P. Moynihan, *The Negro Family: The Case for National Action*, U.S. Department of Labor (March 1965); Carl N. Degler, *At Odds: Women and the Family in America from the Revolution to the Present* (New York, 1980), 127-132.

9. An excellent volume that evaluates the Moynihan report (and includes much contemporary commentary on it) is Lee Rainwater and William L. Yancey, *The Moynihan Report and the Politics of Controversy* (Cambridge, Mass., 1967). See esp. x, 7, 298. William Ryan's critique (1965) is reprinted therein, 220-221, as is James Farmer's (1965), 409-410.

10. Solid sources include President's Commission on Income Maintenance Programs, 1969, *Poverty amid Plenty: The American Paradox* (Washington, 1969), 114; Elizabeth Herzog, "Is There a 'Breakdown' of the Negro Family?" *Social Work*, 11 (Jan. 1966), 3-10; Lee Rainwater, *Behind Ghetto Walls: Black Families in a Federal Slum* (New York, 1970), 498-502; and Elliot Liebow, *Tally's Corner: A Study of Negro Streetcorner Men* (Boston, 1967), 210, passim.

11. See esp. Martin Rein and Hugh Heclo, "What Welfare Crisis? A Comparison among the United States, Britain, and Sweden," *Public Interest*, 33-36 (Fall 1973), 61-83; Hylan Lewis, "Culture, Class, and Family Life among Low Income Urban Negroes," in Arthur M. Ross and Herbert Hill, eds., *Employment, Race, and Poverty* (New York, 1967), 149-174; and Lee Rainwater, "Crucible of Identity: The Lower Class Family," *Daedalus*, 95 (Winter 1966), 172-216.

12. Quote is from Carol B. Stack, *All Our Kin: Strategies for Survival in a Black Community* (New York, 1971), 124. See also Lee Rainwater, assisted by Karol Kane Weinstein, *And the Poor Get Children* (Chicago, 1967). Historical accounts include Frank Furstenberg, Jr., Theodore Hershberg, and John Modell, "The Origins of the Female-Headed Black Family: The Impact of the Urban Experience," *Journal of Interdisciplinary History*, 6 (Autumn 1975), 211-233. The same volume includes Crandall A. Shifflett, "The Household Composition of Rural Black Families: Louisa County, Virginia, 1880," 235-260; see also Herbert Gutman, *The Black Family in Slavery and Freedom, 1750-1925* (New York, 1976), esp. 461-475.

13. Clark, *Dark Ghetto*, 34, 73.

14. Cohen, *Delinquent Boys*, 32. See also the authoritative book by Harold L. Wilensky and Charles N. Lebeaux, *Industrial Society and Social Welfare* (New York, 1965), 121-122, 184-186.

15. Charles Tilly, "Race and Migration to the American City," in James Q. Wilson, ed., *The Metropolitan Enigma* (Cambridge, Mass., 1968), 135-158; P. Neal Ritchey, "Urban Poverty and Rural to Urban Migration," *Rural Sociology*, 39 (Spring 1974), 12-27.

16. Rainwater, *Poor Get Children*, 121; Herzog, "Is There a Breakdown?"; Aaron, *Politics and the Professors*, 52; Hylan Lewis, "Agenda Paper No. V: The Family: Resources for Change," in Rainwater and Yancey, *Moynihan Report*, 314-343; Gutman, *Black Family*, 455-456; Clark, *Dark Ghetto*, 100-102; and esp. Liebow, *Tally's Corner*, 204, 220-221.

17. David Caplovitz, "Economic Aspects of Poverty," in Vernon Allen, ed., *Psychological Factors in Poverty* (Chicago, 1970), 229-241.

18. John B. Williamson and Kathryn M. Hyer, "The Measurement and Meaning of Poverty," *Social Problems*, 22 (June 1975), 652-662; Joseph Ker-

shaw, *Government Against Poverty* (Washington, 1970), 15-16; Robert J. Lampman, "Growth, Prosperity, and Inequality Since 1947," *Wilson Quarterly*, 1 (Autumn 1977), 143-155.

19. Charles Lebeaux, "Life on A.D.C.: Budgets of Despair," in Ferman et al., *Poverty in America*, 401-411.

20. President's Commission, *Poverty Amid Plenty*, 87, 220.

21. Burgess and Price, *American Dependency*, 40-43; Philadelphia *Inquirer* (Sept. 11, 12, 1961).

22. Gilbert Y. Steiner, *Social Insecurity: The Politics of Welfare* (Chicago, 1966), 64, italics added.

23. Department of Labor, *Manpower Report of the President* (Washington, 1968), 96-97; Elaine Burgess, "Focus and Preliminary Findings of 1960 ADC Study," American Public Welfare Association papers, box 5, Social Welfare History Archives, University of Minnesota; Robert H. Mugge, "Aid to Families of Dependent Children: Initial Findings of the 1961 Report on the Characteristics of AFDC Recipients," *Social Security Bulletin*, 26 (March 1963), 3-15.

24. Edward T. Chase, "The Nation's Welfare Dilemma," *Commonweal*, 75 (Nov. 17, 1961), 11 ff.

25. A. H. Raskin, "Newburgh's Lessons for the Nation," *New York Times Magazine* (Dec. 17, 1961), 7 ff.

26. For Mitchell's comments, see Meg Greenfield, "The 'Welfare Chiselers' of Newburgh, N.Y.," *Reporter* (Aug. 17, 1961), 37; and report of speech, Milwaukee *Sentinel*, Nov. 17, 1961. For Goldwater, see *New York Times*, July 19, 1961.

27. Cited in Raskin, "Newburgh's Lessons."

28. Letters to *New York Times*, July 18, 1961; editorial, New York *World Telegram and Sun*, July 19, 1961; *Saturday Evening Post* editorial (Aug. 5, 1961).

29. See esp. Fletcher Knebel, "Welfare: Has It Become a Scandal?" *Look*, 25 (Nov. 7, 1961), 32. A response is Leo Perlis, "Welfare Stories—Have They Become a Scandal?" in APWA papers, box 13. A balanced view is John Davenport (with photos by Walker Evans), "In the Midst of Plenty," *Fortune*, 63 (March, 1961), 107 ff.

30. Reported in Chicago *Sun Times*, Aug. 11, 1961.

31. George Gallup, *The Gallup Poll*, vol. 3, 1959-1971 (New York, 1972), 1919-1921; Washington *Post*, Dec. 15, 1964. See also David J. Kallen and Dorothy Miller, "Public Attitudes Toward Welfare," *Social Work*, 16 (July 1971), 83-90.

32. A useful summary of polls is Jon P. Alston and Dean Imogene, "Socioeconomic Factors Associated with Attitudes Toward Welfare Recipients and the Causes of Poverty," *Social Service Review*, 46 (March 1972), 13-23. See also Joe R. Feagin, "America's Welfare Stereotypes," *Social Science Quarterly*, 52 (March 1972), 921-933.

33. Michael E. Schiltz, *Public Attitudes toward Social Security, 1935-1965* (Washington, 1970), 117-118, 160-161, 195-196.

34. Zavada D. Blum and Peter H. Rossi, "Social Class Research and Images of the Poor: A Bibliographic View," in Moynihan, *Understanding Poverty*, 343-397.

35. Stephen Thernstrom, "Poverty in Historical Perspective," in Moynihan, *Understanding Poverty*, 160-176.

36. Hugh Heclo, "The Welfare State: The Costs of American Self-Sufficiency," in Richard Rose, ed., *Lessons from America* (New York, 1974), 253-282.

37. Leon H. Keyserling, *Progress or Poverty: The U.S. at the Crossroads* (Washington, 1964), 3-7, 87, 97; *New York Times*, Dec. 13, 1964.

38. Quote is from "The Problem of Poverty in America," *Economic Report of the President* (Washington, 1964), 55-83. Other views from economists at the time include Oscar Ornati, *Poverty Amid Affluence* (New York, 1966), esp. 46-50; and R. A. Gordon, "An Economist's View of Poverty," in Gordon, *Poverty in America*, 3-11; and Richard Titmuss, "Poverty vs Inequality: Diagnosis," *Nation*, 200 (Feb. 8, 1965), 130-133.

39. George J. Stigler, "The Economist and the State," *American Economic Review*, 55 (March 1965), 1-18.

40. James N. Morgan, Martin H. David, Wilbur J. Cohen, and Harvey E. Brazer, *Income and Welfare in the United States* (New York, 1962), 3, 7.

41. Aaron, *Politics and the Professors*, 151; Robert J. Lampman, "Poverty: The Historical Approach," *Nation*, 200 (June 7, 1965), 606-609.

42. "The Poor Amidst Prosperity," *Time*, 86 (Oct. 1, 1965), 34-35. Compare "Poverty, U.S.A.," *Newsweek*, 63 (Feb. 17, 1964), 20.

7. A Culture of Poverty?

1. Gunnar Myrdal, "The War on Poverty," *New Republic*, 150 (Feb. 8, 1964), 14.

2. "The Problem of Poverty in America," *Economic Report of the President* (Washington, 1964), 55. A sensible discussion of the question of lower-class culture is Herbert Gans, "Subcultures and Class," in Louis Ferman et al., *Poverty in America* (Ann Arbor, 1965), 302-311. Also Gerald Handel and Lee Rainwater, "Working Class People and Family Planning," *Social Work*, 6 (April 1961), 18-25.

3. See Andrew Levinson, *The Working Class Majority* (New York, 1974); S. M. Miller and Frank Riessman, "The Working Class Subculture: A New View," *Social Problems*, 9 (Summer 1961), 86-97; Richard Sennett and Jonathan Cobb, *The Hidden Injuries of Class* (New York, 1972); Harold L. Wilensky and Charles N. Lebeaux, *Industrial Society and Social Welfare* (New York, 1965), xxix, 192; and esp. the influential article by Hyman Rodman, "The Lower Class Value Stretch," *Social Forces*, 42 (Dec. 1963), 205-215.

4. Lee Rainwater, "The Lessons of Pruitt-Igoe," *The Public Interest* (Summer 1967), 116-123. See also Aaron Antonovsky and Melvin J. Lerner, "Occupational Aspirations of Lower Class Negro and White Youth," *Social Problems*, 7 (Fall 1959), 132-157; Bennett Berger, "Black Culture in Lower

Class Culture," in Lee Rainwater, ed., *Black Experience: Soul* (New Brunswick, N.J., 1973), 131-143; Hylan Lewis, *Blackways of Kent* (Chapel Hill, N.C., 1954) 310-313; and Robert R. Boll, "Lower Class Negro Mothers' Aspirations for Their Children," *Social Forces*, 43 (May 1965), 493-500.

5. Herbert Gans, "Culture and Class in the Study of Poverty," in Daniel Moynihan, ed., *On Understanding Poverty* (New York, 1968), 201-228; Rodman, "Lower Class Value Stretch"; Elliot Liebow, *Tally's Corner: A Study of Negro Streetcorner Men* (Boston, 1967), 208-209. See also David Elesh, "Poverty Theories and Income Maintenance: Validity and Policy Relevance," *Social Science Quarterly*, 54 (Sept. 1973), 359-373; Robert Coles, "Children of the American Ghetto," *Harper's*, 235 (Sept. 1967), 16 ff; and Thomas Gladwin, *Poverty, USA* (Boston, 1967), 79-81.

6. Summaries are Dennis Wrong, "How Important is Social Class?" *Dissent*, 19 (Winter 1972), 278-285; and Barbara I. Coward et al., "The Culture of Poverty Debate: Some Additional Data," *Social Problems*, 21 (June 1974), 621-634. An excellent recapitulation of the view that culture is relevant is Kirsten Grønbjerg, David Street, and Gerald D. Suttles, *Poverty and Social Change* (Chicago, 1978), 93-114. A helpful account of Okie/Arkie/hillbilly cultural forms is Joseph T. Howell, *Hard Living on Clay Street* (Garden City, N.Y., 1973).

7. Michael Harrington, *The Other America: Poverty in the United States* (New York, 1962), 15-18, 159. See also Walter B. Miller, "Focal Concerns of Lower Class Culture," in Ferman et al., *Poverty in America*, 270.

8. Oscar Lewis, "The Culture of Poverty," *Scientific American*, 215 (Oct. 1966), 19-25.

9. Lewis, *The Children of Sanchez* (New York, 1961), xxvi-xxvii.

10. Lewis, *La Vida: A Puerto Rican Family in the Culture of Poverty— San Juan and New York* (New York, 1965), xlii-lii; Harrington, *Other America*, 161.

11. Lewis, *La Vida*, xlii-lii; Harrington, *Other America*, 121-126. Harrington's main source here was August B. Hollingshead and F. C. Redlich, *Social Class and Mental Illness* (New Haven, 1958). For shorter versions, see A. B. Hollingshead, R. Ellis, and E. Kirby, "Social Mobility and Mental Illness," *American Sociological Review*, 19 (Oct. 1954), 577-584; and Hollingshead and Redlich, "Social Stratification and Psychological Disorder," ibid., 18 (April 1953), 163-169. Also Robert Coles, "Psychiatrists and the Poor," *Atlantic*, 214 (July 1964), 104 ff; Robert Coles, "What Poverty Does to the Mind," *Nation*, 202 (June 20, 1966), 748; and esp. Warren Haggstrom, "The Power of the Poor," in Ferman et al., *Poverty in America*, 315-324.

12. Lewis, *La Vida*, xliii-xlviii; Harrington, *Other America* (1969 ed.), xxiv.

13. "The Problem of Poverty," 55; "Can We Abolish Poverty?" *Saturday Evening Post*, 237 (Sept. 5, 1964), 74 ff.

14. Kenneth Clark, *Dark Ghetto: Dilemmas of Social Power* (New York, 1965), 81, made this explicit. "The ghetto [is] institutionalized pathology; it is chronic, self-perpetuating pathology . . . one kind of pathology leads to another." See also the remarks of HEW Secretary Abraham Ribicoff in 1961:

"We are faced with the fact that we are now entering the second or third generation of people on relief." Quoted in Fletcher Knebel, "Welfare: Has It Become a Scandal?" Look, 25 (Nov. 7, 1961), 31 ff.

15. Elizabeth Wickenden, "Notes on Poverty: Cause and Cure," Jan. 23, 1964, White House central files, box 32, Lyndon Johnson Library, Austin, Texas.

16. General critiques of the concept include Charles Valentine, Culture and Poverty: Critique and Counterproposals (Chicago, 1968); Eleanor Burke Leacock, ed., The Culture of Poverty: A Critique (New York, 1971); Zavada D. Blum and Peter H. Rossi, "Class, Status, and Poverty," in Moynihan, Understanding Poverty, 343-397; Elesh, "Poverty Theories"; Coward, "The Culture of Poverty Debate."

17. Lee Rainwater, assisted by Karol Kane Weinstein, And the Poor Get Children (Chicago, 1967), 52. See also Blum and Rossi, "Class, Status, and Poverty"; Peter Marris and Martin Rein, Dilemmas of Social Reform: Poverty and Community Action in the United States (London, 1967), 85-90; Charles E. Silberman, Criminal Violence, Criminal Justice (New York, 1978), 117-120; S. M. Miller, Frank Riessman, and Arthur Seagull, "Poverty and Self-Indulgence: A Critique of the Non-Deferred Gratification Pattern," in Ferman et al., Poverty in America, 285-301; Chandler Davidson and Charles M. Gaitz, "Are the Poor Different? A Comparison of Work Behavior and Attitudes among the Urban Poor and Non-Poor," Social Problems, 22 (Dec. 1974), 229-245; and esp. the withering assault on the notion that the poor are lazy, Leonard Goodwin, Do the Poor Want to Work? A Social Psychological Study of Work Orientations (Washington, 1972), esp. chap. 5.

18. Lee Rainwater, Behind Ghetto Walls: Black Families in a Federal Slum (Chicago, 1970), 476. Other key sources include Vernon L. Allen, ed., Psychological Factors in Poverty (Chicago, 1970), esp. Allen, "The Psychology of Poverty: Problems and Prospects," 367-383, and "Personality Correlates of the Poor," 242-266. Other key articles are Dwight Billings, "Culture of Poverty in Appalachia: A Theoretical Discussion and Empirical Analysis," Social Forces, 53 (Dec. 1974), 315-323; and S. M. Miller and Elliot G. Mishler, "Social Class, Mental Illness, and American Psychiatry: An Expository Review," in Frank Riessman et al., Mental Health of the Poor (Glencoe, Ill., 1964), 16-36.

19. James N. Morgan, Martin H. David, Wilbur J. Cohen, and Harvey E. Brazer, Income and Welfare in the United States (New York, 1962), esp. 198-210. Also Henry Aaron, Politics and the Professors: The Great Society in Perspective (Washington, 1978), 36-37; Stephan Thernstrom, "Is There Really a New Poor?" Dissent, 15 (Jan.-Feb. 1968), 59-64; Thernstrom, "Poverty in Historical Perspective," in Moynihan, Understanding Poverty, 160-186.

20. President's Commission on Income Maintenance Programs, 1969, Poverty Amid Plenty: The American Paradox (Washington, 1969), 30-37.

21. Elesh, "Poverty Theories"; Otis Dudley Duncan, "Inheritance of Poverty or Inheritance of Race," in Moynihan, Understanding Poverty, 85-110; Duncan, "Lifetime Occupational Mobility of Adult Males: March 1962," Current Population Reports, Technical Series, P-23, no. 11 (1962);

Stephan Thernstrom, *The Other Bostonians: Poverty and Progress in the American Metropolis, 1880-1970* (Cambridge, Mass., 1973), 242-244.

22. Morgan et al., *Income and Welfare*, 210.

23. Liebow, *Tally's Corner*, 223.

24. Murrary Hausknecht, "Caliban's Abode," in Lewis Coser and Irving Howe, eds., *The New Conservatives: A Critique from the Left* (New York, 1974), 193-206; Liebow, *Tally's Corner*, 208-209. See also Clark, *Dark Ghetto,* 129-132; Billings, "Culture of Poverty"; and Hylan Lewis, "Culture of Poverty: What Does It Matter?" in Leacock, *Culture of Poverty*, 345-363; Valentine, *Culture of Poverty*, 114-120.

25. Aaron, *Politics and the Professors*, 21-22. The seminar culminated in Moynihan's volume, *On Understanding Poverty.*

8. Girding for War on Poverty

1. Comments of Wilbur Cohen in Robert H. Haveman, ed., *A Decade of Federal Antipoverty Programs: Achievements, Failures, and Lessons* (Madison, Wis., 1977), 189-193; "Office of Economic Opportunity during the Administration of President Lyndon B. Johnson, Nov. 1963—Jan. 1969: An Administrative History," I:8, Lyndon Johnson Library, Austin, Texas.

2. Remarks by William Capron, in "Poverty and Urban Policy" (transcript of 1973 group discussion of the Kennedy Administration Urban Poverty Programs and Policies), I:54-55, John F. Kennedy Library.

3. Quote concerning Ohlin is in James L. Sundquist, *Politics and Polity: The Eisenhower, Kennedy, and Johnson Administrations* (Washington, 1968), 120. Another detailed secondary source is Daniel Knapp and Kenneth Polk, *Scouting the War on Poverty: Social Reform Politics in the Kennedy Administration* (Lexington, Mass., 1971), esp. 56-65, 106-110. For the Kennedy administration and juvenile delinquency, see the relevant documents in box 28, Myer Feldman papers, John F. Kennedy Library.

4. Sar A. Levitan, "Area Redevelopment: A Tool to Combat Poverty?" in Margaret S. Gordon, ed., *Poverty in America* (Berkeley, 1965), 375-385; Sundquist, *Politics and Polity*, 79-83, 97 ff.; John C. Donovan, *The Politics of Poverty*, 2nd ed. (Indianapolis, 1973), 25.

5. Harry M. Levin, "A Decade of Policy Developments in Improving Education and Training for Low-Income Populations," in Haveman, *Federal Antipoverty Programs*, 123-188; Joseph A. Kershaw, *Government against Poverty* (Washington, 1970), 94-97; Sundquist, *Politics and Polity*, 85 ff.; Garth L. Mangum, "The Why, How, and Whence of Manpower Programs," *Annals*, 385 (Sept. 1969), 50-62.

6. Quote is from Robert D. Plotnick and Felicity Skidmore, *Progress against Poverty: A Review of the 1964-1974 Decade* (New York, 1975), 187. Other evaluations include Robert A. Levine, *The Poor Ye Need Not Have with You: Lessons from the War on Poverty* (Cambridge, Mass., 1970), 121 ff.; Earl C. Main, "A Nationwide Evaluation of M.D.T.A. Institutional Job Training," *Journal of Human Resources*, 3 (Spring 1968), 159-170; Robert A. Levine and David W. Lynn, "Studies in Public Welfare: A Review Article,"

ibid., 10 (Fall 1975), 445-466; Barbara Carter, "Can the Job Corps Do the Job?" *Reporter*, 32 (March 25, 1965), 21-26.

7. Hackett oral history interview, Oct. 21, 1970, Kennedy Library, 102. "Ladder" quote is in Thomas Gladwin, *Poverty, U.S.A.* (Boston, 1967), 126-130. See also Peter Marris and Martin Rein, *Dilemmas of Social Reform: Poverty and Community Action in the United States* (London, 1967), chap. 3; Kershaw, *Government*, 90-97; and Hilda Smith, "My Years in OEO: A Seven Year Narrative, 1965-72," Smith papers, box 38, Franklin D. Roosevelt Library, Hyde Park, N.Y.

8. Singletary oral history interview, Johnson Library, 8, 20. Also Sar A. Levitan and Robert Taggart, *The Promise of Greatness: The Social Programs of the Last Decade and Their Major Achievements* (Cambridge, Mass., 1976), 238-284; Sar Levitan, "An Antipoverty Experiment: The Jobs Corps," in U.S. Congress, Committee on Governmental Operations, *Use of Social Research in Federal Domestic Programs*, pt. 2 (1967), 292-300; and S. M. Miller, Pamela Roby, and Alwine de Vos van Steenwijk, "Creaming the Poor," *Transaction*, 7 (June 1970), 39-40.

9. Singletary interview, 10; Levine, *Poor Ye Need Not Have*, 58, 105, 216-219.

10. Figures from Mollie Orshansky, "Recounting the Poor—A Five Year Review," *Social Security Bulletin*, 29 (April 1966), 2-19.

11. Quote re Cohen is in Martha Derthick, *Policymaking for Social Security* (Washington, 1979), 52-54. See also Wilbur Cohen oral history interview, Nov. 11, 1964, 47-48, and May 24, 1971, 69-72; and Wilbur Cohen, "Welfare —A Challenge and An Opportunity," speech of Sept. 13, 1961, in American Public Welfare Association papers, box 4, Social Welfare History Archives, University of Minnesota.

12. Documentary material in box 61, National Social Welfare Assembly papers, Social Welfare History Archives. Also Charles I. Schottland, *The Social Security Program in the United States* (New York, 1963), 183-188. Relevant documents include Raymond Hilliard, "The Road Ahead for ADC," speech, Nov. 29, 1961, APWA papers, box 5; "Public Assistance: Report of the Advisory Council," *Social Security Bulletin*, 23 (Feb. 1960), 10 ff.; and "1962 Legislative Objectives of the National Assn. of Social Workers for Public Welfare—for the Unemployed—and Statement on Work Relief," National Association of Social Workers papers, box 11, Social Welfare History Archives.

13. Gilbert Y. Steiner, *Social Insecurity: The Politics of Welfare* (Chicago, 1966), 80-85; Feldman papers, box 27, Kennedy Library.

14. *New York Times*, July 27, 1962. The basic source on this legislation is Charles E. Gilbert, "Policy-Making in Public Welfare: The 1962 Amendments," *Political Science Quarterly*, 81 (June 1966), 196-224.

15. Marion Folsom, "Cut the Roots of Poverty," *Business Week* (Dec. 24, 1955), 60-64. Also Roswell Perkins (assistant secretary of HEW), "Challenges in Public Welfare," speech, Oct. 15, 1956, APWA papers, box 1; and Martha Derthick, *The Influence of Federal Grants: Public Assistance in Massachusetts* (Cambridge, Mass., 1970), 131.

16. *New York Times*, July 26, 1962; Abraham Ribicoff to J. F. Kennedy, Nov. 1, 1961, President's Office Files, box 79, Kennedy Library. See also box 50, ibid., for extensive documentation; and Sanford Solender to Ribicoff, Sept. 6, 1961, NASW (Washington Office) papers, box 11.

17. "Special Message to the Congress on Public Welfare Programs," Jan. 31, 1962, *Public Papers of the President of the United States, John F. Kennedy, 1962* (Washington, 1962), 98-100.

18. Ribicoff to Kennedy, Nov. 1, 1961, President's Office Files, box 79; Gilbert, "Policy-Making"; Sundquist, *Politics and Polity*, 125-136; Gilbert Y. Steiner, "Reform Follows Reality: The Growth of Welfare," *Public Interest*, 33-36 (Winter 1974), 47-65.

19. Cited in Martin Rein, "Choice and Change in the American Welfare System," *Annals*, 385 (Sept. 1969), 89-109.

20. Derthick, *Influence*, 133-143; Gilbert, "Policy-Making"; M. Elaine Burgess and Daniel O. Price, *An American Dependency Challenge* (Chicago, 1963), 156-157.

21. Martha Derthick, *Uncontrollable Spending for Social Service Grants* (Washington, 1975), 7, 42.

22. Joel F. Handler and Ellen Jane Hollingsworth, "The Administration of Social Services and the Structure of Dependency: The Views of AFDC Recipients," *Social Service Review*, 43 (Dec. 1969), 406-420. For Massachusetts, see Derthick, *Influence*, 143-147.

23. Statement, Jan. 29, 1962, AFL-CIO Community Services Activities papers, folder 78, Social Welfare History Archives.

24. Frances Fox Piven and Richard Cloward, *Regulating the Poor: The Functions of Public Welfare* (New York, 1971), 281. See also Elinor Graham, "The Politics of Poverty," in Ben B. Seligman, ed., *Poverty as a Public Issue* (New York, 1965), 213-249. Contrary views include Lawrence Friedman, "The Social and Political Context of the War on Poverty: An Overview," in Haveman, *Federal Antipoverty Programs*, 21-47; Richard Polenberg, *One Nation Divisible: Class, Race, and Ethnicity in the United States since 1938* (New York, 1980), 193; and S. M. Miller and Martin Rein, "The War on Poverty: Perspectives and Prospects," in Seligman, *Poverty as a Public Issue*, 272-320.

25. Frances Fox Piven and Richard Cloward, "The Great Society as Political Strategy," *Columbia Forum*, 13 (Summer 1970), 17-22; Eugene Durman, "Have the Poor Been Regulated? Toward a Multivariate Understanding of Welfare Growth," *Social Service Review*, 47 (Sept. 1973), 339-359; and the rejoinder by Piven and Cloward, "Reaffirming the Regulating of the Poor," ibid., 48 (June 1974), 147-169.

26. Yarmolinsky in "Poverty and Urban Policy," 162-163. Also William Capron, ibid., 176, 216-217.

27. Quote by William Capron in "Poverty and Urban Policy," 139-141. Walter Heller's views are contained in his memos, "Confidential Notes on Meeting with the President," Oct. 21, 1963, and "Notes on a Quick Meeting with the President and Other Leading Members of the Kennedy Family," Nov. 19, 1963, boxes 13 and 6, Heller papers, Kennedy Library. The Presi-

dent's Office File, box 63a, contains a great deal of documentary material on Heller, Kennedy, and the poverty program. Another important first-hand source relating to Heller is White House Central File, EOA box 1, Johnson Library.

28. Heller to Kennedy, May 1, 1963, Theodore Sorensen papers, box 31, Kennedy Library. For Harrington's lack of direct influence in policymaking, see Henry Aaron, *Politics and the Professors* (Washington, 1978), 53-54; Donovan, *Politics of Poverty*, 181; "Poverty and Urban Policy," 92. For the views of Lampman, a key figure, see Robert Lampman, "Ends and Means in the War against Poverty," in Leo Fishman, ed., *Poverty amid Affluence* (New York, 1966), 212-230.

29. "The Problem of Poverty in America," *Economic Report of the President* (Washington, 1964), 56; Shriver quoted in *Newsweek*, "Poverty, U.S.A.," 63 (Feb. 17, 1964), 38; "Office of Economic Opportunity . . . An Administrative History," vol. I, 33.

30. "Problem of Poverty in America," 15, 73; Aaron, *Politics and the Professors*, 29-30. The focus on "exits" from poverty was Heller's. A critique of this emphasis is Paul Jacobs, "America's Schizophrenic View of the Poor," *Nation*, 207 (Sept. 20, 1965), 196. A critique stressing the role of economic growth is Lowell E. Gallaway, "Foundations of the War on Poverty," *American Economic Review*, 55 (1965), 122-130.

31. Heller to Sorensen, Dec. 20, 1963, White House Central Files, Welfare, box 25, Johnson Library; Heller speech, Jan. 23, 1954, ibid., box 32; "Problem of Poverty in America," passim.

32. W. Willard Wirtz to Sorensen, Jan. 23, 1964, box 37, Sorensen papers; Wilbur Cohen to Sorensen, Dec. 26, 1963, ibid. Erich Tolmach oral history, March 5, 1969, 31-32, Johnson Library.

33. For one comparison of New Deal and Great Society approaches—one that emphasizes similarities—see James Sundquist oral history, 36, Johnson Library.

34. "Problem of Poverty in America," 60. For examples of this optimism see Lloyd Ulman introduction to Gordon, *Poverty in America*, xv-xvi; and Sorensen to Kermit Gordon et al., Oct. 23, 1963, Sorensen papers, box 59. See also Donovan, *Politics of Poverty*, 113; Friedman, "Social and Political Context," 21-47; "Office of Economic Opportunity . . . Administrative History," vol. I, 14-18; and Sar Levitan, "The Design of Antipoverty Strategy," in Ben B. Seligman, ed., *Aspects of Poverty* (New York, 1968), 238-287.

35. Heller, "Notes on Meeting with President Johnson, 7:40 P.M., Saturday, Nov. 23, 1963," Heller papers, box 13. Also Sundquist, *Politics and Polity*, 112, 135-136; Carl Brauer, "Origins of the War on Poverty" (paper delivered at American Historical Association convention, Dec. 1979); Marris and Rein, *Dilemmas*, 38-41. Critics of this faith in planning include Dean C. Tipps, "Modernization Theory and the Comparative Study of Societies," *Comparative Studies in Society and History*, 15 (1973), 199-226; and esp. Daniel Moynihan, whose *Maximum Feasible Misunderstanding: Community Action in the War Against Poverty* (New York, 1963) heaps scorn on wide-eyed social scientists. See also Moynihan, "The Professors and the Poor," in Moynihan, ed., *On Understanding Poverty* (New York, 1968), 3-35.

36. Eric Tolmach oral history interview, March 5, 1969, 15; Robert Kennedy to Theodore Sorensen, Dec. 16, 1963, box 37, and Kennedy to Lyndon Johnson, Jan. 16, 1964, box 37, Sorensen papers. Also R. W. Boone to Franklin D. Roosevelt, Jr., n.d. (late 1963), ibid. Many scholars have stressed this goal of bypassing existing institutions. See Knapp and Polk, *Scouting the War*, 128-154; Piven and Cloward, *Regulating the Poor*, 268-277; Derthick, *Influence*, 225-238. See also David Hackett oral history interview, Oct. 21, 1970, 73-82, Kennedy Library.

37. Lloyd Ohlin and Martin Rein, "Social Planning for Institutional Change," in *Social Welfare Forum* (1964), 85-100. See also Marris and Rein, *Dilemmas*, 53-54, 169-170, 216-217; Andrew Kopkind, "Of, By, and For the Poor: A New Generation of Organizers," *New Republic*, 152 (June 19, 1965), 17; Daniel Moynihan, "What Is 'Community Action'?" *Public Interest*, 5 (Fall 1966), 3-8; Sar A. Levitan, "The Community Action Program: A Strategy to Fight Poverty," *Annals*, 385 (Sept. 1969), 63-75; Louis A. Zurcher, *Poverty Warriors: The Human Experience of Planned Social Intervention* (Austin, Tex., 1970), 63-64.

38. Knapp and Polk, *Scouting the War*, 25-28, 51-52, 196. For historical roots, see Robert M. Mennel, *Thorns and Thistles: Juvenile Delinquency in the United States, 1825-1940* (Hanover, N.H., 1973), 194-195; Thomas Gladwin, "The Anthropologist's View of Poverty," *Social Welfare Forum* (1961), 73-86; Robert Fisher, "Community Organizing and Citizen Participation: The Efforts of the People's Institute in New York City, 1910-1920," *Social Service Review*, 51 (Sept. 1977), 474-490.

39. Knapp and Polk, *Scouting the War*, 9-38. Many writers stress confusion over the meaning of community action. See Earl Raab, "What War and What Poverty?" *Public Interest*, 3 (Spring 1966), 45-66; Nathan Glazer, " 'To Produce a Creative Disorder': The Grand Design of the Poverty Program," *New York Times Magazine* (Feb. 27, 1966), 21 ff.; and esp. Moynihan, *Maximum Feasible Misunderstanding*.

40. Warren C. Haggstrom, "The Power of the Poor," in Louis Ferman et al., *Poverty in America* (Ann Arbor, 1965), 323. Kennedy cited in Donovan, *Politics of Poverty*, 35. See also Charles Silberman, "The Mixed-up War on Poverty," *Fortune*, 72 (August 1965), 218 ff.

41. Richard Cloward, "The War on Poverty: Are the Poor Left Out?" *Nation*, 201 (Aug. 2, 1965), 55-60; Cloward and Piven, "A Strategy to End Poverty," ibid., 202 (May 2, 1966), 510-517.

42. Moynihan, "Professors and the Poor"; Lillian B. Rubin, "Maximum Feasible Participation: The Origins, Implications, and Present Status," *Annals*, 385 (Sept. 1969), 14-29; Miller and Rein, "War on Poverty"; comments of William Capron in "Poverty and Urban Policy," 149.

43. Adam Yarmolinsky in "Poverty and Urban Policy," 287.

44. Moynihan, "Professors and the Poor," 12-13.

9. OEO: A Hand Up, Not a Handout

1. Robert Levine oral history interview, 3, 30-32, 49, Lyndon Johnson Library, Austin, Tex.; Levine, *The Poor Ye Need Not Have With You: Les-*

sons from the War on Poverty (Cambridge, Mass., 1970), 89-90, 186-187. Levine had been an associate director of OEO.

2. "Office of Economic Opportunity during the Administration of President Lyndon B. Johnson, Nov. 1963-Jan. 1969: An Administrative History," vol. 1: 52, 135, Johnson Library.

3. Joseph Kershaw, *Government Against Poverty* (Washington, 1970), 149-161. He was assistant director of OEO, 1965-1966. Other comments on this administrative confusion are Sar A. Levitan, *Great Society's Poor Law* (Baltimore, 1969), 57; David Hackett oral history interview, Oct. 21, 1970, 104, John F. Kennedy Library, Dorchester, Mass.; and James L. Sundquist, "Coordinating the War on Poverty," *Annals*, 385 (Sept. 1969), 41-49.

4. Wilbur Cohen oral history interview, May 24, 1971, 79, Kennedy Library; Council of Economic Advisors, "Draft History of the War on Poverty," 10-11, White House Central File, Legislative Background of EOA, box 1, Johnson Library; Hubert Humphrey to Lyndon Johnson, Dec. 2, 1965, ibid., box 26; Levine, *Poor Ye Need Not Have*, 59.

5. Daniel Moynihan, "The Professors and the Poor," in Moynihan, ed., *On Understanding Poverty: Perspectives from the Social Sciences* (New York, 1968), 3-35; William R. Haddad, "Mr. Shriver and the Savage Politics of Poverty," *Harper's*, 23 (Dec. 1965), 43 ff. (Haddad had then resigned as assistant director and inspector general of OEO); Bertrand Harding oral history interview, 10-11, Johnson Library; James Sundquist oral history interview, 46, Johnson Library. For more mixed evaluations of Shriver, see Levine, *Poor Ye Need Not Have*, 53-54, 61-66, 76-79; John C. Donovan, *The Politics of Poverty*, 2nd ed. (Indianapolis, 1973), 133; and Herbert J. Kramer oral history interview, 16, Johnson Library.

6. Daniel Thursz, "Today's Opportunities for Fighting Poverty," Nov. 14, 1964, in National Association of Social Workers papers, box 2, Social Welfare History Archives, University of Minnesota; NASW, "Poverty," Jan. 1965, ibid.

7. Questionnaire and responses in NASW papers, box 9; Rudolph T. Danstedt to Norman V. Lourie, April 6, 1964, ibid. (Washington office), box 9. See also Frank Riessman, "The Revolution in Social Work: The New Non-Professional," *Trans-action*, 2 (Nov.-Dec. 1964), 12-18; and Aleanor Merrifield, "Implications of the Poverty Program: The Case Worker's View," *Social Service Review*, 39 (Sept. 1965), 294-299.

8. Saul Alinsky, "The War on Poverty—Political Pornography," *Journal of Social Issues*, 21 (Jan. 1965), 41-47. On Alinsky, see R. Young, "Gadfly of the Poverty War," *Newsweek*, 66 (Sept. 13, 1965), 32.

9. Cited in "Office of Economic Opportunity . . . Administrative History," vol. 1: 44-48; and in Herman P. Miller, ed., *Poverty, American Style* (Belmont, Calif., 1968), 235-246; Henry Hazlitt, "The War on Poverty," *Newsweek*, 63 (April 6, 1964), 74.

10. Levine, *Poor Ye Need Not Have*, 56-57, 69-70; "Office of Economic Opportunity . . . Administrative History," vol. 1: 125-126.

11. "Poverty War out of Hand," *U.S. News and World Report* (Aug. 23, 1965), 48-52.

12. Charles E. Silberman, "The Mixed-up War on Poverty," *Fortune*, 72

(Aug. 1965), 223; John G. Wofford, "The Politics of Local Responsibility," in James Sundquist, ed., *On Fighting Poverty: Perspectives from Experience* (New York, 1969), 70-102; William Haddad, "Mr. Shriver"; Donovan, *Politics of Poverty*, 40, 52, 166; Bertrand Harding oral history interview, 19-20.

13. Adam Yarmolinsky, in "Poverty and Urban Policy," (conference transcript of 1973 Group Discussion of the Kennedy Administration's Urban Programs and Policies), 247-248, Kennedy Library; Stephen M. David, "Leadership of the Poor in Poverty Programs," in *Urban Riots: Violence and Social Change, Proceedings of the Academy of Political Science*, 29 (July 1968), 86-100; James Sundquist, *Politics and Polity: The Eisenhower, Kennedy, and Johnson Administrations* (Washington, 1968), 140-151; Robert Levine oral history interview, 10-12; J. David Greenstone and Paul E. Peterson, "Reformers, Machines, and the War on Poverty," in James Q. Wilson, ed., *City Politics and Public Policy* (New York, 1969), 267-292.

14. Wagner cited in Barbara Carter, "Sargent Shriver and the Role of the Poor," *Reporter*, 34 (May 5, 1966), 17-20; for Los Angeles and San Francisco, see Donovan, *Politics of Poverty*, 55-56; for New York official and Daley, see Silberman, "Mixed-up War."

15. Robert Byrd to Lyndon Johnson, Oct. 17, 1967, White House Central File, box 125, Johnson Library; John Connally to Johnson, May 18, 1965, and Johnson to Connally, June 10, 1965, ibid., box 26; Buford Ellington to Johnson, Aug. 2, 1965, ibid. See also Sargent Shriver to Bill Moyers, Feb. 2, 1965, ibid., box 25; and Charles Schultze to Johnson, Sept. 18, 1965, ibid., box 26.

16. Donovan, *Politics of Poverty*, 55-56; Lillian Rubin, "Maximum Feasible Participation: The Origins, Implications, and Present Status," *Annals*, 385 (Sept. 1969), 14-29; Levine, *Poor Ye Need Not Have*, 73-77.

17. Scholar is Kershaw, *Government Against Poverty*, 56. See also Frances Fox Piven and Richard A. Cloward, *Regulating the Poor: The Functions of Public Welfare* (New York, 1971), 266-270.

18. Oral history interviews by Ben Heineman, 29-30, Bertrand Harding, 5-6, and Wilbur Cohen, 9, all Johnson Library. Herbert J. Kramer quotes Johnson as having said to Shriver, "I just want you to make sure that no crooks, communists, or cocksuckers get into this [community action] program." (oral history interview, 21, Johnson Library). Levine, *Poor Ye Need Not Have*, 83-86, contents himself with having Johnson talk of "kooks and sociologists." One OEO official in charge of demonstration projects was known at the office as Dr. Strangegrant. Shriver, reluctantly approving some such grants, supposedly said, "Well, what have you nuts got cooked up for me now? In what funny papers am I going to land?" Eric Tolmach oral history interview, vol. 3: 10-11, Johnson Library.

19. Henry Aaron, *Politics and the Professors: The Great Society in Perspective* (Washington, 1978), 26-28; Donovan, *Politics of Poverty*, 144-146, 170; Robert Sherrill, "De-escalator of the War on Poverty," *New York Times Magazine* (Dec. 13, 1970), 23 ff.; Robert D. Plotnick and Felicity Skidmore, *Progress against Poverty: A Review of the 1964-1974 Decade* (New York, 1975), chap. 1.

20. Levine, *Poor Ye Need Not Have*, 96, 119-150. Other thoughtful evalu-

ations include Aaron, *Politics and the Professors*, 26-32; Henry M. Levin, "A Decade of Policy Developments in Improving Education and Training for Low-Income Populations," in Robert Haveman, ed., *A Decade of Federal Anti-Poverty Programs* (Madison, Wis., 1977), 123-188; and Sar A. Levitan and Robert Taggart, *The Promise of Greatness: The Social Programs of the Last Decade and Their Major Achievements* (Cambridge, Mass., 1976), 265-269.

21. See Pamela Christoffel and Mary Beth Celio, "A Benefit-Cost Analysis of the Upward-Bound Program: A Comment," and Walter I. Garms, "Reply . . . A Comment," *Journal of Human Resources*, 8, (Winter 1973), 110-119; Kershaw, *Government Against Poverty*, 30-40, 50-62; James Sundquist, "The End of the Experiment," in Sundquist, *Fighting Poverty*, 235-251.

22. Evaluations of community action, in addition to those cited above, are Kenneth B. Clark and Jeannette Hopkins, *A Relevant War Against Poverty* (New York, 1969), 125-130, 255-256; George Brager and Francis Purcell, eds., *Community Action Against Poverty: Notes from the Mobilization Experience* (New Haven, 1967); Ralph M. Kramer, *Participation of the Poor: Comparative Case Studies in the War Against Poverty* (Englewood Cliffs, N.J., 1969), 237-238, 266-273; Sar A. Levitan, "The Community Action Program: A Strategy to Fight Poverty," *Annals*, 385 (Sept. 1969), 63-75; and Robert J. Lampman, "Ends and Means in the War against Poverty," in Leo Fishman, ed., *Poverty Amid Affluence* (New York, 1966), 212-230.

23. Kenneth J. and Annette C. Pollinger, *Community Action and the Poor: Influence vs. Social Control in a New York City Community* (New York, 1972); Richard Boone, "New Dimensions for the War on Poverty," April 23, 1968, OEO papers, box 768, National Archives, Washington. See also Peter Marris and Martin Rein, *Dilemmas of Social Reform: Poverty and Community Action in the United States* (London, 1967), 166-175; and Earl Raab, "What War and Which Poverty?" *Public Interest*, 3 (Spring 1966), 45-56.

24. Quote is from Stanley Aronowitz, "Poverty, Politics, and Community Organization," *Studies on the Left*, 4 (Summer 1964), 102-105. See also Robert Pruger and Harry Specht, "Assessing Models of Community Organization Practice: Alinsky as a Case in Point," *Social Service Review*, 43 (June 1969), 123-135; Marris and Rein, *Dilemmas*, passim.

25. Levine, *Poor Ye Need Not Have*, 158 ff.

26. Harold L. Wilensky and Charles N. Lebeaux, *Industrial Society and Social Welfare* (New York, 1965), xlvii; Elizabeth Wickenden to Myer Feldman, Jan. 4, 1964, White House Central File, box 9, Johnson Library; Marris and Rein, *Dilemmas*, 186.

27. James Sundquist oral history interview, vol. I: 8, Johnson Library; James K. Batten, "A Cold Shoulder for the Poverty Program," *Reporter*, 38 (May 30, 1968); Robert Coles, "Rural Upheaval and Confrontation and Accommodation," in Sundquist, *Fighting Poverty*, 103-125.

28. Aaron, *Politics and the Professors*, 27-29; David Hunter, "Poverty and Urban Policy," 29; Charles A. Valentine, "The 'Culture of Poverty': Its Scientific Significance and Its Implications for Action," in Eleanor Leacock,

ed., *The Culture of Poverty* (New York, 1971), 193-225; Nathan Glazer, " 'To Produce a Creative Disorder': The Grand Design of the Poverty Program," *New York Times Magazine* (Feb. 27, 1966), 21 ff.; *New York Times*, Nov. 27, 1978.

29. Leon Keyserling in *New York Times*, May 16, 1964. Also Walter Heller to Johnson, "What Price Great Society," Dec. 21, 1965, White House Central File, confidential file, box 98, Johnson Library; Michael Harrington, "The Will to Abolish Poverty," *Saturday Review*, 173 (July 27, 1968), 10 ff.; Donovan, *Politics of Poverty*, 63-79; Levine, *Poor Ye Need Not Have*, 65-68.

30. Kershaw, *Government against Poverty*, 161-169.

31. Glazer, " 'To Produce a Creative Disorder' "; Daniel Moynihan, *Maximum Feasible Misunderstanding: Community Action in the War against Poverty* (New York, 1970), xxix; Wilbur Cohen oral history interview, 9, Johnson Library. The literature on the role of social science in policymaking proliferated in the wake of the war on poverty. See Irving Louis Horowitz and James Everett Katz, *Social Science and Public Policy in the United States* (New York, 1975), 7-9, 50-51, 139-151; Peter H. Rossi, "Practice, Method, and Theory in Evaluating Social Action Programs," in James Sundquist, *Fighting Poverty*, 217-234; Otis Dudley Duncan, "Social Forecasting—The State of the Art," *Public Interest*, 17 (Fall 1969), 88-118; Frances Fox Piven, "Social Science and Social Policy," in Pamela Roby, ed., *The Policy Establishment* (Englewood Cliffs, N.J., 1975), 215; Martin Rein and Sheldon H. White, "Can Policy Research Help Policy?" *Public Interest*, 49 (Fall 1977), 119-136; Gene M. Lyons, *The Uneasy Partnership: Social Science and the Federal Government in the 20th Century* (New York, 1969), 239-248, 289-292. See esp. the testimony of many experts in U.S. Congress, Committee on Governmental Operations, *Use of Social Research in Federal Domestic Programs*, pts. 1 and 2 (1967); and Leonard Goodwin, *Can Social Science Help Resolve National Problems? Welfare: A Case in Point* (New York, 1975).

32. Adam Yarmolinsky, "Poverty and Urban Policy," 302; Sar A. Levitan, "What's Happening, Baby? Essential Research for the War on Poverty," *Use of Social Research*, 254-260. For Cavanaugh, see Kershaw, *Government against Poverty*, 166.

33. Kershaw, *Government against Poverty*, 167-168; Kirsten A. Grønbjerg, *Mass Society and the Extension of Welfare, 1960-1970* (Chicago, 1977), 158-159.

34. James Sundquist, "The End of the Experiment," in Sundquist, *Fighting Poverty*, 239-240; Piven and Cloward, *Regulating the Poor*, 288-309.

35. Robert Haveman, "Poverty and Social Policy in the 1960's and 1970's: An Overview and Some Speculations," in Haveman, *A Decade of Federal Antipoverty Programs*, 1-19; Levitan and Taggart, *Promise of Greatness*, 57-62; Bertrand Harding oral history interview, 25 Johnson Library.

10. The Revolution in Social Welfare

1. Key sources on poverty and welfare during this period are Robert D. Plotnick and Felicity Skidmore, *Progress against Poverty: A Review of the 1964-1974 Decade* (New York, 1975), 82-83; Joseph Kershaw, *Government*

against Poverty (Washington, 1970), 17-23; Sar A. Levitan, "The Poor: Dimensions and Strategies," *Current History*, 64 (June 1973), 241-246 ff.; Robert J. Lampman, "Growth, Prosperity, and Inequality since 1947," *Wilson Quarterly*, 1 (Autumn 1977), 143-155; Frank Levy, "Poverty by the Numbers," *American Spectator* (May 1978), 24-26; and John B. Williamson and Kathryn M. Hyer, "The Measurement and Meaning of Poverty," *Social Problems*, 22 (June 1975), 652-662.

2. J. Wayne Flynt, *Dixie's Forgotten People: The South's Poor Whites* (Bloomington, Ind., 1979), 110-111; Mollie Orshansky, "Recounting the Poor—A Five Year Review," *Social Security Bulletin*, 29 (April 1966), 2-19; Larry H. Long, "Interregional Migration of the Poor: Some Recent Changes," *Current Population Reports*, Special Studies, Series P-23, no. 73 (Bureau of the Census, Nov. 1978).

3. Long, "Interregional Migration"; Robert Levine, *The Poor Ye Need Not Have with You: Lessons from the War on Poverty* (Cambridge, Mass., 1970), 21-25.

4. Levitan, "The Poor"; Elliott Currie, "The New Face of Poverty," *Progressive* (Jan. 1979), 38-41.

5. Department of Labor, *A Sharper Look at Unemployment in United States Cities and Slums* (Washington, 1966); President's Commission on Income Maintenance Programs, 1969, *Poverty amid Plenty: The American Paradox* (Washington, 1969), 66-67; Kershaw, *Government against Poverty*, 88-89; *New York Times*, March 11, 1979.

6. Mollie Orshansky, "Who Was Poor in 1966?" in Eveline Burns, ed., *Children's Allowances and the Economic Welfare of Children* (New York, 1968), 19-57; Martin Rein, "Choice and Change in the American Welfare System," *Annals*, 385 (Sept. 1969), 89-109; *Poverty Amid Plenty*, 46-47; Wilbur Cohen, "A Ten Point Program to Abolish Poverty," *Social Security Bulletin*, 31 (Dec. 1968), 12.

7. Orshansky, "Who Was Poor?"; Levitan, "The Poor"; Sheldon Danziger and Robert Plotnick, "Can Welfare Reform Eliminate Poverty?" *Social Service Review*, 53 (June 1979), 244-260; Kirsten Grønbjerg, David Street, and Gerald D. Suttles, *Poverty and Social Change* (Chicago, 1978), 72.

8. Mollie Orshansky, "How Poverty Is Measured," *Monthly Labor Review*, 92 (Feb. 1969), 37-41; President's Commission on Income Maintenance, *Background Papers* (Washington, 1969), 12; "Poverty in America: Its Cause and Effect," *Time*, 91 (May 17, 1968), 24-32.

9. Victor R. Fuchs, "Redefining Poverty and Redistributing Income," *Public Interest*, 8 (Summer 1967), 89-94; S. M. Miller, Martin Rein, Pamela Roby, and Bertram Gross, "Poverty, Inequality, and Conflict," *Annals* 383 (Sept. 1967), 18-52; *Poverty Amid Plenty*, 36-40; Robert Plotnick and Timothy Smeeding, "Poverty and Income Transfers: Past Trends and Future Prospects," *Public Policy*, 27 (Summer 1979), 255-272; Martha N. Ozawa, "Issues in Welfare Reform," *Social Service Review*, 52 (March 1978), 37-55; Dwight Macdonald, "Our Invisible Poor," *New Yorker*, 38 (Jan. 12, 1963), 82-132.

10. Grønbjerg et al., *Poverty and Social Change*, 86-88.

11. Lawrence E. Lynn, Jr., "Policy Developments in the Income Maintenance System," in Robert Haveman, ed., *A Decade of Federal Antipoverty Programs: Achievements, Failures, and Lessons* (Madison, Wis., 1977), 55-117; Levy, "Poverty by the Numbers."

12. Quote in Oscar Ornati, *Poverty Amid Affluence* (New York, 1966), 20. A key source is Diana Karter Appelbaum, "The Level of the Poverty Line: A Historical Survey," *Social Service Review*, 51 (Sept. 1977), 514-523.

13. As summarized in *New York Times*, July 17, 1977; and Levy, "Poverty by the Numbers"; Lynn, "Policy Developments."

14. Danziger and Plotnick, "Can Welfare Reform?" 249; Henry Aaron, *Politics and the Professors: The Great Society in Perspective* (Washington, 1978), 39-40.

15. Michael Harrington, *The Other America: Poverty in the United States* (New York, 1962), 9; Mitchell Ginsberg, cited in U.S. Riot Commission, *Report of Advisory Commission on Civil Disorders* (New York, 1968), 457-467; Levine, *The Poor Ye Need Not Have*, 185-186. See also Gunnar Myrdal, "Summing Up," in Margaret S. Gordon, ed., *Poverty in America* (Berkeley, 1965), 438: "Almost all social and economic policies in America . . . have in a queer way . . . been following the perverse line of helping those who are not so poor while leaving the really poor in poverty."

16. David Matza, "Poverty and Disrepute," in Robert K. Merton and Robert Nisbet, eds., *Contemporary Social Problems*, 3rd ed. (New York, 1971), 601-656; Gilbert Y. Steiner, *The State of Welfare* (Washington, 1971), 1; Ozawa, "Issues in Welfare Reform. " Quote in Robert Coles, "Children of the American Ghetto," *Harper's*, 235 (Sept. 1967), 16 ff. Also Paul Jacobs, "How It Is—Getting on Welfare," ibid. (Oct. 1967), 74-75; Richard A. Cloward and Richard M. Elman, "Poverty, Injustice, and the Welfare State," *Nation*, 202 (Feb. 28, 1966), 230-235, and ibid. (March 7, 1966), 264-268; Gilbert Y. Steiner, *Social Insecurity: The Politics of Welfare* (Chicago, 1966), 133-140.

17. Kirsten Grønbjerg, *Mass Society and the Extension of Welfare, 1960-1970* (Chicago, 1977), chap. 3; Social Security Administration, *Social Security Programs in the United States* (Washington, 1968), 91-96; Eveline Burns, "Where Welfare Falls Short," *Public Interest*, 1 (Fall 1965), 82-95; and Martha Derthick, "Intercity Differences in Administration of the Public Assistance Programs: The Case of Massachusetts," in James Q. Wilson, ed., *City Politics and Public Policy* (New York, 1968), 243-266.

18. Frances Fox Piven and Richard A. Cloward, *Regulating the Poor: The Functions of Public Welfare* (New York, 1971). Writings that stress racial considerations include Carol B. Stack, *All Our Kin: Strategies for Survival in a Black Community* (New York, 1971), 127-128; Dorothy L. Newman et al., *Protest, Politics, and Prosperity: Black Americans and White Institutions, 1940-1975* (New York, 1978), 262-264; Grønbjerg, *Mass Society*, 72-82, 163. For other speculations see Steiner, *Social Insecurity*, 246-248; and Nathan Glazer, "A Sociologist's View of Poverty," in Gordon, *Poverty*, 12-26.

19. Thoughtful analyses, set in an international context, include Harold L. Wilensky and Charles N. Lebeaux, *Industrial Society and Social Welfare*

(New York, 1965), xi-xvii; Wilensky, "The Welfare Mess," *Society*, 13 (May 6, 1976), 12-16; Martin Rein and Hugh Heclo, "What Welfare Crisis? A Comparison among the United States, Britain, and Sweden," *Public Interest*, 33-36 (Fall 1973), 61-83.

20. Thomas H. Dye, *Politics, Economics, and the Public: Policy Outcomes in American States* (Chicago, 1966); Ira Sharkansky and Richard I. Hofferbert, "Dimensions of State Politics, Economics, and Public Policy," *American Political Science Review*, 63 (Sept. 1969), 867-879; Grønbjerg, *Mass Society*, 46-48.

21. Quote is Sar A. Levitan and Robert Taggart, *The Promise of Greatness: The Social Programs of the Last Decade and Their Major Achievements* (Cambridge, Mass., 1976), 259-260. Also, Robert D. Plotnick, "Social Welfare Expenditures: How Much Help for the Poor?" *Policy Analysis*, 5 (1979), 271-289; Mayer N. Zald, "Demographics, Politics and the Future of the Welfare State," *Social Service Review*, 51 (March 1977), 110-124; Morris Janowitz, *Social Control of the Welfare State* (Chicago, 1976), 13, 46-47; Robert J. Lampman, "What Does It Do for the Poor?—A New Test for National Policy," *Public Interest*, 34 (Winter 1974), 66-82; James L. Clayton, "The Fiscal Limits of the Warfare-Welfare State: Defense and Welfare Spending in the United States Since 1900," *Western Political Quarterly*, 29 (Sept. 1976), 364-383; Lynn, "Policy Developments."

22. Maurice MacDonald, "Food Stamps: An Analytical History," *Social Service Review*, 51 (Dec. 1977), 642-658; Robert Stevens and Rosemary Stevens, *Welfare Medicine in America: A Case Study of Medicaid* (New York, 1974); Lynn, "Policy Developments"; Aaron, *Politics and the Professors*, 40; Frederick Doolittle, Frank Levy, and Michael Wiseman, "The Mirage of Welfare Reform," *Public Interest*, 47 (Spring 1977), 62-87.

23. Martin Rein, "Equality and Social Policy," *Social Service Review*, 51 (Dec. 1977), 565-587.

24. W. Andrew Achenbaum, *Old Age in the New Land: The American Experience Since 1790* (Baltimore, 1978), 144; Plotnick and Skidmore, *Progress Against Poverty*, 26, 71-72, 182-183; Hugh Heclo, "The Welfare State: The Costs of American Self-Sufficiency," in Richard Rose, ed., *Lessons from America* (New York, 1974), 253-282; Vincent J. Burke and Vee Burke, *Nixon's Good Deed: Welfare Reform* (New York, 1974), 199-205; and *Statistical Abstract of the United States*, 1979 (Washington, 1979), 326-327.

25. Plotnick and Skidmore, *Progress Against Poverty*, 56-57, 112, 140, 164, 179-180; *New York Times*, Jan. 18, 1977; Lynn, "Policy Developments."

26. Wilensky and Lebeaux, *Industrial Society*, xvii, 90-91, 122-123; *Poverty Amid Plenty*, Background Papers, 31-37; Richard M. Titmuss, "The Role of Redistribution in Social Policy," in Titmuss, *Commitment to Welfare* (New York, 1968), 188-199; Ozawa, "Issues in Welfare Reform"; Sidney E. Zimbalist, "Recent British and American Poverty Trends: Conceptual and Policy Contrasts," *Social Service Review*, 5 (Sept. 1977), 419-433.

27. Quote in Arnold J. Heidenheimer, Hugh Heclo, and Carolyn Teich Adams, *Comparative Public Policy: The Politics of Social Choice in Europe*

and America (New York, 1975), 199. See also Norman Furniss and Timothy Tilton, *The Case for the Welfare State* (Bloomington, Ind., 1977), 110-112, 180-181. This is the source for statistics on poverty. Sweden's poor, they estimated, approximated only 4 percent of the population at the time.

28. Richard B. Calhoun, *In Search of the New Old: Redefining Old Age in America, 1945-1970* (New York, 1978), chap. 4; Plotnick, "Social Welfare Expenditures"; Harold L. Wilensky, *The Welfare State and Equality: Structural and Ideological Roots of Public Expenditures* (Berkeley, 1975), 18-19; Henry Aaron, "Social Security: International Comparisons," in Otto Eckstein, ed., *Studies in the Economics of Income Maintenance* (Washington, 1967), 13-48.

29. MacDonald, "Food Stamps." The expert, Robert Nathan, said this in 1980. See President's Commission for a National Agenda for the Eighties, *Government and the Advancement of Social Justice: Health, Welfare, and Civil Rights in the Eighties* (Washington, 1980), 60.

30. Martha Derthick, *Policymaking for Social Security* (Washington, 1979), 12.

31. Stevens and Stevens, *Welfare Medicine*, xv, 23, 53, 65.

11. The Welfare Explosion

1. Lawrence E. Lynn, Jr. "Policy Developments in the Income Maintenance System," in Robert Haveman, ed., *A Decade of Federal Antipoverty Programs: Achievements, Failures, and Lessons* (Madison, Wis., 1977), 55-117; Frederick Doolittle, Frank Levy, and Michael Wiseman, "The Mirage of Welfare Reform," *Public Interest*, 47 (Spring 1977), 62-87; Gilbert Y. Steiner, *The State of Welfare* (Washington, 1971), 32, 296; Frances Fox Piven and Richard A. Cloward, *Regulating the Poor: The Functions of Public Welfare* (New York, 1968), chap. 6; Piven and Cloward, *Poor People's Movements: Why They Succeed, How They Fail* (New York, 1977), 274-275; Henry Aaron, *Politics and the Professors* (Washington, 1978), 5-6.

2. Joe R. Feagin, *Subordinating the Poor: Welfare and American Beliefs* (Englewood Cliffs, N.J., 1975), chap. 5; Martin Anderson, *Welfare: The Political Economy of Welfare Reform in the United States* (Stanford, Calif., 1978), 60-62.

3. Stewart Alsop, "The Dangerous Poor," *Saturday Evening Post*, 239 (July 16, 1966), 18; Alsop, "After Vietnam—Abolish Poverty?" ibid. (Dec. 17, 1966), 12; Michael Harrington, "Close-up On Poverty: O'Haires of Boston," *Look*, 28 (Aug. 25, 1964), 64-72; T. George Harris, "Do We Owe People a Living?" ibid., 32 (April 30, 1968), 25; "Poverty in America: Its Causes and Effects," *Time*, 91 (May 17, 1968), 24-32, and "Welfare: Trying to End the Nightmare," 97 (Feb. 8, 1971), ibid., 14-23.

4. Leonard Goodwin, *Do the Poor Want to Work? A Social Psychological Study of Work Orientations* (Washington, 1972), 124-125; Joe R. Feagin, "America's Welfare Stereotypes," *Social Science Quarterly*, 52 (March 1972), 921-933.

5. "Welfare," *Time*.

6. Cited in Feagin, *Subordinating*, 4-7.

7. Feagin, "America's Welfare Stereotypes"; also John B. Williamson, "Beliefs about the Welfare Poor," *Sociology and Social Research*, 58 (Jan. 1974), 163-175; and Williamson, "Beliefs about the Motivation of the Poor and Attitudes toward Poverty Policy," *Social Problems*, 21 (June 1974), 635-648.

8. Charles Tilly, "Race and Migration to the American City," in James Q. Wilson, ed., *The Metropolitan Enigma* (Cambridge, Mass., 1968), 135-158; Steiner, *State of Welfare*, 86-88; Piven and Cloward, *Regulating the Poor*, 219, 331; Feagin, "America's Welfare Stereotypes."

9. Studies dealing with illegitimacy and family breakup include Heather L. Ross and Isabel V. Sawhill, *Time of Transition: The Growth of Families Headed by Women* (Washington, 1975), 17-18, 101-123; Kirsten A. Grønbjerg, *Mass Society and the Extension of Welfare, 1960-1970* (Chicago, 1977), 108-110; President's Commission on Income Maintenance Programs, 1969, *Poverty Amid Plenty: The American Paradox* (Washington, 1969), 119; Robert A. Levine and David W. Lyon, "Studies in Public Welfare: A Review Article," *Journal of Human Resources*, 10 (Fall 1975), 445-466; Martin Rein and Hugh Heclo, "What Welfare Crisis? A Comparison among the United States, Britain, and Sweden," *Public Interest*, 33-36 (Fall 1973), 61-83.

10. For WIN, see Steiner, *State of Welfare*, 26-27, 44-45, 73-74; Vincent J. Burke and Vee Burke, *Nixon's Good Deed: Welfare Reform* (New York, 1974), 24-35; Goodwin, *Do the Poor Want to Work?* 83-90, 127-128. In practice, the "tax rate" of 67 percent has been closer to 40 or 50 percent, thanks to administrative discretion.

11. Bradley R. Schuller, "Empirical Studies of Welfare Dependency: A Survey," *Journal of Human Resources*, 8, supplement (1973), 19-32; Sheila M. Rothman, "Other Peoples' Children: The Day Care Experiment in America," *Public Interest*, 29-32 (Winter 1973), 11-27; Samuel Z. Klausner, "Six Years in the Lives of the Impoverished: An Examination of the WIN Thesis," Department of Labor study (Washington, 1968); William J. Reid and Audrey D. Smith, "AFDC Mothers View the Work Incentive Program," *Social Service Review*, 46 (Sept. 1972), 347-362.

12. Burke and Burke, *Nixon's Good Deed*, 164-165; Sar A. Levitan and David Marwick, "Work and Training for Relief Recipients," *Journal of Human Resources*, 8, supplement (1973), 5-18; Goodwin, *Do the Poor Want to Work?* 98-105.

13. Levine and Lyon, "Studies in Public Welfare"; Anderson, *Welfare*, chap. 2; Harold W. Watts et al., "The Labor Supply Response of Husbands," *Journal of Human Resources*, 9 (Spring 1974), 181-200; Hirschel Kasper, "Welfare Payments and Work Incentive: Some Determinants of the Rates of General Assistance Payments," ibid., 3 (Winter 1968), 86-110; Peter Rossi and Katharine Lyall, *Reforming Public Welfare: A Critique of Negative Income Tax Experiments* (New York, 1976), 3-12, 184-191; Klausner, "Six Years"; Chandler Davidson and Charles M. Gaitz, "Are the Poor Different? A Comparison of Work Behavior and Attitudes among the Urban Poor and Nonpoor," *Social Problems*, 22 (Dec. 1974), 229-245; H. Roy Kaplan and

Curt Tausky, "Work and the Welfare Cadillac: The Function of and Commitment to Work among the Hard-Core Unemployed," ibid., 19 (Spring 1972), 469-483. More recent experiments suggest a greater impact of guaranteed income on work incentives.

14. Hugh Heclo, "The Welfare State: The Costs of American Self-Sufficiency," in Richard Rose, ed., *Lessons from America* (New York, 1974), 253-282; Rein and Heclo, "What Welfare Crisis?"

15. Gilbert Y. Steiner, *Social Insecurity: The Politics of Welfare* (Chicago, 1966), 244-245; C. R. Winegarden, "The Welfare 'Explosion': Determinants of the Size and Recent Growth of the AFDC Population," *American Journal of Economics and Sociology*, 32 (July 1973), 245-256; Burke and Burke, *Nixon's Good Deed*, 9-10.

16. Daniel Moynihan, "The Crisis in Welfare," *Public Interest*, 10 (Winter 1968), 3-29; Piven and Cloward, *Regulating the Poor*, 192-194. For views offered here, see Eugene Durman, "Have the Poor Been Regulated? Toward a Multivariate Understanding of Welfare Growth," *Social Service Review*, 47 (Sept. 1973), 339-359; Doolittle et al., "Mirage."

17. Sources focusing on the role of eligibility include Ross and Sawhill, *Time of Transition*, 101-108; Martin Rein, "Choice and Change in the American Welfare System," *Annals*, 385 (Sept. 1973), 89-109; Durman, "Have the Poor Been Regulated?"; and (with qualifications), Grønbjerg, *Mass Society*, 51-55, 167-168; and Lawrence E. Gary, "Policy Decisions in the Aid to Families with Dependent Children Program: A Comparative State Analysis," *Journal of Politics*, 35 (Nov. 1973), 886-923.

18. Steiner, *State of Welfare*, 21-22; Feagin, *Subordinating*, 76-78; Ross and Sawhill, *Time of Transition*, 96-98; Piven and Cloward, "Reaffirming the Regulation of the Poor," *Social Service Review*, 48 (June 1974), 147-169.

19. Martin Rein, "Equality and Social Policy," *Social Service Review*, 51 (Dec. 1977), 565-587; Grønbjerg, *Mass Society*, 122-123.

20. Piven and Cloward, *Regulating the Poor*, 196-197; Piven and Cloward, *Poor People's Movements*, 275-277; Piven and Cloward, "Reaffirming."

21. Robert Levine, *The Poor Ye Need Not Have with You: Lessons from the War on Poverty* (Cambridge, Mass., 1970), 184-185; Steiner, *State of Welfare*, 64-65.

22. Martha Derthick, *The Influence of Federal Grants: Public Assistance in Massachusetts* (Cambridge, Mass., 1970), 93-95.

23. For the NWRO, see Piven and Cloward, *Poor People's Movements*, 288-350; Steiner, *State of Welfare*, 280-313; Leonard J. Hausman, "The Politics of a Guaranteed Income: The Nixon Administration and the Family Assistance Plan: A Review Article," *Journal of Human Resources*, 8 (Fall 1973), 411-421; Daniel Moynihan, *Politics of a Guaranteed Income, The Nixon Administration and the Family Assistance Plan* (New York, 1973), 236-238, 247-250, 327-337. For the role of riots, Michael Betz, "Riots and Welfare: Are They Related?" *Social Problems*, 21 (Winter 1974), 345-355; Durman, "Have the Poor Been Regulated?" Ample evidence exists of efforts by the Johnson administration and urban officials to stem rioting by offering better welfare.

See Sargent Shriver to Johnson, Feb. 6, 1968, White House Central File, box 26; Mayor Robert Wagner to Johnson, Aug. 27, 1965, ibid., box 25; Shriver to Johnson, July 20, 1965, box 26; and Hubert Humphrey to Johnson, Dec. 17, 1966, box 25, all Johnson Library.

24. Derthick, *Influence of Federal Grants*, 74-75, 89-90.

25. Ibid., 17-19, 229, 238.

26. Martha Derthick, *Uncontrollable Spending for Social Service Grants* (Washington, 1975), 20-22, 35-36, 71-72; Burke and Burke, *Nixon's Good Deed*, 50-51.

27. Derthick, *Uncontrollable*, chap. 7; Grønbjerg, *Mass Society*, 26-29.

28. Feagin, "America's Welfare Stereotypes"; Williamson, "Beliefs about the Welfare Poor."

29. Grønbjerg, *Mass Society*, 3-4, 96-106, 143-144, 161-162; Herbert Gans, *More Equality* (New York, 1973), 7-13.

30. Grønbjerg, *Mass Society*, 13-17, 106.

31. See Ralf Dahrendorf, "On the Origin of Inequality among Men," in Dahrendorf, *Essays in the Theory of Society* (Stanford, 1968); Daniel Bell, "Labor in the Post-Industrial Society," *Dissent*, 19 (Winter 1972), 163-189; Thomas Halper, "The Poor as Pawns: The New 'Deserving Poor' and the Old," *Polity*, 6 (Fall 1973), 71-86. In varying ways, all stress the rise of expectations and the importance of the sense of relative deprivation.

12. Floors and Doors

1. Comments of S. M. Miller on "doors and floors," *Annals*, 385 (Sept. 1969), 175-178.

2. Robert Heilbroner, "Who Are the American Poor?" *Harper's*, 200 (June 1950), 27-33.

3. William Capron in "Poverty and Urban Policy" (Conference Transcript of 1973 Group Discussion of the Kennedy Administration's Urban Poverty Programs and Policies), 148, John F. Kennedy Library, Dorchester, Mass.; Willard Wirtz in Gilbert Y. Steiner, *The State of Welfare* (Washington, 1971), 8-9.

4. Quote is from Michael Novak, "The Family Out of Focus," *Harper's*, 252 (April 1976), 37-47. See also Daniel Moynihan, "The Crises in Welfare," *Public Interest* 10 (Winter 1968), 3-29; Joseph Kershaw, *Government Against Poverty* (Washington, 1970), 100-110; President's Commission on Income Maintenance Programs, 1969, *Poverty Amid Plenty: The American Paradox* (Washington, 1969), 412-417; and esp. Eveline Burns, ed., *Children's Allowances* (New York, 1967), esp. 3-18, 123-149.

5. Sources discussing jobs programs include Lee Rainwater, *Behind Ghetto Walls: Black Families in a Federal Slum* (Cambridge, Mass., 1970), 536-542; Robert A. Levine, *The Poor Ye Need Not Have with You: Lessons from the War on Poverty* (Cambridge, Mass., 1970), 192-194; Hyman P. Minsky, "The Role of Employment Policy," in Margaret S. Gordon, ed., *Poverty in America* (Berkeley, 1965), 199; Leonard Goodwin, *Do the Poor Want to Work? A Social Psychological Study of Work Orientations* (Washington, 1972), 180-181.

6. Doubts about jobs programs as a total answer include *Poverty Amid Plenty*, 67; Levine, *Poor Ye Need Not Have*, 194, 206-207; Joe R. Feagin, *Subordinating the Poor: Welfare and American Beliefs* (Englewood Cliffs, N.J., 1975), 157-159; Robert D. Plotnick and Felicity Skidmore, *Progress against Poverty: A Review of the 1964-1974 Decade* (New York, 1975), 187-188; Gordon Weil, *The Welfare Debate of 1978* (White Plains, N.Y., 1978), 18-27; John Garraty, *New York Times*, Jan. 3, 1978.

7. Milton Friedman, *Capitalism and Freedom* (Chicago, 1962), 190-195. For background, see Christopher Green, *Negative Taxes and the Poverty Problem* (Washington, 1967); Martin Anderson, *Welfare: The Political Economy of Welfare Reform in the United States* (Stanford, 1978), 72-73; Feagin, *Subordinating*, 144 ff.; Washington *Post*, Feb. 13, 1966. A critique is Alvin Schorr, "Against a Negative Income Tax," *Public Interest*, 3 (Fall 1966), 110-117.

8. Robert Theobald, ed., *The Guaranteed Income: Next Step in Income Evolution?* (Garden City, N.Y., 1966), 229; Theobald, *Free Men and Free Markets* (New York, 1963), 14, 149.

9. James Sundquist, "The End of the Experiment," in Sundquist, ed., *On Fighting Poverty* (New York, 1969), 235-251; Levine, *Poor Ye Need Not Have*, 192-195; Steiner, *State of Welfare*, 99-100. Quote cited in Anderson, *Welfare*, 70-71. Galbraith cited in Vincent J. Burke and Vee Burke, *Nixon's Good Deed: Welfare Reform* (New York, 1974), 18.

10. Edward E. Schwartz, "A Floor on Income for all Americans," speech, Nov. 14, 1964, box 2, National Association of Social Workers papers, Social Welfare History Archives, University of Minnesota; Elizabeth Wickenden for National Social Welfare Assembly, "Statement No. 3, 1967," box 45, NASW papers. These papers contain much information on social workers and poverty in the 1960s. Other sources shedding light on the opinions of social workers include Steiner, *State of Welfare*, 114-116; George Rohrlich, "Guaranteed Minimum Income Programs and the Unfinished Business of Social Security," *Social Service Review*, 41 (June 1967), 166-178; and Eveline Burns, "The Poor Need Money," *Nation*, 200 (June 7, 1965), 613-615.

11. Cited in "Office of Economic Opportunity During the Administration of President Lyndon B. Johnson, Nov. 1963—Jan. 1969: An Administrative History," 624, Lyndon Johnson Library, Austin, Texas. Also Council of Economic Advisers, "Draft History of War on Poverty" (n.d.), White House Central Files, Legislative Background of EOA, box 1, Johnson Library; Wilbur Cohen to Joseph Califano, Nov. 4, 1965, ibid., Confidential File, box 98; Sargent Shriver to Califano, Sept. 21, 1965, ibid., box 364; Shriver to President Johnson, Jan. 4, 1968, ibid., box 26. See also "Report of Task Force on Income Maintenance," Dec. 5, 1966, in Task Forces, box 16, Johnson Library.

For the work experiments see Robert A. Levine and David W. Lyon, "Studies in Public Welfare: A Review Article," *Journal of Human Resources*, 10 (Fall 1975), 445-466; Harold L. Wilensky, *The Welfare State and Equality: Structural and Ideological Roots of Public Expenditures* (Berkeley, 1975), 108-109; Anderson, *Welfare*, 102-115.

12. *Poverty Amid Plenty*, 21, 8; Ben Heineman oral history interview,

Johnson Library.

13. *Poverty Amid Plenty*, 7, 52-53; Commission's *Background Papers* (Washington, 1969), 110-11.

14. Doggerel in H. Ray Kaplan and Curt Tausky, "Work and the Welfare Cadillac: The Function of and Commitment to Work among the Hard-Core Unemployed," *Social Problems* 19 (Spring 1972), 469-483. For criticisms of negative tax plans see Anderson, *Welfare*, 77-78; American Enterprise Institute, *Welfare Reform: Why?* pamphlet (May 20, 1976). For polls, see Washington *Post* (Aug. 7, 1967); and Michael E. Schiltz, *Public Attitudes Toward Social Security, 1935-1965* (Washington, 1970), 182-184.

15. Edward Banfield, *The Unheavenly City: The Nature and Future of Our Urban Crisis* (Boston, 1968), 211.

16. Martha N. Ozawa, "Issues in Welfare Reform," *Social Service Review*, 52 (March 1978), 37-55; Mark Kalman, "The Social Costs of Inequality," in Lewis A. Coser and Irving Howe, eds., *The New Conservatives: A Critique from the Left*, rev. ed. (New York, 1976), 151-164; Martin Rein, "Equality and Social Policy," *Social Service Review*, 51 (Dec. 1977), 565-587; and Eveline Burns, "Social Security in Evolution: Toward What?" ibid., 39 (June 1965), 129-140.

17. Ozawa, "Issues in Welfare Reform"; Kershaw, *Government against Poverty*, 119-122.

18. Basic sources are Burke and Burke, *Nixon's Good Deed*; Moynihan, *The Politics of a Guaranteed Income: The Nixon Administration and the Family Assistance Plan* (New York, 1973); Kershaw, *Government against Poverty*, 127-128; Theodore Marmor and Martin Rein, "Reforming 'The Welfare Mess': The Fate of the Family Assistance Plan, 1969-1972," in Allen P. Sindler, ed., *Policy and Politics in America* (Baltimore, 1973), 2-29; Walter Williams, "The Continuing Struggle for a Negative Income Tax: A Review Article," *Journal of Human Resources*, 10 (Fall 1975), 427-444; Gus Tyler, "The Politics of Pat Moynihan," in Coser and Howe, *New Conservatives*, 181-192; and Steiner, *State of Welfare*, 10-11, 94-95, 314.

19. *Economist* cited in Steiner, *State of Welfare*, 76-77.

20. Gilbert Y. Steiner, "Reform Follows Reality: The Growth of Welfare, *Public Interest*, 34 (Winter 1974), 47-65; Norman Furniss and Timothy Tilton, *The Case for the Welfare State* (Bloomington, Ind., 1977), 179.

21. Richard Nixon, "Presidential Address to the Nation on Domestic Programs, Aug. 8, 1969," *Weekly Compilation of Presidential Documents*, vol. 5 (Washington, 1969), 1105-1107.

22. Moynihan cited in Williams, "Continuing Struggle."

23. Ribicoff cited in James Welsh, "Welfare Reform: Born August 8, 1969, Died October 4, 1972," *New York Times Magazine* (Jan. 7, 1973), 14-17; Williams, "Continuing Struggle."

24. Burke and Burke, *Nixon's Good Deed*, 131; Welsh, "Welfare Reform."

25. Burke and Burke, *Nixon's Good Deed*, 130-138, 161-164.

26. Mau Mau tactics cited in Welsh, "Welfare Reform."

27. Ibid.; and Marmor and Rein, "Reforming 'The Welfare Mess.' " A

favorable account of NWRO is Piven and Cloward, *Poor People's Movements*, 337 ff.

28. Henry Aaron, *Politics and the Professors: The Great Society in Perspective* (Washington, 1978), 3 ff; Anderson, *Welfare*, 143-144; Frederick Doolittle, Frank Levy, and Michael Wiseman, "The Mirage of Welfare Reform," *Public Interest*, 47 (Spring 1977), 62-87.

29. Burke and Burke, *Nixon's Good Deed*, 192-196; Ozawa, "Issues in Welfare Reform."

30. "Revolutionary right" is Burke and Burke, *Nixon's Good Deed*, 155. See also Lawrence E. Lynn, Jr., "Policy Developments in the Income Maintenance System," in Robert Haveman, ed., *A Decade of Federal Antipoverty Programs: Achievements, Failures, and Lessons* (Madison, Wis., 1977), 55-117.

31. Williams, "Continuing Struggle."

32. Edgar K. Browning, "How Much More Equality Can We Afford?" *Public Interest*, 43 (Spring 1976), 90-110; Aaron, *Politics and the Professors*, 68-69; Doolittle et al., "Mirage of Welfare Reform;" and esp. Aaron, *Why Is Welfare So Hard to Reform?* (Washington, 1973), 33-49.

13. Stalemate

1. Edgar Browning, "How Much More Equality Can We Afford?" *Public Interest*, 43 (Spring 1976), 90-110; Robert Haveman, "Poverty and Social Policy in the 1960's and 1970's—An Overview and Some Speculations," in Haveman, ed., *A Decade of Federal Antipoverty Programs: Achievements, Failures, and Lessons* (Madison, Wis., 1977), 18; Sar A. Levitan, cited by Martin Anderson, *Welfare: The Political Economy of Welfare Reform in the United States* (Palo Alto, Calif., 1978), 25.

2. Robert J. Lampman, "Growth, Prosperity, and Inequality Since 1947," *Wilson Quarterly*, 1 (Autumn 1977), 143-155; Sar A. Levitan, "Our Growing Welfare State," *New York Times*, May 16, 1980. Food stamps, ibid., 16; Frank Levy, "Poverty by the Numbers," *American Spectator* (May 1978), 24-26; Larry H. Long, "Interregional Migration of the Poor: Some Recent Changes," Current Population Reports, Special Studies, Series P-23, no. 73 (Nov. 1978); Elliott Currie, "The New Face of Poverty," *Progressive* (Jan. 1979), 38-41; *New York Times*, July 17, 1977.

3. Providence *Bulletin*, Aug. 18, 1980.

4. Statistics on welfare in 1977 are in *Statistical Abstract of the United States, 1979* (Washington, 1980), 326-361. Frederick Doolittle, Frank Levy, and Michael Wiseman, "The Mirage of Welfare Reform," *Public Interest*, 47 (Spring 1977), 62-87.

5. Martin Rein and Lee Rainwater, "Patterns of Welfare Use," *Social Service Review*, 52 (Dec. 1978), 511-534.

6. Henry Aaron, *Politics and the Professors: The Great Society in Perspective* (Washington, 1978), 160; *New York Times*, Aug. 3, 1977; Gordon Weil, *The Welfare Debate of 1978* (White Plains, N.Y., 1979), 53; Anderson, *Welfare*, 60-65; *New Republic* classifieds, 1977.

7. *New York Times*, Nov. 30, 1980.

8. Mayer N. Zald, "Demographies, Politics, and the Future of the Welfare State," *Social Service Review*, 51 (March 1977), 110-124; Sheldon Danziger and Robert Plotnick, "Can Welfare Reform Eliminate Poverty?" ibid., 53 (June 1979), 224-260; Robert Plotnick and Felicity Skidmore, *Progress Against Poverty: A Review of the 1964-1974 Decade* (New York, 1975), 179; Robert Plotnick and Timothy Smeeding, "Poverty and Income Transfers: Past Trends and Future Prospects," *Public Policy*, 27 (Summer 1979), 255-272. "Estimate" from Kirsten Grønbjerg, David Street, and Gerald D. Suttles, *Poverty and Social Change* (Chicago, 1978), 90; Norman Furniss and Timothy Tilton, *The Case for the Welfare State* (Bloomington, Ind., 1977), 169-171; President's Commission for a National Agenda for the Eighties, *Government and the Advancement of Social Justice: Health, Welfare, and Civil Rights in the Eighties* (Washington, 1980), 55-73. The vast majority of the pretransfer poor who escaped poverty relied on social insurance, not public assistance.

9. *New York Times*, Oct. 19, 1980.

10. Providence *Bulletin*, Dec. 31, 1980; *Government and the Advancement of Social Justice*, 55-73.

11. *New York Times*, Aug. 5, 1980; March 14, 1979; Jan. 10, 1978; Martin Feldstein, "The Economics of the New Unemployment," *Public Interest*, 33 (Fall 1973), 3-42.

12. See Irwin Garfinkel, "Welfare Reform," *Social Welfare Forum, 1978* (New York, 1979), 80-95.

13. For welfare reform ideas, Robert A. Levine and David W. Lyon, "Studies in Public Welfare: A Review Article," *Journal of Human Resources*, 10 (Fall 1975), 445-466; Doolittle et al., "Mirage of Welfare Reform"; Martin Rein, "Equality and Social Policy," *Social Service Review*, 51 (Dec. 1977), 565-587; Martha N. Ozawa, "Issues in Welfare Reform," ibid., 52 (March 1978), 37-55. For conservative views, Anderson, *Welfare*; and American Enterprise Institute, "Welfare Reform: Why?" round table discussion, May 20, 1976.

14. The poverty line for such families was $6,660. Weil, *Welfare Debate*, 10-27, 32-35, 77-78, 966-997; *New York Times*, Aug. 7, 1977; Anderson, *Welfare*, chap. 8.

15. *New York Times*, Nov. 8, 1979; April 1, 1979.

16. Ibid., March 18, 1980.

17. Ibid., April 20, 1980.

14. Regression in the Early 1980s

1. U.S. House, Committee on Ways and Means, Subcommittee on Public Assistance, *Poverty Rate Increase* Hearings, 98th Cong. 1st sess., Oct. 18 and Nov. 3, 1983. See also "Poverty in the United States: Where Do We Stand Now?" *Focus* (Institute for Research on Poverty [IRP], Madison, Wis.) (Winter 1984); and *New York Times,* Aug. 28, 1985.

2. In calculating poverty statistics, family income includes both income and cash welfare payments — that is, what economists call "posttransfer payment"

income. Poverty is obviously much greater, statistically speaking, if welfare transfers are not counted in this reckoning. Conversely, the official number of poor people is lower by 15 to 30 percent if estimates of the market value of in-kind benefits such as food stamps is included. See *New York Times,* Aug. 29, 1985.

3. *New York Times,* June 3, 1985

4. See D. Lee Bawden, ed., *The Social Contract Revisited: Aims and Outcomes of President Reagan's Welfare Policy* (Washington, 1984); John Palmer and Isabel Sawhill, eds., *The Reagan Experiment* (Washington, 1984); and "Measuring the Effects of the Reagan Welfare Changes on the Work Effort and Well-Being of Single Parents," *Focus* (Spring 1985).

5. Hugh Heclo, "The Welfare State in Hard Times," (unpublished manuscript, 1985).

6. *New York Times,* June 2, 1985.

7. Charles Murray, *Losing Ground: American Social Policy, 1950-1980* (New York, 1984). See also Murray, "Looking Back," *Wilson Quarterly* (Autumn 1984), 97-139. For an opposing view, see David Ellwood and Lawrence Summers, "Poverty in America: Is Welfare the Answer or the Problem?" paper delivered at IRP conference, Poverty and Policy: Retrospect and Prospects, Williamsburg, Va., Dec. 6-8, 1984. See also Robert Greenstein, "Losing Faith in 'Losing Ground,' " *New Republic,* Mar. 25, 1985, 12-17; and "The Great Society: An Exchange," ibid., Apr. 8, 1985, 21-23. Also relevant is Sheldon Danziger and Peter Gottschalk, "The Poverty of 'Losing Ground,' " *Challenge,* May 6, 1985, 32-38. An early conservative "bible" on the subject, credited with influencing Reagan administration officials, was George Gilder, *Wealth and Poverty* (New York, 1981).

8. *New York Times,* June 10, 1985.

9. See Christopher Jencks, "How Poor Are the Poor?" *New York Review of Books,* May 9, 1985; and Paul Starr, "Health Care and the Poor: The Last Twenty Years," paper given at 1984 IRP conference. A positive overview of Great Society programs is John Schwarz, *America's Hidden Success: A Reassessment of Twenty Years of Public Policy* (New York, 1983).

10. See Eugene Smolensky, "Is a Golden Age in Poverty Policy Right around the Corner?" *Focus* (Spring 1985).

11. Eleanor Holmes Norton, "Restoring the Traditional Black Family," *New York Times Magazine,* June 2, 1985.

12. Cited in Kenneth Auletta, *The Underclass* (New York, 1982), p. 30.

13. Ibid.

14. *Providence Journal,* Apr. 14, 1985.

15. Cited in column by William Raspberry, *Providence Bulletin,* May 20, 1985. See also Mary Jo Bane, "Household Composition and Poverty," and William Julius Wilson and Katherine M. Neckerman, "Poverty and Family Structure: The Widening Gap between Evidence and Public Policy Issues," papers delivered at 1984 IRP conference.

16. *New York Times,* May 23, 1985. Three aspects of this problem tended to be ignored or distorted by alarmists. First, there was no explosion of childbearing in the ghetto: birth rates among black teenagers — as among most American women — decreased in the early 1980s. Second, the feminization of poverty

in the 1970s was a demographic matter; it reflected an increase in the number of female-headed households, not a growing propensity of such households to become poor. And third, the feminization of poverty tailed off in the early 1980s, when a greater "masculinization" of poverty developed, associated with the recession and with conservative federal policies that affected male-headed working families. See U.S. House, Committee on Ways and Means, *Children in Poverty* Hearings, 99th Cong., 1st Sess., May 22, 1985; and Peter Gottschalk, "Overview of Economic and Demographic Factors Affecting Poverty," paper prepared for Food and Nutrition Service, U.S. Department of Agriculture, 1985.

17. Michael Harrington, *The New American Poverty* (New York, 1984).

18. See Wilson and Neckerman, "Poverty and Family Structure"; Bane, "Household Composition and Poverty"; Norton, "Restoring the Traditional Black Family."

19. See Irwin Garfinkel and Sara McLanahan, "The Feminization of Poverty: Nature, Causes, and a Partial Cure," IRP Discussion Paper, April 1985, Madison, Wis.

20. *Providence Journal,* Apr. 14, 1985.

15. Welfare Reform: No Consensus

1. *New York Times,* Nov. 7, 1993.

2. "Indexing" meant adjusting benefits annually to keep pace with changes in the Consumer Price Index.

3. Recovery led to a drop in unemployment to a low of 6.4 percent by late 1993, at which point 8.3 million Americans were out of work, around 3 million of them for 15 weeks or more. *New York Times,* Dec. 4, 1993. The jobless rate was 5.6 percent for whites, 11.5 percent for blacks, and 10.5 percent for Hispanics. For men over the age of 20 it was 5.8 percent, for women over 20, 5.7 percent, for teenagers (16 to 19 years) it was 17.8 percent. *San Francisco Chronicle,* Jan. 8, 1994.

4. Census figures cited in *New York Times,* Oct. 5 and 10, 1993. For commentary on trends see Thomas Corbett, "Child Poverty and Welfare Reform: Progress or Paralysis?" in *Focus* (Institute for Research on Poverty [IRP], Madison, Wis.), 15 (Spring 1993), 1-17; and Robert Plotnick, "Changes in Poverty, Income Inequality and the Standard of Living during the Reagan Years," *Journal of Sociology and Social Welfare,* 19 (March 1992), 29-44.

5. *New York Times,* Dec. 4, 1993.

6. 13.1 percent of midwesterners, 12.3 percent of northeasterners, and 14.4 percent of westerners were then defined as poor.

7. Paul Sniderman and Thomas Piazza, *The Scar of Race* (Cambridge, Mass., 1993), 113.

8. The percentage of whites who were poor, including Hispanic whites, was 11.6 percent (24.5 million people). The percentage of Asian Americans who were poor was 12.5 percent.

9. Donald Huddle, an economist at Rice University, wrote in 1994 that the rate among post-1970 immigrants was 42 percent higher than that for

native-born people. *New York Times,* Jan. 26, 1994. The number of legal immigrants numbered nearly a million a year in the early 1990s.

10. Gary Sandefur, "American Indian Reservations: The First Underclass Areas?" *Focus* (Spring and Summer 1989), 37-42; "Sad Distinction for the Sioux," *New York Times,* Sept. 1992.

11. Corbett, "Child Poverty and Welfare Reform." Also Peter Brandon, "The Connection Between Family Structure and Entitlements Affecting Poor Young Children," *Focus* 15 (Winter 1993-1994), 27–34; and Charles Murray, "Let's Stop Subsidizing Illegitimacy," *Wall Street Journal,* Oct. 29, 1993. Out-of-wedlock births among whites (especially poor whites) also skyrocketed to 22 percent of white births in 1992. In 1992, some 17 percent of white children under 18 were poor. Only 13 percent of black married-couple families (involving 486,000 people) lived in poverty. This was below the national poverty average of 14.5 percent. See *Newsweek,* Oct. 18, 1993, 44.

12. See William Julius Wilson, *The Truly Disadvantaged: The Inner City, the Underclass, and Public Policy* (Chicago, 1987); Marian Wright Edelman, *Families in Peril: An Agenda for Social Change* (Cambridge, Mass., 1987); and Daniel Patrick Moynihan, *Family and Nation* (New York, 1987).

13. See Chapter 14.

14. *New York Times,* Dec. 8, 1993. FBI statistics depended on inconsistent reporting from law enforcement agencies, and were debatable. The overall trends, however, were probably valid.

15. See Reynolds Farley and Walter Allen, *The Color Line and the Quality of Life in America* (New York, 1987); and James Smith and Finis Welch, *Closing the Gap: Forty Years of Economic Progress for Blacks* (Santa Monica, 1986).

16. See Christopher Jencks, "What Is the Underclass—and Is It Growing?" *Focus* (Spring-Summer 1989), 14-26; and Paul Jargowsky and Mary Jo Bane, "Ghetto Poverty in the United States, 1970-1980," in Christopher Jencks and Paul Peterson, eds., *The Urban Underclass* (Washington, D.C., 1991), 251-253, 267-268. Earlier estimates continued to be used. One was Ken Auletta's in *The Underclass* (New York, 1982), 27-30. He settled on a figure of 9 million at that time.

17. David Ellwood, *Poor Support: Poverty in America* (New York, 1988), 193. Ellwood later became a key figure in the design of "welfare reform" in the Clinton administration.

18. See Erol Ricketts and Isabel Sawhill, "Defining and Measuring the Underclass," *Journal of Policy Analysis and Management,* 7 (1988), 316-325; Paul Peterson, "The Urban Underclass and the Poverty Paradox," *Political Science Quarterly,* 106 (1992), 617-638.

19. Estimate by Ronald Mincy of the Urban Institute, as reported in *New York Times,* Oct. 10, 1993.

20. Wilson, *Truly Disadvantaged.* See also Elijah Anderson, *StreetWise* (Chicago, 1990), on African-Americans in Philadelphia; Jay MacLeod, *Ain't No Makin' It: Leveled Aspirations in a Low-Income Neighborhood* (Boul-

der, Colo., 1987), primarily on whites in a northeastern city; and Alex Kotlowitz, *There Are No Children Here* (New York, 1991), on two African-American boys in Chicago.

21. See Sheldon Danziger and Peter Gottschalk, "Earnings Inequality, the Spatial Concentration of Poverty, and the Underclass," *American Economic Review*, 77 (1987), 211-215; Herbert Gans, "Deconstructing the Underclass: The Term's Danger as a Planning Concept," *Journal of the American Planning Association*, 56 (1990), 271-277; Michael Katz, ed., *The "Underclass" Debate: The View from History* (Princeton, 1993); Jacqueline Jones, *The Dispossessed: America's Underclasses from the Civil War to the Present* (New York, 1992); Christopher Jencks, *Rethinking Social Policy: Race, Poverty, and the Underclass* (Cambridge, Mass., 1992); and Nicholas Lemann, *The Promised Land: The Great Black Migration and How It Changed America* (New York, 1991). A thoughtful review essay is Thomas Sugrue, "The Impoverished Politics of Poverty," *Yale Journal of Law and the Humanities*, 6 (Winter 1994), 163-179.

22. See Lawrence Mead, *The New Politics of Poverty: The Non-Working Poor in America* (New York, 1992); and Mickey Kaus, *The End of Equality* (New York, 1992). Although these books differed, they reflected the growing feeling that welfare recipients must learn to work.

23. See Douglas Massey, *American Apartheid: Segregation and the Making of the Underclass* (Cambridge, Mass., 1993); David Ellwood, "The Spatial Mismatch Hypothesis: Are There Teenage Jobs Missing in the Ghetto?" in Richard Freeman and Harry Holzer, eds., *The Black Youth Employment Crisis* (Chicago, 1986), 147-185; and Robert Mare and Christopher Winship, "Socioeconomic Change and the Decline in Marriage for Blacks and Whites," in Jencks and Peterson, *The Urban Underclass*, 175-202.

24. *Providence Journal*, March 17, 1991.

25. Bob Herbert, "Are We Awake Yet?" *New York Times*, Jan. 26, 1994.

26. *New York Times*, Jan. 25, 1994.

27. Andrew Hacker, *Two Nations: Black and White, Separate, Hostile, Unequal* (New York, 1992). For a less pessimistic view, see Sniderman and Piazza, *The Scar of Race*, 64-65, 167-178.

28. Corbett, "Child Poverty and Welfare Reform," *Washington Post*, Nov. 9, 1993; Mary Jo Bane and David Ellwood, "Slipping into and out of Poverty: The Dynamics of Spells," *Journal of Human Resources*, 21 (Winter 1986), 1-23.

29. Western European countries experienced similar upsurges in homelessness. Some advocates for the homeless estimated that there were 400,000 homeless people in France, including 9,000 in Paris. *New York Times*, Dec. 14, 1993.

30. See Christopher Jencks, *The Homeless* (Cambridge, Mass., 1994), who estimates 300,000. A useful survey of these debates is David Rochefort and Roger Cobb, "Framing and Claiming the Homelessness Problem," *New England Journal of Public Policy*, 8 (Spring-Summer 1992), 49-65.

31. See D. L. Bartlett and J. B. Steele, *America: What Went Wrong?* (Kansas City, 1992), 31-39, 88-104, for discussions of foreign competition.

32. See Frank Levy, *Dollars and Dreams: The Changing Nature of American Income Distribution* (New York, 1987). Some jobs in this ill-defined sector were well-paid.

33. *New York Times,* March 31, 1994.

34. For cogent arguments emphasizing the durability of social and occu-pational mobility in the 1980s see Isabel Sawhill and Mark Condon, "Is U.S. Inequality Really Growing?" *Policy Bites* (Washington, D.C., Urban Institute, 1992); and Lowell Gallaway and Richard Vedder, "The Distribu-tional Impact of the Eighties: Myth vs Reality," *Critical Review,* 7 (1993), 61-79. For statistics concerning the distribution of income between 1973 and 1990 see Joel Devine and James Wright, *The Greatest of Evils: Urban Poverty and the American Underclass* (New York, 1993), 31-33.

35. Sheldon Danziger and Peter Gottschalk, eds., *Uneven Tides: Rising Inequality in America* (New York, 1993); Kevin Phillips, *The Politics of Rich and Poor: Wealth and the American Electorate in the Reagan After-math* (New York, 1990).

36. *New York Times,* Dec. 15, 1993.

37. Congress also tried in the 1980s to extend Medicaid coverage to the non-welfare poor, but states tightened eligibility rules (Medicaid was a federal-state program), and a higher percentage of poor people went without Medicaid in 1990 than in 1980. See Theodor Litman and Leonard Robins, *Health Politics and Policy* (Albany, N.Y., 1991), 170-176.

38. This affected roughly 350,000 families by 1992, a small component of the 5 million AFDC families. *New York Times,* Dec. 10, 1993. The pro-gram aided only those AFDC families in which the father had substantial work experience—at least 6 months of the previous 13. It did not aid two-parent poor families mired in long-term unemployment.

39. Some states exempted only parents (mostly women) with children under one year of age. *New York Times,* May 5, 1993.

40. See Committee on Ways and Means, U.S. House of Representa-tives, "Overview of Entitlement Programs," in "1992 Green Book", May 15, 1992, 603-705 for a description of AFDC and the Family Support Act.

41. "What Works?" *The New Republic,* Jan. 3, 1994, 7. For a solid summary of job training efforts, especially on the state level, see Judith Gueron and Edward Pauly, *From Welfare to Work* (New York, 1991), esp. 7-49. It warns against sweeping generalizations, but is cautiously optimistic that flexible programs proved both cost-efficient and beneficial to some poor people.

42. The estimate of Christopher Jencks, as cited in Cloward and Piven, "The Fraud of Workfare," *The Nation,* May 24, 1993, 693-696. Other esti-mates of these costs were lower, but still very high.

43. Mimi Abramovitz, "The New Paternalism," *The Nation,* Oct. 5, 1992, 368-371.

44. Teresa McCrary, "Getting Off the Welfare Carousel," *Newsweek,* Dec. 6, 1993, 11.

45. Corbett, "Child Poverty and Welfare Reform," 7. See also Robert Moffitt, "Incentive Effects of the U.S. Welfare System: A Review," *Journal of Economic Literature,* 30 (March 1992), 1-61; and especially Christopher Jencks and Kathryn Edin, "The Real Welfare Problem," *The American Prospect* (Spring 1990), 31-50.

46. "1992 Green Book," 644-645; *New York Times,* Dec. 2, 1993. Federal contributions to poorer states such as Mississippi were higher (79 percent for Medicaid) than states like Connecticut (50 percent), the result of grant formulas worked out over the years to equalize regional economic health. Though the overall cost of living was less in Mississippi than in Connecticut, the state-by-state variation in the real value of benefits was considerable. (Figures for Alaska, with a much higher cost of living and much higher benefits, are not included.)

47. A useful overview of such programs is Edward Berkowitz, *America's Welfare State: From Roosevelt to Reagan* (Baltimore, 1991).

48. See Theodore Marmor et al., *America's Misunderstood Welfare State: Persistent Myths, Enduring Realities* (New York, 1990), esp. 128-174.

49. *Providence Journal-Bulletin,* Dec. 11, 1993.

50. Michael Kinsley, "Pete's Plan," *The New Republic,* Oct. 25, 1993, 6; Robert Samuelson, "Finally the Right Stuff on Deficits," *Newsweek,* Oct. 11, 1993, 47.

51. See John Schwarz and Thomas Volgy, "Out of Line," *The New Republic,* Nov. 23, 1992, 16-17; Schwarz and Volgy, "Above the Poverty Line—But Poor," *The Nation,* Feb. 13, 1993, 191-192; and Patricia Ruggles, "Measuring Poverty," *Focus* 14 (Spring 1992), 1-9. See also Guy Gugliotta, "Drawing the Poverty Line: A Calculation of Necessity and Self-Image," *Washington Post,* May 10, 1993.

52. Schwarz and Volgy, "Out of Line."

53. See Paul Craig Roberts, "The Scarcest Commodity of All," *Providence Journal,* Jan. 26, 1994.

54. Ibid.

55. *New York Times,* June 8, 1993.

56. For a thorough and wide-ranging defense of Reagan economic policies and of other conservative ideas, see Alan Reynolds, "The Real Reagan Record: Upstarts and Downstarts," *National Review,* Aug. 31, 1992, 25-62.

57. Ruggles, "Measuring Poverty," 4-5. This happened because incomes grew more rapidly than prices (on which the poverty line was based), especially in the 1960s and mid-1980s.

58. Cited in Gugliotta, "Drawing the Poverty Line." Jencks was pointing only to the poorest 5 percent. Government figures estimated that 14.5 percent of Americans were poor in 1992.

59. For Clinton's liberal moves in 1993 and early 1994 see *New York Times,* March 30, 1994. For a conservative critique, see Marvin Kosters, "The Earned Income Tax Credit and the Working Poor," *The American Enterprise* (May-June 1993), 64-72.

60. See Nicholas Lemann, "The Myth of Community Development," *New York Times Magazine,* Jan. 9, 1994, 27ff.

61. *New York Times,* Dec. 3, 1993.

62. *Providence Journal,* Dec. 4, 1993.

63. *New York Times,* Jan. 30, 1994.

64. Some observers thought that job training programs might even attract people to the welfare rolls. Ibid.

65. Ibid.

66. *New York Times,* April 5, 1994; May 12, 1994.

67. *New York Times,* Jan. 19 and 21, 1994. By then 13 states had received such waivers.

68. The New Jersey plan included more liberal provisions concerning job training, educational programs, and family services.

69. *New York Times,* Jan. 14 and 21, 1994. The law was experimental, affecting only two counties.

70. Mimi Abramovitz and Frances Fox Piven, "Scapegoating Women on Welfare," *New York Times,* Sept. 2, 1992.

71. *New York Times,* Oct. 7, 1993.

72. *New York Times,* Nov. 2 and 8, 1993.

73. *New York Times,* Nov. 2, 1993. Other states, including Vermont, Massachusetts, and Colorado, passed or developed similar plans in early 1994. See *New York Times,* Jan. 14, 1994.

74. Murray, "Let's Stop Subsidizing Illegitimacy," *Wall Street Journal,* Oct. 29, 1993. Other relevant commentary on the issue included Robert Samuelson, "Should We Think the Unthinkable?" *Newsweek,* Sept. 13, 1993, 43; William Raspberry, "Murray Raises Tough Issues on Illegitimacy," *Providence Journal,* Dec. 4, 1993; and Mickey Kaus, "Bastards," *The New Republic,* Feb. 21, 1994, 16-19.

75. See Paul Offner, "Target the Kids," *The New Republic,* Jan. 24, 1994, 9-11.

76. See Alan Brinkley, *New York Times,* Jan. 27, 1994.

77. Important statements of liberal/moderate opinion in the early 1990s include Mickey Kaus, *The End of Equality;* Jencks, *Rethinking Social Policy;* and Lemann, *The Promised Land.* A more conservative approach was Lawrence Mead, *The New Politics of Poverty.* More conservative still was Myron Magnet, "Rebels with a Cause: How Did the Underclass Form? We Forgot How to Prevent It," *National Review,* March, 15, 1993, 46-50.

RESOURCES

Because all published sources are cited in full in the notes, I do not list them again here. Instead, I list two main areas: the most important archives, including oral history accounts, and some key documents.

Archival Sources

The main archival sources are the Social Welfare History Archives at the University of Minnesota and the presidential libraries of Franklin D. Roosevelt (Hyde Park, N.Y.), John F. Kennedy (Dorchester, Mass.), and Lyndon B. Johnson (Austin, Texas). Materials cited less frequently are in the National Archives in Washington, D.C., and the Oral History Project at Columbia University.

The Social Welfare History Archives includes vast collections centered about social work. The most relevant were those of the American Public Welfare Association, Survey Associates, the National Association of Social Workers, the National Social Welfare Assembly, and the AFL-CIO Community Services Activities papers. There is much in these papers on the origins of the welfare state in the 1930s, on Social Security and welfare policies in the 1940s, 1950s, and 1960s, and on new governmental programs, including the war on poverty and income maintenance, in the early and mid-1960s.

The most relevant papers at the Roosevelt Library were those of Harry Hopkins and of Lorena Hickok, one of his aides in the field. Official File 444, which concerns relief activities, is equally rich in primary material. The Hilda Smith papers and those of the Social Security Board (OF 1710) and Social Welfare (OF 727) yielded some material. Other collections used were thin: the Committee on Economic Security (OF 1086), the Wilbur Cohen, Charles Taussig, and Aubrey Williams papers, Transient Labor (OF 2037), Unemployment Census (OF 2948), Unemployment (OF 264), and the President's Interdepartmental Committee on Health and Welfare Activities.

Important papers at the Kennedy Library include the collections of Walter

Heller and Theodore Sorensen. Only slightly less relevant are those of John
Kenneth Galbraith. There is much material (some of it duplicated in the Heller
and Sorensen papers) in the voluminous White House Central Files. The Myer
Feldman papers produced some information. A "must" for the war on poverty is the two-volume transcript, "Poverty and Urban Policy," of a conference held at the Kennedy Library in 1973 on urban poverty programs and
policies. Oral histories consulted include those by Anthony Celebrezze, Wilbur Cohen (two), Myer Feldman, David Hackett, and James Sundquist.

The only advice I can give scholars concerning the Johnson Library is to
rely on the archivists: the place is so vast and the filing system so complex
that it is impossible to explain much in a bibliography. Amid the mountains of
paper, there are some relevant documents, especially on the war on poverty
and on income maintenance. Perhaps the place to start is the welfare folders
in the White House Central Files. A helpful in-house history available there is
"Office of Economic Opportunity During the Administration of President
Lyndon B. Johnson, Nov. 1963—Jan. 1969: An Administrative History."
Pertinent oral accounts include those by Wilbur Cohen, Robert Levine, James
Sundquist, Otis Singletary, Bertrand M. Harding, Herbert J. Kramer, and
Eric Tolmach. Less useful oral histories include those by Elizabeth W. Gold-
schmidt, Ben W. Heineman, Mary Keyserling, and Joseph Pechman.

At the National Archives I consulted Record Groups 47 (Social Security),
363 (Social Rehabilitative Services), 235 (Federal Security Agency and HEW),
381 (Office of Economic Opportunity), and 69 (Works Progress Administration). Aside from the papers of the Committee on Economic Security, these
files contain heaps of paper with comparatively little gold among them. The
Columbia Oral History office has a number of memoirs centering about Social Security and Welfare. Those by Eveline Burns and Jane Hoey are helpful,
and those by Wilbur Cohen, Charles Schottland, and Elizabeth Wickenden
are of special relevance.

Documents

Relevant congressional documents, in chronological order, are Senate
Committee on Manufactures, *Federal Aid for Unemployment Relief*, Hearings on Sen. 5125, 72d Cong., 2d Sess., 1933; Special Committee to Investigate Unemployment and Relief (Hearings Pursuant to Sen. Resol. 36), 75th
Cong., 3d Sess., 1938; *Low Income Families*, Hearings before the Subcom-
mittee on Low-Income Families of the Joint Committee on the Economic Report, 81st Cong., 1st Sess. 1949; *Low Income Families and Economic Stability*, ibid., Sen. Doc. 146, March 1950; *Characteristics of the Low-Income
Population and Related Federal Programs*, Subcommittee on Low-Income
Families, 84th Cong., 1st Sess., Nov. 1955; *A Program for the Low-Income
Population at Subsistance Levels of Living*, ibid., Sen. Report 1311, 2d Sess.,
Jan. 1956; *Examination of War on Poverty*, Hearings before Subcommittee
on War on Poverty Program of House Committee on Education and Labor,
89th Cong., 1st Sess., April 1965; and Hearings, Subcommittee on Research

and Technical Programs of the House Committee on Governmental Operations, 90th Cong., 1st Sess., 1967.

Executive documents include: Emma A. Winslow, *Trends in Different Types of Public and Private Relief in Urban Areas, 1929-1935*, Children's Bureau Publication 237 (1937); U.S. Bureau of Public Assistance, *Families Receiving Aid to Dependent Children*, Oct. 1942, Public Assistance Report 7 (1945); National Resources Planning Board, *Security, Work, and Relief Policies* (1942); U.S. Bureau of Public Assistance, *Aid to Dependent Children in a Post-War Year*, Public Assistance Report 17 (1950); Children's Bureau, HEW, *Report to Congress on Juvenile Delinquency* (1960); HEW, *Characteristics of State Public Assistance Plans Under the Social Security Act*, Public Assistance Report 50 (1962); "The Problem of Poverty in America," Annual Report of the Council of Economic Advisers, in *Economic Report of the President, 1964* (1964); U.S. Dept. of Labor, *Manpower Report of the President* (1968); Social Security Administration, HEW, *Social Security Programs in the United States* (1968); President's Commission on Income Maintenance Programs, *Poverty Amid Plenty: The American Paradox* (1969); and ibid., *Background Papers* (1969).

As the notes attest, the most valuable of these documents were the report of the National Resources Planning Board in 1942, the hearings and reports of the subcommittee on low income in 1949-1950 and 1955-1956, the report of the Council of Economic Advisors in 1964, and the findings and background papers of the President's Commission on Income Maintenance in 1969.

INDEX

Aaron, Henry, 124, 205
Abbott, Grace, 66
Addams, Jane, 6, 25
AFDC, *See* Aid to Dependent Children
AFDC-Unemployed Parent (AFDC-UP), 130-133, 174-175, 179, 193, 201-203, 207, 210, 222, 231
Aid to Dependent Children, 67-70, 77; in 1940s and 1950s, 85-88; in early 1960s, 106-108, 111, 120, 153; in 1960s, 162-165; great growth of, 171-181; in 1970s, 197-198, 200-202, 207-208, 210, 212, 218-219, 222; in 1980s and 1990s, 224, 229, 231-235, 236, 237, 239-240. *See also* Categorical assistance
Alger, Horatio, 32
Alinsky, Saul, 111, 139, 144, 145, 149
American Association for Labor Legislation, 26-27, 29, 33, 72
American Association for Old Age Security, 29
American Association of Social Workers, 44
American Federation of Labor, 33, 72
American Public Welfare Association, 44, 89, 130, 182
Appalachia, 120, 123, 127, 134, 150
Area Redevelopment Act, 127-129
Auletta, Kenneth, 216-217, 220

Bakke, Wight, 53-55, 91
Banfield, Edward, 190
Bax, James, 182
Bell, Daniel, 78
Bennett, William, 227
Beveridge report, 92

Bismarck, Otto von, 31
Blacks, 4, 13, 14, 17; in 1930s, 39-40, 41, 49; in 1940s and 1950s, 80, 104; family life of, 101-103; and war on poverty, 134; in 1960s and 1970s, 158, 203-204, 211, 215-222; in 1990s, 226-229, 240-241
Bonus Army, 51
Boone, Richard, 138, 145, 147
Booth, Charles, 6, 7, 8, 9
Boulding, Kenneth, 78, 112
Bourke-White, Margaret, 47-48
Brace, Charles Loring, 21, 136
Brookings Institution, 15-17, 29, 43
Bureau of Family Services, 131-132, 181. *See also* Bureau of Public Assistance
Bureau of Labor Statistics, 82, 87, 159
Bureau of Public Assistance, 67, 85, 87, 131-132, 181. *See also* Bureau of Family Services
Burgess, E. W., 39
Bush, George, 224, 230, 236
Byrd, Harry, 68, 71
Byrd, Robert, 106, 146

Caldwell, Erskine, 46-48
Caprow, William, 186
Carter, Jimmy, 203-204, 206-207, 211-212, 214, 218
Categorical assistance, 60, 77, 93-94. *See also* Aid to Dependent Children
Cavanaugh, Jerome, 152
Charity Organization Society, 21, 24-26, 57, 175, 185
Child Support Assurance, 221-222

Children's allowances, 186-187, 191, 193
Children's Bureau, 100-101
Civilian Conservation Corps, 57, 63, 144, 237
Civil rights movement, 111, 146, 180, 219
Civil Works Administration, 57, 59, 66
Clague, Ewan, 44
Clark, Kenneth, 100, 103
Clinton, William, 224-225, 236-241
Cloward, Richard, 101, 105, 117, 163, 180; and war on poverty, 134, 140
Cohen, Wilbur, 75, 130, 136-137, 143, 152, 154, 189
Cold War, 84, 85, 230
Commission for a National Agenda for the 1980s, 204
Committee on Economic Security, 59-60, 70, 74-75, 130
Community action, 25, 138-141, 145-152
Community Chest, 26
Community Services Administration, 148, 182
Comprehensive Employment and Training Act (CETA), 148, 200, 237, 239
Connally, John, 147
Conway, Jack, 145, 147
Cottrell, Leonard, 139
Couch, W. T., 47
Council of Economic Advisers, 79, 81, 112-116; on culture of poverty, 120, 124; and war on poverty, 134-135, 137-138, 140
Crime, 227-229
Culture of poverty, 12-14, 18, 115-125, 215-216
Cuomo, Mario, 239

Daley, Richard, 146
Depressed areas, 5, 17, 95
Devine, Edward, 8, 22
deVise, Pierre, 218
Disability insurance, 94, 212
Dollard, John, 39
Douglas, Paul, 95

Earned Income Tax Credit, 237
Eastland, James, 145
Eisenhower, Dwight, 95, 100, 131
Epstein, Abraham, 29

Family Assistance Plan, 192-198, 206-207
Family disorganization, 39-40, 101-103, 178, 215-222, 226-228, 240-241
Family Support Act, 231-232, 238
Farm Bureau Federation, 32
Farmer, James, 102

Farm Security Administration, 48
Federal Emergency Relief Administration, 43, 57-59, 60, 62, 64
Female-headed families, 29, 81, 101-103, 159, 218-222, 226-228. See also Family disorganization
Fitzgerald, F. Scott, 118
Folks, Homer, 27
Folsom, Marion, 131
Food stamps, 161, 164-166, 168-169, 183, 196, 198, 200, 206, 208, 210, 212, 224, 232, 233, 235, 237, 240
Ford Foundation, 113, 216, 222
Frazier, E. Franklin, 40, 101, 102
Friedman, Milton, 187-188, 192, 194, 206

Gaffney, Michael, 10
Galbraith, John Kenneth, 83, 95-96, 113, 160
Gallup polls, 109-110, 171
Gans, Herbert, 116
Gardner, John, 182
Gellhorn, Martha, 51, 53
General assistance, 61-63, 164, 198, 200, 206, 207
Gibbons, Cardinal, 20
Glazer, Nathan, 152
Goldwater, Barry, 108, 144
Gompers, Samuel, 33
Griscom, Dr. John, 100

Hackett, David, 127, 128, 138, 140, 145
Harding, Bertrand, 143
Harrington, Michael, 12, 81; on poverty, 99-102, 105, 113-114, 217, 220; on culture of poverty, 118-120, 124-125; on welfare programs, 135, 162, 166, 172
Harris, Patricia Roberts, 202
Hazlitt, Henry, 145
Head Start, 137, 145, 147-148, 214, 237, 238
Health, Education, and Welfare, Department of (HEW), 89, 130, 142, 181-182, 205
Heilbroner, Robert, 185
Heineman, Ben, 189-190
Heller, Walter, 134-138, 147, 153
Hickok, Lorena, 53
Hine, Lewis, 48
Hispanics, 117, 203, 211, 217, 219, 221, 226
Hodson, William, 44
Hoey, Jane, 67
Hollander, Jacob, 23
Homelessness, 229
Hoover, Herbert, 15, 79
Hopkins, Harry, 41 ff, 113, 205

Housing, 4, 18, 37-38, 232, 237
Humphrey, Hubert, 106, 147
Hunter, Robert, 6-12, 15-17, 21, 23, 34, 38, 41-43, 46, 100, 105, 113, 118, 125, 150, 158, 161-162, 184, 199
Hurry, Jamieson, 22

Illegitimacy, 101-103, 111, 173-174, 218-222, 226-227, 240-241
Income distribution, 105-106, 160, 211-212, 230-231
Income maintenance, 66-67, 153, 189-192, 212
Indians, 117-118, 170, 225
Institute for Research on Poverty, 214

Jackson, Jesse, 227
Jencks, Christopher, 236
Jews, 14, 25
Job Corps, 127-129, 137, 141, 142, 144, 145, 148, 212
Joe, Tom, 182
Johnson, Charles, 29
Johnson, Lyndon, 65, 99, 126, 130, 189; and war on poverty, 134-141, 147, 154, 213
Jones, Le Roi, 145
Juvenile delinquency, 100-104, 128

Kellogg, Paul, 26, 44
Kelso, Robert, 22, 27
Kennedy, Edward, 216-217
Kennedy, John F., 79, 96, 99, 101, 153; and poverty (1961-1962), 126-133; and war on poverty, 133-141
Kennedy, Robert, 127, 138, 140
Kerr-Mills Act, 169
Keynes, John Maynard, 43, 83, 85, 94-95
Keyserling, Leon, 112, 113, 151

La Guardia, Fiorello, 53
Lampman, Robert, 135, 188
Lange, Dorothea, 49
Lee, Joseph, 21, 24
Legal services, 148, 153, 179
Lewis, Oscar, 118-120, 124-125
Liebow, Elliot, 117, 123
Local relief, See state-local relief
Long, Huey, 52-53
Long, Russell, 173, 194-195
Lonigan, Studs, 49
Lowell, Josephine Shaw, 21, 26
Lurie, Harry, 44
Lynd, Helen and Robert, 84

Macdonald, Dwight, 99, 159-160
Manpower training, 127-129, 220
McCrary, Teresa, 233

McGovern, George, 168
Medicaid, 153, 161, 179, 183, 191, 198; value of in 1960s, 164-166; passage of, 168-169; in 1970s, 200-201, 203, 210-211, 214, 222; in 1990s, 224, 230, 231, 232, 234, 235, 238
Medicare, 164-165, 167-169, 211, 214, 222, 224, 234, 236
Merton, Robert, 94
Migrant labor, 60-62
Miller, Herman P., 78-79
Mills, Wilbur, 174, 190
Mitchell, Joseph, 107-109
Mitchell, Wesley, 28
Mobilization for Youth, 101, 127, 138-140
Model Cities, 148
Mothers' aid, 27, 29. See also Aid to Dependent Children
Moynihan, Daniel, 40, 102, 103, 125, 143, 231; and war on poverty, 141, 145, 149, 152; and family life, 178, 186, 215, 218, 220, 226; and Family Assistance Plan, 193-194
Murray, Charles, 213-214, 218, 240-241
Muste, A. J., 26
Myrdal, Gunnar, 40, 94, 95, 112, 113, 115, 215

National Advisory Committee on Economic Opportunity, 203
National Association of Manufacturers, 32
National Association of Social Workers, 130, 143-144
National Federation of Settlements, 44, 57
National Resources Planning Board, 41-42, 92
National Social Welfare Assembly, 89, 130, 189
National Welfare Rights Organization, 153, 180-181, 195-196
National Youth Administration, 63
Negative income tax, 187-189, 205-206
Neighborhood Youth Corps, 141, 142-143, 148
Newburgh, N.Y., 107-108, 110, 132
New Deal: relief policies, 57, 67, 72, 76, 83; farm policies, 61; compared to 1960s, 65, 128, 135-137
Nisbet, Robert, 85
Nixon, Richard, 168, 172, 192-197, 207
Norton, Eleanor Holmes, 218, 220

Office of Economic Opportunity, 136, 142-154, 189, 192, 214. See also War on poverty

Ohlin, Lloyd, 101, 105, 117, 127, 138,
  140
Okies, 46, 61, 117-118
Old age assistance, 67-71, 111, 164
Old age pensions, 8, 29, 45, 52; under
  Social Security, 69, 71-75, 77, 85, 94.
  See also Social Security
Old people, 15, 40-41, 72, 81, 84; in
  1960s, 158-159, 167-168; in 1980s,
  214; in 1990s, 225
Omnibus Budget Reconciliation Act,
  212-213
Orshansky, Mollie, 82
Orwell, George, 48, 54

Pauperism, 5, 8. *See also* Poverty
Peace Corps, 139
Perkins, Frances, 75
Perlis, Leo, 133
Perot, H. Ross, 224
Piven, Frances Fox, 134, 163, 180
Poor law (1834), 20-21
Populists, 32
Poverty: causes of, 6, 8-11, 21-23,
  38-43, 129; definitions of, 7, 11-12,
  16, 19, 41, 79-82, 86-87, 91-96, 105-
  106, 115-125, 159-161, 211, 214, 230,
  234-236; extent of, 38-43, 78-82, 157-
  159, 199-200, 203-204, 211, 224-226;
  pre-1800, 9-10; geography of, 11, 104;
  in rural areas, 10-11, 16, 37-40, 61,
  80-81, 150-151, 158; popular conceptions of, 45-50, 89-91, 105, 108-111,
  120-121, 171-173, 177-178, 190, 202-
  203, 208-209; relative, 105-106, 159-
  161, 211, 236
Powdermaker, Hortense, 39
President's Committee on Juvenile Delinquency and Youth Crime, 127,
  138, 145
Pressure groups: before 1940, 29, 31,
  66; in 1930s, 69, 72-73, 77; in 1960s,
  157, 167-170; in 1970s, 182-183, 209;
  in 1990s, 234
Public Welfare Amendments of 1962,
  131-133, 182-183
Public Works Administration, 63

Raspberry, William, 218
Rainwater, Lee, 121-122
Reagan, Ronald, 172, 211-213, 215, 224,
  230, 236
Residency requirements, 62, 87, 179
Ribicoff, Abraham, 131-132, 194
Richmond, Mary, 26
Riis, Jacob, 6 *ff*, 14, 23, 38, 49, 100,
  118, 136, 150, 215, 217
Rockefeller, Nelson, 146
Rodman, Hyman, 116-117

Rogers, Will, 42
Roosevelt, Franklin D., 42, 52 *ff*, 93,
  140, 192. *See also* New Deal
Roosevelt, Theodore, 32
Ross, E. A., 20
Rowntree, B. Seebohm, 6, 7, 9
Rubinow, Isaac, 29, 44-45
Ryan, William, 102

Schuyler, George, 17
Settlement houses, 24-26
Shriver, Sargent, 135-136, 140-141, 142-
  145, 147, 151-152, 169, 189
Singletary, Otis, 129
Smolensky, Eugene, 214, 215
Social insurance, *See* Social Security
Social mobility, 14, 122-123
Social science, 84-85, 91-96, 99-100,
  112-114, 115-125
Social Security: passage of, 60, 67-75;
  in 1940s and 1950s, 85-86, 90, 93-94,
  111; in 1960s and 1970s, 158-159,
  164-165, 166, 170, 198, 207; in 1980s,
  211, 214; in 1990s, 224, 233, 234, 236.
  See also Old age pensions
Social Security Administration, 81-82,
  85
Social work, 25-26, 43-45, 88-89, 143-
  144, 188-189
South, poverty in the, 16, 38-40, 80-81,
  157-158, 217, 225
Sparkman, John, 94-95, 161
State-local relief, 29-31, 56-57, 61-63,
  69, 86-89. *See also* General assis-
  tance
Steinbeck, John, 48, 49, 61
Stennis, John, 145
Stigler, George J., 113
Sundquist, James, 151, 153
Supplemental Security Income (SSI),
  197-198, 206-207, 222, 224, 233, 238
Supreme Court, 71, 75, 153, 179
Survey Research Center, 113, 122-123,
  161
Sviridoff, Mitchell, 216-217

Talmadge amendments (1971), 176, 201
Tawney, R. H., 96, 157
Thatcher, Margaret, 213
Theobald, Robert, 142, 187-188
Thernstrom, Stephan, 82
Tobin, James, 79, 188
Tower, John, 144
Townsend, Dr. Francis, 52, 70-71, 73,
  167
Truman, Harry, 112

Unemployment, 8-9, 17, 18, 37, 40-43,
  211, 220-221, 225, 228

Unemployment insurance, 8, 17, 26-27, 29, 33, 71-74, 164-165, 212
Upward Bound, 137

Veblen, Thorstein, 25
Veiller, Lawrence, 33
Vietnam war, 147
VISTA, 141, 142

Wagner, Robert, 74
Wagner, Robert, Jr. (Mayor), 146
Walker, Francis, 21
Warner, Amos, 6, 8, 21
Warner, W. Lloyd, 91-92
War on poverty, 65, 99, 126, 134-141, 142-154
Washington, Booker T., 24
Welfare: spending for, 27-29, 56-57, 62-67, 68-69, 76-77, 85-88, 148, 164-167, 177, 200, 204, 210-213, 229-232, 237; in states, 29-30; compared to Europe, 30-34, 70, 73-74, 75-77, 83-84, 87, 166-167, 177, 231

Welfare capitalism, 34
Welfare reform, 1960s, 130-133, 210-211, 238-241
Welfare services, 132-133, 182-183
Whyte, William F., 91, 104, 115
Wickenden, Elizabeth, 120, 130, 150
Wiley, George, 153, 195
Williams, John, 196-197
Wilson, William Julius, 227-228
Wirtz, Willard, 136, 141, 143, 186
Witte, Edwin, 70-72, 73, 75
Woods, Robert, 24
Work Incentive Program (WIN), 174-177, 193, 207, 208
Workmen's compensation, 26
Work relief, 63-67, 212. *See also* Works Progress Administration
Works Progress Administration, 43, 46-47, 63-67, 70, 72-73, 92, 141, 144, 186-187, 237, 239
World War II, 79-83, 84, 221

Yarmolinsky, Adam, 134